The Apocalypse of God in Christ

Reconstructions in Lutheran Doctrinal Theology

This series will explore what contemporary theology in the tradition of Luther "should believe, teach and confess" about the God of the gospel. The series will critically engage, explore, and freshly formulate a wide range of topics in dogmatic theology. Every study will ground itself in the doctrinal tradition stemming from Luther's Reformation theology and accordingly will be explicitly focused on the knowledge of God given to faith by the Holy Spirit in Christ according to Luther's pregnant formulation *vera theologia et cognitio Dei sunt in Christo crucifixo*. The studies will articulate the content of faith in formulations which as such propose to be binding upon the contemporary community of faith.

The Apocalypse of God in Christ

A Theology of Theology

Paul R. Hinlicky

CASCADE *Books* • Eugene, Oregon

THE APOCALYPSE OF GOD IN CHRIST
A Theology of Theology

Reconstructions in Lutheran Doctrinal Theology

Cascade Books
An Imprint of Wipf and Stock Publishers
199 W. 8th Ave., Suite 3
Eugene, OR 97401

www.wipfandstock.com

PAPERBACK ISBN: 979-8-3852-2286-5
HARDCOVER ISBN: 979-8-3852-2287-2
EBOOK ISBN: 979-8-3852-2288-9

Cataloguing-in-Publication data:

Names: Hinlicky, Paul R., author.

Title: The apocalypse of God in Christ : a theology of theology / by Paul R. Hinlicky.

Description: Eugene, OR : Cascade Books, 2026 | Series: Reconstructions in Lutheran Doctrinal Theology | Includes bibliographical references and index(es).

Identifiers: ISBN 979-8-3852-2286-5 (paperback) | ISBN 979-8-3852-2287-2 (hardcover) | ISBN 979-8-3852-2288-9 (ebook)

Subjects: LCSH: Apocalyptic literature. | Bible Epistles of Paul—Theology. | Eschatology. | Theology, Doctrinal—History. | Eschatology—History of doctrines.

Classification: BS646 .H56 2026 (paperback) | BS646 (ebook)

VERSION NUMBER 05/22/26

To You-Know-Who; She-Knows-Why

Contents

Reconstruction in Lutheran Doctrinal Theology

Editor in Chief: Paul Hinlicky

Associate Editors: Derek Nelson, Lois Malcolm, Jennifer Hockenbery, Piotr Malysz, Matthew Burdette

General Introduction

The Princeton philosopher of religion, Jeffrey Stout, reflected not long ago on the sorry fate of Christian theology since Barth. He wrote of a doubly cruel loss: both of audience and of theme. Fear of the future, or fear of being left behind by it, cannot but sap theological nerve in a culture for which History-Written-by-Winners is the de facto deity. This failure of nerve must threaten all the more where and when theology still arises in faith alone at the improbable word of the resurrection-vindication of the crucified Jesus. All this points to a crossroads at which the tradition of Christian theology stemming from Luther in particular stands. It does not take much effort or insight to observe how Lutheran theology today either dwindles into irrelevance as the mere defense of an ever-shrinking piece of ecclesiastical turf or dissipates into revisions increasingly distant from, if not antagonistic to, its source. Consequently, it takes *courage* to venture the relevance of this tradition of Christian theology and to pursue its reconstruction in forms that are fresh yet recognizable developments of core affirmations going back to its genesis.

This series of books, therefore, boldly explore what contemporary theology in the tradition of Luther "should believe, teach and confess" (as *The Book of Concord* once admonished) about the God of the gospel. The studies focus explicitly on the knowledge of God in Christ given to faith by the Holy Spirit according to Luther's pregnant formulation, *vera theologia et cognitio Dei in Christo crucifixo sunt* ("true theology and knowledge of God are in Christ crucified"). At the same time, the studies do not ignore, mischaracterize, oversimplify, or otherwise run roughshod over the context in which retrieval takes place. The "theological production of doctrine" (C. Helmer) articulating the knowledge of God is consequently an enormous challenge today after the cultural "death of God" announced by Nietzsche's Zarathustra at the turn into the 20th century. A century later, the ripple effects—varied and far-reaching—of Zarathustra's discovery have hardly subsided. Not only courage, then, but also *insight* into the dramatically transformed spiritual context of "post-Christendom" in the contemporary West is requisite to the theological task today.

With courage renewed, this is a challenge which theology in Luther's tradition can and must undertake in that it has no other claim but that it knows God in the Christ who was once for all truly "crucified, dead and buried"—knowing Creator, and so also creation, only in him, with him, and through him. The theocentric focus on knowledge of God by way of the scandalous "monstrosity" (Hegel) of Christ *crucified*, the Son of God *incarnate*, for the interpretation of topics in doctrinal theology thus demands *critical* retrieval; critical *retrieval* in turn effects a contemporary *pruning* of an overgrown tradition and of necessity entails disciplined experimentation.

A few words by way of introduction to these claims! Lutheran theology flourished in the time of Christendom when Christian theology, including Lutheran theology, undertook the task of promulgating a comprehensive worldview. But Christendom slowly withered under a variety of assaults for this overreach during the Enlightenment. It was buried in the ashes of the 20th century experience of Hitler, Hiroshima and Stalin, moral catastrophes that were perpetrated on the soil of Christian civilizations. Only in retrospect can it be seen how much the enlistment of Lutheran theology in the project of Christendom blunted its critical edge and explosive testimony to the God of the gospel. So nostalgia for those so-called "glory days" of Lutheran theology should also be buried. Let the dead bury the dead!

As may be seen in the 28th article of the Augsburg Confession, the Lutheran Reformation challenged the medieval understanding of Christendom as the political polity of the Christian people under the governing alliance of Pope and Emperor. Yet as a "magisterial" Reformation, it conceived of itself as the proper renewal of the polity of Christendom, although historically this tended, without Pope, to a new "Caesaropapism."

The church became an instrument of the emergent modern nation-state, a "people's church" as opposed to a "confessing church." So a root issue of ecclesial self-understanding was posed during the German church struggle in the 1930s. But with the post-war collapse of Christendom, whether in Protestant or Catholic iteration, the Lutheran version of, and lingering aspirations for, a renewed alliance of throne and altar has become an albatross around the necks of all who would continue Christian theology with insight drawn from Luther. Thus, the task undertaken in this series turns upon a core assumption about the contemporary cultural-spiritual context of *post-Christendom* in Europe and North America, an unprecedented situation which both elicits and requires theological renovation.

Today we reckon with the rise of the natural sciences but also with the conceits of Enlightenment modernity, which ideologically justified extractive colonialism with the racialism of white supremacy, exploitative forms of industrial capitalism, murderous forms of socialism, total warfare, and now threats of economic and/or ecological collapse. The list of disasters on the soil of Christendom could be multiplied, while the real, but tottering achievements of the modern order are today staggering under these accumulated pressures and in danger of disintegration. We enter into a multipolar world no longer dominated by one superpower; willingly or not, we become data sources for the control, manipulation and prediction of surveillance capitalism, whether in alliance with the national security state pretending to defend "democracy" on one side, or, on the other side, with emergent autocracies, bold and powerful, which disdain any very pretense of "democracy."

The forms of Lutheran theology inherited from the passing era of modernity, then, have become not only dysfunctional, but deservingly discredited along with dying Christendom itself. Lutheran theology in the epoch of emergent modernity had oscillated between "modernist" forms of accommodation to rising secularist ideologies and "fundamentalist" forms of resistance to them. Both of these strategies are today in disrepute because each in its own way sought the rehabilitation of the political order of Christendom. Persisting in these lost causes only inhibits theology from facing up to present and future dangers, seeking and finding salutary ways forward.

As Dietrich Bonhoeffer saw from his prison cell, the polity of the Christians, *corpus christianum*, has now dissolved into its components, the body of Christ and "this world," indifferent to "Christ existing as community," if not hostile—yet astonishingly loved by God! The studies in this series take for granted this contemporary cultural-spiritual context and see no particular need to advocate, especially in our Euro-American post-Christendom, the need for a new synthesis. Instead contributions stipulate each author's understanding of this context and proceed to the critical and constructive task of the production of doctrinal articulations of Christian faith's knowledge of God. To be sure, authors will understand this context and the path forward in varying, perhaps even *contrary* ways. But we have sought some measure of coherence for the series by asking authors to give attention to one another's work in constructive dialogue, patient elaboration and charitable critique.

The series attends to the challenges of the world's plurality and multi-polarity in two ways. First, the notion of what constitutes legitimate subject-matter of dogmatic reflection has been opened up. Thus books in this series critically engage, explore and freshly formulate traditional topics in dogmatic theology but also some newer ones. Second, the theological tradition stemming from Luther is not the exclusive preserve of nominal "Lutherans," but bears from its origins an ecumenical intention, appeal, and to some extent influence. Accordingly, this series has deliberately enlisted authors beyond the boundaries of denominational Lutheranism who intend in their own fashion to continue what Luther started. Thus, while every study grounds itself in the doctrinal tradition stemming from Luther's Reformation theology, each proceeds as a critical development of it.

The series has not solicited theologians from the Two/Thirds world, though we think our series will be a richly informative for those who find the complexities and partisanships in current Western theology baffling. The rising generation will happily see a flowering of indigenous Lutheran theologies across the globe which wrestle with problems not identical to the Euro-American context of the demise of Christendom. Perhaps our wrestling in the series can serve as a cautionary tale in certain respects for global partners in the Lutheran theological tradition. Perhaps these new Lutheran theologies will shed light in turn upon our own Euro-American perplexities.

The situation of post-Christendom, in parallel to "post-modernism" but not identical with it, thus forces a winnowing so that what is essential for theology as a discipline is clarified as knowledge of the God of the gospel such that other dimensions of Christian doctrine are clearly developed as corollaries of the saving, therefore essential, knowledge of God. In arguing cognitive claims about God, the studies articulate the content of faith in formulations which as such propose to be binding upon the contemporary community of faith in that they are integral to the gospel of God which authors and authorizes Christian faith, community and mission. Such proposed formulations neither repudiate nor repeat formulations of the past but seek freshly to articulate their pertinent content, rationale and relevance.

This series originated after the publication by Cascade Press of Paul Hinlicky's *Lutheran Theology: A Critical Introduction*, when Cascade queried whether he would be willing to edit a series of books on Lutheran theology. Hinlicky gathered together theological colleagues, most of whom had worked with him on the *Oxford Encyclopedia of Martin Luther*, to form an editorial advisory group. He also recruited an editor who would reflect the series' ecumenical orientation. The group brainstormed prospective authors and topics and began solicitation of interest. The response has been overwhelming as the series launches with thirty some authors with topics under contract to appear over the course of the next seven years. We have deliberately sought out a rich mix of senior and junior scholars from a variety of backgrounds holding to various positions within contemporary systematic theology, experimentalist *and* retrievalist, deliberately breeching denominational walls and crossing old battlelines.

Systematic theology is, even at best, an ambiguous good, reflecting our status as wayfarers on a pilgrim way. In a better world yet to come, we would not labor to articulate the knowledge of God, but simply worship the God of the gospel who in the cross of Christ has sought and found *us*, and so come to *know* us. But here and now, between the already of the resurrection-vindication of the Crucified and the not yet of his final victory for us and for all, we write *about* the God whom *we know as knowing us* that we may serve *intelligently in this fateful interim time*. Such is our task, neither hankering after the fleshpots of Egypt nor storming the kingdom to take it by force. In the end (pun intended), true theological statements are doxological, finding their correction and vindication in the great doxology of the creation rescued and fulfilled at the Pauline "redemption of our bodies." In this confidence we offer this series to the glory of God and for the edification of the Body of Christ in its mission to the world.

Editor in Chief: Paul Hinlicky

Associate Editors: Derek Nelson, Lois Malcolm, Jennifer Hockenbery, Piotr Malysz, Matthew Burdette

Preface and Acknowledgments

IT WAS NOT THE plan originally for me to author the book on the nature of doctrine in the series Reconstructions in Lutheran Doctrinal Theology of which I am the general editor. But when R. David Nelson, the contracted author, had to withdraw, I decided to offer authorship for this important book so that it would appear early in the series and without inordinate delay. I had given a lecture in the fall of 2023 to The Society of the Holy Trinity in Mundelein, Illinois, with the title, "The Nature of Doctrine 2.0," which provided a template for the book proposal which, being endorsed by our editorial group, was subsequently contracted with the proposed title, "Praise, Proclamation, and Militancy." But as often happens in the course of writing a book, the focus clarified and the project radicalized, as readers will discover. In short, with the arrival of postmodernity in the contemporary maelstrom of contending propagandas, "modern" theology must be reconstructed from the root up. Uprooting and replanting is both possible and desirable with "the apocalyptic turn in contemporary theology,"[1] particularly for the tradition of Christian thought concerning deity which stems from Luther.

Since the publication of my *Beloved Community: Critical Dogmatics after Christendom* in 2015 in the academic category of "systematic theology," my perplexity about the troubled nature of the discipline of theology has only increased. The cumbersome retitling as "critical dogmatics" for the discipline already then signaled that discomfort. I recall an anecdote from graduate student days that may illuminate the difficulty. I had been reading the English translation, *No Rusty Swords*, of some of Bonhoeffer's writings from the 1930s and was particularly struck by

1. Ziegler, *Militant Grace*.

his discussion of Barth's theology. In a paper I submitted I formulated the gist of the claim for the sovereignty of divine revelation in this unfortunate way: "Israel has no theology because Israel does not know God in the flesh."[2] I do not at this time regard this dictum as a wholly apt characterization of Judaism, i.e., "the body of faith: God in the people Israel."[3] But at that time around 1980 I found Bonhoeffer's judgment insightful for explaining the striking difference between thinking the simplicity of the *Shema* and the complexity of thinking something like the Nicene Creed, and hence of the strange, sprawling, and conflicted discipline of Christian theology that ensued. When I issued that statement in a paper to make that point for an avowedly progressive professor, I was excoriated for anti-Semitism (no matter Bonhoeffer's credentials in this regard!). For me the force of the statement was to underscore the scandalous improbability of *Christian* theology as an academic discipline. So, the argument before you, long simmering in my head, is that although Christian theology deploys a scholarly method as an exercise in humility before God, generosity toward fellows and as an internal check against propaganda, it is not an academic discipline so much as an apocalyptic one—and this on the precedent of Luther.

This book has benefited from generous and insightful feedback, first from R. David Nelson who found the time to read the penultimate draft of the work from whose authorship he had resigned. His counsel on reader friendliness along with that of others, I have no doubt inadequately attempted to follow. I seek clarity in writing, but on intrinsically difficult matters clarity can be even more taxing on readers in requiring them to rethink matters familiar and presumably long settled. Substantively, I have been gratified to receive critical approbation from my fellow editors in the series, especially Lois Malcolm and Peter Malysz. I confess that many times I felt that these two comrades have understood me better than I understand myself. To a lesser degree but in ways important at critical junctures in this book's argument, I am indebted to feedback from Jennifer Hockenberry, Derek Nelson, and Matthew Burdette. I am grateful to Shaun Brown for a helpful discussion and clarification of several points in the interpretation of Lindbeck's theology. Finally let me gladly acknowledge a dear group of peers, the "Beerologians:" Bishop emeritus James Mauney, Rev. Dave Delaney, Rev. David Drebes, Rev.

2. Bonhoeffer, *No Rusty Swords*, 362–66.

3. Wyschogrod, *Body of Faith*.

Paul Henrickson, Father Ned Morris, Prof. Michael Hackenberg, and Prof. Fritz Oehlschlaeger. We have met over craft beer for years to discuss theology and these friends invested three months of effort into slow and careful discussion of the draft book, providing for me an invaluable focus group with a target audience. Finally, as is as usual by now, daughter theologian Sarah Hinlicky Wilson honored me with reading the draft and recording a podcast about it for our queenofthesciences.com.

I shamelessly take over a statement on inclusive language from a fellow author in this series, Dr. Cheryl Peterson, from her recent book, *The Holy Spirit and the Christian life:*

> For the technical discussion of the doctrine of the Trinity in this [book], I have chosen to use the church's traditional terms for the three persons (Father, Son, and Holy Spirit) and affirm the use of this traditional formulation in the sacrament of Holy Baptism and the historic creeds because it ties us to the church throughout time and space. However, I agree with feminist theologians that our language for God must expand beyond the traditional Trinitarian formula (especially in preaching, testimony, prayers, and hymnody) to include non-male and non-masculine images *from the Bible and Christian tradition* because God is both inclusive above and beyond human gender categories, per Genesis 1:27. Alternative Trinitarian formulas should be measured according to how well they identify God, not only by God's saving acts for us but also by God's internal relations that distinguish the persons from one another and, at the same time constitute the triune unity.[4]

The language for the deity in the whole of this book, and the crucial analysis of the grammatical distinction between name and title, illustrate what is at stake in employing language which does not pass muster with Peterson's stipulations.

After fifty years of partnership in life, this book is dedicated to Ellen in (a one-year-belated) thanksgiving for our golden anniversary.

Paul Hinlicky

Time after Pentecost, AD 2025

4. Peterson, *Holy Spirit in the Christian Life,* 24n2, emphasis added.

Abbreviations

BoC	*The Book of Concord: The Confessions of the Evangelical Lutheran Church.* Edited by Robert Kolb and T. J. Wengert. Minneapolis: Fortress, 2000.
CD	Karl Barth, *Church Dogmatics*, 4 vols. Translated by G. W. Bromiley and T. F. Torrance et al. Edinburgh: T. & T. Clark, 1969—).
DBW	*Dietrich Bonhoeffer Works*, 12 vols. Minneapolis: Fortress, 1997–.
LW	*Luthers Works: The American Edition.* 58- vols. St. Louis: Concordia & Philadelphia: Fortress, 1955–2025.
NPNF	*Nicene and Post-Nicene Fathers.* Edited by P. Schaff and H. Wace. Grand Rapids: Eerdmans, 1979.
OREML	*Oxford Research Encyclopedia of Religion: Martin Luther.* 3 vols. Edited by Derek R. Nelson and Paul R. Hinlicky. New York: Oxford University Press, 2017.
WA	*D. Martin Luthers Werke*, Kritische Gesamtausgabe Weimar: Bohlau, 1883-

Introduction

THE TITLE MAY SEEM overly bold. On the face of it, seemingly sensationalistic appeal to the "apocalyptic turn" in contemporary theology together with an argument that this improbable turn leverages renewal in the tradition of theology stemming from Luther seems reactionary at worst, quixotic at best. Debunking "click-bait" sensationalism in theology today, which has lost both audience and theme,[1] however, is a major burden in what follows. The gravity of the situation facing the Christian message and its theological articulation in contemporary post-modernism is twofold. Embarrassed at literalism on one side of polarized theology yet indulging undisciplined imagination on the other side, Christian doctrine and its salutary assertion seem a lost cause and a lost art, respectively. Failure of nerve is endemic. This book seeks to restore sanity and nerve in the production of Christian doctrine in the tradition of theology stemming from Luther. It offers accordingly an apocalyptic theology of theology as of the word of God spoken in the resurrection-vindication of the crucified Jesus, confessed in faith, lived in hope and operative in love.

A long simmering crisis in the doctrine of the word of God stands behind today's crippling demoralization. It should not have been this way. Early on in the Reformation controversies, Luther discovered that opponents could challenge his interpretations of Scripture by construing texts differently, questioning his selection of texts, or pointing to contradictions in the Bible resulting in *rabies theologorum* ("theological rabies"), i.e., unending contention that could only be settled in turn by the teaching authority invested in the papal magisterium.[2] Opponents

1. Stout, *Flight from Authority*.

2. LW 31:307–25.

asked: How can you appeal to *the* Word of God when they are so *many* words of God? Luther replied by articulating a *norming norm* by which *Scripture interprets Scripture*; this is the apostolic word of God that speaks to gentiles in the originating event of joining them to the Israel of God (Gal 6:16), namely, citing Rom 1:3–5, "the gospel concerning his Son . . . ."[3] The Romans text references the word of God spoken on Easter morn by the sanctifying Spirit powerfully declaring the divine Sonship of Jesus as Israel's Messiah. This *gospel concerning the Son* manifests the *resurrection power* of God, which brings about an "exchange of things" (*rerum metaphora*)[4] in the world. Here Christian theology arises in that this singular and powerful word of God both authors and authorizes the new life of community "in Christ," including the discipleship of the mind that is its theology. The sanctified community in the world constituted in these gospel beliefs in turn holds them as epistemically primary, as access to the knowledge of God in articulating essential, trust-enabling beliefs which cannot be lost without the dissolution itself of holy community in Christ.[5] The primitive confession of faith in

3. "You may ask, 'What then is the Word of God, and how shall it be used, since there are so many words of God?' I answer: The Apostle explains this in Romans 1. The Word is the gospel of God concerning his Son, who was made flesh, suffered, rose from the dead, and was glorified through the Spirit who sanctifies. To preach Christ means to feed the soul, make it righteous, set it free, and save it, provided it believes the preaching. Faith alone is the saving and efficacious use of the Word of God, according to Rom. 10[:9]: 'If you confess with your lips that Jesus is Lord and believe in your heart that God raised him from the dead, you will be saved.' Furthermore, 'Christ is the end of the law, that everyone who has faith may be justified' [Rom. 10:4]. Again, in Rom. 1[:17], 'He who through faith is righteous shall live' The Word of God cannot be received and cherished by any works whatever but only by faith. Therefore, it is clear that, as the soul needs only the Word of God for its life and righteousness, so it is justified by faith alone and not any works; for if it could be justified by anything else, it would not need the Word, and consequently it would not need faith." LW 31:346.

4. "Et in hac translatione non solum est verborum, sed et rerum metaphora. Nam vere peccata nostra a nobis translata sunt a posita super ipsum, ut omnis qui hoc credit, vere nulla peccata habeat, sed translata super Christum, absorpta in ipso, eum amplius non damnent." ("And in this transference [that 'Christ was made to be sin'—2 Cor 5:21] it is not only a metaphor of words but of things. For truly our sins are transferred from us and placed on Him, so that all who believe Him truly have no sins but they are transferred onto Him, absorbed in Him, no longer damning him." Author's translation, WA 8:87; cf. LW 32:200. See the compelling analysis of Vind, "Christus factus est peccatum metaphorice."

5. Marshall, *Trinity and Truth*. "Epistemic primacy" designates what belief is necessary to a community's survival, what is least dispensable, what one is least willing to give up (44). As a belief, it is a sentence held to be true, a truth claim (45), in relation to which other beliefs are logically subordinate, depending for their truth on their

his resurrection thus acknowledges Jesus as Lord just as this church-identifying confession of the Easter word of God marks the constituting iteration of Christian doctrinal theology.

Yet, racked with controversies concerning its proposed "doctrine on which the church stands and falls"[6] in the years after Luther's death, the well-meaning Formula of Concord fundamentally confused the matter. Principally opposed to papal magisterium as the antichrist, it distinguished categorically between the sacred Scriptures of Old and New Testaments and all other writings; canonical Scripture, not the pope nor other human traditions, is *solely* to be acknowledged as the judge, norm and rule of Christian doctrine, that is, as the norming norm. The intention here, linking Old and New Testaments as rule of faith, was well-meaning insofar as the gospel makes itself known in the act of distinguishing itself as gracious promise of divine favor and rectification of sinners on account of Christ's reconciling work in distinction from the righteous demand on them and holy prosecution of them by the law *of God*. But a doctrine of *sola sacra scriptura* (in the Latin nominative case from the *Epitome*[7]) was thus enunciated *in place of* Luther's apocalyptic event of Christ's vindicated work creating this purposive movement and consequent distinction *within* the living word of the *one God* and its messaging to the nations as the "gospel concerning his Son."

The confusion is subtle and therefore plausible, as the Formulators acknowledged that already in the time of the still living apostles (i.e., well before New Testament canonization) false teachers and heretics invaded the church requiring the formulation of doctrinal "symbols" to articulate the one faith of catholic Christians against deviations. As we shall see, however, this is historically backwards and hermeneutically misleading. The threefold confession of the Father, the Son, and the Spirit by which baptismal candidates professed their new allegiance and renounced the kingdom of the devil had expanded upon the primitive post-Easter acknowledgment of Jesus as Lord; this summary in proto-Trinitarian confession of the gospel word of God poised against the tyranny of the devil in turn began to function as the rule of faith, just as baptismal confession publicly marked out Christ-formed membership in his new and true humanity. As such, it served as the criterion by which early Christian literature was assessed for inclusion in the emergent New Testament to

coherence with the primary one (46–47).

6. Vainio, *Justification and Participation in Christ.*

7. Dingel, *Bekenntnisschriften der evangelisch-lutherischen Kirche*, 769:7.

form the canonical Bible in union with the Scriptures of Israel.[8] Thus, the apocalyptic gospel of the Lord Jesus coming as victor over the kingdom of the devil, just as Luther intuited, is in truth the norming norm of canonical Scripture, making canonical Scripture in turn its primary *normed norm*.[9] The canonical Genesis-to-Revelation narrative emerges as in fact the first dogmatic judgment of catholic Christianity, not incidentally formulated against the gnostic/docetic teaching which attributed the material creation to the work of an evil deity and consequently denied the embodied humanity of the Lord Jesus. But apocalyptic had attributed the woes of the good creation to its seduction and oppression by the foe of God against whom the exalted Lord battles for creation's redemption and renewal.

What difference does this clarification of the doctrine of the word make for the tradition of theology stemming from Luther for us today? The difference may be posed in the form of a rhetorical question. Is the apocalyptic foe forever to be identified with the papacy and its overreaching claim to magisterium as *the* antichrist? Or was the papacy of the sixteenth century one of the powers and principalities usurped by the apocalyptic foe yet capable of redemption and reordering in service under the Lordship of Jesus?[10]

There are a few today who will seriously affirm tout court that the papacy is antichrist (and those who still do should be excoriated for it), just as it is right to work in hope for a reformed papacy.[11] Rather, the naming of the apocalyptic foe is and remains an urgent problem that this book will tackle in chapter 4. To get to that problem, however, the present study works with an important distinction between three orders of theological work:[12] first, the historically descriptive and theologically interpretive account of the word of God uttered in the resurrection of the crucified Jesus; second, the historically descriptive but theologically expansive account from the primitive confession of faith, Jesus is Lord, to its explication in Trinitarian doctrine, oriented ultimately to the eternal confession of praise; and third, deliberative theology in which interlocutors, competent in the foregoing determination of the terms by which any debate is Christianly meaningful, argue for and against adequacy

8. This claim is argued in detail in Hinlicky, *Divine Complexity*, 69–108.

9. Hinlicky, "Prima Scriptura."

10. See forthcoming in this series Volker Leppin, *Antichrist in Lutheran Theology*.

11. Hendrix, *Luther and the Papacy*.

12. For the sources in Luther, see Hinlicky, "Luther and Systematic Theology."

in formulation. Such third-order deliberation includes the possibility of doctrinal reformulation in seeking salutary correlations with the human realities of contemporary contexts in which the gospel is proclaimed. This book is an exercise in all three interlocking orders of theology in that it argues for definite reconceptualizations, if not reformulations of received doctrine in order better to enable the multifaceted missiological engagement indicated in the third order. As indicated, the most basic reconceptualization involves rethinking the classical Protestant doctrine of *sola scriptura* by re-situating the "external word" in the apocalyptic gospel of the resurrection-vindication of the crucified Jesus. In tandem with this comes the task of rethinking the creedal doctrine of God in relation to the confession of Jesus as Lord, taken as the embryonic confession in Christian doctrine.[13]

Thus, the reader may expect a series of interlocking arguments: about christologically modified apocalyptic; theology as rule of faith or catechesis, and as freed thinking in distinction from freethinking; about the tension between resurrection as vindication and incarnation as disclosure; about the Gospel of John as the bridge between the synoptic accounts of Jesus as Christ and Lord and the creedal doctrine of the Trinity; about the vagaries of "free will" and the certainty of faith as freedom in the sanctifying Spirit; about the proper meaning of docetism in Christology in view of the unity of Christ's person enabling his presence in the joyful exchange of righteousness for sin, life for death, peace with God for enmity with God; above all about replacing the unbaptized God of Platonic impassibility with the apocalyptic intervention of the passionate God of the gospel. Moreover, transversing the siloed contemporary disciplines of systematic theology, philosophy of religion, history of doctrine, missiology, and biblical studies, all of these methods are deployed in the interlocking arguments. All this, moreover, is filtered through a theologian for whom the pastoral vocation, bearing the concrete responsibility to deliver the word of God in liturgical proclamation, is not incidental to the theological *subjectivity* required by this proposal for the reconstruction of *objectivity*[14] in Lutheran doctrinal theology that is being made in this book rebuilding amid the ruins of Christendom.

13. I am grateful to Lois Malcolm for full clarity on this point.

14. *Fides quae creditur*, "the faith which is believed, the object of faith." "First, what one should believe, that is, the objectum fidei, that is, the work or thing in which one believes or to which one is to adhere. Secondly, the faith itself, or the use which one should properly make of that in which he believes. The first lives outside the heart and

Yet it is said that pastors today no longer read theology, not to mention the laity. In the judgment of this author that failure in the discipleship of the mind makes a precise diagnosis of the sickness of contemporary Christianity in Euro-America. To be sure, much of the fault for this intellectual decline lies in the pretensions of the modern discipline usually named "systematic theology" which today is forced by declining health to downsize and morph into so-called "constructive theology." Systematic theology was the modern reinvention of the dogmatic tradition, piggybacking upon Hegel who wanted to convert theology into a latently Christian philosophy of religion. So, theology became philosophy by other means, pretending to construct a comprehensive view of reality, a vast metanarrative, a Christian "worldview" of history as salvation. Over time this impossible and endlessly qualified ambition became so esoteric, complex and distant from the gospel and its scriptural matrix, and thus from the basic language of faith, that practitioners of Christianity became uninterested. But constructive theology today, if by that one means undisciplined freedom to reimagine Christianity at will in a desperate bid to drum up business, must by nature abandon the unitive function of church doctrine to bind together in common confession of Jesus as Lord. Thus, my preferred name for the renewed discipline is "critical dogmatics," by which I most simply mean the intelligent, contemporary teaching of the canonical deposit of faith. What critical dogmatics means for the audience of this book is to project for the future of vital Christianity within a post-Christendom world the rejuvenation of scholarly pastors, who will be valued and supported by their communities of faith as gospel preachers, Bible teachers, and thusly equipped public intellectuals in their localities—practical experts in the missiological domain of third order theology.

The scholarly method by which the argument will be made should be held in mind by the reader working through the aforementioned series of interlocking arguments. Lutheran theology has always been coupled with the vocation of the educator, on the model of those Renaissance

is presented to our eyes externally, namely, the sacrament itself, concerning which we believe that Christ's body and blood are truly present in the bread and wine. The second is internal, within the heart, and cannot be externalized. It consists in the attitude which the heart should have toward the external sacrament . . . Up to now I have not preached very much about the first part, but have treated only the second, which is also the best part. But because the first part is now being assailed by man, and the preachers, even those who are considered the best, are splitting up into factions over the matter . . . the times demand that I say something on this subject also." LW 36:335; WA 19:482–483.

humanists, Luther and Melanchthon. Consequently, this book argues chiefly by way of exposition, so-called "deep reading" of selected texts, by which the points relevant for the case being made are pushed to the surface.[15] The credibility of this method, of course, depends on fair, even generous interpretation of these sources especially when critique is being executed. Whether the book succeeds in this intention is for the reader to judge. But if one is looking for a fast and easy take on the case being made, one impatiently deprives oneself of the deliberative process of theology which luxuriates in deep dialogue with competent interlocutors as something intrinsically worthwhile. As mentioned, the perhaps jarring juxtaposition in what follows of evidence and argument from the varying modern disciplines of biblical studies, history of doctrine, philosophy and contemporary theology is quite deliberate. Overcoming the siloing of these disciplines instituted at the turn of the eighteenth century in the desperate effort to have Christian theology recognized as an academic science in the modern university is fundamental to the retrieval of doctrinal theology from the tradition of Luther since its natural habitat is the confessing church of the Lord Jesus.

All the same, my selection of interlocutors may also be questioned, particularly with respect to the limited number presented for careful treatment within the confines of this book. Suffice it here to acknowledge that comprehensiveness is impossible and that the selection is determined both by the author's finite limitations and his aim for the renewal of dogmatic theology as the critical discipline of a confessing church. May those who feel overlooked in this book rise to the challenge of responding with their own deep reading and critique of it! The tradition of Luther, in any case, is not the proprietary domain of nominal Lutherans but has, and, indeed, intends ecumenical scope, a fact which justifies inclusion of important interlocutors who are not denominationally Lutheran. It is an irony that ought to provoke some holy jealousy that some of the best work in doctrinal theology out of the tradition of Luther today is coming from Reformed and Anglican theologians!

If the reader desires an overview of how the interlocking arguments running through the book cohere, they may look ahead to the italicized paragraph(s) at the outset of each chapter for a summary of each's purpose. Reading these seriatim provides the desired overview. But the basic proposal of the book is to relocate a cultural-linguistic interpretation

15. Thanks to Dave Nelson for this insight.

of the nature of doctrine as regulative instruction for properly speaking and enacting an "external word" concerning the originative event authoring and authorizing the being and mission of the community of faith. Relocating this model into New Testament apocalyptic in order to disambiguate the external word of God and its confession serves better missiological engagement in the world in third-order theology. As we shall see, however, this relocation entails important amendments to the cultural-linguistic model of doctrine to rescue it from a perceived liability to fideism and to specify pneumatologically Christian experience with its proper account and place in doctrinal theology.

I would stress from the outset, however, that this study is not an exercise in "second naïveté" remythologization as might be imagined over against the criteria established for contemporary Lutheran theology in the influential 1941 essay of "radical Lutheran" Rudolf Bultmann, "The New Testament and Mythology."[16] True, if speech about "God," based no less upon "the act of God," were itself the last, devious refuge of mythology, any theology that intends knowledge of God would be guilty of remythologization as charged (and strictly in that sense one may so indict this book as "remythologization"). But Bultmann himself pleaded not guilty and insisted that he was speaking non-mythologically of the act of God in Christ as "external word" by soberly elaborating its anthropological effects in the fashion that Schleiermacher had established for modern theology after Kant: we cannot see the noumenal divine cause, but we can imagine and symbolize it from the effects apparent in religious or existential experience. In fact, Bultmann argued, this happened in primitive Christianity. In the essay Bultmann pinned together Hellenistic Gnosticism and Jewish Apocalyptic as two influential mythologies in which the Christian message of the New Testament was expressed, as if they provided the catalog of available symbols for the articulation of experience. As prescientific "worldviews," however, these ideologies are no longer credible and had become a false stumbling block to faith, casting an unconscionable burden upon conscience if proclamation required adherence to fantastic and outmoded beliefs. But the kernel of authentic existence can be shucked free from the husk of mythological beliefs: that is the *theological* task of demythologization. Yet, as the Greek word, *mythos*, translates into English as a story or tale, demythologization inevitably shades into denarrativization,

16. Bartsch, *Kerygma and Myth*, 1–44.

a procedure which cannot but render canonical Scripture inoperative as primary normed norm.

The objections to Bultmann's program are twofold, historical and hermeneutical. First, Bultmann misunderstands Gnosticism after Harnack as the "extreme Hellenism" attending the ideological environment of the early Greek-speaking congregations. He thusly fails to see that early Gnosticism is historically connected with the disillusionment of Jewish apocalyptic, most likely following the destruction of Jerusalem by the Romans.[17] This misunderstanding profoundly influenced his interpretation of the Gospel of John as a liberation *from* fleshly and unspiritual Judaism with the help of Gnosticism rather than reflecting a painful schism *within* post-Temple Judaism over the Messiahship of the crucified Jew Jesus, as J. Louis Martyn has shown.[18]

Bultmann's hermeneutical attempt to decode the cosmological statements in the New Testament as symbols of existential human possibilities was illuminating to the extent of setting off the characteristic anthropological dualism of mind/spirit vs. flesh/body in gnostic (and, by extension, in broadly Platonic traditions) from the apocalyptic opposition of the eons of darkness and light. Yet in discarding apocalyptic as equally suspect mythology, Bultmann failed *theologically* to deliver the New Testament's intended knowledge *of God the creator regaining a usurped creation* for life, righteousness, and peace. This knowledge of God is delivered by the New Testament's christological modification of the apocalyptic dualism of the ages. In Christ the self-donating God of the gospel has broken into a strong man's house to bind him and plunder his goods, a counter offensive against the creation's prior invasion and hostile occupation by the anti-divine powers of Sin, Death, and Devil. When this insight into the theological intention of the New Testament writings is sustained, the apocalyptic metaphors are not to be *demythologized* reductively as symbols of individual existence but rather are to be *deliteralized* to tell of the God who gives life to the dead and calls into being worlds that do not yet exist in the very act of subduing contra-divine powers. The blunder here is not only to take metaphor literally but also to imagine that metaphor is without reference to something in the world. Deliteralized, metaphors refer and that reference is the meaning of the metaphor. The extended metaphor of apocalyptic's

17. Robinson, "Introduction," 1–26.

18. Martyn, *History and Theology in the Fourth Gospel*; cf. Ashton, *Understanding the Fourth Gospel.*

conflict of the eons is deliteralized in Christ to refer to the coming of the creator God to redeem and fulfill, and by this work of interpretation, theology produces faith's knowledge of God.

The need for this alteration of the program of one of the last great New Testament scholars who took theological production seriously as incumbent upon vocational dedication to the particular texts of the New Testament is indicated by the fact that the famous essay was first published in Germany just as the triumphant swastika flew from the Atlantic Wall to the outskirts of Moscow. Stronger medicine is needed than existentialist theology and it is the cosmological metaphors of apocalyptic that provide it, when deliteralized for understanding by the Christ event to produce knowledge of God: not the end of time but the time of God's end for life, righteousness and peace breaking in to liberate and redeem a usurped creation. Just this gospel is the word of God which authors and authorizes the ecclesia as the beachhead of the originating event which ever orients the work of theology. It provides the theology of theology to be worked out in this book.

It is hermeneutically important here to interpret apocalyptic as a genre of metaphorical narrative referring to deity. The precedent for deliteralization of metaphor over against Bultman's program of demythologization may be found in Luther's well-known rendering of the ascension narrative of the risen Christ to the right hand of God: a metaphorical narrative referring to the Crucified Jesus's exaltation to lordship over the powers and principalities structuring human life on the earth, not a rocketship ride up to a local place within the cosmos seated on a velvet cushion surrounded by dancing angels next to a right-handed potentate, as Luther satirized. Grammatically, metaphor is not simile.[19] The comparative statement of simile, "God is *like* a rock," refers literally to the less familiar deity by comparison with a mundane familiar, a rock, to signify God's substantiality in the fleeting world of becoming. In simile, the linguistic sign refers away from itself, rock, to the signified thing in the world, God, to make in this way a meaningful statement about reality that can either be affirmed or denied. But if I state a metaphor, "God *is* a rock," I literally produce an absurdity (unless there actually are rock worshipers in the world) in that the copula literally *identifies* God with a rock. In metaphor the sign is united with the thing signified. When such intentional absurdity in metaphor goes unrecognized and is taken literally, the literal identification produces

19. Soskice, *Metaphor and Religious Language.*

nonsense that strictly speaking can neither be affirmed nor denied because no one knows what in the world is being asserted. In metaphor, then, new language is created. Here "rock" becomes a new word with a new signification, the Rock of Ages.

Of course, and in practice, metaphors can be taken literally, but the intended novelty of the metaphor is then lost and the result pernicious, particularly in the case of the battle imagery of apocalyptic. But in every case the meaning of a statement in human language is its signing something there in the world, a *being there*, subject to clarification by descriptive ontology, if not to speculative metaphysical comprehension. In the metaphor, the sign is identified by the copula with the signified to issue, not in literal nonsense, but in a novel term grasping something newly *there*. "The Rock (of Ages) is there to found one's transient human life upon." Taken rightly by way of deliteralization as an illuminating transfer in the meaning of word-signs, metaphor's novelty yields a literal reference to something there in the world, e.g., God is there for creatures in immutable fidelity, and so makes a meaningful statement. According to Luther, metaphor in theology expresses something in the world for which there is little existing vocabulary. So deliteralization is a hermeneutical operation in second-order theology which does not discard the apocalyptic narrative of the creator God reclaiming the usurped creation from dark forces as does the program of demythologization, but interprets it to refer to the being there of the Father in heaven who sends the beloved Son into the depths of our troubled world in the power of his Spirit to liberate and redeem. It thus produces a meaningful statement, a confession of faith, which can be affirmed in faith or denied in unbelief.

The critical edge and constructive fruit of this move from demythologization to deliteralization of misunderstood metaphor eventuates in a critical differentiation within this book. In that the "became flesh" (John 1:14) of the divine Logos seems literally absurd as a confusion of natures, Christology premised upon incarnation as a starting point conceives instead of a unique and paradigmatic similitude of the divine in the humanity of Jesus and this as intrinsically salutary; incarnation saves by revealing what the deity is like. The familiar Jesus qua human tells what the unfamiliar deity is like. Incarnation-premised theology thus produces an analogy to sustain the "grace and truth" claimed for it: Jesus is to God as the eternal Son is to the eternal Father. This starting point for Christology, however, obscures the Jewishness of the event of Jesus Christ in that it presumes precisely what the Torah forbids: a Christianly permissible association, unique and salutary, of a creature with the Creator, no matter how "low" on a scale of divinity, no matter the difference required by the analogy between the son of Mary and the Son of God. It is just this tacit assumption of a permissible range of idolatry in Christology which finally makes imperceptible the resurrection of Jesus as the vindication of a unique divine Sonship lived out in a unique and controversial human obedience, yet enacting the Torah's proto-Christology of the "servant of God."[20] Here the metaphorical paradox of the gospel, crucified Jesus *is* the Christ, the Son of God, saves by telling what God does in the world and *only so* revealing God's self in this action; in gospel proclamation Jesus becomes a new word in the world for a new thing in the world, telling who God is in doing creation's salvation.

Christology premised upon resurrection as vindication thus provides the epistemic avenue to the Trinitarian knowledge of the God of the gospel precisely from out of (and not in spite of) the scriptural matrix of Israel. Here the compassion of God motivates the Lord's coming down to rescue, having heard the cry of his people (Exod 3:7–8). Here the compassion of God grows warm and tender even to overturn white-hot anger at the ruin of Jacob by the cruel sins of the chosen people (Hos 11:8–9). According to the same narrative reasoning concerning divine character and intentionality,[21] already in Paul[22] one of the divine three fittingly, not necessarily but voluntarily, was sent in the compassion of God to make his very own the humanity singled out in the name, Jesus of Nazareth. In the cause of the God of Israel's sovereignty, Jesus befriended alike sinners and the sinned-against. In this scriptural matrix of divine *hesed*, we have to speak exclusively and with rigorous discipline of resurrection as the Father's act of self-identification by the Spirit with the crucified Son, revealed on Easter morn *simultaneously with* the creation of faith by the same Spirit, with all that this complex event of the coming of God to reign upon this earth portends for the being of God. Only so do we come doxologically to the confession of the incarnation (as John 20:28 actually teaches). For here the gospel word *is* the action: the incarnation is not a similitude of ascent to the divine, but a metaphor of descent to the lost and perishing. The christological

20. Hinlicky, *Joshua*, 53–54, 100, 264–65, 272.

21. For contemporary Jewish theology recognizing the narrative shape provided by the Hebrew Bible to the understanding of Hashem, and its affinities with Christian doctrine of God, see Wyschogrod, *Body of Faith*.

22. Hill, *Paul and the Trinity*.

paradox of the Christ crucified or what is the same, this body risen and glorified, asserts a new meaning representing a new reality in the world: Jesus is "Lord and God" (John 20:28). The abstract idea of incarnation is not the premise the theological thinking, but a concrete conclusion to which it comes, if and when the particular humanity of the controversial Jesus is not elided but forthrightly asserted.

The irony of prioritizing the idea of incarnation in Christology is that it eclipses the specifically Trinitarian doctrine of the being of God with an abstract notion of salvation as the sheer contact of immutable with mutable being; it does so by displacing the apocalyptic framing of the originative event of the gospel with a more or less Platonic framing relating mind to matter. But not only that! At length, it turns incarnation itself into a simile that transforms theology into a toothless program informing the ignorant what the divine is like. The enfleshment of John 1:14 which designated the tabernacling of the Lord in the new sanctuary of the body-and-soul who is the man Jesus, crucified for our sins but raised for our justification, declines into a routine metaphor for the realization of an idea imposing form upon matter. Having an "incarnational faith" comes to mean that we are to not just talk but put words into action. This idealism posing as Christian theology will be the object of critique throughout this book. But enough by way of introduction—onward to an apocalyptic theology of theology wherein the gospel word *is* divine action!

I

Gospel in the World of Propaganda

Propaganda is the machine by which the "father of lies" continues his murderous tyranny in secularism. This chapter unpacks the postmodern predicament of doctrinal theology in today's climate by an analysis of the total system of propaganda which surrounds and indeed permeates theology in the ruins both of Christendom and of its erstwhile rival, secular modernity now breaking down into postmodernity. Akin to the Gospel of Luke's parable of the return of the unclean spirit to a spiritually vacated home (11:24–26), it argues that "secularism" is dialectically related to the apocalyptic conflict of the eons as the repudiation of Christianity's eschatological ordering of the temporal kingdom to the eternal kingdom. As an exclusive affirmation of "this age only," secularism cast out the unclean spirit of Christendom triumphalism only to open the door to "seven other spirits more evil than itself." This theological analysis of the modern ideology of the secular provides a better account than shallow indictments of "secularity," because it attends to the emergence of "political religion" as propaganda machines within "secularism." Political religion actually precludes the holy secularity of newness of life on this earth lived conscientiously before God in responsibility for the creation. This chapter accordingly retrieves from a generation ago George Lindbeck's proposed cultural-linguistic model of doctrine, as he conceived the future of theology rehomed in a righteous remnant that would be sociologically sectarian but catholic in its self-understanding. By this relocation of the communal setting of theological work, the model in principle charts a path of integrity for Christian theology through the propaganda predicament. Yet seemingly the question of truth in the sense of valid reference to reality is dodged in the model. This apparent evasion, however, flags a deeper problem in the received tradition of "catholic" doctrine, fingered by Robert Jenson's diagnosis of the "unbaptized God" (as also his own failure to remedy it). The diagnosis that secularism re-admits the demonic also extends to the roots in the antecedent Christendom triumphalism on account of a compromised doctrine of God.

Understanding the Propaganda Machine

HOW DO WE PROPAGATE the gospel in a world awash with propaganda? What if the gospel itself becomes propagandized? The verb, "to propagate," derives from the Latin and was ordinarily used in a completely benign sense to indicate natural increase by the dissemination of seed, perhaps in Christian imagination recalling of the Parable of the Sower. Making a metaphor of this benign meaning, the Roman Catholic Church in 1718 organized a committee of cardinals to oversee foreign missions and, using the gerundive form of the Latin verb, titled it *Congregatio de Propaganda Fide*. By the late eighteenth century, the meaning of propaganda shifted to the political sphere, referring to the promotion of emergent nation-state ideology without necessarily connoting manipulation or deception. But by the mid-twentieth century our familiar understanding of propaganda became current, as Jacques Ellul defined in 1961: "Propaganda is a set of methods employed by an organized group that wants to bring about the active or passive participation in its actions of a mass of individuals, psychologically unified through psychological manipulations and incorporated in an organization."[1]

French Protestant and lay theologian, sociologist Ellul's postwar book could have been written yesterday to describe the Christian theological predicament amid the current postmodern, i.e., "post-truth" descent into a global maelstrom of contending propaganda, religious and secular. Indeed, he diagnosed that in both dimensions "propaganda is one of the most powerful factors of deChristianization in the world through the psychological modifications that it affects, through the ideological morass with which it has flooded the consciousness of the masses, through the reduction of Christianity to the level of an ideology,

1. Ellul, *Propaganda*, 61.

through the never-ending temptation held out to the church—all this is the creation of a mental universe foreign to Christianity. And this de-Christianization through the effects of one instrument—propaganda—is much greater than through the anti-Christian doctrines."[2] Sucked into a culture of propaganda, propagation of the gospel becomes one manipulative narrative alongside others, albeit hardly as effective. For Ellul, however, this is the one thing the gospel of Jesus Christ cannot endure without self-destructing theologically. But why? Where can we now find the insight and the nerve to resist the "never-ending temptation" to resort to propaganda? How do we de-propagandize the gospel? How do we propagate the gospel in the world awash with propaganda?

Of course, the phenomenon is not new even if the terminology is. We see across the broad spectrum of New Testament literature a similar concern doctrinally to define rightly and, accordingly, to propagate ethically the glad news of the resurrection-vindication of the crucified Jesus for human salvation and creation's redemption. The need to define the gospel doctrinally is a matter of ascertaining the integrity of proclamation in correspondence to its originating event and, being properly defined, the requirement ethically that proclaimers proceed in the cruciform fashion of the Lord they represent as propagators of the gospel. The Pauline epistles are surfeit with his apostolic defense against interlopers and opportunists, the apostle presenting his apostolic credentials as his sufferings from persecution and anxieties over the churches. The little apocalypse of the Synoptic Gospels similarly warns against false prophets and pseudo-messiahs who would summon the people of God to violent resistance rather than the Jesus way of suffering witness by courageous confession of his name. The Johannine literature admonishes believers to test the spirits to see whether they are of God by the criterion of the coming of the Christ as Jesus crucified in the flesh. From the beginning, distinguishing in this way the gospel and its proper proclamation from propaganda and its hucksters mandates the work of doctrinal theology with its corresponding ethic "in the theology of the martyrs."[3]

But in contemporary culture, the perennial problem of the gospel amid propaganda is intensified by a magnitude. We experience this today in the promise and peril of social media, now magnified by the rise of AI,[4]

2. Ellul, *Propaganda*, 231–32.

3. Hinlicky, *Divine Complexity*, 92–105.

4. The profound peril of the monetization of the Internet as opposed to its early promise of democratizing public discourse is acutely analyzed by Zuboff, *Age of Surveillance Capitalism*.

but Ellul understood the technological amplification of propaganda as it was aborning more than sixty years ago. "The study of propaganda must be conducted within the context of the technological society" but not in a way that we might superficially think. Rather, "propaganda is called upon to solve problems created by technology, to play on maladjustments, and to integrate the individual into the technological world. Propaganda is a good deal less the political weapon of the regime (it is that also) than the effect of the technological society that embraces the entire man . . . "[5] The analysis here is subtle but also profound: modern people, atomized in mass society, *need and desire propaganda* as psychological protection against the ceaseless, overwhelming bombardment of information ("facts" or "data") assailing them and pushing them in multiple, often contrary directions.

Thus, working like an umbrella holding off a chaotic downpour to see the way through the storm, "propaganda has become an inescapable necessity for everyone." It is not just the technology amplifying information but also our modernity of "mass society" which creates the craving for propaganda. How so? Modern people have come to worship "facts"—that is, they accept "facts" or "data" as the ultimate reality. They are convinced that what is, is good. The modern individual "believes that facts in themselves provide evidence and proof, and he willingly subordinates values to them; he obeys what he believes to be necessity, which he somehow connects with the idea of progress . . . inevitably result[ing] in a confusion between judgments of probability and judgments of value. Because fact is the sole criterion, it must be good."[6] It is a kind of secular fundamentalism: The fact *is*. That settles it. End of discussion.

The problem, however, is that there is a practical infinity of facts so that whenever one appeals to facts, one is in reality executing a *selection* which is pre-determined by a judgment of value, namely, the value of relevance to an agenda. A hidden value judgment lurks behind a selection of facts claiming relevance as the really real. That is the root deception and manipulation involved in propaganda, which is less a "big lie," according to Ellul, than a selective assortment of actual facts stitched together in a cunning narrative. Propaganda conceals its value-laden, agenda-driven selection highlighting some facts and obscuring others

5. Ellul, *Propaganda*, xvii.

6. Ellul, *Propaganda*, xv.

to concoct an ideologically compelling narrative as a substitute for laborious, inconvenient discernment.

Ellul characterizes the modern mentality of mass society in four points: 1) our aim in life is happiness, 2) we are naturally good, 3) history develops in endless progress, and 4) everything is matter.[7] Much of this mentality, ironically, can be traced to the success of the Reformation.[8] What makes theological discernment so difficult in this cultural climate, then, is that in large part this modern mentality represents the *success* of Protestant liberalism, as David A. Hollinger has argued incisively. "As the heavily Christian foundations of modern science and of the Enlightenment are now widely acknowledged," Protestant liberalism initiated accommodations to its own child, consisting in *demystification* in theology (the sovereignty of "facts" discrediting "opinion," i.e., "superstition") and *diversification* ("cosmopolitanism") in ecclesiology, i.e., the modernized mission of building the "kingdom of ends" on the earth by transmuting the parochial church into the avant-garde of the ideal of the global family of humanity.[9] Religiously, this has been the dominant propaganda of the modern period now staggering into its postmodern death rattle. On many fronts ranging from religious studies and the philosophy of religion to the rise of the "nones" among the masses, the triumphalist assumption of the superiority of the Christian religion cum civilization embedded in Protestant liberalism is being named and exorcised as the propagandistic bias of a fading hegemony.

What difference does this accommodation of the gospel to "modern science and the Enlightenment" make? In modern mentality "the average individual, the ordinary man of our times . . . is not sensitive to what is tragic in life; he is not anguished by a question that God might put to him; he does not feel challenged except by current events, political or economic." Consequently, "only isolated individuals are interested in religion. It is part of their private opinions, and no real public opinion exists on the subject."[10] Indeed, the little that is known of historical Christianity in contemporary public opinion are the (polemically selected and

7. Ellul, *Propaganda*, 39.

8. Hegel, *Lectures on the History of Philosophy*, 3:147.

9. Hollinger, *After Cloven Tongues of Fire*.

10. Ellul, *Propaganda*, 49. The privatization of religion is an accommodation to mass society in the technological era. Religious conscience would interfere with the routinization of life required by the technological juggernaut driving the total organization of society. See Hinlicky, "Complicity and the Truth of the Christological Path of Ecclesial Resistance."

highlighted) "facts" of Inquisition and Crusade, colonial conquests and forced conversions, heresy trials and ecclesiastical opposition to scientific discovery. Indeed, such ever-reiterated "facts" demoralize (and, as propaganda, are *intended* to demoralize!) would-be proclaimers of the gospel, reduced now to a diminishing band of church "survivalists" (Hollinger). Laying a heavy burden of guilt on Christianity's history of bad "facts" for resorting—ironically enough—to propaganda and its violence, this new propaganda of secularism renders the contemporary proclamation of the church, even in the church, an unlikely source for any alternative to the present paralysis. But Christianity's very real guilt, it shall be here argued, betrays in the first place an antecedent decline in the church's consciousness of its ongoing task of *critical* dogmatics by which it *tests* for integrity its proclamation and behavior by the gospel of God.

Further analyzing our present malaise, Ellul in his other expertise as a sociologist dissects the correlation between atomistic individualism and mass society. The "first move towards liberation of the individual is to break up the small groups that are an organic fact of the entire society. In this process the individual frees himself completely from family, village, parish, or brotherhood bonds—only to find himself directly vis-à-vis the entire society . . . in their isolation, [their] identities are determined by their relationships with one another,"[11] i.e., by forming *factions* as new social shelters, each with its own propaganda within the overarching propaganda of secularism. Mass society has the great problem of

> adjusting the normal man into a technological environment—to the increasing pace, the working hours, the noise, the crowded cities, the tempo of work, the housing shortage, and so on. Then there is the lack of personal accomplishment, the absence of an apparent meaning of life, the family insecurity provoked by these living conditions, the anonymity of the individual in the big cities and at work. The individual is not equipped to face these disturbing paralyzing traumatic influences. Here again he needs a psychological aid; to endure such a life, he needs to be given motivations that will restore his equilibrium. One cannot leave modern man alone in a situation such as this.

The propagandist provides a needed service;[12] propaganda creates factions as ersatz community.

11. Ellul, *Propaganda*, 90.

12. Ellul, *Propaganda*, 143.

In the broadly regnant propaganda of mass society composed of atomistic individuals, to be sure, "freedom" (even as "security," i.e., freedom from threat) is the common coin rationalizing the anomie: "the individual has eminent value, man is the master of his life; in individualist reality each human being is subject to innumerable forces and influences and is not the master of his own life."[13] In fact highly determined but claiming to be free, the atomized individual is forced to find a new identity/social cohesion over against mass society as a whole and other indifferent or hostile factions within it. In loneliness modern people feel

> the most violent need to be reintegrated into a community . . . The loneliness inside the crowd is perhaps the most terrible ordeal of modern man; the loneliness in which he can share nothing, talk to nobody, and expect nothing from anybody, leads to severe personality disturbances. For it, propaganda, encompassing human relations, is an incomparable remedy. It corresponds to the need to share, to be a member of the community, to lose oneself in a group, to embrace a collective ideology . . . . *Propaganda is the true remedy for loneliness.*[14]

We moderns, therefore, welcome this service of propaganda. The best defense against the infinity of information bombarding via information technology is propaganda; it is "a necessary protection against being flooded with facts without being able to establish a perspective":

> News loses its frightening character when it offers information for which the listener already has a ready explanation in his mind, or for which he can easily find one. The great force of propaganda lies in giving modern man all embracing, simple explanations and massive, doctrinal causes, without which he could not live with the news . . . Just as information is necessary for awareness, propaganda is necessary to prevent this awareness from becoming desperate.[15]

Note well! Modern people have not outgrown the human need either for community or for doctrine but satisfy the need with faction and propaganda.

This is why theologians who remember the Reformation alternative of the *studia humanitatis* are *educators*, not propagandists. These

13. Ellul, *Propaganda*, 91.
14. Ellul, *Propaganda*, 148.
15. Ellul, *Propaganda*, 147.

would inculcate the intellectual virtues, requiring students to look for the difficulties, i.e., the ignored or obscured "facts" that work against any thesis they are arguing. The qualitative superiority of any genuine argument is shown by its striving to deal with *all* the evidence, especially the evidence that goes against one's thesis, providing an argument that anticipates disagreement and speaks openly to the "bad" facts, even if the accomplishment is finally only to achieve a qualitatively better disagreement with a perceived opponent. Genuine educators do not simplify but in this way "complexify" understanding in pursuit of the truth which corresponds to our conflicted human reality in a world yet unredeemed. Scholarly method, rooted in the Renaissance *studia humanitatis* which catalyzed Reformation theology by the cultivation of such intellectual virtues, is a significant resource in resisting propaganda, not only of opponents but also one's own.[16] The stellar Reformation example of this is Philip Melanchthon's spirited but methodologically irenic *Apology of the Augsburg Confession*.

But against the rigors of intellectual virtue, there is a felt *need* today for propaganda to fight fire with fire, and thus to secure one's faction in a faux "identity," also in contemporary theology. Nevertheless, a fatal delusion attends propagandistic warfare by way of identity politics (of many types, not just postmodern, e.g., "Critical Race Theory" or "White Nationalism" but including Continental "confessionalism" and American "denominationalism"), namely, that one "can resist *one* particular propaganda, not the general phenomenon of propaganda, for the development of the groups takes place simultaneously with the development of propaganda. These groups develop inside of society propagandized to the extreme; they are themselves the loci of propaganda; they are instruments of propaganda and are integrated into its techniques."[17] One utterly misunderstands Ellul's argument, or deliberately misunderstands it, if one thinks that it is the *other* side in our debased politics, one's civil *opponents*, who indulge in propaganda while one's own side "follows the

16. "And let us be sure of this: we will not long preserve the gospel without the languages. The languages are the sheath in which this sword of the Spirit is contained; they are the casket in which this jewel is enshrined; they are the vessel in which this wine is held; they are the larder in which this food is stored; and, as the gospel itself points out, they are the basket in which are kept these loaves and fishes and fragments. If through our neglect we let the languages go (which God forbid!), we shall not only lose the gospel, but the time will come when we shall be . . . unable to speak or write a correct German or Latin, and have well-nigh lost . . . natural reason to boot." LW 45:360.

17. Ellul, *Propaganda*, 97.

science," objectively stating the facts and aiming objectively at truth, let the chips fall as they may. Propaganda is a system embracing all. It offers no way out of its totalizing embrace, only a way through it, itself dependent on an apocalyptic break-in from outside its system.

Modern humanity pays the high price of captivity to faction and an accompanying moral disintegration of personhood for the palliative of propaganda. People float along in the current, blown about by every wind of "news" selected and bull-horned by some "doctrine." Addiction to propagandistic news helps one "to forget the preceding event. In doing so, man then denies his own continuity; to the same extent that he lives on the surface of events and makes today's events his life by obliterating yesterday's news, he refuses to see the contradictions in his own life and condemns himself to a life of successive moments, discontinuous and fragmented."[18] A biographically fragmented self, "the propagandee is by no means just an innocent victim. He provokes the psychological action of propaganda, and not merely lends himself to it, but even derives satisfaction from it . . . There is not just a wicked propagandist at work who sets up means to ensnare the innocent citizen. Rather, there is a citizen who craves propaganda from the bottom of his being and the propagandist to respond to this craving."[19]

Theologians here may take note here of the dominical saying in Mark 13 regarding the appetite for propaganda: "Take heed that no one leads you astray. Many will come in my name, saying, 'I am he!' and they will lead many astray . . . And then if anyone says to you, 'Look, here is the Christ!' or 'Look, there he is!' do not believe it. False Christs and false prophets will arise and show signs and wonders, to lead astray, if possible, the elect."

With the help of Reformation theology in this apocalyptic vein, Ellul, now wearing the hat of theologian, pushes his analysis to the depths of our human predicament. "Finally, as a result of all the threats and contradictions in contemporary society, man feels accused, guilty. He cannot feel that he is right and good as long as he is exposed to contradictions, which placed him in conflict with one of his group's imperatives no matter which solution he adopts . . . " One propagandistic home remedy for this endemic feeling of guilt comes by the false consciousness of virtue-signaling:

18. Ellul, *Propaganda*, 47.

19. Ellul, *Propaganda*, 121.

> man needs to be right in his own eyes . . . He feels the need to belong to a group. What matters is not to be just, or to act just, or that the group to which one belongs is just—but to seem just, to find reasons for asserting that one is just, and to have these reasons shared by one's audience. This corresponds to man's refusal to see reality—his own reality first of all—as it is, for that would be intolerable . . . Before himself and others, man is constantly pleading his own case . . . [20]

The modern person, then, no longer fears the judgment of God which would scrutinize "his own reality" in truth but wants desperately to be seen on the so-called "right side of history," *as if* history in the voice of peer pressure were God. Any capacity, then, to stand against the stream, any Luther at the Diet of Worms professing a conscience bound to the word of God, vanishes—or this very Luther image is retooled for religious propaganda!

If Ellul's analysis is right, how mistaken is the twentieth-century theological cliché that modern humanity no longer asks the question of justification. In fact, the question of justification is omnipresent and becomes all the more urgent but also equally unanswerable in the total world of modern propaganda. As secularist idolatries, the answers which propaganda provides lead over time to the moral disintegration of the person or *in extremis* to the fanatical violence of one's faction lashing out against the systemically unjust world composed of all the other "lying" factions. Propaganda, providing a desperate but illusory self-justification, does not allow anyone to see that truth about themselves which comes, according to the Sermon on the Mount, from the scrutiny of the Father in heaven who sees in secret, there to unmask the hidden treasurings of the human heart (as we shall learn again from Howard Thurman in chapter 3).

Preaching such an *apocalypse* of the heart with integrity before the modern audience, therefore, would excavate hermeneutically *the divine pressure* on the human creature (as we shall hear from Augustine and Simeon Zahl in chapter 5) which is experienced in the conscientious need for some justification in order to expose the false consolations provided by propaganda. It would penetrate to this underlying hopelessness of finding justification in surrender to propaganda and its factional faux identities. It would enunciate the reality of the Father of the beloved Son Jesus Christ who by the sanctifying Spirit is prosecuting anyone who

20. Ellul, *Propaganda*, 121.

"needs to be right in his own eyes." In this way it would challenge the foregoing web of assumptions in the mental world of secularism that modern propaganda creates and sustains: the illusions about happiness in this life, the authority of mere data, the default innocence of humanity and the overriding myth of moral progress. In all these ways it would necessitate for the disillusioned of postmodernity the righteousness and salvation declared and delivered in Jesus Christ.

But "obviously, church members are caught in the net of propaganda and react pretty much like everyone else. As a result, an almost complete disassociation takes place between their Christianity and their behavior. Their Christianity remains a spiritual and purely internal thing."[21] For them, reality outside their pious feelings is the "panorama of the various propagandas [taken] for living political reality, and [they] do not see where they can insert their Christianity in that fictitious panorama. Thus, like all the others, they are stumped, and this fact removes all weight from their belief . . . "[22] Propaganda thus confronts the church with an excruciating dilemma: either

> *not* to make propaganda—but, then, while the church slowly and carefully wins a man to Christianity, the mass media quickly mobilize the masses, and churchmen gain the impression of being "out of step," on the fringes of history, and without power to change a thing. Or to make propaganda—this dilemma is surely one of the most cruel with which the churches are faced at present for it seems that people manipulated by propaganda become increasingly impervious to spiritual realities, less and less suited for the autonomy of Christian life.[23]

By the "autonomy" of Christian life, Ellul refers to the Pauline "freedom for which Christ has set us free," as in Martin Luther's claim that the justified sinner is "Lord of all, subject to none," as heir of a defiant hope that trumps the intimidations, even death threats of any Leviathan claim to sovereignty. To be sure, this Christian autonomy is immediately coupled in Paul and in Luther after him with its paradoxical complement of being slaves to one another in love. In providing a genuine alternative to propaganda, including denominational Christian propaganda, theology must be rigorous in attending to both poles of new life in Christ:

21. Ellul, *Propaganda*, 228.

22. Ellul, *Propaganda*, 229.

23. Ellul, *Propaganda*, 229.

freedom and love, doctrine and ethos, witness and service, the reality of the redeeming God and the reality of the afflicted creation. The theology of the martyrs (witnesses on trial!) is doctrine for life in exodus from the total system of propaganda of "the dark Egypt of this world" (Menno Simmons). So, Luther: "Out of the blood of Christians always grow other Christians, who imitate and marvel at their faith, confession of Christ, patience under the cross, and steadfastness, and who turn to the Christian faith and are saved."[24]

The need for such discipleship, such training of heart and mind, is because "propaganda is a total system that one must accept or reject in its entirety. If the church accepts it, two important consequences follow. First, Christianity disseminated by such means is not Christianity. . . . Christianity ceases to be an overwhelming power and spiritual adventure and becomes institutionalized in all of its expressions and compromised in all its actions. It serves everybody as an ideology with the greatest of ease and tends to be a hoax. In such times there appear innumerable sweetenings and adaptations, which denature Christianity by adjusting to the milieu."[25] Platitudinous celebrations of the Christian "idea" of God as "love" to clobber a competing faction as "haters" accomplish little but to bless disintegrating modernity by posturing for a place of esteem within it. Scripture in fact admonishes that love be sincere by hating what is evil (Rom 12:9), beginning with what is evil in oneself.

One may fear that Ellul's analysis of propaganda reduces us to a night in which all cats are gray: to abject relativism leaving us nothing but blind choices. It surely does in one sense level the playing field into a new cultural pluralism. Yet, as George Lindbeck has wisely observed: "Antifoundationalism, however, is not to be equated with irrationalism. The issue is not whether there are universal norms of reasonableness, but whether these can be formulated in some neutral, framework-independent language."[26] It seems not. Prima facie for theology, knowledge of the word of God provides a framework stipulating universal norms of reasonableness although it is hardly a neutral and independent language. Rather, a pungent little apocalyptic parable of Jesus disrupts our postmodern vertigo: "No one can enter a strong man's house to plunder his goods unless he first ties up the strongman" (Mark 3:27). Breaking free within the world of modern propaganda on account of

24. LW 62:30–31.

25. Ellul, *Propaganda*, 230.

26. Lindbeck, *Nature of Doctrine*, 130.

the in-breaking gospel will work a deep reformation in demoralized churches which have bet everything for the last several centuries on accommodating themselves to modernity's illusions. It will require a new birth to theological subjectivity, a conscientious and principled life lived in the presence of the God of the gospel. Such subjectivity does not *take* sides in the identitarian world of modern propaganda but *makes* sides as indicated in Gal 3:26–28. Propagating the gospel will not be an exercise of propaganda (which would be proselytism, soft or hard), but a proclamation in word and deed of the God of the gospel with its own agenda cutting through the claims and counterclaims of propaganda to create beloved community inclusive especially of those polarized or alienated by the technocratic juggernaut. How are we to proclaim the gospel in a world awash with propaganda? That is what is at issue. Robust doctrinal theology provides answers instructing how to speak and act the gospel with integrity. Ellul's analysis suffices to describe in broad strokes the situation in life of the present effort at the reconstruction of doctrinal theology in the tradition of Luther; to this we now turn.

Theology as Discipline in the Rule of Faith

We have indicated that doctrinal theology resists propaganda both within the church and outside the church by self-critically testing the church's proclamation and mission in the world by the gospel of God. Is the church saying the same thing that it has heard in the gospel? That same-saying would be the church's timely and therefore non-identical repetition or *confession of the word of God*. Is the church doing what the gospel mandates? That question would measure and assess the integrity of the church's practice in thought, word and deed as discipleship of the crucified Lord.

Doctrinal theology conducts its business with a scholarly method that exemplifies intellectual virtues and exposes intellectual vices, a methodological defense against propaganda, including the propagandization of gospel and its doctrine. To be sure, scholarship today is also vulnerable to co-optation in the total system of propaganda. Accordingly, as Jennifer Hockenberry emphasized in her commendation of the church father Augustine's scholarly method,[27] theology is driven to its most daring and most risky belief *in truth* just as *it believes in God*, indeed trusts in

27. Hockenberry, *Wisdom's Friendly Heart.*

the friendliness of God's truth inviting and aiding its pursuit. Augustine, believing this promise, broke free of cult (faction) and conspiracy theories (propaganda) just as he exposed the *libido dominandi* of Imperial Rome (*and* its rebels and opponents) in a way that anticipates our present situation of reconstructing doctrinal theology within postmodernity. Augustine was following the apostle Paul who was informed by Second Temple Jewish wisdom literature. This confidence in the faithful use of human reason in theology has its basis in the biblical wisdom literature. When the apostle Paul linked Lord Jesus Christ to the God and Father as mediator and source of creation respectively in 2 Cor 8:6, he initiated the decisive movement in early Christian theology away from emerging Gnosticism's dualism in the doctrine of God along with its occult rather than public rationality. This material cosmos was both the creature of the creator and the object of its redeeming act in Christ. The Epistle to the Colossians would later add the thought that the cosmos was not only made through the Lord Jesus but it was made for the Lord Jesus, indicating that creation itself is eschatologically determined and destined to a fulfillment, thus not a fixed or perfected given. This linkage was not only expressed in the kerygma's affirmation of the bodily resurrection of the Lord Jesus as sign and pledge of the redemption of our bodies together with the whole groaning creation, as in Romans 8. The linkage was also made, as it were, "from above" by affirming that the creator is the redeemer and that the redeemer redeems the creation. We can observe the same theological move in the prologue to the Gospel of John and in the treatise we know as the Epistle to the Hebrews.

Lois Malcolm in this connection has helpfully pointed to the biblical figure of Wisdom from the predominantly apocryphal literature (aside from the canonical book of Proverbs) of Second Temple Judaism as an important resource for patristic Christianity's articulation of the Trinitarian hypostasis of the Logos/Son with its mediatorial role in creation and hence its fittingness as the agent mediating the redemption of the afflicted creation.[28] She urges that the Nicene Creed, in articulating the doctrine of the Trinity, should direct us back to these Jewish sources of the doctrine to regain the sense and inspiration of the teaching for "contemporary reconstruction of creedal dogmas in view of the biblical sources."[29] Malcolm discovers necessary nuances in this way for contemporary interpretation

28. Malcolm, "No Wisdom, No Trinity."

29. Malcolm, "No Wisdom, No Trinity," 226.

of the Trinity, especially "to clarify the nature of the Father-and-Son relationship within the Trinity."[30] This clarification, or perhaps better, qualification, of the New Testament's predominant linguistic deployment of the Father-and-Son relationship in the gospel narrative to articulate the redemptive engagement of the Creator with the fallen and oppressed creation was complemented and thus qualified by the figure of Wisdom. Wisdom alongside the Word and Torah of God was imagined "as a pre-existent tool or plan through which the world was created"[31] and now in Christ to be re-created. Human reason and love for wisdom was thusly grounded theologically, not in itself, but in Israel's creation faith.

Were Logos/Wisdom, however, to displace rather than qualify the Father-Son language of the gospel narrative, which provides a *social* metaphor in thinking the Trinity, the Logos metaphor could instead imagine a mental operations model of Trinitarian life: "the mental production of the word, or wisdom coming forth from the mind" as occurred in Neo-Platonism. Indeed, "early Christian understandings in Jesus as the Logos were often interpreted in relation to a middle Platonic sense of the Logos as the divine principle of reason linking the human mind to the mind of God and cosmic order."[32] In spite of this vulnerability, Malcolm argues we can rather relate the "sapiential themes" of Second Temple Jewish literature "to biblical narrative and law."[33] The qualification of the Father-Son language arising from the gospel narrative in this scriptural way helpfully identifies Jesus as the wisdom and word of no other God than the God of Israel. Consequently, the figure of Wisdom as such does not occupy, Malcom argues, some ontological "middle ground" between creator and creature (as in Platonism) but is rather the Creator in the office of wisely forming and ultimately reforming the creation. So it is that in this faith human reason can be faithfully utilized for the understanding of what is believed.[34]

Moreover, the biblical figure of Wisdom helpfully qualifies the New Testament language of Father-and-Son: "The plethora of wisdom-related terms and images used in tandem with Father-Son language to depict these relations within the Trinity point in the direction of a kind of

30. Malcolm, "No Wisdom, No Trinity," 223.

31. Malcolm, "No Wisdom, No Trinity," 223.

32. Malcolm, "No Wisdom, No Trinity," 225.

33. Malcolm, "No Wisdom, No Trinity," 226.

34. Relevant here and very helpful is Zimmerman, *Recovering Theological Hermeneutics.*

baffling of gender literalism."[35] Malcolm's account of the "baffling" is accurate as well as theologically complexifying: "The Father gives birth to a Son; Jesus is both the messianic king and the feminine personification of God's Sophia; and the Spirit is both a masculine-like figure in the conception of Jesus in Mary's womb, and a feminine-like figure who 'groans' like a mother giving birth, amid creation's and our own sighs and groans."[36] In short, Malcolm's argument for the role of wisdom in theology is akin to the rule interpretation of the notion of divine "simplicity" in doctrinal theology.[37] Simplicity as a qualification of all kataphatic speech regarding the gods began with the pre-Socratic philosophers demythologizing of the Olympian tales; in its developed Christian usage, it requires recognition of the metaphorical nature of the New Testament apocalyptic genre, with its narrative figures of the Father, the Son, and the Holy Spirit presented as discrete and interacting agents on the plane of immanence; simplicity as a rule requires that these be deliteralized for understanding yet not abandoned. They are rather qualified as speech about the ineffable Creator of all that is not God in accord with the first Table of the Decalogue.[38] Malcolm sees that the Jewish-Hellenistic Sophia concretely works in this way to qualify the Son language in the doctrine of the Trinity, clarifying that it refers to something ineffable.

The wisdom literature of Second Temple Judaism was itself strongly influenced by Hellenistic culture by its broad diffusion of Platonic themes, as can be seen in the contemporary of Jesus and Paul, Philo of Alexandria. Consequently, the affinity of Jewish sapiential themes with second- and third-century Christian Logos theology is not accidental. Yet Malcolm registers a reservation about the realized eschatology of the letter to the Colossians "with its emphasis on Christ as the risen Lord glorified as *pantocrator*," i.e., defining the risen Lord in relation to "the Wisdom that created all things and brings them into cohesion and harmony." The reservation is that the apocalyptic dualism of the ages is only breached in Christ, as the hostile powers are not yet wholly defeated nor is Christ yet fully triumphant over them. It is for this reason that natural reason, long habituated to the creation's subjugation to anti-divine powers, cannot comprehend the things of the Spirit apart from the apocalypse and

35. Malcolm, "No Wisdom, No Trinity," 227.
36. Malcolm, "No Wisdom, No Trinity," 227.
37. Hinlicky, *Divine Simplicity*.
38. Hinlicky, *Divine Simplicity*, 197–209.

falls victim to (and subsequently perpetrator of) of propaganda under the hegemony of the father of lies. So, a "tension" of discontinuity and cosmic disharmony remains and is reflected in the "eschatological proviso" found in Paul's undisputed letters" which is not "easily harmonized" with the Platonizing Logos doctrine or the Colossians *pantocrator*.[39]

We have here is a subtle and difficult historical problem. Early Christianity, faced with the radical ontological discontinuity of pessimistic Gnosticism, welcomed help from the cosmic optimism of Platonism to link the mediator of creation with the mediator of redemption.[40] But in time, the same Platonism funded the Arian subordination of the Logos as "a second God" in the great chain of cosmic being, a metaphysics which indeed proved incompatible with the apocalyptic mediation of salvation as resurrection from the dead. The Arians were even able to celebrate the figure of Wisdom as "the first of God's creatures" (Proverbs 8:22). With all this in mind we can grasp the ambivalence in Luther's teaching on human reason, at once God's greatest gift and at the same time the prostitute which sells itself to the highest bidder. For Luther it is essential to grasp that the human being is not a sinner in its lower, animal being but rather in its highest dignity and power. Human reason and the love of wisdom is a field of battle in the apocalyptic duel.

Within modernity, no one so insisted upon rigorous scholarly method in theology as insightfully as Lutheran philosopher Georg Friedrich Wilhelm Hegel. In the following passage, he deploys the term "philosophy" in a traditional sense as the love of wisdom in pursuit of truth, similarly to Hockenberry's Augustine and his early scholastic disciple, Anselm.[41] He underscores the hermeneutical nature of such "philosophical" method in theology as faith seeking understanding, just as the Reformers had appropriated Renaissance humanism for scholarly method.

> Philosophy has been reproached for placing itself above religion. But as a matter of fact this is surely false because philosophy has only this [i.e., religion] and no other content, although it gives it the form of thinking; it places itself only above the *form* of faith, while the *content* is the same in both cases . . . Philosophy *thinks* what the subject as such *feels*.[42]

39. Malcolm, "No Wisdom, No Trinity," 226.
40. Hinlicky, *Divine Complexity*, 159–200.
41. Rogers, *Neoplatonic Metaphysics and Epistemology of Anselm of Canterbury*.
42. Hegel, *Lectures on the Philosophy of Religion*, 488n265.

Since Hegel's time, of course, few in the modern academic discipline of philosophy would agree that it has the same content as the Christian religion. In any case, Hegel is affirming that the thinking of faith—whether we call it systematic theology or philosophy of religion or critical dogmatics—is as necessary as inevitable:

> Just as soon as religion is no longer simply the reading and repetition of passages, as soon as what is called explanation or interpretation begins, as soon as an attempt is made by inference and exegesis to find out the meaning of the words in the Bible, then we embark upon the process of reasoning, reflection, thinking; and the question then becomes how we should exercise this process of thinking, and whether our thinking is correct or not. It helps not at all to say that one's thoughts are based on the Bible. As soon as these thoughts are no longer simply the words of the Bible, their content is given a form, more specifically a logical form.[43]

Even worse, religiosity that despises such rigorous method involves itself in self-deception. Thinking based on pure feeling and/or a naïve reading of the Bible in fact "reserves for itself the option to think as it chooses, in contingent fashion."[44] This fault particularly damages biblical studies today. Unable to give any definite theological answer to what the historically-critically atomized Bible says to any contemporary question, the biblical scholar is asked, "Well, nonetheless, based on your expertise what should we say about X?" To this the biblical scholar then holds forth with nothing but an *opinion* channeling some current of the zeitgeist. On the other side, so-called "systematic theology," faced with this theological vacuum in biblical studies, loses any grip on Scripture as primary matrix of theological thinking and presents itself as an ostensibly Christian philosophy of religion, preoccupied in modernity with foundationalist epistemology but of little interest to the churches which have their hands full with ambulance chasing, if not mere survival. Genuine thinking according to Hegel, by contrast, proceeds by "immersing ourselves in the subject-matter." That means self-forgetfulness on the part of the exegete, "giving up our particular opinions and beliefs and allowing the subject matter to hold sway over us." With this deployment of reason in elucidation of faith Hegel retrieves the motto and method of Anselm of Canterbury, "faith seeking understanding."

43. Hegel, *Lectures on the Philosophy of Religion*, 400.

44. Hegel, *Lectures on the Philosophy of Religion*, 400.

In definite distinction, however, from Hegel's own transformation of the antecedent theological tradition into his idealist philosophy of religion, in dogmatics as a critical discipline doctrine in the final analysis articulates the praise of God[45]—the endless praise of God by the church triumphant: when in the power of the Spirit we are brought to full conformity with the risen Son ecstatically to sing victory lauds to the Almighty Father. That eschatological note of the confession of praise provides the ultimate orientation for the entire theology of Christian doctrine. It has been this way from the beginning. "The Lord is a warrior, the Lord is his name," rescued Israel sang exuberantly on the far side of the Sea of Reeds, even though Israel was to learn through bitter experience that the Lord who fights for us must often enough also fight against us.[46] Nor is it different with the people of the new covenant whose anticipatory praise of God in the eucharistic meal is necessarily tempered in this interim time by a proper fear of God. "For as long as you eat this bread and drink this cup you proclaim the Lord's death until he comes again" (1 Cor 11:26).

No vague feeling awkwardly expressed in inadequate images or misleading language, doctrine in the end is the *articulate* praise of God as befits redeemed humanity. In the interim, the church militant holds together by its *articles* of faith which is the subject matter of doctrinal theology. Beginning at the end this way, we can see that one of the reasons why doctrinal theology is misunderstood and neglected in contemporary churches of North America and Europe is that the praise of God (together with the fear of God, for these two go together this side of the eschaton) has profoundly declined in the consciousness of churches so far as they have succumbed to the total system of propaganda. Nervous liturgical sloppiness and reckless revisionism reflect a "this age" only anxiety about whether the targeted audience is getting the proper vibe which the worship leader orchestrates. Hymnody becomes increasingly about us and our struggles or triumphs rather than what the Father has done in Christ the beloved Son by his sanctifying Spirit that his kingdom come, his will be done on earth as in heaven. Doctrinal assertion regarding the confession of faith rings hollow when there is little confidence of faith in face of the propaganda maelstrom to break forth in joyful praise, in unison celebrating who and what the God of the gospel is in anticipation of the final victory.

45. Pannenberg, *Basic Questions in Theology*, 1:202–5.

46. Hinlicky, *Joshua*.

To be sure, *just because* in final perspective doctrine articulates the fulfilled praise of God, in the interim the articles of faith are vulnerable as they must pass through many trials and tribulations on the church's pilgrim way. "Orthodoxy" which thinks, speaks and walks true to the gospel of God without deviation is the Spirit's work in progress. Yet this vulnerability, as Pannnenberg puts it, this vulnerability to doubt and hence the *disputability* of the articles of faith,[47] firmly locates the task of doctrinal theology. In this interim of trial and testing, the social location of doctrine is the embattled eucharistic community, the redeemed people of God in the midst of an as yet unreconciled world, defiantly anticipating in hope against hope the final ecstasy when they will directly know God in endless praise even as they have been known by God.

Christian theology, which a millennium ago created the university, is for the most part exiled from it today; it seeks a return home to the community of faith where for various reasons its welcome remains uncertain. Critics there ask: "Is churchly theology all talk and no action, talk that inhibits action, talk that divides actors?" Words, words, words! Theology is a matter of words: the *word of God* spoken on Easter morning, the *word of God heard and confessed from Pentecost onward, our words in doctrinal theology* about the words of the hearing, believing and confessing church in mission responding to the calling of the word of God! This is humanly fitting. An ancient but common description of our humanity is of "the animal having word." Scriptural religions instantiate this truth about us, preserving and handing down oral testimonies to an originating and authorizing event of a culture, requiring always fresh appropriations in new circumstances, themselves mediated by more and more words. Theology is wordsmithing in practice, syntactical and grammatical analysis in reflection, the more precisely to understand and efficiently to communicate the central and enduring import of the originating event in novel situations for the purpose of cultural renewal. Of course, words can become empty, communicating nothing. Symbols can die. Words can deceive, miscommunicating truth, even subverting it. Words can be performative, doing what they say but, just so, also weaponized to work verbal violence. Yet, in every case, language is the matrix and medium of the distinctively human life on the earth, just as canonical Scripture read, studied and interpreted is the matrix of the form of life which is the Christian community of faith. To be frustrated

47. Pannenberg, *Systematic Theology*, 1:50.

with words is to be frustrated at broken communication but to despair of words is to become deeply misanthropic.

As mentioned in the Introduction, this study will accordingly distinguish three orders of theological discourse to aid clarity in communication. First comes the descriptive theology of the word of God by way of theological exegesis of Scripture; second follows the hermeneutical theology of the confessing tradition with respect to the word of God as it has been heard, believed and taught in temporal-spatial context and handed onward; and third, the deliberative theology which queries the adequacy of the foregoing orders of theology for the sake of doctrinal reform and/or for communicating the word of God freshly in unanticipated situations. Importantly, the first two orders of theology are inheritances that provisionally determine *the terms* by which any debate in third-order theology is meaningful.[48] In every order, the scholarly discipline of doctrinal theology tends to the language of the church with verbal formulations of the central and enduring beliefs in their claim to truth originating from the Christ event, the external word from God that comes to the human self from outside of itself in order to transform it into the true humanity of Jesus Christ. It may do so in confidence of the sanctifying Spirit who tends to the word of God and its proclamation to the end of the age.

Such *precise* location of doctrinal theology in the language-behavior of the pilgrim church, taken as a "cultural-linguistic" community, was the great contribution of George Lindbeck a generation ago. Chiefly, his model accounted for the *unitive* function of common discourse as akin to the way a common vernacular unites otherwise diverse people with the means of articulate interchange of meaning, including equipment for negotiating conflict, at least in principle. His book, *The Nature of Doctrine*,[49] was a breakthrough into emergent postmodernity, or in Lindbeck's more narrowly theological conceptuality, our "post-liberal" (and post-Christendom) historical epoch. Perhaps the apex of that cultural modernism which Lindbeck was seeking to leave behind for a better understanding of the nature and function of Christian doctrine was the assault by the mid-century logical positivists who influentially argued against the troubling logical ambiguities besetting ordinary human language in general. Pioneers of the notion that faulty human language could be replaced by computation, they insisted that mathematically enabled falsifiability, as

48. Hinlicky, "Scripture as Matrix, Christ as Content."

49. Lindbeck, *Nature of Doctrine.*

in experimental science, is the criterion of meaningfulness. If a proposition is not in principle capable of being scientifically articulated, mathematically measured, empirically tested and as such capable in principle of being disproved (if not yet proved), it is not a meaningful statement at all and need not be taken with cognitive seriousness. One cannot say yes or no to statements in principle incapable of proof; they are simply meaningless. Obviously, this criterion of falsifiability would be devastating for Christianity—just as the logical positivists intended.[50] One cannot say yes or no to Christian doctrine because no one has any idea of what it means. What *in the world* is it talking about? Doctrine is mere opinion, scientifically idle chatter.

The interesting twist, however, is that Lindbeck argued convincingly that both liberal and conservative theologies in modernity had tacitly internalized modern positivism in their understanding of the traditional articles of faith. They wished Christian theology to maintain its academic status in the modern university as a "science." Either historically or metaphysically, conservative theologians thought that doctrinal claims were propositions that had to establish their meaningfulness by demonstrating evidential capacity for scientifically established truth. Such theological "propositionalism," as Lindbeck tagged it, in time had morphed into "evidence that demands a verdict" apologetics: searching for the remains of Noah's Ark, looking for gaps in evolution to find a place for intelligent design or supernatural intervention, in desperation arguing that the fossil record was planted by God to test the faith of "Bible-believers." In another permutation, propositionalism turned to classical metaphysics, especially the ontotheological doctrine of divine simplicity, to assert the reasonableness of postulating the necessary being of the First Cause as a rational foundation of general validity on which to erect the Christian doctrine of the revealed God. For Lindbeck, an antifoundationalist, these kinds of conservative apologetics had shipwrecked on the reef of reality in the twentieth century.

Liberal theologians by contrast embraced that conservative shipwreck and shifted ground to human spirituality as a positive fact empirically accessible to the human sciences, claiming that doctrine was to be understood as symbolic objectifications of the primal feeling for life; this *Lebensgefühl* counted as the evidential reference point. But this resort to feeling and its symbolization in images or representations was a

50. Berlinski, *Devil's Delusion.*

slippery slope: empirical resort to putative feelings reflected in "religious consciousness" uncovered such a pluralism of objectifications of spiritual experience that the unifying function of doctrine for healthy community life was utterly eclipsed by a proliferation of identity theologies declining into factions with their self-referential propaganda. These subsequently amounted to so many languages each with their distinct, indeed, virtually incommensurable jargon and grammar, attempts at "intersectionalism" notwithstanding, that liberal theology increasingly morphed into "religious studies"[51] of the diverse spiritualities.

For Lindbeck, theology wishing to be science, whether in conservative or liberal forms of accommodation to modernity had *both* shipwrecked, not only on the alleged empirical or metaphysical reality claimed, but on the very shoal of the would-be criterion of falsifiability: the proposition that falsifiability is the criterion of meaningfulness is itself not falsifiable, and so the program of the Logical Positivists collapsed in a self-contradiction on the path to our current postmodernism.[52] But Lindbeck's analysis of this common fate of conservative propositionalism and "experiential-expressivism," as he named the liberal alternative, exposed a shared misunderstanding of the nature of Christian doctrine. Christian doctrinal theology is neither systematic apologetics nor a particular branch of religious studies, each aspiring to credibility as understood by "science" in the modern academy. It is the scholarly "dogmatics" of a religious tradition attending to integrity by the production of stipulations about authentic behavior in word and deed. Doctrines may prima facie bear a claim to truth but that is not their doctrinal function. As doctrine they are rather rule of faith instructing proper usage of the terms of faith; accordingly, doctrinal disagreement rarely occurs over the terms of faith which are inherited from the originating event and its propagation by an external word. Rather, doctrinal disagreement is understood as rooted

51. For the birth and eventual separation of religious studies from idealistic theology in Germany, see the outstanding study of Zachhuber, *Theology as Science in Nineteenth Century Germany.*

52. Modernity was marked by "the conviction that there is a universal, rational order to the world that is in principle knowable by human beings." Greene, *Imagining Theology*, 35. The postmodern disillusionment comes to "a radically revised picture of science, that is of one that understands scientific research to be rooted in cultural commitments and social intercourse, dependent on the persuasive power of shared paradigms that give shape and focus but that cannot themselves be justified by appeal to universal principles" (37).

in differences over priority in the ordering of doctrines, i.e., what is the *norma normans* and what is *norma normata.*

Lindbeck's differentiation opens up the possibility of freshly seeing the real differences between Christian theology and the sciences, as Garrett Greene has argued, specifically "between knowing the things of this world and knowing those aspects of reality that transcend our cognitive abilities."[53] Knowledge of genuine transcendence, not "the watered down, domesticated God of modern deism and religious apologetics, but the biblical God, the holy one of Israel . . . " is "not simply quantitative but qualitative" as the difference between "time and eternity, earth and heaven, creature and creator, immanence and transcendence, contingency and necessity, this world and the world to come."[54] In Christian understanding of deity, the One who is God truly is categorically the creator of all that is not God, a notion that funds the doctrine of all humanity made in the image of God for likeness to God and thus of abiding value in spite of sinful deformation. As universal creator, true God is by distinction from creatures exclusively *ab se*, from itself and not any other. Calling upon Katherine Sonderegger's case for divine *aseity*,[55] Greene argues that the central error of modernist theology has been putting God into the ontotheological role of cosmic causality (*Alleinwirkamseit Gottes*) which "forces divine will off the stage, compromising God's freedom by deifying the notion of "absolute cause, an efficient power that can brook no rival."[56] Greene associates divine aseity with Karl Barth's virtually untranslatable German term, *Unverfügbarkeit,* denying that true God can ever be instrumentalized by creatures. "God is not at our disposal but sovereignly free."[57] Divine freedom is the insignia of the true transcendence of the creator of all that is not God—just as Luther maintained against Erasmus. Aseity means that God is determined by God and not any other, especially not by the creature's ideas of what constitutes a perfectly divine being. Like divine simplicity, aseity is here understood as a stipulation for thought and speech to refer to the one creator of all that is not God as God truly. Doctrine that attends the ongoing life of the freely elected community

53. Greene, *Imagining Theology,* 9.

54. Greene, *Imagining Theology,* 9.

55. Sonderegger, *Systematic Theology,* Volume 1, *The Doctrine of God.* See this author's contribution to the symposium on Katherine Sonderegger, *Systematic Theology,* Volume 1, *The Doctrine of God,* in *Pro Ecclesia.*

56. Greene, *Imagining Theology,* 10.

57. Greene, *Imagining Theology,* 11.

arising from the Christ event must regulate its thought, speech and behavior in such fashion in order to sustain its identity and mission through the changes and chances of time. Doctrines in this light function like grammatical rules for clarifying articulate speech, the matrix of human thought and behavior. For example, another Lutheran, Lindbeck's friend Robert Jenson, thusly expressed the Reformation doctrine of justification by faith as a rule: "So speak of Jesus and his love that nothing in all creation can defeat it." For both Lindbeck and Jenson, this postliberal understanding of doctrine as communal rules for properly Christian word and deed in the conduct of life was particularly amenable to the causes of liturgical and eucharistic renewal and thusly facilitated Lutheran-Roman Catholic doctrinal reconciliation. Catechetical training in this light intends formation of competent speakers of ecclesial Christianity in the same way that a knowledge of grammar empowers speakers to employ language clearly and compellingly in social interaction.

The present book stands in definite continuity with Lindbeck's model but also requires the development, indeed *amendment* of it in several respects. This book for the most part consists in meeting these criticisms by providing an apocalyptic theology of theology, which continues in Lindbeck's anti-foundationalism. The criticism, however, is twofold. First, critics have complained that Lindbeck's understanding of the nature of doctrine is ghettoizing even as Lindbeck himself had projected the Christian future in the West as sociologically sectarian, although catholic in its self-understanding. While this prediction regarding post-Christendom is at least partially coming true, it can also serve to open up a clearing amid the haze of propaganda to point the forward path of integrity in the propagation of the gospel.[58] Yet the objection may immediately sound: what *in the world* are you talking about? Surely there is a danger of losing "catholic self-understanding" in abandoning historical and/or metaphysical propositional claims to truth as reference to extra-linguistic reality, as critics charged, if the seemingly inward turn of the cultural linguistic model undercuts the authentic need of Christian doctrine to relate to new developments in history, science, and philosophy in the common world. Indeed, for reasons internal to the doctrinal tradition, these developments *must* be theologically acknowledged and comprehended under the doctrine of creation and preservation. By the same token, Lindbeck's rejection of doctrine as the expression of religious

58. Lindbeck, *Nature of Doctrine*, 124–28.

feeling seemed to many critics dryly to expect salutary change in human affect to occur mechanically, *ex opere operato*, by rote participation in the community's worship life, bypassing connection with and concretion in the lived experience of contemporary people as the human reality to which the gospel is ever freshly addressed.

For our purposes, Simeon Zahl has executed the better critique of the cultural-linguistic model of doctrine for failing to account for the affective salience of gospel doctrine to capture the heart and to reform desire, as it must, if doctrine in an other than propagandistic way is to unite hearts-and-minds in common confession and doxological wonder. We will amend Lindbeck's model with his help in chapter 5. The succinct and incisive critique of Lindbeck's model for its reticence regarding truth claims in propositional form was provided by Sarah Coakley in a discussion of the christological doctrine of the Council of Chalcedon.[59] She expertly rejects three misleading representations of this classical statement of doctrinal theology: 1) that it merely regulates language about Christ without making any direct truth claims; 2) that its metaphorical speech is not at all cognitive but only expressive of believers experience of Christ; and 3) that its claims are literally true in a modern positivistic sense. Having cleared the ground in this way, her own position is that Chalcedon sets boundaries about that which can and cannot be said of Christ; hence with Lindbeck, doctrine regulates. But it regulates in such a way that *it refers* to the "mystery of his person." As the reader will see, this book concurs with all three of these judgments. Quite specifically, she faults the model for implying "that Chalcedon is attempting not an ontological proposition but a more modest set of linguistic 'rules of predication'" for the sake of a dubious apologetic advantage consisting in retreat from reality into the hermeneutical circle of the community of faith. Doctrine as regulation assures a sectarian *way of speaking*; it does not speak publicly to attest *a way of being*, neither of the person of Christ nor of the "very reality of *experienced* salvation."[60] Thus, her critique dovetails with Zahl's. We shall amend Lindbeck's model with this help from Coakley in chapter 6, picking up support from Luther along the way.

Lindbeck himself, however, noted that his model *does* allow for ontological claims of a modest, descriptive sort and tacitly held that historical reference to the fact of the Christ-event was *sine qua non* of

59. Coakley, "What Does Chalcedon Solve and What Does It Not?"

60. Coakley, "What Does Chalcedon Solve and What Does It Not?"

his model, entailed insofar as the cultural-linguistic community depends upon an "external word," i.e., the "news" in the good news of the gospel. But he left the development of these possibilities to others. Sharing in his generation's general disaffection from the legacies of pietism and revivalism, he had little to say about the experiential dimension of doctrine as ecstatic experience in anticipation of the Lord's promised victory—as already signaled here in the claim that in final perspective doctrine articulates the praise of God's victory for us and for all. But certainly, no one learns to speak a language by studying grammar rules nor employs a learned language *not* to make meaningful reference to something in the world, the very utility of the sign being its ostensive function to point to something signified. How then? Particularly when the language and culture in question require a perpetual, counterintuitive *conversion* from an antecedent state of being? The apostle Paul in the earliest extant Christian literature described his Thessalonian converts as those who have "turned from to God from idols, to serve a living and true God, and to wait for his Son from heaven, whom he raised from the dead—Jesus, who rescues us from the wrath that is coming" (1 Thess 1:9–10). The function of Christian doctrine is similarly to witness, to attest, to point to such "mystery" as the apostle here proclaims in full apocalyptic raiment. It will be argued that its abiding regulative force depends upon a basic theological claim to truth.

How doctrinally does that change in human affect and loving loyalty of mind come about? To answer such objections to the cultural-linguistic model and in the process further to develop it, it must be relocated from "propositions borrowed from philosophy" (as in Schleiermacher)[61] to New Testament apocalyptic which frames the originating event giving rise to the external word, the news of the gospel which forms the new self of the theological subject. Philip Ziegler, following Calvin, argues

> that, while affirming the essentially formal architecture of the human subject as a creature possessed of reason and will by nature, more important by far is what becomes of this nature through the adventitious history of fall and redemption. For this history is the history of the unmaking and remaking of the moral subject, the transit of the human creature from the *status corruptionis* in which genuine moral subjectivity is an impossibility to the *status gratiae* in which it becomes newly

61. In Lindbeck's case, Wittgenstein and Geertz.

> possible solely by virtue of the effective working of Christ and the Spirit on us and in us.[62]

To articulate the efficacious working of the present Christ by the sanctifying Spirit in the transformation of human subjectivity to the newness of life on the earth by the capture of desire to the impending reign of God is the amendment needed to meet the objections to Lindbeck's model of doctrine. And just this articulation enables the reading of Scripture in the apocalyptic way that disrupts even venerable theological tradition by renewing the articulate claim to truth *about God* in doctrinal theology.

62. Ziegler, *Militant Grace*, 139.

II

Resituating Doctrinal Theology in New Testament Apocalyptic

This chapter argues that the deficits in the cultural-linguistic model identified in the previous chapter can be remedied by resituating the "religion" Lindbeck described with sociological and philosophical conceptuality in the apocalyptic theology of the New Testament as the ecclesia authored and authorized by, and hence also enlisted in service of, the good news of the resurrection-vindication of the crucified Jesus. This is from the outset a christologically modified apocalyptic in that, asserting the resurrection of the crucified Jesus already now, ahead of apocalyptic expectation, this knowledge of God is inaugurated with the embattled reign of Christ in advance of the eschaton, breaching the dualism of the ages of the antecedent apocalyptic literature of Second Temple Judaism. Yet this proposed relocation immediately raises its own set of difficulties, most acutely the problem here and now in the fog and friction of apocalyptic contestation of naming, both of Jesus and of his diabolic foe (Mark 3:22–27). Contemporary objections to such naming for demonizing human opponents, exemplified in the negative by Martin Luther's apocalyptic invective, give pause. Nevertheless, the very difficulty of naming Jesus apocalyptically in conflict with the regnum diaboli indicates a deep problem in the received doctrine of an unbaptized God, also lying behind Luther's rhetorical violence, that is to be explored, exposed and remedied throughout the rest of this book. In short, the burden of perfection in the tradition of Christian Platonism imposed upon Luther as well as others an absolutism in theology which could tolerate little humility in the otherwise bold articulation of doctrine.

The deep problem consists in the supposed metaphysical certainty attained by thinking the idea of the perfect being in substitution for the vulnerable dubitability of faith in the promising God, the God who promises himself, at once the agent, the content, and the medium of the gift. The reconstruction of doctrinal theology in the tradition of Luther, accordingly, requires of us today a threefold move to be executed in this chapter: 1) resituating doctrinal theology in the apocalyptic setting of the gospel narrative;[1] *2) working through the immediate perplexities and objections to the foregoing move and in the process qualifying Lindbeck's sociological notion of religious community to locate doctrinal theology in that "cultural linguistic community" specifically authored and authorized by the apocalypse of the resurrection-vindication of the crucified Jew Jesus;*[2] *3) and following from the foregoing, the diagnosis and execution of a probing critique of the basic flaw in the received tradition's doctrine of God.*

The procedure in this chapter recognizes the respective virtues of the heretofore divergent contemporary theological tendencies of the "radical Lutherans" and the "evangelical catholics"[3] *and works to unite them for a new formation of theological work. The task of doctrinal theology today in the ruins of Christendom will be to rule in a path of integrity in speaking and acting true to the gospel by ruling out the seductions of propaganda in the community of faith confessing Jesus as Lord.*

THE PRECEDING CHAPTER'S ANALYSIS from Ellul served to explicate the broad cultural context of the postmodern West for reconstruction in

1. Ziegler, *Militant Grace*; Morse, *Not Every Spirit*; Davis and Harink, *Apocalyptic and the Future of Theology.*

2. Portions of this chapter are adapted from Hinlicky, "New Language of the Spirit: Critical Dogmatics in the Tradition of Luther."

3. Ziegler invokes the radical Lutheran Gerhard Forde's monergism of grace, *Militant Grace*, 5. Witness the sharp critique by Mark Mattes of the thin, existentialist interpretation of Luther on behalf of "the embodiment of the Word" which in turn "acknowledges that faith at its core is markedly aesthetic, awakening the senses, opening receptivity, kindling wonder, and evoking gratitude. Such an aesthetic core of faith is expressed in worship that is sensitive not only to the ecstatic joy but also to the complaint or accusation against God when life seems terribly unfair . . . " Mattes, *Martin Luther's Theology of Beauty*, 3.

Lutheran doctrinal theology by showing what is at issue. The account which followed of the "cultural-linguistic" model of doctrine along with its need for revision and further development indicates, however, that it would be a major mistake to build this book's argument on mere reaction against the now totalizing system of propaganda in which we find ourselves today. The temptation to fight fire with fire is too strong while counter-fire only implicates theology in the same systemic mendacity. We are *against* propaganda because we are *for* propagation of, and in behavior that is proper to, the gospel of God; *consequently*, as "judgment begins in the household of God," we are self-critically on guard against *ecclesiastical* propaganda wherein the Lordship of Christ is swallowed up by partisan, factional, denominational ecclesiologies involved in the usual fight for recognition in a fallen world (Mark 10:35–45). We learn to propagate the gospel properly, even if not especially in our contemporary world, let alone in our compromised churches, by attending to the gospel and learning to speak it on its own terms according to its own purpose, in the process proposing doctrinal rules to safeguard our speaking of it with integrity, guarding especially against our own betrayals of its intended meaning.

The Apocalyptic Setting of the Gospel Narrative

As Lindbeck wrote in muted reference to his own Lutheran tradition, "to become a Christian involves learning the story of Israel and of Jesus well enough to interpret and experience oneself and one's world *in its terms*. A religion is above all an external word, a *verbum externum*, that molds and shapes the self and its world, rather than an expression or thematization of a pre-existing self or preconceptual experience."[4] The terms, as we shall see, are "Jesus," "Lord," and the copula which unites them into one person, "the one Lord Jesus Christ the Son of God." In accord with the external word of adoption by union with this beloved Son, the sanctifying Spirit bears witness to our spirits that we are indeed the children of God. "Spirit" does not, then, designate contemporary "spirituality"—putatively "common experience diversely articulated in different religions"[5]—but names the selfsame divine Agent who initiated, conducted, and finally vindicated the saving mission of the Son

4. Lindbeck, *Nature of Doctrine*, 34, emphasis added.

5. Lindbeck, *Nature of Doctrine*, 34.

of God incarnate. This *Spiritus Creator*[6] is at work and may manifest outside the visible Christian community, but that possibility is a matter for discernment by those who know the sanctifying Spirit whom the Father breathed upon the beloved Son. Thus, the primary form of doctrinal theology is its account of this external word, the gospel of God, precisely as propagated by the sanctifying Spirit.

To explicate Lindbeck's latent Lutheranism, however, requires us both to identify his "external word" as the good news of the resurrection-vindication of the crucified Jesus and to understand it, with its properly apostolic propagation, in the setting of New Testament apocalyptic which is, according to Ernst Käsemann's famous claim, "the mother of Christian theology."[7] In a preliminary way, the previous chapter already located doctrinal theology in the Christian community's anticipation of the victory of God for sinful and suffering humanity. This anticipation means that doctrine is ultimately doxological, the victorious *confession of praise* reciting in jubilation the saving deeds of the Lord. To be sure, such confession is penultimately assertive in a world saturated with pseudo-prophets and pseudo-messiahs with competing claims to human liberation "to deceive even the elect" (Mark 13:22), inspired as they are by alternative constructions of deity than that One who justifies the ungodly, "raises the dead and calls into existence the things that do not exist" (Rom 4:17). As the closing citation from 1 Thessalonians in the previous chapter indicated regarding conversion, a battle of patient expectation is underway for hearts and minds and bodily obedience. Accordingly, there is an urgent need already now for the clear *confession of faith*, sustaining by scholarly analysis and argument the news of the saving deed of the Lord communicated in the gospel; indeed, clarity is gained in the fog and friction of engagement with integrity-threatening deviations from within and the hostility of the idols and their propaganda from without. Consequently, to make concrete what Lindbeck denoted abstractly by the "cultural-linguistic model of religion" we now describe the social location of doctrinal theology in the ecclesia as figured in the apocalyptically fraught world of Mark 13.

In the thirteenth chapter of the Gospel, we learn that Mark is writing to churches that are being overrun with miracle workers, messianic pretenders, and false prophets trying to read the signs of the times and

6. Prenter, *Spiritus Creator*.

7. Käsemann, *New Testament Questions for Today*, 102.

claiming to speak in the name of the risen Lord. They are saying that they have the mind of Christ, that they speak in the voice of the Spirit. They preach an attractive but deviant message that evades the necessity of publicly confessing, especially under duress, the incriminating name of Jesus with the attendant willingness to suffer for that naming of him as saving Lord. We can see this concretely in the words which Mark's Jesus addresses to an urgent situation of war and persecution (Mark 13:5–8) in which Mark's suffering community looked for the coming of the Lord Jesus in clouds of heaven to rescue them: "And if anyone says to you at that time, 'Look! Here is the Messiah!' or 'Look! There he is!'—do not believe it. False prophets and false Messiahs will appear and produce signs and omens . . . " (Mark 13:21–22a). For Mark, informed faith knows the One in whom it is invested; it is thusly able to distinguish true from false prophets, the true from false messiahs. Demonstration of wonder-working power does not suffice for this task. The problem runs far deeper.

As commentator Joel Marcus has it, "if Mark 13:22 ["false messiahs and false prophets will produce signs and omens, to lead astray, if possible, the elect"] is taken seriously, the majority of the Markan Christians will be enmeshed in the realm of demonic delusion—perhaps not only a tendency to follow false Christs (13:22) but also a related propensity to despair over the return of the true one (cf. 4:38, 6:48 . . .)." But the true Messiah by his passion and death on the cross has already fulfilled the prophecies of the end time in Mark 13: "the elect fall asleep (14:37, 40–41) and go astray (14:50–52, 66–72), the sun is dimmed (15:33), the temple suffers damage that portends its destruction (15:38), and the Son of Man passes through an all-night vigil until finally, on the other side of cosmic death, he returns as the herald of new life and a new age."[8] "Apocalypse now" comes by the gospel narrative that reveals the crucified one as the Son of God (or does not reveal him at all, Mark 4:11–12), thusly beginning end time judgment already now within the household of God. Apocalypse comes now, not as the literal end of time but as the time of the end breaking into the strong man's house. Christians therefore may struggle too, holy if so liberated, to follow their Lord in bearing their own crosses, not only against the outside world but even also within the church, because their Lord has already struggled, pioneering the way, winning the victory for them. In his light and truth as the *Crucified* Messiah (1 Cor 2:2), they know

8. Marcus, *Mark 1–8*, and Marcus, *Mark 8–16*, 922–23.

the holy way forward (Luke 22:24–27)—*true* progress in holiness and specifically *Christian* progressivism, if you will.

The false prophets indeed have a "gospel," a contemporaneous emancipatory message; in working wonders it even resembles Jesus's own beginnings. But decisively the false prophets are now promising escape from the impending tribulations closing in on the community. This message of liberation *as escape*, tested against Mark's story of Jesus's way to the cross, is what the Gospel judges theologically false and spiritually ruinous. For the same reason, the sanctifying Spirit, who led Jesus on his path to the cross, is no source of new and independent revelations, introduced by "signs and omens," but, as the same One who anointed Jesus, leads disciples in their vulnerability, just as he had led Jesus, into mortal combat with Satan and his legion unclean spirits (Mark 1:8, 12–13, 23–27). This Spirit gives courage and words of truth to suffering disciples so that they testify truly in the time of trial (Mark 13:11). Against the deep-seated human inclination to which the false prophet's message of escape appeals, the counter-intuitive truth that God's salvation comes not in escape from sufferings, but through enduring the cross, had to be articulated and expressly taught: "You will be hated by all because of my name. But the one who endures to the end will be saved" (Mark 13:13). "But be alert; *I* have already told you everything" (Mark 13:23). The gospel narrative thus elicits express teaching about the "name" of Jesus, if the "I" of Jesus is to be identified, heard and understood truly, and thus to be obeyed faithfully. Faith must be informed about Jesus in order to recognize his voice. For this first-order descriptive task the word is mediated by the Spirit and the Spirit is given by the word in a virtuous circle to establish thereby knowledge of the controversial Jesus who authors and authorizes the community of faith's confession of his name, provoking in turn the time of trial in the world.

This social location in the beleaguered community of faith implies that in large part such doctrinal or confessional assertions as words about the word of God are regulative, i.e., they arise from reflection on practice in naming and recognizing Jesus and behave like grammatical rules for proper speech in the world about the God of the gospel, e.g., "do not name Jesus the Son of God nor understand his Lordship apart from his destiny on the cross." Such second-order regulative usage depends upon the primary theology of the external word of God spoken on Easter morn to reveal him who was crucified as the very Son of God. In first-order discourse regarding the external word, theology describes the *divine* cognitive act of identification, the *apocalypse* of resurrection, vindicating the one named by it. "Crucified Jesus is indeed my beloved Son" is the very word of God, the gospel. In immediate dependence by the sanctifying Spirit on that word of God, theology in second-order discourse confesses in faith that "Jesus is Lord," singing glory to the Father for sending the beloved Son into our midst to save; before the world, the confession, "Jesus is Lord," pointedly and provocatively affirms that this Servant of the Lord is Messiah of Israel, not a zealot insurrectionist, let alone the imperial tyrant who sits on Caesar's throne. In yet a third level of discourse, such as this book, theologians inquire into and debate about the foregoing definition of terms to discern its contemporary contextual sense in our world of propaganda machines and systemic mendacity.

The Gospel of Mark does its second-order confessing climactically in its dramatic portrait of the beloved Son's Godforsaken death. Here, of all things unexpected, the church's confession of faith is voiced by *the executioner* to show that it is not in the power or possession of stumbling disciples and failed followers but given from above where and when it pleases God, stopping every mouth to put an end to religious boasting, granting truthful same-saying of the word of God no matter how improbable the human source. Certainly, the executioner is not being lifted up as a moral model but rather as a rebuke to pious boasting, being the first human being to know and to say the full truth about Jesus. The centurion's confession represents Mark's formulation of Spirit-evoked Christian doctrine. Rebuked and silenced now is the demonic attempt hitherto to identify Jesus as the Son of God, i.e., *apart from this precise termination of his mortal history, apart from this unlimited solidarity with failed disciples in their justly experienced "bitter weeping" as unfaithful failures.*

In a world of contending stories that promise liberation, the Spirit thereby simultaneously implicates all truthful confessors of the name of Jesus in his very destiny, thereby freeing them in the process from their own willful and persistent incomprehension (Mark 8:33). The name of Jesus is not magical incantation, but a real object in the Spirit of theological knowledge. In turn, the person of Jesus (*not* in the modernizing sense of inner psychological processes, but in the sense of the *public persona* of the man in mission as rendered in the gospel narrative) displays the leadership of the Spirit (Mark 1:12!). At the Spirit's bidding in turn and as humbled by the awe-some depiction of the executioner telling the truth, same-saying by Easter-redeemed disciples henceforth of the originative identification of crucified Jesus as God's Son and saving

Lord in fresh circumstances of the conflicted world constitutes a second cognitive task of theology, making its regulative function clear, as in Luther's characterizations: *Vera theologia et cognitio Dei in Christo crucifixo sunt. Sola crucis nostra theologia est.*

Of course, the originative apocalypse and corresponding confession of faith as we have seen in the Gospel of Mark is historically conditioned; concretely it affirms that neither imperial Roman hegemons nor Jewish insurrectionists of first-century Palestine represent the Messiah of Israel. Recognizing this ineradicable historicity of the originative event, the notion of doctrine as "confession" is concrete and thus needs ever to be contextually apt. Just as the word of God spoken in the originative event is inextricably historical, confession of this authorizing and hence authoritative word of God is always historical, a nonidentical but recognizable repetition of the word of God as it is heard in a particular time and place, asserting here and now regulative force within the community of faith over speech and behavior. Only so is the church the creature of the gospel and only so does it remain so in its own self-understanding.

Such a view of confession was integral to early Lutheran theology and its refusal of papist claims to exclusive stewardship of Christian truth. This usage retains its apocalyptic sense according to the word of Jesus in Matt 10:32–33, just as this meaning was retrieved in Germany during the church struggle in the 1930s to identify the church in the concrete act of confessing Jesus as Lord over against a politically subservient people's church raising the arm in salute with Nazism.[9] This apocalyptic sense of confession with its sensitivity to historical context is not identical, then, with post-Reformation "confessionalism" as a sectarian ideology marking out and justifying ecclesiastical boundaries in a fractured Christendom. But confession of praise is the beating heart of the community's life according to the gospel mandate to gather for thanksgiving in proclaiming the Lord's death until he comes again; confession of faith articulates the abiding conflict with spiritual forces of wickedness in high places resisting the risen and ascended Lord Jesus who must battle until he subdues those forces under his feet. Whenever and wherever Jesus is confessed as Lord, the strong man's house has been broken into, binding him, and the despoiling of the dark Egypt of this world has begun.

Confession as the very being in act of the church—answering Bonhoeffer's question, "who do *we* say Jesus is" *is strictly a reply* to *Jesus*

9. Hinlicky, "Confession." Günther Bornkamm, "Das Wort Jesu vom Bekennen."

questioning us, "who do you say that I am?" It gives no license to making Jesus over in our own preferred way. Rather, this dialectic between first-order and second-order theology raises acutely the christological question: Who really is Jesus Christ? Which spirit is his Spirit by which our confession corresponds to his self-giving? Which story of deliverance really is *Jesus's* story? What difference does the *name* of Jesus make, that it cannot be substituted by another name?—that "no other name under heaven is given by which we must be saved" (Acts 4:12)? What does the name of Jesus name?

Yet notice the *derivative* status of these oftentimes acute theological questions of today. They arise only because of the antecedent *terms* of the external word reporting Jesus as divinely given good news and echoed in churchly traditions of confession of praise, faith and service. Lindbeck allowed, as mentioned, the question of propositional correspondence within his cultural-linguistic model just as he also allowed the question of symbolic correspondence with religious experience but subordinated such third-order theological inquiry to the second-order grammatical rules of ecumenically intended doctrine *in terms of which* "truth claims are made and expressive symbolisms employed." Doctrinal rules, in other words, do not do the actual work of affirming here and now that "Jesus is Lord" nor of efficacious transformation to a corresponding subjectivity but only assert *the terms* by which that confession is a meaningful statement and human transformation is authentic such that these can be in principle be affirmed or denied, explicated or misconstrued, verified, nuanced, or falsified.[10]

Third-order theology, of course, may vigorously affirm or even deny by evidence and argument the doctrinally meaningful confession, Jesus is Lord, in answering the derivative but acute questions of our post-Christendom context. Christianly speaking, that is as it should be. The church's received confession of faith establishes a solid platform for meaningful inquiry. The orientation provided is of widest scope because knowledge of the Creator of everything that is not God entails that everything under the sun is theologically relevant. Second-order theology, to be sure, tests the church's speech and behavior by the word of God as understood in the terms of the received confession of faith, but third-order theology experiments, testing out new modalities of speech and behavior in fresh and challenging circumstances posed by the dynamism of historical

10. Lindbeck, *Nature of Doctrine*, 48.

change. Yet even exploratory doctrinal theology is not freethinking but freed thinking, thus bound to its liberating Lord. Only the honest, resolute and persistent denial of the confession, Jesus is Lord, excludes one from the theologically meaningful circle of revelation and faith.

This reflexivity of being at once bound and freed in theological thought, i.e., of being free*d* rather than *free*thinkers, reflects an axiomatic truth integral to serious speech about God: only the promised fulfillment of God definitively validates the Christian confession of faith, "Jesus is Lord." In the interim the confession is controversial and thus subject to doubt within the very posture of faith. The confession of faith articulates faith, not sight, to be sure, but gospel-thinking of the Father who spared not the beloved Son but gave him up for us all is *informed* faith. The doctrinal rule of theological humility instructs that only God can speak of God and so also that only God can definitively validate any human creature's speech of God, even confessing speech. Thus, the fear of God accompanies confidence in God. The church's confession of Jesus as Lord depends for its truth not on what Christians think, nor even on what Jesus thought, but on what his God and Father thinks of Jesus and so also of us identified with Jesus by Spirit-given faith in him as liberating Lord. This is the knowledge of God indicated for faith in, and so informed by, the resurrection vindication of Jesus which, however, remains publicly disputable until its final victory. Short of that, second-order rule-making of ecumenically intended doctrine goes to work by means of which "truth claims are made and expressive symbolisms employed." It stipulates the cognitive content of both terms of the originative confession, Jesus is Lord. We cannot deliberate any contemporary truth claims of the confession in third-order theology until we know what the several terms, and their combination, mean. How so? Grammatically, it is crucial to distinguish between titles and names with respect to speech concerning God.

"The recognition that stands at the heart of the Old Testament" is that Israel is "to know that God [YHWH] is indeed God [*Elohim*]."[11] R. W. L. Moberly argues that Israel is both gifted and burdened to know in faith that YHWH is the One who is truly divine. This creedal claim of Israel to theological truth, as such, makes a meaningful *synthetic* statement, not only in laying claim for YHWH to the title, *Elohim*, but also in the act clarifying the true oneness of God, the sense of the title, God, telling what kind of divinity YHWH is amid the idols of the world. The

11. Moberly, *God of the Old Testament*, 208.

content of the particular name, YHWH, spelled out by the narratives of the history of liberation from bondage to *false* gods which YHWH initiates with his covenant people Israel, provides epistemic access to the apprehension of what the divine One truly is; it moves Israel from vague notions of a higher power according to a generic *sensus divinitatis* to that of the One and only who is universally the Creator of all that is not God, whose history with Israel, then, may provide the template of his history with all humanity.

A prima facie objection arises from the theological tradition of Christian Platonism. Is it meaningful to ask the question, what kind of God is God? Does such a question sneakily subordinate God to some worldly category, some notion of "kind?" Or project upon God human-all-too-human ideals or virtues? Must not answer to this question upon analysis dissolve into the tautology of pure being, God is God, such that a formal analysis of persistent sameness over against temporal becoming gives the meaning of the term? As transcendent self-same identity, *actus purus*, That Which Is, defiant not only of slings and arrows of outrageous fortune but of any creaturely conceptualization, let alone real cognition? It may seem so, if we are willing to reify an apophatic boundary-rule into an ontology of perfect or supreme being.[12] But how can we then use this strange title as a proper name, as habitually we do? *Elohim* should be translated, The Divine One or The Holy One, *ho theos*, "the Deity." This translation reflects Elohim's original reference to the sphere of the gods and Israel's careful usage deploying the plural noun, the gods, with singular forms of verbs, literally, "the gods *is* or the gods *does* x, y, or z." Israel turns the term into the title for the One who is truly divine as creator of all.

The habit of using the title, God, as a name, a grammatical personal subject bearing character-informative predicates, rather than as a title, an impersonal grammatical predicate indicating kind, inclines towards metaphysical doctrines of divine simplicity more or less rigorously to insist upon a mind-numbing tautology: God is simply God. Yet in Moberly's welcome exploration of the scriptural affirmation that believers are to know that YHWH is *the* God, he argues to the contrary that it is meaningful and important to ask what kind of God YHWH is. Most basically such inquiry involves sorting out Israel's differentiated usage of

12. Hinlicky, *Divine Simplicity.*

the divine name YWWH from the divine title, *Elohim*. Being clarified, the distinctive terms interpret each other.

Indeed, predicates of the divine explicate the title, telling that one and only God is wise, just, mysterious to the point of inscrutability, yet trustworthy and so forth; as such, these predications do not reduce to various creaturely relations to and representations of timeless self-identity, but issue important instruction from the creator for creatures made in its image and therewith summoned to attain likeness or correspondence. Reading the Old Testament as Christian Scripture yields theology, knowledge of God for those called to likeness to true God. And since the God of Israel so understood is the Father of our Lord Jesus Christ, as Moberly concludes, specific characterizations of Israel's YHWH together with this One's titular claim to be God truly, are highly salient theologically for Christians.

What kind of God is God, then, if knowledge of the divine nature, i.e., kind too is a matter of divine self-revelation? If answer to the question *who* God is requires a corresponding conceptualization of *what* God is? Answering the latter question is really the gravamen of Moberly's undertaking. As such the book makes a contribution to an important debate recently opened up by Katherine Sonderegger, as Moberly expressly acknowledges in conclusion. Sonderegger's contention is that Christian Trinitarianism must not abandon Israel's monotheism; as Moberly understands her, the topic *de Deo uno* must be considered alongside the topic *de Deo trino*. Yet for Moberly in turn, Israel's "monotheism" may not be taken without further ado as the philosophers' "God beyond the gods" in such a way that ultimately undercuts the self-revealing God who names himself to Israel as YHWH and so to all other humans as Israel's God who is in fact and will be recognized as truly God of all.

It's the other way around: theological knowledge of the revealed God learns *its own* limit in this *named* God's claim to *universality*, YHWH's claim to the title of true deity. Moberly accordingly finds "striking" the "confidence" which some "commentators have in the adequacy and appropriateness of modern interpretive categories, especially 'monotheism' . . . It is at least possible that certain philosophically formulated conceptions of monotheism may so privilege the universality of the one God that they do not know how to do justice to particular modes of access to that universality."[13] For "other gods" remain in contention for the title of

13. Moberly, *God of the Old Testament*, 184.

true deity in one way or another, a permanent challenge to allegiance to YHWH. Biblical "monotheism," if we must call it that, is accompanied by "the recognition of the problematic presence and persistence of 'other gods' both within and beyond Israel."[14] By the same token, believers are challenged by the claim to universality of the particular God of the gospel, who has claimed them for his own, to regard all others as equally precious creatures of the same God. Consequently, we learn from the Scriptures of Israel not only who God is but what it means to be the One who is God truly—creator of all that is not God. The claim to universality thus functions as an inbuilt limitation to faith's humanly particular knowledge of the revealed God—lest believers boast of their election in place of the electing God who is and will be the same God of all.

Titles like "Lord," or even "God" are not personal names but offices, like "Mayor" or "Lieutenant." An inheritance from Old Testament Scripture, the title "God" (*Elohim*, *Adonai*) designates the One and only, the Holy, who proves truly to be creator and redeemer of all that is not God. In this sense God is *the* One and only, whose Lordship is yet contested and so hoped for. Aside from such preliminary remarks, we will attend to this sense of this term of the confession, Lord, in the final chapter when we ask the question, What in the world does the word *God* mean? Our present concern is with the other term, Jesus (etymologically, YHWH-saves), particularly as this historical naming is framed by the apocalyptic theology of his day. Names, by contrast to titles, have references to someone or something appearing in the creation; they are words that work ostensibly, by pointing to something other than the sounds they make or letters forming a written word. Apart from this work of pointing, a name can become a clanging gong, a magical incantation, as if sounding "Jesus, Jesus" effected his promised presence to lead and to liberate (Matt 7:21). But the reference of the name of Jesus is to the personal identity rendered in the gospel narrative to which it points; accordingly, the truthful *voicing* of the name of Jesus is that which accords with Jesus's *journey* in our time and space and the personal *intentionality* it exhibits. Only so can disciples know the "mind" of this rabbi for an intelligent *imitatio mentis*, not a wooden *imitatio carnis*. One does not follow Jesus by turning over the Girl Scout cookie table in the narthex! But one does follow Jesus by critiquing the religion business in favor of the business of his Father's reign.

14. Moberly, *God of the Old Testament*, 201.

Lindbeck famously illustrated this requirement for spiritual and ethical correspondence in naming Jesus truthfully when he asked about "*Christus est dominus!*"—is it *true* when the Crusader cries it out in a war-whoop, cleaving the infidel's head? Lindbeck's attention to doctrine as grammar-like rules for linguistic usage, in this case about naming Jesus as the Christ, denies that it is true in this case. Any possible ontological correspondence between the terms, Jesus and Christ/Lord, depends on *Christianly* coherent usage of the confession. Such coherence is a necessary, though not sufficient condition for this very particular truth claim of the gospel in *referring to Jesus* as Christ the Lord. In other words, *Christus est dominus* acquires propositional meaningfulness as part of a specifically Christian performance in language, which performance itself helps to create the very correspondence—a point Lindbeck particularly credits to Luther and Paul.[15] Lindbeck acknowledges, then, that there is a place for correspondence in his model, when a lived religion "as a whole" corresponds to the being and will of God,[16] in light of which manifest non-correspondence such as the Crusader's war-whoop can be identified and rejected in the work of doctrinal theology testing the church's speech and behavior by the word of God. The rule does not and cannot affirm that in fact Jesus is the Lord but only that if it is Jesus who is the Christ, the Crusader's performance—precisely in Christian perspective—violates the sense of the confession's identification of the terms. It takes in vain the name of Jesus who was crucified for his witness.

Lindbeck's view of the anticipatory, eschatologically definitive location of correspondence in the fulfilled confession of praise has the merit of protesting realized eschatology and ecclesiastical triumphalism in that it acknowledges the ambiguous, *simul iustus et peccator* being of Christianity *qua* religion,[17] no matter the abstract truth of doctrine or the profundity of pious feeling. It underscores that this linguistic community is elected to the freedom of faith for the service of love.[18] Doctrinal theology thus gives attention to the *usus*, making an issue of what we are doing with the language of belief contextually. Lengthy discussion of Lindbeck's question about the Crusader brought about the clarification that it is the speech-act of the Crusader which is false to the reference the sentence bears, since the proposition points as to one of its two terms to the Man

15. Lindbeck, *The Nature of Doctrine*, 66.
16. Lindbeck, *The Nature of Doctrine*, 51.
17. Lindbeck, *The Nature of Doctrine*, 60.
18. Lindbeck, *The Nature of Doctrine*, 61.

of Sorrows who was nevertheless vindicated by God, not by his disciples' sword.[19] The letter must be used in conformity with the Spirit if it is to assert the truth. But that redoubles the problem. How shall we know Jesus in his personal intention, according to the Spirit of his personal identity? So that we know what we mean when we confess, *Jesus* is Lord?

The historically first evangelist took the formative early step in answering this question. Assembling traditions about Jesus, he commits them to writing in a definite plot on which early Christianity built in order to give narrative account of the name of Jesus as for a public figure in the world. Matthew and Luke (and even John), for all their important differences from Mark in emphasis, material, even criticism and correction of him (Luke 1:3!), are nevertheless his theological children. Essentially, they only build on what he has begun, and this especially in the central matter of Christology. The profound reason for this is that they owe to Mark the narrative framework of their own Gospels (also in John's rearranging of the Synoptic plot with which he assumes his audience's familiarity[20]). Recall again that plotline.

Mark's story begins with the baptismal calling of Jesus, in which Jesus is identified from above as beloved Son upon whom the Spirit descends and remains, propelling him into conflict with the unholy spirits. The narrative proceeds with Jesus's proclamation of the approach of the reign of God in Galilee, which he manifests in healings, exorcisms, parables, and the calling, instruction, and commissioning of disciples. This activity, however, comes into conflict with the Law of God given through Moses and this conflict provokes questions of credentials: by what authority does Jesus work healing on Sabbath, overrule Moses on ritual practice, forgive sins? At the turning point of the story, Jesus himself poses the question of credentials to his disciples, "Who do you say that I am?" In rapid succession, then, Peter confesses Jesus to be Israel's Messiah, Jesus responds by disclosing his obedient way to the cross only to be met with Peter's incomprehension and disbelief. Nevertheless, the

19. A Lutheran who remembers Augsburg Confession V, could qualify Lindbeck's performative analysis of the proposition, "Jesus is Lord," that even correct performance does not guarantee, nor does false performance prohibit God from sovereignly granting correspondence, i.e., the truth, independent of the human-all-too-human speech act. Thus, the Gospel of Mark's confession of Jesus on the lips of the executioner tells the truth even as the performance of the executioner as such contradicts it. AC V affirms that gospel predication succeeds in eliciting justifying faith as a truthful correspondence to the fidelity of God in Christ "where and when it pleases God."

20. Hoskyns and Davey, *Riddle of the New Testament*.

Transfiguration story divinely validates both Jesus's messianic status and his unheard-of announcement of messianic destination to suffering, rejection, death and resurrection in Jerusalem. Now everything turns toward Jerusalem. The crowd led on by the still uncomprehending disciples welcomes Jesus as a warrior king, but Jesus immediately heads to the temple. His business is with the temple. In a prophetic action, he cleanses it of profiteering, demanding that the temple resign its lucrative trade in the religion business and rather become fruitful for the reign of God, i.e., to acquire the praise and prayer of the gentiles for the Lord. Disappointed at this turn away from insurrectionary violence, one of Jesus's own betrays him to secret arrest in dark of night. The temple authorities try him, find him a blasphemer for making himself out the Son of the Blessed, and denounce him to the Roman governor as a political rebel. Roman justice bows to the demands of the mob disappointed in Jesus and inflamed by the temple authorities. Jesus thus dies in the place of Barabbas, a condemned insurrectionist whom the mob preferred to him. Jesus dies alone, forsaken, taunted, disgraced. He is buried without ceremony on the eve of the Sabbath. Nevertheless, on the third day, his tomb is discovered empty by grieving women. What can this mean? A divine messenger declares, "Do not be alarmed; you are looking for Jesus of Nazareth, who was crucified. He has been raised; he is not here. Look, there is the place they laid him. But go, tell his disciples and Peter that he is going ahead of you to Galilee; there you will see him, just as he told you" (Mark 16:6–7). As such, the Gospel suddenly ends with the women fleeing in terror saying nothing to anyone.

In tersest outline, this is the plotline of the first Gospel. This plot is what is christologically decisive in rendering the public *persona*. The motif of the secrecy of Jesus's identity indicates that, as Jack Dean Kingsbury has argued, "hearing aright the Gospel-story of the divinely wrought destiny of Jesus, which has its center in the cross, is indispensable for understanding aright his identity."[21] The narrative's purpose was to establish that the name of Jesus refers to the one who in Spirit-inspired obedience to his Abba-Father, the God of Israel, went to the cross as a testimony and as a ransom. This counterintuitive story of the inauguration of the reign of God on the earth, told as the beginning of the gospel (Mark 1:1), provides the apocalyptic touchstone of true Christology.

21. Kingsbury, *Christology of Mark's Gospel*, 174.

This is all the more the case if the Gospel of Mark ends deliberately at 16:8 with the women disciples fleeing the tomb in terror. For this ending leaves the reader with no human and historical vehicle to communicate the Easter message as a human tradition, but only recourse to the pattern of episodic apocalypses recorded at baptism, transfiguration, and Golgotha, culminating in the angelic summons to meet Jesus again in Galilee, there to resume the mission where he had begun the messianic battle against Satan and his legions. In fact, then, the resurrection-vindication of the crucified Jesus as the *gospel concerning the Son* has been the silent presupposition of the whole narrative telling of the "beginning of the gospel." It motivates the evangelist's quest to fill in the name Jesus with narrative content. Like any narrative it consists in a selection of facts from a particular point of view based upon a judgment of value. Even if one should wish theologically to deconstruct the gospel narrative, one will only erect a new narrative based on another selection of facts from a particular point of view based upon another judgment of value. So, *what* judgment of value stands behind the gospel narrative, and by what right does it so identify Jesus?

Bearing in mind that to "construct" is *not* to create out of nothing, but to fashion out of existing materials that themselves admit of varying appropriations, the gospel narrative constructs this reality of the messianic agent Jesus crucified and risen and draws the audience to him, not to evade the present circumstance, but drastically to alter perception of it by asserting *his* saving presence with the community there in distress. This accompaniment of *Jesus* empowers them to engage the difficult present time in the different way of following *Jesus*, here and now, in the vulnerability of witness to an improbable word heard putatively from God. And that reference to a divine judgment of value is key to the right understanding of the gospel narrative. Mark's strange conclusion deliberately excludes human vivification, so to speak, of the truly dead Jesus. What happened is not even in the power of humans to communicate. A so-called historical Jesus, consequently, considered apart from his intense relation to the God of Israel as vivifier, is an ahistorical fiction. The *historical* judgment on this person with its termination on godforsaken Golgotha effected an apparent rupture, that is, *disillusionment* of that perceived relationship to the Abba-Father. This rupture in turn necessitated the stark reversal of Easter resurrection-vindication as the divine judgment of value presupposed in Mark's Gospel. It is only the *divinely*-crucified-and-*divinely*-risen Jesus who can be present with his people in their trials for disciples to follow him in the here and now. Anything else is merely human propaganda.

Albert Schweitzer classically expressed the stark alternative in judging the historical Jesus an apocalyptic fanatic who tried to turn the wheel of fate only to have it catch and crush him.[22] Human beings in Mark's church finally know what it means in their own dire circumstance to call their risen and vindicated Lord Jesus the Son of God, when they, in the person of the executioner, behold apocalyptically Jesus's God-forsaken death as in solidarity with *them*, indeed *all, even* Roman *crucifiers*, all who are in sinful complicity under the thrall of the unholy spirit. Only then are the sufferings of the present time comprehended and understood in their true significance of human solidarity in sinfulness before the judging God who justifies the ungodly—*only* the ungodly.

Or to make the same point from the opposite direction, human beings come to think about Jesus as God thinks about Jesus, not as existing humanity would think, nor as Satan entices. The confrontation between Jesus and Peter in Mark 8 illustrates this. After Jesus informs that he will exercise the Messianic office by way of the cross, Peter "rebukes" Jesus (Mark 8:32)—a technical term in Mark for silencing a demon (e.g., Mark 3:12). And Jesus in turn "rebukes" Peter in a statement that should be translated: "Get behind me, Satan, because you are not thinking the things of God but those of humans" (Mark 8:33). Disciples, then, are *being taught* to think of Jesus as God thinks of Jesus, i.e., to identify the crucified as the beloved Son with all that implies for knowledge of one's self ransomed from one's enthralled world. That knowledge, however, is and *must be* bestowed by the apocalypse and received in Spirit-generated faith confessing: "Truly this was Son of God!" Just this identification/evaluation from above signifies the new human solidarity as subjects together of divine redemption and fulfillment

From its origins, gospel story-telling as begun by Mark yields in the course of its history certain claims to truth about deity, regulatively about proper "God talk"—teachings that instruct Christian speech and behavior, "dogmas" that bear into the world the claim to truth of the Easter word of God—which must be affirmed along with gospel storytelling, if the story is to continue to be told properly before its final validation. It is all here *in nuce*. The trinity of personal agents, Father, Son, and Holy Spirit as the one who is God truly; mysterious Jesus, somehow divine but

22. Schweitzer, *Quest of the Historical Jesus*.

also somehow human, yet the one public figure of the beloved Son in battle with unholy spirits; sinful human beings drawn from Satan's grip into Jesus's relationship with his Abba-Father by the grace of the sanctifying Spirit who pointedly singled out the denier Peter for the Easter good news, not by merit, then, of his own failed discipleship but by ransom-won forgiveness of sin. All this may be truly proclaimed in deeds, sermons, even in visual images as the narrative prompts, like Mark's precious verbal portrait of the unnamed woman anointing Jesus beforehand for burial. Just as surely it may be truly articulated in human words of confession and elaborating theological concepts.

Objections and Initial Clarifications

But what kind of logical or conceptual status do these characteristic Christian doctrinal ideas have? All sorts of problems and objections arise for us here. For example, that any demand to affirm doctrinal teachings beyond "simple trust" in the heavenly parent is an intellectual form of works-righteousness, which makes faith conditional on something other than that parent's "unconditional acceptance." Or, that the gospel story as told cannot be true: mental illness is not caused by demons, the forgiveness of sins is an imaginary solution to an imaginary problem, God does not "act" within the closed system of the physical universe, people do not come back from the dead, and so forth. Nor can gospel narrative, even sans miracles, be taken at face value as corresponding to what really happened in history. In fact, the criticism of the gospel narrative by the reconstruction of what really happened in history presents itself as the allegedly liberating alternative in modernity to traditional doctrinal theology. In due course, all such objections will be dealt with in this book.

The most searching objection to doctrinal theology to ponder, however, yet most profitable for present purposes, is the one posed by Dietrich Bonhoeffer in the opening salvo in his *Discipleship*:

> Cheap grace means grace as a doctrine, a principle, a system. It means the forgiveness of sins proclaimed as a general truth, the love of God taught as the Christian "conception" of God. An intellectual assent to that idea is held to be itself sufficient to secure remission of sins. The Church which upholds the correct doctrine of grace has, it is supposed, ipso facto a part in that grace. In such a Church the world finds a cheap covering for its sins; no contrition is required, still less any real desire to be

> delivered from sin. Cheap grace therefore amounts to a denial of the living Word of God, in fact, a denial of the Incarnation of the Word of God.[23]

Ziegler has rightly protested that "unconditional grace" is "a too abstract" way of putting the matter. Echoing Bonhoeffer here, he continues, "Crucially, the truth from which the militancy of faith derives is not a proposition but a *life*"[24] in encounter with which a new subjectivity is formed by the God who kills to make alive, a self which thus "knows itself to be dislocated, wrenched out of phase with the 'form of this world,' which is 'passing away.'"[25] The cosmological metaphors of apocalyptic make the human self a microcosm of the apocalyptic turn of the ages. "Grace" is not delivered in the gospel narrative as a comfortable idea, but as a followable person, provided that disciples are baptized in the same Spirit as was the author and pioneer of their faith.

Thus, this passage from Bonhoeffer is as misunderstood as it is famous. It is a penetrating attack on pseudo-Lutheran ethical idealism stemming from the nineteenth century. Bonhoeffer here takes aim at the interpretation of theological doctrine *as ideas* in the sense of German *idealism*. Held in the human mind, they populate a religious worldview of costless grace on the grounds of the idea of God as love and the inference therefrom of indulgent forgiving as a virtually involuntary reflex of divine nature. So understood, "doctrine" is an ecclesiastical ideology mounting a sophisticated denial of the risen Word of God whose costly incarnation won the surprising grace of mercy surpassing well-merited wrath that now commands and enables the radical lifelong conversion of the whole human being in contrition and repentance for newness of life. Bonhoeffer's critique of merely intellectual assent to the flattering religious ideas of a church conformed to the present age with its denatured notion of God as a benign idea, then, in truth *presupposes* "right doctrine" as the public confession of praise, faith and service formed by the external word announcing the resurrection-vindication of the crucified Jesus. This is doctrine for life, identifying Jesus as present and active, therewith enabling contemporary discipleship. Bonhoeffer's critique of cheap grace is an exercise in doctrinal theology properly understood according to the argument of this book. His commitment in this

23. Bonhoeffer, *Cost of Discipleship*, 43.

24. Ziegler, *Militant Grace*, 163.

25. Ziegler, *Militant Grace*, 166.

regard is demonstrated abundantly by his co-authoring with Herman Sasse of the original draft of the Bethel Confession, sabotaged before publication by Nazi sympathizers.[26]

Naming Jesus

In any event, it is important here to emphasize that the enumerated contemporary objections are *not* the problems that were being addressed at the formation of the gospel's narrative genre in primitive Christianity, and which, according to the present argument, ought to reframe our necessary consideration of objections for whatever truth may be found in them. Neither Mark nor his opponents had objections to miracles. Indeed, Mark's opponents performed them (or claimed to perform them) "to lead astray, if possible, even the elect" (Mark 13:22b). This was a plausible deception among early Christians including Mark's community, since Mark's Jesus also works wonders ("Who then is this that even wind and sea obey him?" Mark 4:41). The problem Mark is dealing with, however, is that opponents are *remythologizing* the gospel, so to say, by *etherealizing* Jesus. By this term, one does not refer either to the simple fact of the widespread belief in miracles, nor particularly to the fact that under the inspiration of the Spirit early Christian prophets of the post-Easter church spoke "in the name of the Lord" and in this way gave voice to new words that came to be placed in the mouth of the earthly Jesus (or generated stories about Jesus to give a home to isolated and, as it were, free-floating dominical sayings).[27] Mark himself is willing to contemporize Jesus in this way and does so dramatically in making Jesus speak directly to his own community's dire situation as reflected in Mark 13:37. Indeed, belief in the contemporaneity of Jesus, being there as the risen-to-be-active-and-communicative agent of salvation for the troubled community was a necessary implication of the universal scope of unsurpassable agency attributed to him by the titles Christ, Son of God, Lord, as given with the announcement of his resurrection-vindication as the decisive word of God for the whole creation. Jesus is for these early Christians alive and no longer dead, the living subject, *not only* the object of their faith (and thus, as *only* objectified, a waxen

26. Hinlicky, "Verbum Externum."

27. Käsemann, *Essays on New Testament Themes*; Käsemann, *New Testament Questions for Today.*

nose vulnerable to being molded by their agency to satisfy their religious needs). Consequently, all true preaching was for them prophecy in "the name of the Lord" to and for the community of faith (and as it will also become again in a post-Christendom church of doctrinal integrity). Naming Jesus truthfully is thus a matter of knowing his subjectivity, his own purpose, his public "I," his intentional *obedience of faith* by which preaching/prophecy in the name of Jesus may be tested.

Accordingly, the problem is that within this circle of resurrection faith there have arisen some prophets speaking in the name of the risen Lord Jesus who have distanced, if not detached their message of salvation from the public *persona* of the one crucified *sub Pontio Pilato*. They are *remythologizing* Jesus in the sense that they are using his name magically, i.e., as an incantation no longer referred strictly to the narrative content of Jesus's historical life as demarcated by his earthly coming, ministry, obedience and fate which Mark's narrative conveys as the formative "beginning" of the gospel (Mark 1:1). As in Paul, this minimal list of events in common history suffices to secure *reference* to the "historical" Jesus of Nazareth as one term in the confession that *Jesus* is Lord. More importantly, what accounts for Mark's resistance to the *remythologizing* of Jesus is the apocalyptic event of the crucifixion referring to no other Jesus Christ the Son of God than to the crucified Jew. It is quite striking, then, to observe in this light how the very first deviation in doctrine against which early Christianity had to battle was christological *docetism*.

> Beloved, do not believe every spirit, but test the spirits to see whether they are from God; for many false prophets have gone out into the world. By this you know the Spirit of God: every spirit that confesses that Jesus Christ has come in the flesh is from God, and every spirit that does not confess Jesus is not from God. And this is the spirit of the antichrist, of which you have heard that it is coming; and now it is already in the world. (1 John 4:1–3)

The Johannine text reckons apocalyptically with the *surd* of positive evil as that which effectively contradicts God in the here and now of creation, in the present case the "antichrist," denying the flesh of Jesus. Contesting such false prophecy entails the knowledge of God in the flesh of Jesus. One can hardly reckon with the actual evil which contradicts the gospel's God apart from logically coincident knowledge of God's grace and truth manifest in this tabernacling in human flesh (John 1:14).

Yet this is not theoretical knowledge, gazing on a timeless form as in Platonic traditions, seeing *through* the flesh of Jesus to a divinity other than this mortal man, nor following in speculation the forward movements of the divine Idea unfolding in human history as represented by Jesus; so Hegel thinks and continues to think in much of modern theology. It is knowledge of the crucified and risen Lord as only begotten Son sent by his Father's love for those in thrall of alien powers, sent with his Father's own Spirit to set free prisoners trapped in a prison house of mendacity under the propagandistic regime of "a liar and murderer from the beginning" (John 8:44). This is *militant* knowledge of those engaged in battle by the sanctifying Spirit who anointed Jesus's flesh, and their flesh also as joined to Jesus, to form the community of commissioned disciples amid legion spirits of implacable malice. But denying the flesh of Jesus severs this linkage and thus threatens community disintegration as the living body of Christ. Doctrinal theology thus contends for the flesh of Jesus as the enfleshment of the only begotten Son of the Father and against the docetic etherealization of Jesus.

In the account of the descent of the Spirit on Jesus at his baptism, as Mark tells it, the Spirit immediately "drove" Jesus into contest with Satan (Mark 1:10,12). Following this apocalyptic framing of the origin of the gospel in describing the Spirit-anointed flesh of Jesus, we are presently sustaining the critical break with nineteenth-century progressivist theology of history as salvation descending from Kant's transcendentalism through Hegel's philosophy of history, signaled when the Ritschlian Johannes Weiss realized to his dismay that Jesus's preaching of the reign of God involved an "antithetic, not a thetic notion."[28] Jesus's reign of God is *not* Kant's kingdom of ends which we posit and build, no longer waiting immaturely for supernatural fulfillment, but rather it is a veritable declaration of war against superhuman usurpers of God's good earth such that creation groans in travail awaiting the cosmic new birth.

Heiko Obermann has argued that in general this is the correct way to read Luther's theological legacy,[29] and he was accordingly careful to distinguish Luther's contribution, as Obermann wanted it to be appropriated, from "the origins of anti-Semitism."[30] In his better mind, Luther named the name of Jesus as "born a Jew."[31] Yet, understanding how Luther

28. Chilton, *Kingdom of God*, 7–8.

29. Obermann, *Luther*.

30. Obermann, *Roots of Anti-Semitism in the Age of Renaissance and Reformation*.

31. LW 45:199–229.

lost his mind to anti-Judaism has not a little to do with Luther's taking apocalyptic literally on account of the Trojan presence of the Platonic God in Western Christianity. When the sanctifying Spirit is depersonalized and reduced to an impersonal energy equated with intense religious feelings in general, it's decisive role in forming the messianic identity of cross-bound Jesus and in turn of Christians to battle the spiritual forces of wickedness in high places rather than flesh and blood is supplanted by propaganda for "our Jesus" against "your Moses" (or Mohammed). Taking apocalyptic literally, i.e., as non-metaphorical speech, means inevitably to posit Christendom as a religion over against the world religions[32] rather than to behold the creator breaching walls to liberate the creation from its oppressors. Rightly understood the apocalyptic metaphor refers literally to the reconciling, rectifying coming of the Creator to regain a usurped creation, precisely not to crusaders.

There is little doubt, however, that we are here treading on dangerous ground. Luther, exuberant in devil talk, is the preeminent apocalyptic theologian of the antecedent Christian tradition, yet his appropriation of New Testament apocalyptic *as knowledge of God* suffers from lingering precritical *literalism* which fails to understand gospel narrative as christologically modified apocalyptic, theologically, then, *as metaphorical speech*, specifically, the *catachrestic* metaphor which invents new words for speaking, thinking and enacting the hitherto unknown and unspoken reality of God in Christ the crucified and risen Son reconciling the world to himself.[33] This move of christologically modified apocalyptic to theological metaphor was pioneered in the Johannine rereading of the Synoptic tradition to reconstitute the gospel's apocalyptic framing, *not* as a literal timetable scheduling the end of "the late, great planet Earth," but as *kairos*, the time of the end breaking in upon us in the crisis that occurs with the Johannine coming of Jesus Christ the Son of God into our present darkness through the external word of the gospel, by the animating power of the Spirit. Ironically, Luther himself not only understood and deployed theology as metaphorical speech about God, especially in his conflict with Zwinglian literalism confining the risen Lord to the compendious and undoubtedly cozy right hand of God in heaven, thus geographically unavailable to us on earth, but also in some of the profounder later disputations. Luther's notorious failures in demonizing

32. Greggs, *Theology Against Religion*.

33. Hinlicky, "Metaphorical Truth and the Language of Christian Theology."

theological opponents can be traced to his relapses from apocalyptic theology's metaphorical usage into dangerous apocalyptic literalism. But this descent into dangerous literalism following Luther's construction of the papacy as antichrist was virtually required by Protestant retention of Christian Platonism's doctrine of deity, casting biblical narrative now as the perfect revelation of the perfect Being.

Naming the Devil: The Special Problem of Luther's Rhetorical Violence

Mark U. Edwards Jr. located Luther's notorious verbal violence against peasant, pope, Turk, and Jew in apocalyptic literalism, which burst into flames after his excommunication by Leo X and the disaster of the Peasants' War. To a Luther despairing over the forces he had unleashed, these traumatic events were signs of the approaching end of time according to an apocalyptic timetable which he actually tried to reconstruct from the Bible[34] (prefiguring a future preoccupation in Protestantism). "Luther understood his disagreement with [opponents] in the context of this struggle between God and Satan. Behind them all loomed the figure of the devil, the father of lies. Often Luther directed his attacks not at his human opponents but at the devil whom he saw as their master, and, of course, no language was too harsh when attacking the devil."[35] Luther spewed noxious tirades, to be sure, within a *Christendom* frame of reference; he does not single out Jews exclusively, let alone racially, as opposed to others for invective. But given the disintegration of Christendom for which he was in part responsible, in practice the distinction between Satan and his various human minions collapsed and, in the process, the ethical restraint of Eph 6:12 fell with it. Luther rationalized his verbal violence on the grounds that his scatological defense of true doctrine was not physical violence but a "battle of the Word," and as such is exempt from the martyrs' ethos of suffering witness. In Luther's mind, verbal violence is just war, a limited counterattack against overt persecutors or crafty subversives intended to protect the innocent from deception. Verbal violence rationalized in this way, however, slid imperceptibly into sanction

34. *Supputatio Annorum Mundi* (1541); see University of Cambridge, "Lutheran Timeline."

35. Edwards,"Luther's Polemical Controversies," Edwards, "Supermus"; Edwards, *Luther's Last Battles.*

of physical violence, as in the disgraceful *On the Jews and Their Lies*.[36] In the long march of history to the Holocaust, theological demonization, not just Luther's, stemming from John 8:42–47 provided the bridge to racial theory's reification in the picture of the incorrigibly malicious, racially hardened Jew. In light of this humiliating *Wirkungsgeschichte*, one may well be inclined to ditch apocalyptic devil-talk altogether—indeed, one hesitates *only* with the thought that forfeiture of talk about the devil might be yet one more victory for the devil. We will return to "diabology" in chapter 5. For the present we consider it only in relation to naming Jesus as one term in the Christian confession of faith, Jesus is Lord.

If the polemical task of theology as a conflict discipline contending for the confession of faith, Jesus is Lord, as we see in Luther, is to be continued at all today, it must be coordinated with, if not subordinated to, the irenic task, short of full convergence, of achieving a mutual disagreement with apparent opponents in theology according to a scholarly method as stipulated in the first chapter of this book. This irenic mode of doctrinal theology was exemplified in our times by the doctrinal dialogues between divided confessions regarding the ecumenical church's central beliefs. But what are central beliefs? As Bruce Marshall has argued quite precisely in this regard:

> The epistemic priority of the church's central beliefs does not depend on the apparently hopeless suggestion that the gospel is opposed to most or all of the beliefs which the rest of humanity holds true, but only on the contrast between the gospel and the epistemic *priorities* human beings are otherwise inclined to have.[37]

This is surely right, not only as a helpful explication and application of his teacher Lindbeck's regulative theory of doctrine but also as interpretation of Luther's epistemic priority in affirming the *solus Christus*, which Marshall conceptualizes as the universal scope of Jesus's reign (= Lindbeck's "unsurpassability").[38]

But even granting the unrestricted scope of Jesus's agency, what can this mean for the persistence of sin in the life of the redeemed, the scandalous failures of the historical Christian religion, the world's continuing unbelief—or to sum all these up: the incorrigible malice of the biblical

36. *LW* 47:137–306.

37. Marshall, *Trinity and Truth*, 157.

38. Marshall, *Trinity and Truth*, 108.

figure of the Evil One who wills nothing but to contradict the will of God? Marshall argues for eschatological correspondence as the theological possibility of the rectification of all true beliefs in Christ with the notable exception of evil. Marshall turns to the time-honored privative account: evil is the nothing which does not correspond to God's will and as such cannot be rectified, only exposed and left behind, forgotten forever, annihilated.[39] Yet somehow, like the privative doctrine of evil itself, this does not satisfy our sense from the gospel narrative—certainly Luther's very vivid sense, not to mention Mark's—of evil as actual, the positive reality of a massive yet cunning, trans-individual, superhuman, albeit creaturely contradiction (not just failure to correspond) which God, moreover, in willing this very world in which his Son would be crucified, permits actually to exist. The devil figures, not the absence of the good, but the actuality of evil as a surd in the good creation of the good God.

If that spells out a deep perplexity in the narrower sense, certainly there is also a burning rhetorical problem. Luther's antithetical preaching of the apocalyptic battle framing the gospel requires a "devil" (recall the lyrics in his battle hymn, "A Mighty Fortress") just as it did of its apostolic author. J. Louis Martyn, who with and after Ernst Käsemann in our times contended for the "apocalyptic" interpretation of Paul, notes the problem of receiving Luther's Paul interpretation today at the outset of his insightful commentary on Galatians. Even though we have to repudiate "Luther's pejorative and indefensible references to 'Jews, Turks, papists, and sectarians,'" and register "notable reservations related to Luther's portrait of Judaism," nevertheless Luther's captivation "by the message of God's free and powerful grace" produced an "interpretation that has happily influenced—to one degree or another—most readings of the letter since his time."[40]

Yet, one must query whether these two aspects of Luther's legacy are so easily separated. The proclamation of the free and powerful grace of God *and* the reduction of those who do not surrender themselves to it in trust and hope to the status of hardened hearts, incorrigible reprobates, captivated instruments of the devil, the damned? If not, is Paul's apocalyptic theology, as appropriated by Luther, indeed guilty of "historicizing the eschatological"[41] in the very notion that in Christ Jesus the ages

39. Marshall, *Trinity and Truth*, 274.

40. Martyn, *Galatians*, 35. See particularly the Comment # 51, "The Apocalyptic Antinomies and the New Creation," 570–74.

41. Ruether, *Faith and Fratricide*, 246ff.

have turned, the new creation begun (and there with the execution of the old age)? The difficulty is not wiped away by attributing it to Paul's or Luther's personal limitations. The "apocalyptic antinomies" (Martyn) of the greatly appreciated Gal 3:27 engendered by the inbreaking of new creation provided Luther the ground upon which he refused and sharply criticized the traditional anthropological dualisms of mind and matter, soul and body, male and female, civilized and barbarian as merely *temporal arrangements once made to hold sin in check* but now passé. Apocalypse as promise of inclusion in the coming reign is the reason, moreover, why he can conceive of the doctrinal beliefs brought with the gospel *not theoretically* as adequate *representations of, but metaphorically* as adequate *references to*, the extramental reality of the imminent God, with all the advantages that holds over untenable propositional claims to objective mental mirroring in doctrine corresponding to the world as it yet is, let alone to ineffable deity hidden in majesty.

Can this new language of the Spirit be retrieved without hauling along with it the theological potential for invective, which Luther also imports from Paul (cf. Gal 5:12; Phil 3:2). It can be retrieved, to anticipate a little, with fresh understanding of the *sanctifying* Spirit, the distinct divine agent generating the new language of doctrinal confession in making newborn theological subjects.[42] The Spirit is a distinct personal agent yet essentially related to the equally distinct personal agent of the incarnate Word of whom it speaks, incorporated into whom by the Spirit theological subjects hear and believe. In the formative early theology of the martyrs, the sanctifying Spirit *forbids*, indeed in holy wrath condemns to death, trafficking in religion (Acts 5:1–11), i.e., any departure from the vulnerable posture of witness with sole reliance on the sanctifying Spirit. Naming Jesus of Nazareth, who spoke and enacted parables of the impending reign of God and at length was crucified for it as Son of the living God and King of the Jews, executes a catachrestic metaphor by which something familiar in our world, this Jesus in the flesh, signs immediately something not familiar: saving Lord, Messiah of Israel, Son of the living God. So, Jesus as named in the flesh becomes a "new word" naming the divine agent of salvation. How this confession can be reiterated today in retrieval of the theology of

42. Hinlicky, "Luther's Anti-Docetism in the Disputatio de divinitate et humanitate Christi (1540)," employing the translation of Christopher Boyd Brown from WA 39/ 96:27–30.

the martyrs after a ruinously violent history of apocalyptic literalism is a huge question and will occupy us throughout this book.

Equally difficult, the previously alluded dialectic of Word and Spirit seems circular in reasoning, perhaps viciously so and guilty to boot of special pleading. Noting that difficulty, for the present we may recall the ecumenical-Lutheran Lindbeck's argument that doctrinal statements may include truth claims of literal correspondence to extra-linguistic reality as articulated in a propositional form but chiefly consist in regulative service for properly communicating the external word concerning the saving person of Christ Jesus, who unites God and humanity in a new covenant of mercy. What disrupts the theological circle from the outside and keeps its dialectic from becoming viciously insular is the disruptive surd, the assaults of Luther's *Anfechtung*, adventitious attacks of utter despair attributed to the Evil One. In re-rooting Lindbeck's regulative model of doctrine in New Testament apocalyptic as appropriated by Luther, we have identified the sanctifying Spirit as the divine agent poised to tell truth against Satan's deception, who would divide anew this saving unity of God and humanity by attacking Christ's person through deviant doctrine denying his enfleshment. Doctrinal regulation in this apocalyptic light concerns the entire narrative complex to be spoken and understood with integrity according to its divine and saving purpose even as it is the lived narrative complex as a whole, inclusive of its performance by theological subjects, which may or *may not* (so far as corrupted by the Evil One) be found ultimately to correspond with the divine reality.[43]

With this regulative antithesis in mind, the problem of figuring "Satan" may be reframed by resort to the source of creedal-catechetical theology in the gospel narrative, as we have been proposing in this chapter. That reframing would indicate a helpful change in manner of doctrinal presentation, if not a more fundamental hermeneutical revision at the basis of dogmatics, bringing it closer to Luther's *Great Catechism* than to Melanchthon's *Loci Communes*. That innovation would find a starting point for the presentation of Christian doctrine with the article on the person and work of the Holy Spirit in order to identify the theological subject who apprehends the Word incarnate to the glory of the God of Israel, the Abba-Father of Jesus Christ. It would proceed in that order of presentation from the Spirit through the Son to the Father to conclude with the doctrine of the eternal Trinity as claimant

43. Lindbeck, *Nature of Doctrine*, 51.

to the title of the One who is God truly. Beginning this way, a teleologically ordered and positive dialectic is issued by the Spirit, traditionally named "Law and Gospel," which specifies how moral instruction and gospel narrative are *used* by the self-surpassing God of love when taken from human hands for self-justification into the Spirit's hands for the judgment and justification of the ungodly. This ordering means that the gospel needs to be understood in relation to the law of God just as the law of God must be understood in relation to the gospel. The law of God, concretely summarized as the double love commandment of Jesus, functions as a hermeneutic of human experience on the earth targeting the proclamation of the gospel to real-world human experience as theologically interpreted by the holy demand of God for righteousness, life and peace. So, likewise, with Augustine, the gospel is rightly understood to give what the law of God demands by the mediation in Jesus Christ. This ordering of the law and gospel of the one God reflects a positive dialectic of love, not sentimental but militant, as love must be against what is against love before it can and does achieve the new and surpassing love of mercy for the loveless. In this way the Holy Spirit exposes the actual evil of the unholy spirit which knows and works only by a parasitical dialectic of negativity, damning the very human failures whom it has lured into the self-destruction of sin, blocking from perception the surpassing love of mercy for them achieved and communicated in Christ Jesus. This is, to be emphatic, not a contest of ideas but of spiritual forces. And it is not settled but remains in process so that doctrinal theology as the work of the sanctifying Spirit equips theological subjects for this battle with the "whole armor of God" (Eph 6:10–17). The characterization of "the devil" in personifying and perpetrating actual evil as the opponent of the sanctifying Spirit anointing Messiah Jesus might be further explored theologically in regard to its ontological status since it will be important to restrict its being to finitude, as a bizarre creature driven by *envy* (so Luther[44]) to destroy creatures destined for redemption and fulfillment. This perplexing question of the ontology of the devil will be considered in chapter 5.

Most immediately pertinent, however, to bring this section to a close, is a particularly deep problem in the received doctrine of God blocking perception and hence utilization of the positive dialectic of love in the sanctifying Spirit's use of moral instruction and gospel narrative,

44. LW 1:82.

namely, that of understanding the equally dialectical relation between the Son incarnate and the sanctifying Spirit. Not a few New Testament scholars argue today that the Spirit is simply Jesus in post-earthly form, an etherealized Jesus. Thus, there is no real, "personal," difference between them, just one and the same X of generic divine spirit manifesting in different forms. To be sure, in the gospel narrative these two distinct figures are *inseparably* related, *not* identified. And this inseparable relation of the distinct agents corresponds to the hermeneutical problem of understanding the Word in the words and the letters in the Spirit, concretely, Jesus in the gospel narrative and the gospel narrative in and for the Spirit's working of beloved community: "Jesus was having dinner at Levi's house, many tax collectors and sinners were eating with him and his disciples, for there were many who followed him" (Mark 2:15).

This dialectic of incarnate Word referring itself to Spirit for right understanding and Spirit referring itself to Word incarnate for true content is needed for grasping holy Jesus "who knew no sin" in saving but counter-intuitive solidarity with those who cannot by their own reason or strength believe that they are sought, found, claimed, won and restored as living subjects in God's reign. They cannot believe because the unholy spirit works in every way to render trusting faith in Jesus, true friend of Luther's "real, not imaginary" sinners, incredible. A fresh account of the personal distinction and relation of the beloved Son and the sanctifying Spirit can overcome a debilitating pneumatological deficit in the tradition of theology stemming from Luther with a more robust Trinitarian personalism, as we will see in chapter 5. This move corresponds to the apocalyptic turn in contemporary theology as we have argued from the Gospel of Mark in this chapter. So, Ziegler contends in accord with the Gospel's depiction of the failure of disciples under their own understanding and willpower: "people are no more the agents of their coming to faith than they are of their creation or recreation. Such talk of the Spirit is a crucial element in a proper Trinitarian person of the monergism of saving grace. When we praise the Spirit in this way as the sufficient cause of the advent of saving faith, we rightly tether 'the efficacy of calling' to the very 'motion of God'"[45]—the apocalyptic invasion!

But for the same reason, the monergism of divine grace is co-equally effectuated "in a properly Trinitarian person," Jesus Christ the Son of God. This was Luther's great contention for the full implications

45. Ziegler, *Militant Grace*, 76.

of the patristic "communication of idioms" in Christ by which this single agent in the world enjoys and deploys the capacities of both creator and creature in his life's mission to overthrow the devil's tyranny by boldly enacting the free and sovereign forgiveness of sins, thusly to pioneer the path of faith for the faithful to follow. This communication of idioms in Christ was certainly a way of speaking, preached concretely in Luther's "joyful exchange," but not only a way of speaking. It was for Luther a *valid* way of speaking (*verborum metaphora*) just because and only because it was Christ's way of being as the man for others (*rerum metaphora*). Robert Jenson, probably the most significant doctrinal theologian in the tradition of Luther in recent times, undertook this gravamen of Luther's Christology. In large he succeeded in raising and pressing the issue, but overreached, as we shall see in the remainder of this chapter.

Trojan Horse: With and Beyond Jenson's *Unbaptized God*[46]

In important ways, Jenson's theological project answers several critical objections raised against Lindbeck's cultural-linguistic model as previously noted, as over the course of his theological life he moved away from the salvation history optimism informed by a youthful right-wing reading of Hegel's philosophy of history to a more apocalyptic perception of the end of Christendom and its justified but perilous consequences. He agreed with Lindbeck that the church of the future would be sociologically sectarian but catholic in its self-understanding and applied himself increasingly to this future church in his theology. Recall the propositionalist objection to Lindbeck that it turns the church inward in self-concern for survival, abandoning engagement with the contemporary world outside the church bunker (which world, for his critics, in fact sets the agenda for the church and theology, whether to accommodate its traditional claim to truth to it, or, apologetically to justify itself before its tribunal). The expressivist objection was that the banishment of feeling as a theological resource relies with unjustified confidence on ritual to reform human affect when liturgy rather stifles expression and open exploration for healing of repressed emotion. Neither of these objections can justly be raised against Jenson's theological project, including his appropriation of Lindbeck's cultural-linguistic model of the church

46. Jenson, *Unbaptized God.*

as the locus of Christian doctrine and the regulative understanding of doctrine articulating the rule of faith.

No theologian has engaged so deeply and explicitly with the danger of recurrent fascism as a genuinely *theological* problem as Jenson has.[47] And he grounded his confidence in liturgical and sacramental *renewal* (precisely *not* the ersatz worship forms of mutually antagonistic fragments of divided Christendom, let alone the private spirituality of contemporary gnostics) to form human affect by a rare theological doctrine of beauty built upon his reading of Jonathan Edwards[48] and his love for Johann Sebastian Bach. One may disagree, of course, with Jenson's third-order explorations, but objections about disengaged cultural insularity in principle are met by the very fact of these theologically dense and nutrient-rich engagements from the angle of Lindbeck's model of doctrine. Moreover, he devoted himself to the habitat of doctrinal theology that was current in his lifetime which were the ecumenical dialogues proceeding from the Second Vatican Council onward. Just as with Lindbeck, this commitment to ecumenical theology of doctrine obscured for many Lutheran partisans (although not for ecumenical partners!) his standing as a Lutheran. Some work must be done in this section to excavate those credentials, above all by showing how his kind of theological exegesis of Scripture disrupted theological tradition, as had Luther's before him.[49]

It was not Jenson's intention, quite the contrary, but in effect he predicted the stasis to which the doctrinal dialogues have come in our so-called "ecumenical winter." He did so by putting his finger on a deep fault of the post-Vatican II doctrinal dialogues in the assumption that the Great Tradition, so-called, could, as if a monolith, provide a solid basis of unity. What his theology accomplished, however, was to expose and diagnose a deeply disturbing incoherence in the Great Tradition, namely, that the reinterpretation by the gospel of the antecedent doctrine of the divine in Hellenistic philosophical theology was left unfinished. This is a nuanced iteration of the so-called "Constantinian betrayal" of Christianity transforming the gospel and its gathered people into a religion organized for the preservation of an imperium.[50] Jenson resisted shallow

47. Jenson, *Systematic Theology*, 2:143–45.

48. Jenson, *America's Theologian*.

49. Hinlicky, "How Theological Exegesis Disrupts Theological Tradition."

50. An exceptional counterargument to this indictment by Jenson, equally critical of Platonism, may be found in Meyendorff, *Byzantine Theology*. Indeed, the problematic Jenson fingers may more properly be traced to the *Western* tradition.

understandings of this historical phenomenon. Charitably interpreted, what occurred was the evangelization of Hellenism (Pelikan), not the Hellenization of the gospel (Harnack), just as in any missionary situation the goal is the enculturation of Christianity. But incompatible purposes were joined as a result in that the Hellenistic doctrine of the divine was meant to undergird the precarious achievement of Hellenic civilization against the ravages of time. But the gospel doctrine of the divine, signified by the subversive image of the Crucified, signaled the apocalyptic turn of the ages, let the political chips fall as they may. Consequently, in the most basic topic of theology concerning God, there were tied together antithetical elements that have regularly reappeared to express themselves in contradictions dividing the church doctrinally. And there is a further irony, which Jenson only began to recognize towards the end of his career: that in spite of his aspiration to write as an ecumenical theologian for the post-Christendom church of the future, this most critical insight of his work about a basic flaw in the ecumenical doctrine of God was in fact the product of a Lutheran intuition. Not that opponents overlooked this Lutheranism! Rather, they could dismiss his disturbing thesis as idiosyncratic Lutheranism along the lines of Hegel, producing a kenotic collapse of transcendent deity into human history.[51]

Jenson's method in his book *Unbaptized God*, prefacing the appearance of his two-volume *Systematic Theology*, amounted to an impressive reading and analysis of the entirety of the doctrinal dialogues to date in 1992, amply documented. From this immersion in the literature his thesis emerged organically, namely, that in case after case partners in dialogue could contextualize and clarify sufficiently mutually contradictory doctrinal formulations so that each side could understand the Christian concern underlying the traditional opponent's formulation of doctrine which hitherto they had condemned. On this basis, both sides could achieve a convergence around a nuanced reformulation of the disputed doctrine by acknowledgment of the other's theologically legitimate concerns. Each side would still register its traditional worries and warnings about dangers to which the new convergence formulation of the doctrine was vulnerable, and as such could recommend to the divided churches that on the basis of the convergence formulation that there were no doctrinal grounds in it as such for continuing visible disunity between the churches. And yet, despite this seemingly significant achievement, with

51. Keating and White, *Divine Impassibility and the Mystery of Human Suffering.*

every new convergence a newly divisive issue popped up, requiring further work and so on and so on.

For example, in the Lutheran-Catholic dialogue there could be a convergence on real presence, but that immediately raised the issue of the sacrificial nature of the mass; and then there could be a new convergence on eucharistic sacrifice as the real presence of the Jesus who offered himself to the Father for us, but that immediately raised the issue of the priestly character of eucharistic presidency; there could be convergence even on the priestly re-presentation of Christ in his self-sacrifice, but then that raised the issue of holy orders and so on and on, seemingly to infinity. At the root of this continual frustration, Jenson identified a problem of temporality. How can an event endure? Should an event of the advent of God in the gospel endure? If gospel is good news of the Christ event, thus itself an event of the Spirit in its proclamation and confession, what binds events purporting to be gospel together in recognizable continuity across time and space? Or is the gospel purely episodic? But then how are we to test new events purporting to be gospel for authenticity if no accumulation of recognized precedents truly exist to enable present discernment?

Analysis of the doctrinal divisions of the churches can in fact be organized around diverging answers to such questions about the time that remains between Ascension and Parousia. Is a ministry of oversight in historically discernible succession going back to the origin necessary for the apostolicity of the church? Do the bread and the wine of the Eucharist remain the body and blood of Christ beyond their intended use in communion and immediate consumption? Is preaching every new time a bolt-from-the-blue invasion of the New Age, leaving behind nothing but a crater on the earth? Or in liturgical preaching may the assembly of the baptized and catechized be presupposed? Are there irreversible developments in the presumably Spirit-led history of Christianity? Or is the historical, empirical, institutional Christian religion a betrayal of the Spirit? Not only Protestant/Catholic divisions can be organized around this axis but also intra-Protestant and intra-Catholic divisions.[52]

52. It is fascinating to observe here that David Bentley Hart has moved in Jenson's direction in his recent *Tradition and Apocalypse: An Essay on the Future of Christian Belief.* The book executes a withering critique of "sacred tradition," worthy of an Adolph von Harnack, as if it were a palpable historical succession not only in orders but especially in doctrine; it justifies the Nicene doctrine of the Trinity not by its precedents but by its innovation, the novelty inspired by the new perception of apocalyptic salvation as deification.

At root, Jenson argued, these dilemmas of Christian disunity exhibit dramatically the problem of the delay of the Parousia. What are we to make of the disappointment of the earliest Christians when Jesus did not literally return in glory on the clouds of heaven as expected? What are we to do, consequently, with all this time? Jenson for his part tried to solve the problem by regarding Pentecost as the new initiative of the Spirit who resources and binds the mission of the church to its origin in the event of Christ, which binding is also its unity—substantively, a none too Lutheran iteration of the *satis est* of Augsburg Confession VII. Yet Jenson's solution of the new initiative undertaken by the sanctifying Spirit in spreading the gospel to the nations goes beyond traditional Lutheran ecclesiology. The following bare-boned synopsis can hardly substitute for study of this rich and Jensonian-dense text, the persuasiveness of which consists in its detailed expositions of the ecumenical dialogues and sharp logical analyses. Doctrinally, Jenson argued, to reunify the fragmented churches divided by underlying differences in the experience of time and its doctrinal interpretation, we need a new synthesis which does not merely ameliorate the traditional divisions (as attempted in the convergence formulations) but transcends them.

His attempt is rooted in the Lutheran *finitum capax infiniti* according to which creator and creature, though ontologically distinct as infinite and finite in being respectively, are conceived correlatively not antithetically. God does not need to be creator but becomes one; if God becomes creator, there must be creatures. This correlative distinction indicates divine temporality, the *becoming* of God as creator, redeemer and ultimately as fulfiller of the promise of creation. This proposed new synthesis in the doctrine of God intends to solve the root problem diagnosed in the failure of the ecumenical dialogues regarding the relationship to time of the God of the gospel.

Consequently, Jenson critiques common understandings of the default linear model of time, particularly the pessimistic version of it which he interprets as a secular demythologization of the Olympian myth of Cronus who devours his children, i.e., linear time as one damn and depressing thing after another in infinite succession, going nowhere. By contrast, the God of the gospel is Lord of time which is in turn his creature destined to fulfillment through its lived history with the God who blesses his creatures and makes them children. Jenson is sympathetic, then, with an optimistic interpretation of linear time, even suggesting that Jonathan Edwards's post-millennialism was likely true as this also corroborated his affinities for Hegel's philosophy of history and the correlative conception of the creator-creature relation. In any case, the eternal liveliness of God, Creator of time, is time-like in the sense that God lives a purposeful life in anticipation of goals upon which God has freely determined, faithfully innovating along the way to accomplish his purposes. The life of God, Creator of space, is also space-like in the sense that God relates to God in God by an eternal conversation of persons which in turn can and does make space within its own life for creatures other than God. This capacious God initiates, embraces, sustains and brings to fulfillment the time of creatures other than God, especially human creatures addressed by God in his word and responding by prayer in the Spirit so that by this interaction they forge a common history.

Metaphysically the idea of the divine is not to be attained in Christian theology by the negative way of identifying the contrary of temporal imperfections. In fact, this negative idea of divinity, ultimately as persistent, utterly timeless, spaceless self-identity (*esse ipsum subsistens*) is the Trojan horse of a sublime idol, the divine *ousia* of classical Hellenism sneaking into the city Troy of the Trinity. Its persistent existence there constitutes the basic flaw in ecumenical theology because it forces a non-adjudicable choice between *eternity interrupting* time episodically but recognizably and *eternity sacralizing* some particular time while profaning the rest. The metaphysics of the God of the gospel, however, is a metaphysics of anticipation, namely, that God will be all that God purposes to be for himself as also for us in the coming of his reign in creaturely time and space. Corresponding to a Trinitarian mapping of divine temporality, Jenson proposes that in parallel to the doctrine of God the Father as the font of the deity there should be a new recognition of the Holy Spirit as the goal of deity. Notably, this means that we achieve the doctrine of the *unity* of God not by way of a naturally timeless self-identity, a natural and qualitative "oneness," abstract divine *ousia*, but by God's accomplishment of God's own goals, showing "the One" who alone is God truly as the Spirit brings the creation redeemed in Christ the Son to the glorification of God the Father forever. Importantly and in profound distinction from the Hellenistic divinity, the latter understanding of divine unity keeps faith's knowledge of God in the posture of faith and hope urgently active in love, while the former can avoid the risk of faith in God to rest in the supposed metaphysical certainty of rational knowledge that true God is blessedly above it all, the perfection and supremacy of being.

As mentioned, Jenson did not entirely succeed in concealing his Lutheranism when it came to his decisive intervention against the concealed flaw in ecumenical theology: "Every confessional group supposes it is the exception to the scheme by which it classifies the other groups. I am Lutheran, at least in conviction that the Reformation was needed and that in the process Luther and a few of his coworkers achieved certain new theological insights. Perhaps I may this once allow this bias to appear. Luther and some of his followers were driven by the doctrine of justification to amend the standard Christology drastically and in a hyper-Alexandrian direction."[53] What is this christological amendment? The Western understanding of Chalcedonian Christology, informed by the *Tome of Leo*, regarded the suffering of Christ strictly as the suffering of the human nature, as if something quite separable from the divine person of Christ himself. Against this Western tendency towards the Nestorian error, Jenson quotes from Luther's treatise against Zwingli: "For if I have to believe that only the human nature has suffered, Christ is too feeble a Savior for me." One notes, here, decisively that a divine incapacity for suffering is regarded by Luther as *weakness*! On the other hand, and centrally for the sacramental controversy: "Where you can say, 'here is God,' you must also say, 'and so the man Christ is also here.'"[54] Luther asserts: Christ crucified *is the same person as* Jesus bodily risen and glorified. Person, not nature.

Yet focusing only on this pitched polemic against the Nestorian implications of the Christology of Luther's opponent, Jenson draws the conclusion that a second generation Lutheran, Johannes Brenz, drew from it, namely, of a two-way communication of natural idioms, so that mortal suffering of human nature is "really," i.e., not figuratively communicated to the divine nature of the Logos, i.e., not only to the Logos qua person but also qua divine nature, just as God's infinite "energies" are in turn really communicated to the man Jesus (the standard position in Eastern Christianity in contrast to the Western doctrine of the created graces attending the humanity of Christ). This Brenzian doctrine gives rise to the crucial innovation Jenson makes in that he discards the very notion of the eternal hypostasis of the Son of God/Logos to make the humanity of Jesus directly the second Trinitarian "identity." Hence, for Jenson Lutheran tradition in its Brenzian iteration suggests divine suffering on

53. Jenson, *Unbaptized God*, 128. Cited from LW 37:161–372.

54. Jenson, *Unbaptized God*, 129.

the one side and the ubiquity of Christ's body on the other, even if there had been a failure of nerve actually to teach this officially in historical Lutheranism. The soteriological point is that such an incarnation *as a profound exchange of natures* can "really" negotiate the purposeful movement from God as origin to God's future within the life of the one God mediated by the present Jesus Christ who *is* this exchange. Thus, the past is ever surpassed for the sake of the promised future by the mediation of the "hyper-Alexandrian" Christ event in which God takes on what is human in order to give what is divine.

The would-be reformatory implications of this christological amendment for contemporary Christianity in the ruins of Christendom are quite striking:

> If the church's liturgical and institutional life actually honored the Spirit as equal in deity with the Father, the experience in shaping self-understanding of the church would be very different than it is in the West. Then eternity would be apprehended as the dramatic mutuality of Father and Spirit, of God as God's origin and God as God's goal, and therefore not as immunity to change but as *faithfulness* in action. Being would accordingly be apprehended not as persistence in what is but as *anticipation* of what is not yet. The church would know herself as the temporal mission not of resistance to time but as faithful change in time and know her own continuity in the mission not as hanging onto what is already there but rather is receiving what must come.[55]

Before offering a critique of Jenson's overreach in the foregoing, it is necessary to locate this dissent within a far wider context of appreciation for his accomplishment of the program outlined in *Unbaptized God*. Jenson belongs to a group of twentieth-century Lutheran theologians who have been so exasperated by the paralyzing "doubling" of the God of the gospel and the Divine of classical Greek metaphysics deeply embedded in Western traditions of orthodoxy, that they have cut the Gordian knot in Christology where they see doubling reiterated between the impassable divine Son and the pathetic human Jesus. Jenson dispenses, therefore, with preconceived ideas of divinity as timeless, spaceless self-identity. Instead, he identifies the human Jesus of first-century Palestine *as such* as the second "identity" of the triune God, i.e., the God of the gospel who, liberated from divine timelessness, is in turn *eternally* capable of time as its creator. The motives for doing this drastic surgery include

55. Jenson, *Unbaptized God*, 138.

greater appreciation of Luther's insistence on the indivisible personhood of Christ, picking up on the neo-Chalcedonian reiteration of the "*one* Lord Jesus Christ" as that "*one* of Trinity who suffered in his human nature." This dramatic move, however, bans from further consideration any preexistent Logos *asarkos*, and perhaps even the notion of an antecedent, so-called "immanent" or eternal Trinity. For Jenson, the Trinity of revelation, the "economic" Trinity, *is* as such the immanent and eternal Trinity and vice versa, but by way of anticipation.[56]

As mentioned, Jenson achieves this rather profound revision of the orthodox tradition by way of an eschatological ordering of eternity to time to solve the problem of God's relationship to time. The event of Jesus Christ *is* (and thus always has been) the *divine* anticipation of the eschaton, not only for us, then, but also in the life of the Creator in relation to the creation. So, the economic Trinity of revelation will prove to be the immanent and eternal Trinity when the kingdom arrives in fullness and power and God is all things to all. The pivot on which this theological revision turns is the wholly temporal event of the godforsaken death of Jesus at the nadir of the scriptural story of God with humanity. This true death of the beloved Son, shrouded in the sin of the world, generates a crisis and turning point in the eternal life of the living God in relation to the wayward creation. As Jenson put it in his *Systematic Theology*, in raising, vindicating and exalting the crucified Jesus, God decides what kind of God God will be.

It is not wrong for Jenson to source himself here in Luther, even if Jenson's Luther exegesis is rather truncated and one-sided.[57] What for Luther is especially dramatic is the spiritual suffering of Jesus the beloved Son in obedience to his Father's strange will that he drink the bitter cup of abandonment by God on account of his loving solidarity with sinful and perishing humanity. How will this crisis be resolved? With the Father's recognition by the mediation of the Spirit that the crucified, dead, and buried Jesus, shrouded in the sin of the world which out of love he has borne personally albeit in true, holy obedience to the Father—this strangely righteous Jesus clothed in human sin, suffering and death is indeed his beloved Son. And this love for dying sinners is decided as also the Father's own. "Therefore, God has highly exalted him . . . "

56. This Trinitarian revisionism at the heart of Jenson's proposed remedy is relentlessly driven home in Harvey, *Jesus and the Trinity*.

57. Luy, *Dominus Mortis*.

So far—with further help from Luther—so good. So understood theologically, the resurrection-vindication is first of all an event within the life of the one God over its relation to the creation. To his credit, Jenson aims to affirm that the identity of Jesus Christ the Son of God does not consist in assuming an abstract human nature but in living a coherent and complete human life offered to God in self-entrusting faith.[58] It is as such that this particular Son of Man is indeed the Son of God. But at just this decisive juncture there is indeed a danger in Jenson's reconstructed doctrine of the Trinity of a Hegelian collapse of the deity into human historical process. Although this is not his intention and he consistently denied that it is an implication of his theology, it involves a key innovation, his substitution of the term "identity" (= "recognizable self-sameness through time") in place of the classical term *hypostasis*, particularly as the latter gained its dogmatic meaning as "concrete way of being" in distinction from generic being, *ousia* or *physis* (nature). Identity concerns self-relation through time but Trinitarian hypostasis indicates other-relation within the divine space. The sense of hypostasis in Trinitarian Christology is to affirm that Jesus the beloved Son is indeed creator with his heavenly Father, but creator in *the concrete way of being Son of his Father. Sonship* is *not* the same predication as saying Jesus of Nazareth is the second identity of a divinity. Contrary to express intention, Jenson's "identity" affirms little more than that the human creature Jesus is truly divine, albeit in a second showing out of three.[59] Unlike the hypostasis of Sonship, "identity" does not immediately tell us how this one is related in particular to the other Trinitarian "identities" nor account for their inseparable relationships other than as exhibiting a common divine being. Dispensing with the Trinitarian concept of hypostasis for defining the unique character in inseparable relation to the other characters in the gospel narrative of God cuts the ground from under the ex post facto inference, the "induction,"[60] of the

58. Piotr Malysz, personal correspondence, May 8, 2025.

59. "The term 'identity' is not without problems, as it can be used in the modalistic sense (e.g., I am one person with several identities: daughter, wife, friend, etc.). Others have proposed alternative language including Karl Barth and Karl Rahner, respectively 'modes of being' and 'distinct matters of subsisting.'" Peterson, *Holy Spirit in the Christian life*, 24n3. The usage employed in this book to paraphrase hypostasis in contemporary English as "concrete way of being" is to facilitate description of *something in the world* as opposed to intellectual imagination of generic being, particularly if the latter is thought to be the really real of the former.

60. Hinlicky and Adkins, *Rethinking Philosophy and Theology with Deleuze*, 209–11.

eternal Trinity of persons as the ground for the free economy of God in creation, redemption, and fulfillment.

And that is a problem. Jenson in fact explicitly dispenses with the concept of hypostasis in Christology as redundant: Chalcedon's doctrine of one person (*hypostasis)* in two natures verges, he says, on "vacuous circularity. The hypostatic union is only permission to speak of Christ in the way stipulated by the doctrine of communication of attributes, but such speech, it turns out, can be true only by way of a detour through the hypostatic union." Evidently, for Jenson, the communication of attributes as such can substitute for the hypostatic union; this substitution amounts, however, to an unnuanced identification of deity and humanity *as* Jesus, begging the question of his personal relationship to his Abba Father and the sanctifying Spirit sent upon him. Jenson's revisionism is not right, either theologically or historically. The doctrine of the one person/hypostasis, i.e., the one concrete way of being which is Jesus Christ *the Son* of God, was developed to distinguish and to relate this humble way of obedient being within the life of the one God *as Son* vis-a-vis the other concrete ways of being God as Father and as Spirit. Moreover, the divine subjectivity of Sonship is essential for affirming the person's capacity for fitting yet *voluntary* obedience (not a necessity of self-same "identity") just as this free subjectivity remains important for understanding correctly the reciprocating communication of divine and human attributes as a *personal* exchange of will, not a natural or metaphysical process, such as is needed to accomplish the saving mission. By contrast, it is difficult to conceive of an "identity" as a personal agent or patient; an identity just is whatever it is, more like the timeless "nature" which Jenson is otherwise concerned to exorcise from Christian theology in favor of the lively eventfulness of the God of the gospel.

Jenson's reading of Luther in this regard is one-sided, influenced by his reading of Brenz in which the *personal* communication of attributes (defended by Chemnitz and later Gerhard against Brenz[61]), exercised in the personal obedience of the Son to the Father's will to save, seems to be replaced by an *impersonal, i.e., natural* exchange of attributes from eternity—a major stumble on the way to downfall into Hegel's logical dialectic with whose pantheistic error Jenson is often charged. The real culprit, however, is the Chalcedonian concept of "nature" (*physis* or *ousia*) as some kind of master category of reality by means of which

61. For the full and detailed argument see Hinlicky, *Beloved Community*, 547–65.

to comprehend for comparison the contrary beings of the supposedly ontologically perfect deity and ontologically imperfect creature. Here theology could receive real help from Hegel who pointed out that this un-dialectical juxtaposition of perfect and imperfect under a shared concept of nature or being, inevitably produces a "false infinite," i.e., a perfect being constructed by contrast with imperfect being, but in the process limited or negated by finitude and thus not truly infinite in being. This "false infinite" is the perfect and so supreme being of ontotheology.

Essentialism, in any case, has come under justified critique today for important reasons, above all the presumption that by a process of abstraction one can pigeonhole phenomena, be they human, animal, angelic, inanimate, or divine, in generic ideas supposedly more real than the phenomena themselves. But as we must learn in theology *what* God is from *who* God is in Jesus Christ, we also learn what it is to be human from the new Adam in whom God is inhominated by the Spirit from the Virgin Mary. The concept of "nature," *physis*, generic categories of being, is the bastion of preconceived ideas of fallen humanity about itself and the divine which eternalize the alienated experience of fallen humanity. The concept must be used with great caution in theology.

Closer to home is the associated usage of *ousia* in Trinitarian theology, the "same being" confessed of the Son with the Father. Jenson's worry is about metaphysical *oneness* (as opposed to the numerical One who alone is God truly, i.e., numerical *singularity*). For Jenson this metaphysical oneness, as previously discussed, is the sublime idol of Hellenistic theology sneaking into the understanding of the Trinity. It neutralizes the hypostatic distinctions and relations as the living reality of eternal divine unity in the perichoresis of love. Unbaptized, *ousia* is easily imagined as pure being, being itself, pure perfect act without any unrealized possibilities and thus incapable of change in *any* ontological sense; as such it may be taken as that which the three persons of the Trinity possess in common as some fourth thing and indeed must have in equal measure if they are to be God equally. This move makes the personal distinctions of the Trinity a bafflement, if not *utterly* incomprehensible, overshadowed by the requirement to think them the self-same divine thing. Having traveled so far from the gospel narrative, the resulting doctrine of God is pronounced the "mystery" that one perfect being should somehow be the three of the gospel narrative, a mathematical, not to mention *narrative* muddle. But de facto this suggests a practical "quaternity" in which the really real God is the oneness of nature behind the phenomenal three persons, remote and utterly inaccessible.[62] As Christopher Steed pointed out a generation ago, however, the genuinely *theological* use of the term, being or substance, means merely *to point* to the irreducible reality in and for itself, theologically, of the numerical One who is creator of all that is not God. And thus, the creedal, "same being with the Father," means only to point to this Son together with his Father as that one creator of all that is not God.

Jenson, therefore, should have regarded these terms "nature" and "being" as logical placeholders, stripped of their metaphysical baggage from Hellenistic philosophical theology to stand biblically for the discrete realities of unbounded creator and bounded creature and yet relating their respective capacities engaged in the unique person of Christ's redemptive mission and work according to his free decision to love unworthy and helpless creatures. Their theological function is grammatical, not classically metaphysical. Consequently, we would see with clarity that the divine Son personally bore sin and the curse on account of our humanity which he has made his very own inseparably and forever; likewise, just as this humiliated humanity of the divine Son was vindicated and exalted we would see clearly the *divine* love that was hidden in the *human* obedience. So, the concrete and particular two-way *personal* communication of attributes of the one *person* in its historical passage through cross to exaltation (as seen in the Christ hymn of Phil 2) becomes visible and articulate to inform the proclamation/confession of the church in the Spirit anticipating final victory: Jesus is Lord to our human good and the glory of God the Father.

We need not, then, go so far as Jenson does in dispensing with the immanent and eternal Trinity as the condition for the possibility of the historical event of the incarnation and with it the role of the Holy Spirit in giving human birth to the eternally begotten Son of God. The blessed life of love of the eternal Trinity provides for theological understanding the superabundant divine life that funds creation, inclusive of its redemption and fulfillment, as a free and generous act, indeed, one that proves costly to God. One should not give up lightly this divine freedom to love that voluntarily costs God, secured by the doctrine of the immanent Trinity. The problem of doubling can in fact be resolved with a rigorous Trinitarianism which takes the divine *Sonship* far more seriously

62. Hinlicky, "Quaternity or Patrology?"

in Christology.[63] In other words, it is not "feeble," no diminution of the deity of the eternal Son, to come to us by becoming truly human, but it is rather the free and fitting exercise of the almighty power of divine Sonship willingly to learn obedience by suffering in his own humanity. This indicates in turn a proper understanding of *divine* suffering, unlike the pathetic suffering of creatures. Divine suffering is voluntary for purposes of redemption of what is other than God. Voluntary!—even to the ignominy of being delivered into the dirty hands of sinners and subjected to their outrages. The passion of Christ indeed sums up and recapitulates the entire providential history of God's loving patience with sinful humanity in the Hosea 11 resolve of love, not to retaliate but rather to take the satisfaction of divine justice upon itself, sin-bearer and only so also punishment-bearer. This divine patience *is* incarnate as the helpless faith of the man Jesus in his passion, surrendering absolutely to the Father's pledge of vindication beyond the human finality of death. The humble Son of God *is* the crucified and risen son of Mary.

Jenson indexes the eternal sequence Father, Son and Holy Spirit to the temporal succession from origin through mediation to goal. That would be (Hegelian) salvation history as the enactment in profane history of the eternal idea, actualizing in creation the eternal being of the triune God. It seems on the contrary, however, that in the biblical witness the Spirit gathers up redeemed humanity in union with Christ to the eternal glorification of God the Father who sits upon the throne victoriously declaring all things new. Is not the teleology of this circulation of love breaking apocalyptically into human time that of a return to origin in the theological sense of redemption and fulfillment of *creation's* promise according to the Father's purpose? Is not the adventitious invasion of the contra-divine powers of Sin and Death disrupting divine and creative purpose overlooked here? Or, *felix culpa*, integrated into history as salvation? How do we say that the Spirit, not the Father, is the goal of God without re-admitting "God" as naming a fourth player behind the Trinity? "God" as the Father is origin and as such not God as goal which is the Spirit? But "God" is not a name, the subject of predicates, but rather a predicate. "God" is the title for the creator of all that is not "God," the one who is truly "God" over all. Such a true God, according to the gospel, is the Father of the Son on whom he breathes his Spirit so that in the Spirit the Son, joined now to redeemed humanity, returns the glory to

63. Hinlicky, "Incarnation of the Eternal Son"; Hinlicky, "Luther and the 'Repair of Chalcedon.'"

the Father. This teleology of returning all things to the Father's purpose of blessing would follow out the problem of the delay of the Parousia to its full deliteralization in apocalyptic theology which tells instead of the episodic in-breaking to the strong man's house to bind him and plunder his goods *ubi et quando Deo visum est.* To be sure, giving up history as salvation is a tough sell within modern theology. But, as we shall see, it can be sold without giving up holy secularity.

In other words, to put it bluntly, no matter how humanity on the earth turns out, the fulfillment of the creation consists in every prodigal's return to the Father's waiting arms in the eternal life of the triune God. The truth of the gospel does not depend upon the fate of humanity on the earth which, in defiance of the Triune purpose, we may surely in our malice and injustice destroy. Avoiding the ghettoization theology suffers in the contemporary academy, which can be reinforced by the cultural-linguistic model, Christian doctrinal theology for its own integrity wrestles in its third order of discourse with the implications of scientific cosmology about the eventual death of the universe and takes this as an indicator theologically of the mortal finitude of creation. Can the physics, not ideology, of linear time proceeding from the Big Bang really be overridden by a theological fiat? Should the methodologically unscientific speculation of a multiverse to avoid this mortal finitude of the cosmos go uncontested by theology? What is salvation history in relation to scientifically measurable chronology? Admittedly, this questioning could undermine Jenson's solution to the problems of continuity and discontinuity in the church's self-understanding on its historical way.[64]

64. I am not sure. Perhaps for my taste there is too much in Jenson of salvation history mediated by right-wing Hegelianism and not enough of Pauline-turned-to-Johannine apocalyptic! When I think of Jenson's endorsement of Jonathan Edwards's postmillennialism, I also think back to Joachim of Fiore regarding the coming age of the Holy Spirit on the earth. I wonder if youthful Jenson's 1960s idealism/utopianism (I once debated him on nuclear deterrence when he advocated for unilateral disarmament vis-à-vis the Soviet Union) is at play in his solution to the relation of God and time. My apocalypticism has the Niebuhrian flavor of Christian realism. Christians are placed into a real battle for the redemption of the creation, and we cannot in finite history see beyond the fog and friction of it. Our hope is "hope against hope," transcendent of creaturely possibilities. I tend to favor the demythologized apocalyptic of the Gospel of John over salvation history readings of Luke-Acts. I think with Luther that the gospel comes and goes like a thundershower, while the church in Advent-tide solidarity with Israel awaits healing rain upon our parched land. But that may be a generational difference between the Age of Aquarius in which Jenson was formed and my own postmodern disillusionment at the 1970s "Me Generation."

Given the ecumenical winter and given the correctness of Jenson's diagnosis of the basic flaw, including the "Lutheran" genesis of the insight, doctrinal theology in the tradition of Luther has little choice but to forge ahead with the reform of Chalcedon in the direction of a Trinitarian Christology as we shall see in chapter 6. One undertakes this work in dogmatics in the ecumenical hope that it forges a way forward towards a new kind of Christian "unity," reflective of the self-surpassing of the Triune God for human salvation—one that traverses stale lines of demarcation to find partners in the most surprising places. The visible unity of the churches will not be achieved in an institutional way by paper convergences on hitherto divisive doctrine, but by convergence around the apocalyptic demand to become again the confessing church responding conscientiously to the gospel of the resurrection of the crucified Jesus.

III

God's Word as the Resurrection of the Crucified Jesus

This chapter exposits Christ Jesus along the lines of the Barmen Declaration's one "word of God" which we are bound to believe and obey in life and in death for the good reason that it is he who delivers us from the grip of ungodly power by the forgiveness of sins; in delivering the truth of God's costly grace, Christ Jesus bequeaths his Spirit for faith and newness of life in joyful service to the ends of God for righteousness, life and peace on the earth. Critical dogmatics in this light obediently puts the why question to any putative word of God. In this way doctrinal theology exposes authoritarianism posing as Christian theology (the underlying issue at Barmen vis-vis the Führerprinzip*), disrupting even venerable doctrinal tradition for purposes of its reform(ulation). Chiefly, however, it discovers blind spots in the task of naming Jesus and fills them in by theological exegesis accounting for his controversial human faith and earthly ministry as that which provoked opposition and eventuated in his death by crucifixion; this destiny provides in turn the very sense of his resurrection-vindication. But this re-situating of the naming of Jesus in Second Temple Jewish apocalyptic seems at the same time to problematize the venerable doctrine of the Incarnation by identifying instead the Easter word of God as that declaration in power of the divine Sonship of the Crucified. Thus, the deeper problem of the naming of God is raised again. The chapter concludes with initial probing of the meaning of Incarnation connected with the second chapter's exploration of Jenson's "basic flaw in ecumenical theology."*

"TAKE AWAY ASSERTIONS," LUTHER famously wrote against the skeptical Erasmus, "and you take away Christianity."[1] In a polemical reversal, Luther's antithesis became the battle strategy of agnostic forces in the European Enlightenment—one thinks especially here of Hume and Kant—seeking to neutralize, if not "take away" dogmatic Christianity. Likewise, in a reversal of the Enlightenment's polemical reversal of Luther, the antithesis between revealed dogma and freethinking became the raison d'être of modern fundamentalism's defiant boast: "God said it. I believe it. That settles it. End of discussion," never bothering to ask whether one had understood what God had supposedly said. Assertion can be uninformed *obiter dicta*, ignorant, bigoted and self-privileging as if to exempt one's claim to truth from critique or examination. Dogma, which originally designated the instruction essential to Christianity as the mission into the nations delivering the gospel of God, becomes dogmatism in modern fundamentalism and for just this reason richly merits the attack of agnostics wishing to "take away [such!] Christianity." *Tertium non datur*?

In a world surfeit with propaganda, especially the modern "culture war" positioning of theology as religious fundamentalism against secular agnosticism, Luther's actual point disappears from consideration. The "assertions" which Luther wished to make for the sake of the certainty of trust in the Word of God incarnate as infused into human hearts by the sovereign election of the sanctifying Spirit, have fallen out of the picture. Yet, as Luther countered Erasmus, it is no less dogmatism to rule out of bounds claims to truth without a fair hearing appropriate to the subject matter in question.[2] It is the task of this chapter to specify the terms of the subject matter in question to determine what constitutes fair hearing of its claim to truth.

Why Has God Said So?

Methodologically, to begin with, Christian doctrinal theology in the tradition of Luther looks for the reason good enough to assert the good news of the gospel. It cannot and does not spare any effort to give good reasons for its hope, never forgetting that faith with its hope and love remains faith, not sight. A fair hearing of the claim to truth in this domain bears in mind

1. Luther, *Bondage of the Will*, 67.

2. For the contemporary case against the skeptic's dogmatic "prejudice against prejudice," see Gadamer, *Truth and Method*.

that faith is the correct human posture in relation to the One who is God truly, i.e., beyond our control, manipulation or prediction, yet worthy of trust for a good reason. It warrants trust in this uncanny subject by pursuing the question *why*, never abandoning the ethical posture of vulnerable witness whose claim to truth cannot be imposed by force, including by supposedly knock down arguments of intellectual force. Yet precisely as grounded in the apocalyptic event of Christ, Christian doctrinal theology is informed assertion, that is, assertion in the form of a response to a message that has been heard, providing good reason to believe, thus knowing what and in whom it believes. This message is "the gospel of God." Doctrinal theology is responsible for the stewardship of this message. It stewards the message for its truth and purity by pressing the why question regarding asserted words of God heard and confessed, that is, repeated in new circumstances: "Perhaps God has said so, but why has God said so? What is God's good reason for saying so?" Asking this critical question, doctrinal theology cuts the ground out from under dogmatism with its merely authoritarian notion of deity (*Deus exlex*) in order to uncover the divine ground of all divine words to humanity in, as Luther once put it, "the fiery furnace—aflame with love for us."

The why question, of course, seems audacious. It assumes that inquiring theologians are theological subjects. As newborn children of God they have, as Scripture attests, "the mind of Christ" by way of the sanctifying Spirit, searching the deep things of God, thusly to understand spiritual things opaque even to supersmart freethinkers who have not been freed in this way of conformation to Christ. Theology is freed thinking, Spirit-inspired thinking after the lively word of God which is the gospel on its way through ages and cultures. Indeed, the boldness of vulnerable witness to ask and answer such an intimate question about the deity is professedly a kind of madness in the eyes of the unspiritual: an ecstasy of the mind rapt in Christ, a folly reflecting the folly of proclaiming the best of news in an untransformed world: the oxymoron of the Christ crucified and in that very body vindicated, risen and exalted to saving authority of universal scope. Doctrinal theology is not for the faint of heart. It withers and dies from failure of nerve unfortified by the sanctifying Spirit. Drawing upon Col 2:2, 1 Thess 1:5 and Heb 6:11, 10:22 to respond to Erasmus's preference for agnosticism in difficult matters, Luther immediately referenced *plerophoriam*, "full conviction,"[3] as the

3. Luther, *Bondage*, 67.

spiritual gift empowering the theological subject to assert the gospel of God intelligently and in life to confess it in word and deed.

Apparent madness notwithstanding,[4] doctrinal theology utilizes a rational method of scholarly hermeneutics. In this fashion it stewards the proclamation and confession of the gospel message, supremely, as mentioned, by putting the subject-appropriate why question to the putative word of God. The Latin word translated "to preach" comes into English as "to predicate," i.e., to affix a descriptor to a subject via the copula. As predication, the proclamation of the word of God and its doctrinal confession are parsed for interpretation by grammatical and syntactical analysis on the hermeneutical way to interpretation for missiological purposes of translation and communication. Hermeneutical interpretation looks for the Spirit in the letters, the mind at work in the words, and finds answers to this inquiry in pursuing the why question. Predication is what liturgical preaching is as a recognizable repetition of the originating message, as in the absolution: "Be of good cheer, child of God, you are forgiven for Jesus's sake who suffered your sins and was vindicated for your release." Note how this nonidentical absolution repeats the word of Jesus in forgiving sins and how the why question to this putative word of God puts the same question behind the Mark 2 objection protesting the right of mortal Jesus's declaration of forgiveness for usurping the sole right of the deity. Enabling description of this originating message, kerygma or proclamation, which the gospel is as an external word, and its testing by the question why it is good news from God, is the primary form of doctrinal theology as it resources and then enables by regulative instruction such concrete but recognizable repetition in ever new contexts.

Note, moreover, the qualification of preaching as "liturgical." This qualification is necessary to supply the link between proclamation of the word of God and the work of the sanctifying Spirit. Proclamation of the gospel is enabled by the Spirit, to be sure, in preachers who have been given "the mind of Christ" by which always they enunciate the good reason for the words of God they have been entrusted to deliver. But the hearing of the proclamation is also enabled by the Spirit, who joins proclamation to the real existing community of faith as the proper context for hearing with

4. ". . . A sublime madness which disregards immediate appearances and emphasizes profound and ultimate unities." Niebuhr, *Moral Man and Immoral Society*, 255. "Nothing but such madness will do battle with malignant power and 'spiritual wickedness in high places.' The illusion is dangerous because it encourages terrible fanaticism. It is therefore must be brought under the control of reason. One can only hope that reason will not destroy it before its work is done" (277).

faith within the wider context of time and place. The Spirit gives the same mind of Christ to the community so that they are empowered to hear and obey the voice of the Good Shepherd in the words of their preachers, eschewing the voices of strangers and hirelings. So Luther taught: the sanctifying Spirit "first leads us into his holy community, placing us in the church's lap, where he preaches to us and brings us to Christ . . . [The Spirit] has a unique community in the world, which is the mother that begets and bears every Christian through the word of God, which the Holy Spirit reveals and proclaims, through which he illuminates and inflames hearts so that they grasp and accept it, cling to it and persevere in it." Kerygma and ecclesia go together, hand in glove, reflecting the Trinitarian circulation of Word and Spirit as the church, both creature and mediator of the gospel, exists in mission to the nations.

This chapter proceeds with elaborating the critical implications of the foregoing chapters, namely, that doctrinal theology today first of all orients itself by accounting in first-order theology for the originating event which gave rise to the proclamation with its exclusive doctrinal predications as produced and articulated in the tradition of theology stemming from Luther by asking the why question—namely, why faith alone in Christ alone by the grace of the Spirit alone to the glory of God alone according to the Scriptures accounts for the authoring and authorizing word of God.[5]

Yet we meet a grave difficulty in this contemporary task which we face in this chapter. Twentieth-century biblical scholarship discovered that the Gospels of the New Testament are not biographies that explore the inner life of Jesus or histories that detail comprehensively or reflect precisely the twists and turns of some thirty years in his earthly way. Rather, the Gospels present Jesus for the purpose of faith in his Messiahship. This is no hidden agenda; it is openly professed. Presupposing the Easter faith in Jesus as risen, they render by their narrations the character, Jesus Christ the Son of God, as a single-minded man on a Spirit-driven mission such that his proclamation and enactment of the approaching reign of the God of Israel brought him to Golgotha. At that nadir, in the experience of Godforsakenness, this Jesus of Israel understood his destiny in the lights of Psalm 22 and Isaiah 53. Easter, then, enunciates the primal gospel predication; it is the very word of God: "This Jesus, crucified, dead and buried, is risen from the dead."

5. For the fulsome account, see Hinlicky, *Beloved Community*, 108–92.

That divine assertion is the original enunciation of the gospel: Jesus who suffered in solidarity with the sinners whom he forgave by taking their sins from them and upon himself before God was raised for—*answering the question why*—their justification, life, and salvation. Resurrection is the divine proclamation which vindicates Jesus as God's beloved Son and validates his messianic mission even as it also identifies the God of Israel as his Abba Father and their Spirit as the sanctifying Spirit who works holiness in calling to faith by a corresponding crucifixion of the old self for resurrection into the trust of newborn children of "our Father in heaven." The resurrection is not an arbitrary miracle, not the supernatural warrant of an authoritarian claim to establish a true religion, but the Father's vindication and exaltation of the person Jesus which as such defines the creation's salvation which this gospel has to offer by baptism into this very Son's death and resurrection. Resurrection to eternal life in the reign of God is the good reason for all the words of God to humanity. Showing this as the primary theology of the word of God in response to the why question is the task of this chapter.

Incarnation?

What could be the problem with the foregoing? The central dogma in the ecumenical tradition of the "incarnation" seems to be sidelined in this account of the originating event. We pick up here where we left off in the last chapter, critically receiving Jenson's exposé of the deep flaw in the so-called Great Tradition along with a critique of his proposed solution. Writing this book in the 1700th anniversary year of the Nicene Creed, which became the dogmatic standard of ecumenical Christianity, the venerable confession of faith acknowledged an eternal "Son of God, eternally begotten of the Father, God from God, light from light, true God from true God, begotten not made, of one being with the Father, through whom all things were made. For us and for our salvation he came down from heaven and by the power of the Holy Spirit he became incarnate from the Virgin Mary and was made man." The Creed teaches an eternal Trinity in which the Christ event of human history is grounded as the sending to and for us of this eternal Son by the heavenly Father in the power of the Spirit who sanctifies. The originating event in human history of the resurrection of the crucified itself originates, then, in the eternal counsel of the triune God, as Luther expressed in his hymn, "Dear

Christians, One and All Rejoice." The key verses in this connection read: "But God had seen my wretched state before the world's foundation, and, mindful of his mercy is great, he planned for my salvation. He turned to me a father's heart; he did not choose the easy part, [it cost] his dearest treasure. God said to his beloved Son: ''Tis time to have compassion. Then go, bright jewel of my crown, [be salvation to the poor]; from sin and sorrow set them free; slay bitter death that they may live with you forever.' The Son obeyed his Father's will . . . "[6]

A number of issues arise at this juncture for us today in the reconstruction of Lutheran doctrinal theology. The "economic Trinity" of revelation, i.e., the gospel narrative, tells of Jesus, the God of Israel whom he addressed as Abba-Father and from whom he heard himself addressed as beloved Son, and the sanctifying Spirit whom the Father breathed upon his Son that by this sanctification the Son returned—along with the redeemed host he has won to be his own—all glory to the Father. Yet the baptismal Creed which the West knows as the "Apostles Creed" suffices for confessing this. Epistemically, how is it possible and why would it be necessary to go from here to the immanent ontology of an eternal Trinity resourcing an incarnation? What why-question is being asked and answered here? Lindbeck seems skeptical: "[R]ule theory does not prohibit speculations on the possible correspondence of the Trinitarian pattern of Christian language to the metaphysical structure of the Godhead but simply says that these are not doctrinally necessary and cannot be binding. . . . Ontological interpretations of the Trinity do not, or should not, be made communally normative for the way Christians live and think."[7] But, strictly speaking, that precisely is what the Nicene Creed, howsoever tersely, requires and delivers as seen in Luther's hymn cited above. To be sure, already in early New Testament literature like Philippians 2, the letter to the Hebrews, and the prologue to John one witnesses the movement of Christ Jesus from above to below expressed in the notion of incarnation requiring in turn some doctrinal proposition concerning the eternal Son. But predominantly in New Testament literature and especially the Synoptic Gospels we meet a "Spirit-Christology" of the new Adam who by his Spirit-enabled obedience demonstrates "sonship" in his earthly journey. The question can be posed biblically: how do we unite theologically the Synoptic Gospels

6. Cited from Hinlicky, *Luther and the Beloved Community*, 122–25.

7. Lindbeck, *Nature of Doctrine*, 106.

and the Gospel of John? And for what good reason would that synthesis be necessary as a matter of ecumenical dogma as per the Nicene Creed?

Correcting a Blind Spot

The plot thickens and the difficulties increase. Another issue that arises today regarding *both* early creedal formulations was acutely voiced during the social gospel movement and came to poignant expression in Howard Thurman's influential little book *Jesus and the Disinherited*,[8] namely, the creeds' apparent omission of the "religion of Jesus," i.e., his own life of faith, hope and love as disclosed in his ministry which inspires discipleship in those whom he calls. There was a good reason historically for the seeming omission. The original motive of the relative clauses in baptismal creeds was to exclude docetic Christology and gnostic doctrine of God, i.e., positively to identify the truly human Jesus by the marks of birth and death and thusly to define salvation he brings as the redemption of our bodies and fulfillment of the material creation. What mattered therefore was to accentuate the marks of human finitude of the human Jesus believed as Christ and Son of God. Moreover, predicating this human as the Son of the Father, Almighty Creator of heaven and earth, made the positive correlation that this material world, as the good but oppressed and groaning creation, is the object of the Creator's reconciling work. Anyone who reads the creedal theologians of early Christianity, moreover, knows how earnestly they dealt with the faith-enacted ethic of the man Jesus in that for them the lived faith of Jesus implicated believers as witness-martyrs in an epoch of cultural hostility and state-sponsored persecution. Seemingly, all this was lost from view in the period following imperial establishment of Christianity as the state religion when a contextually apt selection of data from the Gospels inadvertently but fatefully produced a blind spot in the creedal identifications of Jesus.

And this loss from consciousness of the "religion of Jesus" is what grieves Howard Thurman and for a good reason. As Vincent Harding wrote in his introduction to Thurman's book, "[T]here was never any doubt in [Thurman's] mind that the life and teachings of Jesus, 'the poor Jew' of Nazareth, the disinherited, threatened subject of Roman power, was especially relevant to the ever present contingent of black men and women in America. So, he could unhesitatingly declare that 'the striking

8. Thurman, *Jesus and The Disinherited.*

similarity between the social position of Jesus in Palestine and that of the vast majority of American Negroes is obvious to anyone who tarries long over the facts.'"[9] This correlation of poverty in power with fresh perception of the courageous and dignified religion of the human Jesus became theologically significant not only for Thurman but through his influence on Martin Luther King Jr. and in the subsequent rise of Black Theology in James Cone. Thurman's exploration of the faith/religion of Jesus had immediate relevance for a critique of the predominant Christian religion that rationalized a race-based slavery and supported Jim Crow segregation; this critique flagged the creedal blind spot regarding the life Jesus lived for us, a resource validating the humanity of the poor and in this way empowering them. It poses for us today not only the need for a necessary correction of a creedal blind spot, however inadvertent. More profoundly, recovering the faith and faithfulness of Jesus raises the thorny problem of the motive of the crucifiers and its role in the economy of God which, according to the Nicene Creed's naming of Pontius Pilate, takes place "for us and for our salvation." Taking up Thurman's complaint here, in any event, illustrates how fresh theological exegesis undertaken in critical dogmatics can disrupt and repair doctrinal tradition in testing the church's speech and behavior for its correspondence to the gospel word of God. The second-order work of doctrinal theology is unfinished, as the confession of faith is not yet the fulfilled confession of praise; it is the Spirit's work in progress. The question of the church's confession of Jesus Christ is freshly answered in every new situation—for good or for ill.

Thurman's inquiry raises for us the dogmatic issue of the *pistis Christou*, the faith/faithfulness of the messianic man Jesus as that which provoked his crucifixion and consequently provides the sense of his resurrection-vindication. "For years it has been a part of my own quest so to understand the religion of Jesus that interest in his way of life could be developed and sustained by intelligent men and women who were at the same time deeply victimized by the Christian churches' betrayal of his faith."[10] Pointedly, "my interpretation of the meaning of the religion of Jesus . . . [is] as religious subject rather than religious object."[11] Jesus as human subject of faith—a one-sided, to be sure, but necessary correction to a long-standing tendency reductively to objectify Jesus as an

9. Thurman, *Jesus and the Disinherited*, ix.

10. Thurman, *Jesus and the Disinherited*, 19.

11. Thurman, *Jesus and the Disinherited*, 6.

ethereal "Savior," a contemporary example of docetism objectifying Jesus as a "spiritual" deliverer to meet to perceived religious need in disregard of his concretely historical human being.

Thurman's particular interpretation of the faith of Jesus, consequently, does not traffic in cheap grace or hawk the sugarcoated pill of docetism. On the contrary, the message of Jesus to the poor who gathered to hear him "focused on the urgency of a radical change in the inner attitude of the people. He recognized fully that out of the heart are the issues of life and that no external force, however great and overwhelming, can at long last destroy people if it does not first win the victory of the spirit against them."[12] For all the proper emphasis on social sin solidified in structures of malice and injustice as the injurious source of dysfunction in oppressed communities, "Jesus saw this with almighty clarity. Again and again he came back to the inner life of the individual. . . . A profound piece of surgery has to take place in the very psyche of the disinherited before the great claim of the religion of Jesus can be presented . . . "[13]

To be sure, Thurman's analysis of the "spiritual" injury inflicted by oppression is penetrating. He speaks to his own audience, the poor in power: "The disadvantaged know that they cannot fight back effectively, that they cannot protect themselves, and that they cannot demand protection from their persecutors." It is not simply the fear of physical death that works in the souls of the disinherited but the

> deep humiliation arising from dying without benefit of cause or purpose . . . Merely being killed or being beaten . . . [by] indifferent sadism, without the dignity of being on the receiving end of a premeditated act hammered out in the white heat of transcendent moral passion. The whole experience attacks the fundamental sense of self-respect and personal dignity, without which man is no man . . . , contemptuous disregard for the personhood is the fact that is degrading.[14]

The religion of Jesus, however, makes the demoralized among the disinherited into fearless children of God. "Such a man recognizes that death cannot possibly be the worst thing in the world. There are some things that are worse than death." Slavishness is worse than death as is its merely apparent opposite, fanatical, retaliatory hatred. "The awareness

12. Thurman, *Jesus and the Disinherited*, 11.
13. Thurman, *Jesus and the Disinherited*, 11.
14. Thurman, *Jesus and the Disinherited*, 28.

that man is a child of the God of religion, who is at one and the same time the God of life, creates a profound faith in life that nothing can destroy. . . . Here we reach the high watermark of prophetic religion, and it is of the essence of the religion of Jesus of Nazareth."[15] No matter the terrestrial outcome, inspiration from Jesus to live as a fearless child of God is good news to and for the poor.

Belief in God in the religion of Jesus is belief in truth and its universal vindication. "There must always be the confidence that the effect of truthfulness can be realized in the mind of the oppressor as well as the oppressed. There is no substitute for such a faith."[16] The source of this confidence is living life before the Father in heaven of the Sermon on the Mount, as Jesus preached, who knows and sees in secret:

> Unwavering sincerity says that man should always recognize the fact that he lives always in the presence of God, always under the divine scrutiny, and that there is no really significant living for man, whatever may be his status, until he has turned and faced the divine scrutiny. Here all men stand stripped to the literal substance of themselves, without disguise, without pretension, without seeming whatsoever. No man can fool God.[17]

Propaganda is of no avail before the truth exposed in the sight of the Father in heaven. Following in the faith of Jesus, the disciple likewise lives life conscientiously, naked and exposed before the gaze of the heavenly Father. Yet the one who fears God has nothing else in all the world to fear.

Thurman does not, therefore, give a pass from the divine scrutiny Jesus attests in the Sermon on the Mount to the rage, however righteous, of the oppressed.

> In many analyses of hatred it is customary to apply it only to the attitude of the strong towards the weak . . . Such an assumption is quite ridiculous . . . Hatred, in the mind and spirit of the disinherited, is born out of great bitterness—a bitterness that is made possible by sustained resentment which is bottled up until it distills an essence of vitality, giving to the individual in whom this is happening a radical and fundamental basis for self-realization.

15. Thurman, *Jesus and the Disinherited*, 45.
16. Thurman, *Jesus and the Disinherited*, 16.
17. Thurman, *Jesus and the Disinherited*, 61.

Hatred in this way becomes a pure but demonic energy. "Hatred becomes for you a source of validation for your personality"[18] against the assaults and debasements of the oppressors. Hatred is thus an elixir, but like any intoxicant it finally consumes its consumer. "When hatred serves as a dimension of self-realization, the illusion of righteousness is easy to create. Often there are but thin lines between bitterness, hatred, self-realization, defiance, and righteous indignation . . . [yet when] hatred becomes a device by which an individual seeks to protect himself against moral disintegration," it works a furious disintegration. "Hatred bears deadly and bitter fruit. It is blind and nondiscriminating . . . once hatred is released, it cannot be confined to the offenders alone . . . Hatred cannot be controlled once it is set in motion."[19] Rage is a tsunami which drowns both hater and hated.

Thus, hatred must be purged from those who follow Jesus. "It is clear that before love can operate, there is the necessity for forgiveness of injury perpetuated against a person by a group. This is the issue for the disinherited. Once again, the answer is not simple. Perhaps there is no answer that can be completely satisfying from the point of view of rational reflection,"[20] i.e., on account of the antecedent irrationality of hateful bigotry issuing in acts of gratuitous injury. Ultimately, Thurman concludes, we may forgive because "God forgives us again and again for what we do intentionally and unintentionally . . . "[21] The ultimate ground in the religion of Jesus is that "there is forgiveness with God." On this basis, "for the privileged and underprivileged alike, if the individual puts at the disposal of the Spirit the needful dedication and discipline, he can live effectively in the chaos of the present the high destiny of the son of God,"[22] knowing Jesus and following him as exemplar. "Such a figure was Jesus of Nazareth"—grand prototype, eternal presence, the divine moment in human sin and misery, the man most worthy of honor and praise," a model "for what he did all men may do. Thus interpreted, he belongs to no age, no race, no creed. When men look into his face, they see attached the glory of their own possibilities, and their hearts whisper, "Thank you and thank God!"[23]

18. Thurman, *Jesus and the Disinherited*, 69.
19. Thurman, *Jesus and the Disinherited*, 72.
20. Thurman, *Jesus and the Disinherited*, 97.
21. Thurman, *Jesus and the Disinherited*, 98.
22. Thurman, *Jesus and the Disinherited*, 99.
23. Thurman, *Jesus and the Disinherited*, 101.

It is evident that, as in the social gospel theology in general, there is as much ethical idealism in Thurman's portrait of the Jesus of history—"grand prototype" in whom anyone can discover "the glory of their own possibilities"—as there is of the New Testament witness to the controversial figure of Jesus. Yet, in Thurman the prophetic concern for justice for the poor in power within human society couples with a bracing doctrine of personal transformation of those very poor even, if not especially, under the duress of oppression. The forgiving love of God is melded to penitent, transforming love for God, thusly fearing death less than slavishness by fearing God above all, lest unholy rage overtake or meek cowardice subvert the dignity of true children of God. Faith in God cashes out as faith in truth and its vindication over against the debilitating propaganda of an unjust world. Even Thurman's claim that this Jesus belongs to "no age, no race, no creed" may be substantiated in that there are many relations to this Jesus (Thurman mentions Gandhi) other than that of the Christian faith in him, crucified and risen and so revealed the Son of God in the flesh.[24] We will return to the problem of such an anti-docetic account of the humanity of Christ in chapter 6's consideration of Schleiermacher's *Life Of Jesus*.

The Faith of Christ

What matters for present purposes is that an account of the earthly faith of Jesus and its enactment fills in the apparent omission in the baptismal creed to provide the missing link between his coming and his destiny. In brief, Jesus taught parables, drawn from the matrix of the Scriptures, of the impending reign of God of Israel and Jesus was consequently crucified as would-be "King of the Jews." Quests for this "historical Jesus" come and go with varying results and are profoundly problematic hermeneutically speaking, given the nature of the New Testament sources as motivated by resurrection faith, not to mention the cognitive motives, other than pure "disinterested science," of historical questers. The meaning and significance of anti-docetism in Christology for the doctrine of God, as mentioned, will be treated in detail in chapter 6. What matters presently for the reconstruction of doctrinal theology in the tradition of Luther are two salient facts.

24. Ochs, *Another Reformation*. The holy book of Islam also has a relationship to Jesus and his mother, Mary. Through its global spread Christianity has brought many non-Christians into some relation to Jesus other than that of Christian faith in him.

First, the faith of the man Jesus is articulated for us to know and to share in the Lord's Prayer which substantially conveys it. Alongside the baptismal creed, the Lord's Prayer informs the faith of the church in conformity with the faith of Jesus. For that reason, it has belonged to the catechetical tradition, teaching disciples to pray with Jesus and at his invitation.[25] The opening petitions imploring the coming of God's reign, making the petitioner a theological subject, and the concluding petitions asking in the interim to be spared trial by the Evil One form apocalyptic brackets around the needs of daily life in the afflicted creation for sustenance and forgiveness. The Synoptic linkage between the petition that God's will be done on earth as in heaven and Jesus's iteration of this petition in Gethsemane establishes the connection between the lived faith of Jesus and his destiny.

Second, the recent rediscovery of the Pauline *pistis Christou* profoundly challenges the polemical antithesis between an ethical Jesus and a dogmatic Paul that sabotaged the theology of the social gospel.[26] *Pistis Christou* rather puts on display the intrinsic linkage between the creedal identification of the human Jesus and the enacted proclamation of this man in his own faithful obedience. *Pistis Christou* is an ambiguous construction grammatically. Paul employs the unusual formulation in the genitive case which in Greek serves to put a leading noun into relation with another noun, most commonly a possessive relationship. Literally transposed into English this unusual formulation is "the faith, or faithfulness (the Greek word can mean either) of Christ." The question is whether this expression denotes Christ's own faith or faithfulness (grammatically, the genitive of the subject) or the faith which is put in Christ by human beings (grammatically, the genitive of the object). Does the phrase, faith of Christ, say something about Jesus Christ whose faith or faithfulness saves us or about those who believe in him, whose faith saves them? Or somehow both?

In the following texts, however, Paul employs this curious *pistis Christou* construction in order immediately to relate the "faith of Christ" to those who believe in him. Note further that these examples are found only in Galatians, Romans, and Philippians where Paul is engaged in controversy regarding the doctrine of justification. Note further how

25. Hinlicky, "Retrieving Luther on Prayer."

26. Thurman took a nuanced position on this cleavage by calling attention to Paul's Roman citizenship which located him socially in a place other than among the disinherited audience of Jesus.

differently the same Greek phrase is translated by the King James version and by the Revised Standard Version.

> KJV Gal 2:16: Knowing that a man is not justified by the works of the law, but by the faith of Jesus Christ, even we have believed in Jesus Christ, that we might be justified by the faith of Christ, and not by the works of the law: for by the works of the law shall no flesh be justified.
>
> RSV Gal 2:16: Yet we know that a man is not justified by works of the law but through faith in Jesus Christ, even we have believed in Christ Jesus, in order to be justified by faith in Christ, and not by works of the law, because by works of the law shall no one be justified.
>
> KJV Gal 3:22: But the scripture hath concluded all under sin, that the promise by faith of Jesus Christ might be given to them that believe.
>
> RSV Gal 3:22: But the scripture consigned all things to sin, that what was promised to faith in Jesus Christ might be given to those who believe.
>
> KJV Rom 3:22: Even the righteousness of God which is by faith of Jesus Christ unto all and upon all them that believe . . .
>
> RSV Rom 3:22: the righteousness of God through faith in Jesus Christ for all who believe. . . .
>
> KJV Phil 3:9: And be found in him, not having mine own righteousness, which is of the law, but that which is through the faith of Christ, the righteousness which is of God by faith
>
> RSV Phil 3:9: And be found in him, not having a righteousness of my own, based on law, but that which is through faith in Christ, the righteousness from God that depends on faith.

The exegetical question about the interpretation of *pistis Christou* has precipitated "a proxy war between a corporate participationist reading of Paul and an individual, forensic reading."[27] The arguments to and fro over the years indicate that the question cannot be resolved solely on the basis of semantics, grammar or non-theological exegesis. In some exchanges, it appears as a proxy war between the Christologies of Rudolf Bultmann and Karl Barth. In this author's first academic book, *Paths Not*

27. Bird and Sprinkle, *Faith of Jesus Christ*, 6.

Taken, he sided with Barth, arguing alongside Olli-Pekka Vainio[28] that the doctrine of justification by faith already in the sixteenth century fell into hopeless conundrums (faith abstracted from its work of love or faith incarnate in love?) when parsed exclusively on the plane of anthropology. The sense of justification by faith could only be resolved, I argued, by elevating discussion to the plane of Trinitarian Christology. And this was also the gravamen of Richard Hays's seminal book, *The Faith of Jesus Christ*,[29] namely, that Paul's kerygma presupposes a gospel narrative by which Christ is identified as the just and faithful one, hence indicating the subjective genitive reading: "the faith/faithfulness of Christ."

We see in all these cases that Paul introduces the ambiguous genitive construction "the faith of Christ" in order immediately to relate it to the benefit of those believing *in* Christ (for which he employs a different Greek construction). This excludes any one-sided interpretation of the expression which downplays or even excludes the importance for the apostle of human faith in Christ as a real correspondence on the earth to the faith/faithfulness of Christ. God does not justify on account of (*propter*) human faith in Christ, as if this were the causal factor that merited God's approval, but *propter Christum.* Yet certainly for Paul the faith *of* Christ is given for the sake of human faith *in* Christ.

As mentioned, the expression, faith of Christ, is introduced in the context of Paul's justification controversies. Here we face an interpretive choice. Is the genitive "disambiguated" by the context as nothing but a stylistically alternative way of expressing faith in Christ as redundancy supposedly makes clear? That would support the objective genitive reading that "faith of Christ" really means and should be put in English as "faith in Christ." Or should we regard the introduction of this unusual and innovative language, faith of Christ, as a deliberate nuance in the justification controversy, specifying how justifying human faith wholly consists in the *Christus pro nobis.* That is how Karl Barth understood it. Quoting Gal 2:19–20, he writes:

> The fact that I live in the faith of the Son of God in my faith in him, has its basis in the fact that he himself, the Son of God, first believed for me, and so believed that all that remains for me to do is to let my eyes rest on him, which really means to let my eyes follow him. This following is my faith. But the great work of faith has already been done by the one whom I follow in my

28. Vainio, *Justification and Participation in Christ.*

29. Hays, *Faith of Jesus Christ.*

> faith, even before I believe, even if I no longer believe, in such a way that he is always, as Hebrews 12:2 puts it, the originator and completion of our faith in such a way, therefore, that every beginning and fresh beginning of our faith has its only starting point in him, indeed, the only basis of its awakening.[30]

The undisputed references, equally significant in Paul's exposition of his doctrine of justification, to the act of righteousness in the obedience of Christ (Rom 5:18–19) are conceptually indistinguishable from the subjective genitive reading of the faith of Christ. The occurrence of the subjective genitive in Philippians likewise coheres with the humility and obedience of Christ Jesus celebrated in the hymn of chapter 2. The theological subject portrayed in Gal 2:20 likewise indicates that the believer's personal faith is a participation in the faith active in the love of the Son of God who loved and gave himself for the believer. This participation for Paul, of course, is not in a metaphysical principle but rather, by the sovereign election and work of the sanctifying Spirit, incorporates the believer's faith into Christ's faithfulness: as Jesus believed for me, so I believe in him—the same Spirit inspiring us both. For Barth too

> the reality of Christian existence is to be explained by the Spirit as the power of participation. Through the Spirit, the Christian is caught up in the history of Jesus; she participates in Jesus's own faithful obedience, and the event of this participation launches her into a new freedom, the freedom "to be faithful to God as God is faithful to her."[31]

The role of the sanctifying Spirit in incorporating believers into the faithful love of Jesus Christ that they may believe bears particular emphasis because the anxiety running through this controversy is that attributing faith to the Son of God somehow diminishes his divinity. Faith is a deficiency, an imperfect form of knowledge which in any case should be attributed only to Christ's humanity. For many reasons theology in the tradition of Luther has to reject this anxiety about the humility of God leading to various kinds of Nestorian division of labor between the needless Son of God and the beggarly son of Mary. Over against abstract preconceptions of natures, divine or human, in Trinitarian Christology Jesus is God precisely in the way of being Son, for whom the humility of trust and obedience is the fitting and powerful

30. *CD* II/2, 559.

31. Miters, "From Faithfulness to Faith in the Theology of Karl Barth."

expression of his particular divine hypostasis. Indeed, and more broadly, we may speak of the humility of the triune God in the act of creation itself wherein God hides behind the mask of nature to give time and space for creaturely growth. There, in contrast to the neo-Platonic deities, God needs no medium other than God's self to be present to the creation immediately and thusly to be revealed there as human need requires. The point is that God is antecedently the humble God, capable of being present in revelation *as creature.*[32]

We now add to the foregoing elaboration of the *pistis Christou* the insightful work of Teresa Morgan. She sees that Paul uses *pistis* in Galatians "to refer to the relationship of trust/belief between God, Christ, and the faithful, the pledge or assurance secured by Christ which binds them together, the bond formed by the pledge, and the community formed by the bond."[33] Surely, this is the certainty that Luther contended for, not a modern epistemological foundation but an experienced ecstasy of the heart set free in being bound to a trustworthy and liberating Lord now joined by his Spirit to the community of his liberated. This reading of the faith of Christ cuts in every direction against the debate, as noted earlier, which has seemed a proxy war between corporate participationist readings Paul and individualistic forensic interpretations. Morgan maintains, however, that, when trust is understood as a relationship, the primacy of trust (*fiducia, fides ex corde*) in primitive Christianity is articulated christologically, i.e., in the doctrine of Christ Jesus. She finds the faithfulness/faith of Jesus Christ rendering him trustworthy operative in multiple relational dimensions, inclusive of eliciting personal faith to be lived out communally in the ecclesia. This discovery of the christological articulation of faith as a social reality, moreover, proves to clarify the rise of creedal Christianity, the "We believe . . . " enunciating the *fides quae creditur*. Any act of informed trust, Morgan repeatedly reminds, implicitly but necessarily entails beliefs about who and what is trustworthy. Such confidence-building beliefs must become explicit and articulate in trial and testing if trust is to persevere under duress. Writing in reference to the Gospel of John, for example, she observes that propositional "believing occurs within relationships, potential or actual, between Jesus and the elect, and its content is no more nor less than the identification

32. Piotr Malysz, personal correspondence, May 17, 2025.

33. Morgan, *Roman Faith and Christian Faith*, 290.

of Jesus which leads the elect to trust in him" in spite of the enmity of the "unbelieving world" with the doubt it insinuates.[34]

Paul likewise is deliberately introducing the unusual locution of a subjective genitive, meaning "the faith of Christ," to indicate a relationship between the lived faith of Christ, baptized in the Spirit for his messianic work of love for others, and the Spirit-induced faith of believers in him also operative in such love for others. Morgan identifies a mediating "model of Jesus as doubly faithful to and trusted by God and humanity to explain how his death and resurrection save those believing from their sins."[35] In other words, the faith/faithfulness of Jesus was simultaneously his relation of filial obedience to his Abba Father and of loving loyalty to sinners whose sins he had forgiven in the name of the Father's coming kingdom. In sending his Son to this uncanny end, God trusts, indeed entrusts his own fatherhood[36] to the Son's faithful course, even to death on a cross, and so by the Spirit vindicates their mutual relationship of trust by his resurrection/exaltation. Resurrection is vindication and fulfillment of the faith of Christ. The proclamation of this event of divine victory for us consequently extends the event in eliciting the new community in this multidimensional trust. The ecumenical, "*We* believe . . . ," prefacing the Nicene Creed, is thereby scripturally corroborated. Thus, Paul uses *pistis* in Galatians "to refer to the relationship of trust/belief between God, Christ, and the faithful, the pledge or assurance secured by Christ which binds them together, the bond formed by the pledge, and the community formed by the bond."[37] The Christian faith thereby is recovered as a social faith, the faith of the "Israel of God," an inchoate beloved community generated and constituted in new bonds of trust, established and so centered upon the enacted faith of Christ. Fulfilling a wish of Dietrich Bonhoeffer, one may at last see fulfillment in Morgan's account of the "social intention of all the basic Christian concepts."[38] That indeed points the way forward. Its reformatory potential for the moribund churches of Euro-America, fragmented and in the throes of a nigh-lethal legitimacy crisis, is evident.

Recall that we have been entertaining the creedal question of the dogmatic necessity of the Nicene Creed's teaching of the immanent and

34. Morgan, *Roman Faith and Christian Faith*, 439–40.

35. Morgan, *Roman Faith and Christian Faith*, 437.

36. Cf. CD IV/1:419.

37. Morgan, *Roman Faith and Christian Faith*, 290.

38. Bonhoeffer, *Sanctorum Communio*, 21.

eternal Trinity as the ground of the economic Trinity at work in creaturely time and space. Biblically, it is the question of the necessity of reading the Gospel of John as a theological commentary on the Synoptics in parallel to the Pauline "faith in Christ" as alike capturing theologically the significance of the obedience of Jesus portrayed in the gospel narrative. Dogmatically, we are at the same time posing the question of how resurrection faith at length yields faith in the incarnation. What are the reasons good enough for these formative moments in the originative second-order theology of the word of God? Here too we must work through difficulties. Nothing seems as dubious as "resurrection" today after the bloodied mass murderers of the twentieth century and consequently a renewed awareness of the historic criminality of our human race, not to mention massive and irreplaceable loss. What good does pie-in-the-sky in the sweet-by-and-by do in face of actual evil on this earth? But perhaps in our bafflement over this, we are like the disciples in Mark descending from the Mount of Transfiguration with no idea of what "resurrection from the dead" could mean (Mark 9:10).

On the Way to the Confession of Doubting Thomas

N. T. Wright is the rare bird these days of a highly skilled biblical scholar who also thinks and writes theologically. The interpretation of "resurrection" in his *Surprised by Hope*[39] has the great merit of insisting upon its Second Temple setting in Jewish apocalyptic. This positioning removes resurrection from the characteristic modern framing that puts it in the category of miracles in general, whether as implausible proofs good only for fooling the credulous or as supernatural intervention substantiating a religion's claim to authority in doubly offensive violation of the causal nexus of the physical order and cultural plurality in the moral order. The issue then becomes the scientific plausibility of the Easter assertion legitimating the Christian religion. But, by historically and critically locating the sense of resurrection in Jewish apocalyptic, an entirely other issue emerges. In Wright's words, voiced in direct address to the reader: "Are you going to worship the creator God and discover thereby what it means to become fully and gloriously human, reflecting his powerful, healing, transformative relation to the world? Or are you going to worship the world as it is, boosting your corruptible

39. Wright, *Surprised by Hope*.

humanness by gaining power or pleasure from forces within the world, merely contributing thereby to your own dehumanization and the further corruption of the world itself?"[40]

That is what is at issue in the gospel's assertion of the bodily resurrection of Jesus: asserting and defining a defiant Christian "hope against hope." Easter is "the foundation of the Christian stance of allegiance to a different king, a different Lord. Death is the last weapon of the tyrant . . . Resurrection is not the redescription of death; it is its overthrow and, with that, the overthrow of those whose power depends on it."[41] The moral and broadly political sense of the resurrection of Jesus is divine vindication of him who was crucified by those possessing the power of death.

> Easter has a very this-worldly, present-age meaning: Jesus is raised, so he is the Messiah, and therefore he is the world's true Lord; Jesus is raised, so God's new creation has come—and we, his followers, have a job to do! Jesus is raised, so we must act as his heralds, announcing his Lordship to the entire world, making his kingdom on earth as it is in heaven![42]

Accordingly, the doctrinal battle of the early church against docetism/Gnosticism recurs in Wright's sustained polemic against etherealizing interpretations of the Risen One. "If the promised final future is simply that immortal souls leave behind their mortal bodies, then death still rules—since that is the description not of the defeat of death but simply death itself, seen from one angle."[43] The sustained polemic against the modern Gnosticism of the soul "going to heaven when you die" by virtue of the other-worldly lobbying of an equally ethereal Savior represents a deficient salvation that is essentially away from this world in contrast to the primitive Christian hope for God's new creation of it, for new heavens and a new earth which has been inaugurated, *pars pro toto*, in the bodily resurrection of Jesus Christ. When the world tells the church to get back to its proper business of saving souls "that radical distortion of Christian hope belongs exactly with the quietism that leaves the world as it is and thus allows evil to proceed unchecked."[44]

40. Wright, *Surprised by Hope*, 185.
41. Wright, *Surprised by Hope*, 50.
42. Wright, *Surprised by Hope*, 56.
43. Wright, *Surprised by Hope*, 15.
44. Wright, *Surprised by Hope*, 269.

Wright positions his argument for the contemporary salience of the apocalyptic meaning of resurrection in current postmodernism's questioning of Enlightenment secularism (i.e., "this-age-only-ism[45] as opposed to apocalyptic's new-age-aborning):

> The totalitarianisms of the last century were simply among the varied manifestations of a larger totalitarianism of thought and culture against which postmodernity has now, and rightly in my view, rebelled. . . . And *this is the point where believing in the resurrection of Jesus suddenly ceases to be a matter of inquiring about an odd event in the first century and becomes a matter of rediscovering hope in the 21st century.*[46]

To sustain this apocalyptic interpretation of the meaning of the bodily resurrection of Jesus inaugurating his messianic kingship over the new creation of God advancing on the earth, Wright makes apologetic arguments for plausible evidence of it. He holds that the empty tomb and the appearances of the risen Lord are historically credible data while acknowledging that the meaning of this data is not self-evident. He argues that it is a choice, not "something called scientific historiography forces us to" make, to maintain dogmatically on behalf of secularism, reminiscent of the Sadducees of the temple establishment at the time of Jesus, that dead people do not rise and therefore there must be some other explanation of Easter. But neither is resurrection an arbitrary miracle; it signifies the turning of the ages. In the actual historical context of Jesus's conflict with the temple establishment in Jerusalem in cahoots with Rome, resurrection enunciating divine vindication cannot be taken "as an odd event within the world as it is but as the utterly characteristic, prototypical, and foundational event within the world as it has begun to be. It is not an absurd event within the old world but the symbol and starting point of the New World."[47]

For our purposes in this chapter probing the difficulty caused by the originative event of the gospel in the resurrection of the crucified for the Nicene Creed's doctrinal endorsement of the immanent and eternal Trinity in warranting the Christology of incarnation, we can leave to the side Wright's apologetic for the historical probability of the bodily resurrection as a third-order concern of theology. His excavation of

45. Asad, *Formations of the Secular.*

46. Wright, *Surprised by Hope*, 75, emphasis original.

47. Wright, *Surprised by Hope*, 67.

the meaning of the claim is what matters for second-order theology. Although it is not fully developed, the connection Wright indicates between the *bodily* resurrection of Jesus and the doctrine of the in*carn*ation is of one piece with the anti-doceticism we have discussed along the way as the very first challenge in Christian doctrinal history. "To put it bluntly, creation is to be redeemed; that is, space is to be redeemed, time is to be redeemed, and matter is to be redeemed."[48] "Heaven and earth, I repeat, are made for each other, and at certain points they intersect and interlock. Jesus is the ultimate such point. We as Christians are meant to be such points, derived from him. The Spirit, the sacraments, and the Scriptures are given so that the double life of Jesus, both heavenly and earthly, can become ours as well, already in the present."[49]

Christologically modified apocalyptic, then, for Wright is an *inaugurated* eschatology still in struggle and not yet arrived. Just so, "what we do in the present matters enormously," drawing upon the Pauline encouragement and consolation concluding his teaching on the resurrection in 1 Corinthians: "Therefore, my beloved, be steadfast, immovable, always excelling in the work of the Lord, because you know that in the Lord your labor is not in vain" (1 Cor 15:58). As such "historicizing of the eschatological," resurrection funds the doctrine of baptismal vocation as signing creation's redemption. In the same Spirit, the apocalyptic event of Jesus Christ the Son of God proclaimed as very word of God in the Easter gospel opens up a theological path from the originative event of the resurrection of Jesus to the Johannine intimation of the eternal Word become flesh, just as John has the apostolic figure representative of docetism in early Christianity, Thomas, kneeling before the risen Lord upon seeing his glorified wounds to exclaim, "my Lord and my God!"[50]

Ambiguities of "Incarnation"

What difference does it make, however, whether the christological confession of faith orients itself with the ambiguous notion of incarnation (the realization of an idea? aka the "Logos" which became flesh, as some have taken in John 1:14) or with that of the vindication of Jesus, born in David's royal line, as the Son of God (as in Rom 1:2–4)? Both motifs

48. Wright, *Surprised by Hope*, 211.

49. Wright, *Surprised by Hope*, 252.

50. Riley, *Resurrection Reconsidered.*

exist in the biblical sources and are at play in the traditions of Christian theology. The question posed is thus not a matter of a for-and-against choice between these motifs; it is rather a matter of orientation, of epistemic priority and access, by which one of these motifs has primacy and therefore will govern the other, in particular by construing differently the theological sense of resurrection, whether as moral vindication of a controversial act of solidarity or as supernatural confirmation of the authority of the founder of a religion.

The incarnation orientation will interpret resurrection as datum alongside others, serving significantly as miraculous confirmation of the presence of God expressed in the figure of the incarnate one, a miracle of confirmation overcoming obstacles to faith in his authority to found a new and true religion. The vindication orientation, by contrast, will interpret resurrection as the exaltation of the abidingly controversial Jesus, not least of all controversial for his death in solidarity with sinners, to saving, albeit still contested authority of universal scope—but particularly here and now in the ecclesia, understood as the community of those elected by the sanctifying Spirit to share in the sufferings of Christ in hope of sharing his glory.[51] As Christian theology is reflection on a "word given prior to thought" (Jüngel).[52] in the first case, incarnation serves as the dogmatic premise of christological thinking about the founder; in the second case, incarnation marks the doxological conclusion of christological thinking which is premised instead on the Easter proclamation of the divine Sonship of this crucified Jew (Rom 1:2–4), in the act revealing the inauguration of the reign of the God of Israel over a new humanity. In a nutshell, for the incarnation orientation resurrection *overcomes* the scandal of the cross, not to mention of the Jewishness of Jesus, while the vindication orientation *asserts and prosecutes* these very scandals without remainder (1 Cor 1:8–25).

The alternative just sketched has many ramifications, although we should note from the outset a definite ambiguity that haunts the incarnation orientation and thus may confuse the issue. This ambiguity is usually masked by an alleged contrast between "high" and "low" Christologies of incarnation, as if varying degrees of divinity might be assigned to the manifestly human Jesus so far as and to what extent he incarnates the divine. But even so-called low Christologies, which think

51. Dalferth, *Crucified and Resurrected: Restructuring the Grammar of Christology*. See Hinlicky, "Ingolf U. Dalferth, Crucified and Resurrected."

52. See Hinlicky, "Metaphorical Truth and the Language of Christian Theology."

of Jesus as a human being with a special or extraordinary consciousness of God, think fundamentally in terms of incarnation for telling *that* "God is present" with reassuring affirmations of "*what* God is like." On this basis a normative idea or image of God is generated, traditionally but not unproblematically, as our doting heavenly parent.[53] Such disclosure with its assertion of timeless truth which in any event antecedently and universally prevails, even if obscured and little known, is what is decisive for an incarnation orientation, no matter whether conceived highly "from above" or lowly "from below." In contrast, vindication tells what God is doing in the novelty of raising Jesus, bringing to naught the things that are in order to evoke new creation *ex vetere*.

Moreover, since each orientation may interpret the other biblical motif, it is not always clear how the governing christological logic is at work incorporating the other motif into its own framework. Both orientations claim revelation of God, for example, but for the incarnation approach revelation is *disclosure* by way of *similitude* which clarifies so far as possible an essentially unknowable divine reality which clarification the resurrection miracle in turn, alongside other miracles, is thought to confirm. For the vindication approach by contrast revelation is an apocalyptic incision executed in the resurrection of the crucified Jesus which gives and demands knowledge of God by proclaiming reconciliation through the cross of God's Son and on that basis promising fulfillment of the suffering creation in a resurrection like his.

Centrally for the question of christological doctrine, neither the personal characteristic of the eternal Son nor his human-historical particularity as the Jew Jesus of Nazareth determine essentially the portrait (Gal 3:1) or pastoral function (Gal 5:1) of incarnation. In incarnational Christology, the name, Jesus, survives only so far as everything historically particular about him is demoted to accidental status in favor of his being disclosive of the universal presence of God, denying everything "Jesus" about himself to his being as the revelation.[54] All that matters here is connection of divine being with mortal being, no matter whether the connection is taken materially as divinization of mortal human flesh or cognitively as disclosure of what God is like through the consciousness of the incarnate One. By contrast, for the vindication Christology not only does the historical particularity of Jesus who was crucified matter

53. Kunieriková, *Acting for Others*.

54 Tillich, *Systematic Theology*, 2:123.

centrally for specifying the Jewish, i.e., messianic content of Easter vindication (Rom 1:2–4!), but brings with it inescapably the personal distinction of the divine Son, "Christ Jesus" (Phil 2:6) in relation to the God of Israel whom he addressed as Abba Father and from whom he received the sanctifying Spirit for the accomplishment of his mission to reconcile estranged humanity and redeem the frustrated creation.

Vindication Christology consequently must understand resurrection first and foremost as a moral event within the life of God, a resolution of the dramatic tension of Good Friday which left the Father without his Son, shrouded in death by the sin and woe of the world which he had assumed in daring to forgive sins and so taking responsibility for them upon himself before his God and Father. Thus, in the resurrection, the Father decides *what kind of* God he will be.[55] This decision comes about in answer to the divine dilemma classically articulated by Athanasius, "What was God in his goodness to do?" Ignore sin and let the creation go to ruin? Judge sin and in the process destroy the sinners and thus merely confirm the ruin of creation?[56] At the heart of the resurrection gospel is the divine decision to be God who *justly* justifies the ungodly and gives life to the deservedly dead, indicating in the process an eschatological metaphysics of anticipation (Jenson) with a relational ontology of divine being on the way to the articulate doctrine of the eternal circulation in love of the Father and the Son in the sanctifying Spirit. That can only mean that Jesus, in anticipating by faith his vindication as the beloved Son in doing the Father's will, has already been what he will prove to be.

If so, however, that portends a reformation in the Christian understanding of the being of God away from the Hellenistic metaphysics of persistence, the natural habitat of the incarnation orientation. But this exposes an even deeper fault line: for the vindication is of a persona in the world, a "who," owning human body and soul, "the Son." But for the incarnation orientation, it is variously an idea, a form, a logic, or a plan which becomes incarnate, i.e., realized, "the Logos." From its re-appropriation in medieval scholasticism, the incarnation orientation is defending the Christian faith against the particular criticism (by the heirs of Greek

55. "The Crucifixion put it up to the Father: Would he stand to *this* alleged Son? To *this* candidate to be his own self-identifying Word? Would he be a God who, for example, hosts publicans and sinners, who justifies the ungodly? The Resurrection was the Father's Yes. We may say: the Resurrection settled that the Crucifixion's sort of God is indeed the one God; the Crucifixion settled what sort of God it is who establishes his deity by the Resurrection." Jenson, *Systematic Theology*, 1:189.

56. Athanasius, "On the Incarnation of the Word," in NPNF 6:7.

philosophical theology especially as represented by the Jewish minority within Christendom and ascendant Islam on the border), namely, that it is absurd for the perfect to become imperfect, the substantial to become insubstantial, the infinite to become finite, and so on.

When such purely *logical* "paradoxes" are embraced in a celebration of Christian irrationalism or dodged with resort to "mystery," the sharp edge of *rhetorical* paradox subverting the dominant system of values expressed by the vindication of the crucified Jew Jesus is lost from view. As in all systematic apologetics, the tail comes to wag the dog as philosophical assumptions about simple, perfect and substantial being are unwittingly taken over into Christian theology as self-evident axioms. By contrast what is recovered in the vindication orientation is the root of the Trinitarian perception of God in that here theology must simultaneously distinguish and relate in the very being God the judgment on sin in the Father's sending of the beloved Son into the company of the damned to the ultimate solidarity of the cross and the justification of sinners in the Son's vindicated and victorious of love for the them by the Easter work of the sanctifying Spirit. Vindication Christology simultaneously distinguishes and relates the God who sends, the God who is sent and the God who accomplishes these purposes in humanity and for the redemption and fulfillment of creation.

Thus, incarnation Christology understands resurrection as a miraculous confirmation of Jesus's exemplification of God, helpfully telling what God is like where the notion of God is self-evidently presupposed in terms of the metaphysics of persistence: transcendent, self-identical and thus the Beyond, a fundamentally unknowable ground of cosmic becoming. So, purportedly, revelation tells us what God is like. This line of thought can be traced back to the pre-Socratic Greeks up to Plato's announcement in the voice of Socrates *that* the divine One *is*, as such, can be rationally known, but it is impossible to tell *what* the divine One is.[57] So, the disclosure in the incarnate God telling analogically "what God is like" is helpful. Yet the gap between what the deity really is in and for itself and what its revealer assures about it in similitudes leads alternately to the domestication of God into an idea or to disillusionment with such intrinsically inadequate representation and consequent religious uncertainty.

Modern theologies double down on the problem when they assert Christologies of incarnation as "absolute paradox," as Karl Barth

57. Plato, *Republic*, Book X.

described the existentialist revival of the late medieval/early modern doctrine of God as sheer unfathomable omnipotence, *Deus exlex*, arbitrary freedom bounded neither externally nor internally. According to these theologians, God reveals Godself in a majestic display of daunting, cognitively paralyzing but rhetorically overpowering contradictions such as the "infinite is finite" or the "impassable suffers." The theology of absolute paradox, as it were, ups the ante in a risky bet against the mundane but forceful logical criticism of "incarnation of God" as a contradiction in terms: nonsense is proof that we are actually talking about inscrutable, hence true deity.

Inevitably, however, the bet fails. Such intentional nonsense posing as Christology finally bows to the recognition that all our metaphors, including "incarnation" (however paradoxically conceived), fail to declare the ineffable. Not knowing what in the world is being claimed in the "dialectical" proclamation of absolute paradox, one can neither affirm nor deny it. Sheer apophasis becomes preferable; "that whereof we cannot speak we must remain silent."[58] The would-be exclusive claim for revelation in Jesus in the Christology of absolute paradox thus slowly dies the death of a thousand qualifications until it collapses into ironic agnosticism. So also, only more slowly and painfully, with the incarnation orientation, as it is not the incarnation of the Father's Son for the messianic mission of redemption but the ultimately vacuous instantiation of a transcendental idea.

What survives this collapse is not Jesus, or even his name, but the thin gruel of a christological pattern supposedly exemplified in him, namely, incarnation as emancipatory paradox, spoken on the lips of the defiant defeated. Jesus's naming of the God of Israel as Abba Father, or this Father's naming of Jesus as indeed his beloved Son in the Easter vindication, are left behind as time-conditioned images that may safely fall from usage in favor other metaphors more aptly telling us what God is like in contemporary images, provided as is alleged, that they display the same pattern: deconstructively exploding binaries perceived to be oppressive by logical paradox justified by an emancipatory intention: death is life, destruction is creative, bondage is liberation. Ironically, then, for incarnation Christology the doctrine of the Trinity, which insists linguistically upon the personal distinctions in the life of God as the eternal Father of the Son in the unity of the sanctifying Spirit, now grasping hold

58. The famous last words of Ludwig Wittgenstein's *Tractatus Logico- Philosophicus* (1922).

of perishing human creatures through the gospel of the incarnate Son, becomes dysfunctional and inoperative. All that matters is that by means of some provocative new incarnational metaphor an idea of divinity makes allegedly liberating contact with humanity in the pattern of alleging sense to be nonsense. That is the good news, an up-to-date religious ideology. But if Jesus survives this Christology only as a paradigmatic similitude of the unknowable God so that on his precedence some emancipatory idea of the divine can make equivalent contact with those lost in the darkness of matter and the flesh, why not a fresh "paradox" like, say, "Stalin is risen"? "Stalin tells us what God is like"? Death is life, destruction is creative, bondage is liberation, indeed.

Incarnation Christology has a Nestorian inclination, distinguishing sharply between the God who was revealed once upon a time and the son of Mary, figure of the past; as categorically distinct agents these two only functionally correlate, again no matter whether the correlation is strong or weak with a high or low dose of divinity manifest in the creaturely vehicle of incarnation. Taken to its logical extreme, not only for such thinking could any of the traditional Trinitarian three have become incarnate (since they are equally, i.e., interchangeably divine), while incarnation can occur with varying degrees of intensity anywhere and in anyone, not confined or localized in the flesh of Jesus.

But vindication Christology will read the Christ hymn of Phil 2 by contrast as the story of a singular divine person passing in obedience from an antecedent state of glorious proximity to deity into a state of humiliation and indeed dereliction on account of which he is now exalted as the saving Lord of the humiliated of the earth whose plight he has made his own. What is good news, then, is that the Jew Jesus, the same person as this eternal Son, the one "Christ Jesus" of Phil 2:5, fulfilled all righteousness in this obedient act of loving solidarity up to and including ignominious death on an imperial stake. By his filial obedience there he has won the right to be saving Lord of the disobedient for whom he has taken personal responsibility and thus has been given this title, *Kyrios*, by his God and Father, who is YHWH, the God of Israel. If that is so, anything like "Stalin is risen" is ruled out (Mark 13:5, 21–22). Only *Jesus* is risen, marking him out as the only Son of Man who *is* the Son of God in that he came not to be served like a king, but to serve like a slave, giving his life for the ransom of many held captive in a strong man's house (Mark 10:45).

One comes to the fulsome Trinitarian and christological confessions of early Christianity by receiving their witness as a guide to the trajectory in which doctrinal theology that intends orthodoxy must go. This reception proceeds by retracing (as in this book) the footsteps leading to these dogmas of ecumenical Christianity, owning them by a process of critical reception, including repair and amendment as needed. On the other hand, it is uncritical dogmatism to assume the letter of these creeds as an inviolable norm that may be deployed over the gospel word of God and its scriptural witness. The creeds are secondary *norma normata*. That hermeneutical differentiation in the method of doctrinal theology is made manifest as we resituate the resurrection gospel into the matrix of Jewish apocalyptic in this way advancing the task of de-Platonizing Christian theology in the situation of post-Christendom.

The Jewish Matrix of Resurrection-Vindication

We turn now to corroborating the foregoing questioning of the Western theological tradition in favor of the thesis that the resurrection vindication of the crucified Jesus as the only Son of God launches the path to the Trinitarian knowledge of God and consequently to the right understanding of incarnation. Here essentially two points must be argued. The first we have already seen: resurrection as vindication is intelligible on its Second Temple Jewish background. Apocalyptic is the mother of Christian theology[59] as a theology of the martyrs.[60] Second, resurrection as vindication entails strong personal distinctions in the relational being of God, namely, being God as the Father who sends; being God as the Son who is sent and freely obeys; being God as the sanctifying Spirit who unifies the Father and the Son even as he unites lost humans with the Son and so incorporates them into the Son's own relationship to the Father.

This "fittingness" of the incarnation *thusly premised on resurrection Christology* is the real import of the seminal little tract published a generation ago by Jewish theologian Pinchas Lapide, rich with illuminating parallels from rabbinic literature. The book was sensationalized as recognition by an Orthodox Jew of the historical reality of the resurrection of Jesus, but the account provided by Lapide is more subtle than the headline indicated. The actual argument, in Jewish voice now filling in

59. Käsemann, *New Testament Questions of Today*, 108–37.

60. Boyarin, *Dying for God.*

the historical-contextual setting argued by N. T. Wright as previously discussed, was that in the theological climate of Second Temple Judaism, the rise of the early Christian resurrection faith is entirely intelligible on its native Jewish terms—indeed, that intelligibility depends upon the Jewish prophetic-apocalyptic framing of theology as knowledge of the God who comes to judge and to save. "Expiatory suffering, a martyr's death and resurrection belong to that Jewish doctrine of salvation which until today is expressed in the examples of the patriarch Isaac who sacrifices himself voluntarily, of Isaiah's suffering servant of the Lord, and of the death-defying valor of the Maccabean blood witnesses."[61]

Lapide was careful to observe that there is no narration whatsoever in the New Testament literature describing the Easter event as such. As an event within the life of God, no human witnessed what transpired between the crucified, dead, and buried Jesus and the God of Israel whom he had addressed as his own to the end, even as the manifestations of the risen Lord were likewise confined to a select company of chosen witnesses. Something happened, to be sure. Something happened to turn defeat into victory and consequently turned the disciples who had fled and denied from grief to joy, rising up to a new agency. Something happened—yet what happened becomes cognitively accessible as "resurrection" only to those in whom its proclamation works a corresponding trial of Gethsemane surrender unto resurrection in faith by the Spirit's echoing in them of Jesus's own resurrection from the dead. There is a subject-object correlation here between a believer's faith and Jesus's resurrection that can neither be denied nor comprehended as each is a work of God the Holy Spirit. Indeed, it is one and the same work of the Lord and giver of life.

Naturally then there are other explanations of the "empty tomb" or the Easter "appearances" than "resurrection." These other explanations are plausible ways of assimilating the unfamiliar report of Easter to the familiar world where the dead are dead and do not rise except as delusions or propaganda. Moreover, we must observe and acknowledge critically how the Easter reports acquired midrashic expansions through the telling and retelling of the Easter announcement, "He is not here. He is risen!" This narrative filling out occurred on the familiar pattern of Hebrew Scripture's narrative theology. These interpretive embellishments

61. Lapide, *Resurrection of Jesus*, 132; see also Lapide, *Jewish Monotheism and Christian Trinitarian Doctrine*. More recently Levinson, *Death and Resurrection of the Beloved Son*.

consolidate in the resurrection narratives of the Gospels, often reflecting an anti-docetic stress on the identity of the Jesus who had died and was buried with the risen one who now appears speaking peace (and even snacking on some fish). Knowing these things today, we may come to the skeptical conclusion that these stories are not intended as a proof of anything and certainly cannot serve as proofs that what happened was God's act of resurrection.

But we may also come to the insight that these midrashic expansions explicating the Easter announcement intend to extend the action of God in Jesus, upon Jesus, and now through Jesus into the here and now of proclamation. When we grasp just this conviction of the action of God upon Jesus such that it is Jesus who is now made to be present to continue to speak to faith[62] by means of continually expansive proclamation of his vindication (as happens in every sermon), we see how that Easter action of God was intelligently named resurrection in the faith which arose by the Spirit at its announcement. The good news is indeed news in that its content is the vindication and exaltation of the crucified Jew Jesus by his Father, the God of Israel, who raised him from the dead. Because it is this news, it is ever made new in the retelling of it as good news which articulates the reason why this is the very word of God addressed to the entire creation. One may disbelieve this of course, but so far as we attend rigorously to the Jewish context of primitive Christian theology the intelligibility of the claim and proclamation of the resurrection vindication of the crucified Jesus is the starting point—whether of knowing disbelief or knowing faith. So, we have specified one term of the subject matter in question and the copula which unites it with the other term to illuminate what constitutes fair hearing of its claim to truth.

Trinitarian Christology: Understanding Incarnation as the Personal (Hypostatic) Union

To corroborate now the claim that resurrection as vindication entails strong *personal* distinctions and yet *essential* relations between the Father, the Son and the Holy Spirit, we turn to a pioneering exploration in this regard, Walter Künneth's 1951 *Theologie der Auferstehung* (subsequently

62. See "Sentences of Holy Law in the New Testament," in Käsemann, *New Testament Questions for Today.*

translated into English and published in 1965).[63] Unfortunately for Künneth's reputation, his polemical spirit led him into battle against the increasing purchase of Rudolf Bultmann's program of demythologization in postwar Germany, as he was a leader in the "No Other Gospel" movement in the 1950s and 1960s. Yet it was the same polemical spirit that had led Künneth into ferocious theological combat against Nazi race ideologist Alfred Rosenberg's *Myth of the 20th Century* in the 1930s. After his 200-page tract against Rosenberg had sold 36,000 copies, the Gestapo banned it and took away Künneth's right to teach. These are credentials of moral credibility that the influential Bultmann had not attained.[64]

Künneth was active in the Confessing Church but as a traditional Lutheran he distinguished between the religious conflict for the soul of the church against its coordination with the National Socialist worldview and the open question of political obedience to governing authorities. Be that stance of all too traditional Lutheranism as it may, Künneth saw his battle against Bultmann as continuous with his battle against Rosenberg because in either case theological anti-Judaism was eclipsing both the particularity of Jesus and thus the sense of his resurrection as vindication. And there is evidence for Künneth's perception of continuity in these polemics in Doris Bergen's observation[65] that the anti-doctrinal Nazi Christians found a pretext for readmission to the postwar church in Bultmann's program for demythologization as providing the same liberation from Jewish myths and legalisms that they had sought in Nazism.

What is important for our purposes is Künneth's "resurrection Christology" and its affirmative, apparently innovative (in the context of the Western tradition) treatment of divine Sonship. Künneth, to be sure, directly posed divine Sonship against the "Logos Christology of the Greek councils and of early Protestant dogmatics." On analysis we shall see, however, that Künneth fails in this to differentiate sufficiently between Eastern and Western doctrines of the Incarnation. "Logos Christology" for Künneth is an iteration of the incarnation orientation previously discussed. According to Künneth, "the human and divine natures exist side-by-side yet at the same time are also one in the unity of person." This paradoxical combination, however, "radically breaks down

63. Künneth, *Theology of the Resurrection*.

64. But Jack Forstman in *Christian Faith in Dark Times* lifts up Bultmann's critique of the notorious Ansbach Memorandum of Althaus and Elert in the context of the church struggle.

65. Bergen, *Twisted Cross*.

because of its failure to grasp adequately the concept of 'divinity.'" The "divinity" is conceived substantially as the unchanging metaphysical essence of the Logos, and this essence implies the immobile character of a natural state of ontological perfection. The immutability of the divine nature of the Logos inevitably gives rise to speculation about the relation of the two natures in the incarnation of the Logos and especially about the nature of the union. Such speculation "forces Christology into unhistorical abstraction, without being able to make clear any living relationship between the humanity and divinity of the Christ. But above all, the Logos Christology does not make it possible to bring out the reality of God in its relation to Christ"[66] i.e., the saving assertion of God's reign in the event of Christ. The Logos only, as previously discussed, uses the human Christ as a disclosure vehicle to tell what the ineffable God is like, providing an authoritative metaphor of perfect being so far as possible within a cosmic structure taken as fixed and unchanging. Resurrection is the supernatural wonder confirming the authority of the disclosure.

A "high" Christology, in light of Künneth's critique, is one which insists on the absoluteness of the paradox that God is this man while a "low" Christology (a "Spirit Christology" as Künneth terms it) wants to lessen that severe cognitive tension by saying that in this man the absoluteness of God is somehow specially and authoritatively conceived in consciousness. But neither high nor low Christologies satisfy because the orientation to the problem is confused, if not profoundly mistaken: "the choice of starting point is in fact decisive for the treatment of the Christological problem" and as a result "our answer to the question takes its cue from the basic insight of the primitive Christian message and declares: the resurrection of Jesus. Christology has to take its basic starting point in the raising of Christ. With that, the theme of Christology is summed up as 'God's action on Christ in the resurrection', in which is given the decisive point of reference and direction"[67] for the production of christological doctrine (indeed, Trinitarian doctrine).

What "resurrection Christology" thus grasps firmly and essentially is that "the divine action upon Christ in the resurrection requires a thorough grounding" within the eternal life of God, i.e., that Christ's obedience in the state of humiliation should be not taken as a contradiction to, but rather as an expression of, his true divinity, i.e., his being God

66. Künneth, *Theology of the Resurrection*, 114.

67. Künneth, *Theology of the Resurrection*, 117.

in the way of being Son. This grounding is what the concept of eternal divine Sonship provides: precisely as the divine Son of God Christ does not send or raise himself but is sent and raised by his Father. To be sure, one cannot be a father without a son nor a son without a father. The correlative concept of sonship thus first of all expresses "the personal, spiritual and essential homogeneity with the Father . . . This essential divine sonship of Jesus lies beyond all possibility of human comparison and means absolute transcendence." The eternal generation of the Son is ineffable. Yet, by the same token, Sonship indicates "also the difference between Son and Father, the dependence of the Son and the fact of his being conditioned by God" such that there is not "an identity of power, rank and dignity with the Father." The Sonship of the "preexistent one," then, is to be theologically understood and "used [both] to safeguard the uniqueness of Jesus's filial status as transcendence and yet not as an expression of divine sovereignty."[68] In this way of implicating a divine temporality, Künneth challenges Western theology's misleading obsession going back to Augustine with the abstract equality in nature of the Trinitarian persons to insist upon genuine personal distinctions and yet essential relations in the threefold way of being God in and for God as well as in temporal relation to the creation.

For the one who was in the form of God did not count "equality" with God something to be coveted but was able as this form of God to let go of any natural claim to status as Son, thus heir to the sovereignty God as Father possesses. The Christ hymn of Phil 2 indicates that the preexistent Son "possesses divine being and essence, i.e., . . . 'identity of being with God' and in that sense 'divinity'. But he does not yet possess . . . the function of divine authority, the divine sovereignty of Matthew 28:18, which is first bestowed upon the Son through the resurrection." This exaltation to the right hand of divine power occurs in the Christ hymn as the awarding of the name above every name, that of *Kyrios*, to the vindicated Jesus, the incarnate Son of God.

Künneth's exegesis thus provides the transcendent ground of Jesus's Sonship: "God raises Jesus from the dead because he is his "preexistent" Son"[69] who now has truly lived out divine Sonship in and as the human obedience of the man Jesus, even to death upon a cross. Accordingly, however, the much-discussed *kenosis* in the Philippians passage "does not

68. Künneth, *Theology of the Resurrection*, 119.

69. Künneth, *Theology of the Resurrection*, 121–22.

mean emptying himself of the divine sovereignty—which in fact the Son does not yet possess" as heir to the Father's throne but will rather attain on account of his enduring the test of divine Sonship in the humbled form of an incarnate life. Kenosis has not to do with a metaphysical metamorphosis but rather to do with the "change in the status of the Son in relation to God, as also to the world," what the old dogmatics called the "state of humiliation." Bound to God as the sinless one, he also binds himself in love to the sinful humanity whose sphere of estrangement from God he has entered; thus, he goes incognito into the ignominy of his sufferings. "Having become flesh, he shares with a brother's solidarity in the curse of sin and its effects in destruction and punishment, suffers in his 'servant form' with his fellows under the distress of humanity, and knows himself like all creatures subject to the laws of transience and the necessity of dying." Yet precisely here the humiliated Son stands "the test of obedience," "filial obedience in the giving, suffering and dying."[70] This obedience of Jesus the eternal Son now found in the likeness of sinful flesh is thus identical with relinquishing his filial right by nature to inherit the sovereignty in favor of the filial choice for solidarity with the disobedient, indeed with the rebels from his own kingdom, a voluntary grace. So it is by the grace of this undertaken ignominy, complete in a death from which the Son cannot raise himself, that "the sonship of Jesus comes to its perfection": willingly he goes into the powerlessness of death to complete his solidarity of love with unworthy others; in the utter darkness of true death, silenced, he helplessly awaits his Father's vindication.

There are problems with Künneth's pioneering critique of Western theological tradition: a child of his times, he dismisses too simplistically the patristic Logos Christology as a Hellenization of the gospel rather than as an evangelization of Hellenism (J. Pelikan). Misled in this way to read the prologue of the Gospel of John as an instance of the mediating Logos of middle Platonism, he fails to grasp the thoroughly Jewish atmosphere of the Gospel of John as well as the utter predominance within it christologically of the father-son relation. Had Künneth understood this he would have seen how that prologue serves to introduce and exposit nothing other than this relationship: "No one has ever seen God, but the only Son, who is in the bosom of the Father, has made him known" (John 1:21). Still lacking a genuine Trinitarianism, Künneth also succumbed to the Western tendency to interpret the Holy Spirit as nothing but a nonphysical presence of

70. Künneth, *Theology of the Resurrection*, 123.

Jesus rather than as a distinct person at work (also in the earthly sojourn of Jesus!) in the same sense as Künneth has exposited the distinct persons of the Son and the Father. Conceding all that, Künneth has nevertheless broken through to the crucial differentiation in Eastern Trinitarianism between *ousia* and *hypostasis*, i.e., between abstract being and social being in concretely particular or personal ways of being together with others, whether divine or human in being.

You cannot have a resurrection without first a death, nor the justification of the sinner without first the holy judgment on sin, nor can you have the loving God of the gospel apart from the holy wrath of divine love against what opposes love. To be sure, the God of the gospel is deeply, darkly hidden in the wrath of his love, in executing accusation, conviction, and condemnation. For this very reason the same God, so hidden, is revealed in the surpassing mercy by which he has sought and found the way to the justification of the ungodly as the new and certain basis for the renewal of life. Paul's letter to the Galatians reverberates with these themes. The God of the gospel is the Father who sent forth his Son, born of a woman, born under the law, in order to redeem them who were under the law. The Son became a curse for them in order that the blessing of Abraham might fall upon them. The blessing is the sanctifying Spirit whom they have now received by faith apart from the works of the law, the Spirit of this Son sent into their hearts crying, Abba Father! The God who revealed his Son in raising him from an accursed death for us and our redemption is revealed as the Father of this Son where and when their Spirit works resurrection to faith by the proclamation of crucified Jesus's resurrection. The gospel-revealed God is the Trinity and Christology of the incarnate Son is the enactment of this way of divine being for us and for our salvation, inaugurated in the resurrection the crucified Jesus.

As mentioned, the Gospel of John solidifies its own meaning of "incarnation" in the climactic resurrection story of so-called doubting Thomas. The high priestly prayer of consecration at the end of the farewell discourse in John tells how believers come to dwell in Jesus, as in Jesus the Logos dwells in the flesh, as henceforth the Incarnate Logos dwells anew in the Father (17:20–23). So linking incarnation with ascension at the end of the Gospel, the evangelist has Thomas fall down before the Risen Lord Jesus who bears the imprints of nail and spear acclaiming, "My Lord and my God!", providing in conclusion the very picture of the rightly worshiping and rightly believing community (as opposed to the docetist community claiming the authority of the apostle

Thomas for its denial that the crucified and risen body of Jesus is Lord and God).[71] As Athanasius saw, the Johannine community worships "the Lord who is in the flesh as in a temple." For the Gospel of John, the persona of "the Word made flesh" accomplishes the reconciliation and communion of God with humanity to which the temple in Jerusalem had been appointed but failed to achieve. To the extent then that theological exegesis thusly disrupts and reforms theological tradition as we have seen in this chapter, doctrinal theology today may proceed from the apocalyptic framing of the originative event of the resurrection of the crucified Jesus as the external word that not only authors and authorizes the community of worship and faith, but culminates in confession of the Nicene Creed in the path pioneered by the Johannine rereading of the Synoptic tradition, the first in the series of theological disruptions of theological tradition by scriptural midrash. This claim will be elaborated and solidified in the final chapter of this book, in answer to the question, "What in the world does the word *God* mean?"

71. Riley, *Resurrection Reconsidered.*

IV

Regnum Diaboli

This chapter explores a basic absurdity besetting Christian theology, not only in acknowledging the actuality of diabolical evil effectively contradicting the will of the Creator on the field of the creation but of personifying this evil in the figure of "the devil." Minimally, this figure remains rhetorically necessary in any narrative account of the deliverance proclaimed in naming Jesus Christ the Son of God, Mark's "Holy One of God" (1:24), or Paul's, "who was rich but for our sakes became poor" (2 Cor 8:8). But this figure of negation at the same time resists ontological theorizing and cognitive capture; only its modus operandi can be described on the basis of its exposure, flushed out by the intrusion of Christ Jesus into the space it invisibly occupies. The demonic operation is exposed by antithesis to "the generosity of our Lord Jesus Christ," to be the motivated in the malice of envy perverting and even usurping, not only hapless lost souls, but the social institutions of creation designated by the biblical notion of "powers and principalities." This usurpation can extend even to the total depravity of "one concretion of power"[1] *in structures of malice working injustice e.g., the Atlantic slave trade, the Trail of Tears, the Nazi machines of death, the Soviet Gulag; yet powers and principalities can also be reordered for service to the ends of God by the militant reign of the ascended Christ. This account of "the malice of envy" as the "radical" evil at work in the world indicates an eschatological, rather than protological conception of the doctrine of creation as groaning in labor for the revelation*

1. Wink, *Naming the Powers.*

of the glorious liberty of the children of God, the redemption of our bodies, according to Rom 8.

Signs of Apocalyptic Discontent in Modern Theology

If faith lives in the highly contested Mark 13 interim between the originating event of Easter promise and its fulfillment at the Parousia, this interim is the Holy Spirit's time of militant grace. In her work to rehabilitate the doctrine of the sanctifying Spirit, Cheryl Peterson puts her finger on this militancy.

> Luther believed that the church's gospel witness would be opposed, even by the devil himself. His references to the devil in his writings are numerous and well-known, and Luther often spoke of the opposition of the devil to the word of God. . . . [but was] equally confident in the power of the Holy Spirit to defend and strengthen the church's witness in the face of such opposition. In such situations, the Holy Spirit [citing Luther] "will fill us with the courage that is called a divine holy bold defiance." As the Spirit of truth, the Holy Spirit not only teaches us about the one who is truth (i.e., Christ) but also gives us the courage needed to stand in and testify to the truth and to oppose all lies and false gospels.[2]

The salience of this observation for the reconstruction of doctrinal theology in the tradition of Luther is that Christian doctrinal theology takes basic form as catechesis just as *catechesis is an act of apocalyptic warfare* against the *regnum diaboli.* Instruction in the incipient "rule of faith" in preparing candidates for baptism, the first developments of second-order doctrinal theology in early Christianity (beyond polemical and apologetic elaborations) are to be found in the "catechetical lectures" of local overseers (bishops). The apocalyptic nature of early Christian baptism entailed the renunciation of the kingdom of the devil with its pomp and circumstance by the threefold counter-confession of the Father, the Son and the Holy Spirit in their respective but integrated works of creation, creation's redemption, and the creature's fulfillment.[3] A conversion so drastic for combat this difficult required serious training.

2. Peterson, *Holy Spirit in the Christian Life*, 128–29.

3. See the treatment of the catechetical lectures of Cyril of Jerusalem below.

Thus, apocalyptic battle frames the positive inculcation of the gospel faith in God as the spiritual and moral formation of the theological subject putting on the whole armor of God.[4] Centuries later Martin Luther recovered this framing for his catechisms as "a brief digest and summary of the entire holy Scriptures."[5] He admonishes by way of preface that "you will offer up no more powerful incense or savor against the devil than to occupy yourself with God's commandments and words and to speak, sing, or think about them. Indeed, this is the true holy water and sign that drives away the devil and puts him to flight."[6] Luther invoked the precedent of the Book of Deuteronomy as scriptural model[7] for catechetical training in faith and life, as it once instructed Israel to guard against seduction by the idolatries of Canaan through strict adherence to the Shema's summons of love for "the Lord, the Lord alone." Just this summons is non-identically reiterated in the New Testament confession, "Jesus is Lord"; it is punctuated with doxological outbursts along the way upon forcing the surrender of the foe by the baptismal exorcism: "Jesus is the victor!"

But since the Enlightenment,[8] modern theology has been framed in another way and consequently caught on the horns of a dilemma. The turn for academic credentials to the rising and methodologically self-conscious disciplines of historiography and/or philosophy of religion as scientific forms of the *studia humanitatis* under the Tribunal of Reason put the theological tradition into the position ultimately of choosing between sacred and profane history, the latter now understood by self-consciously modern philosophy modelling itself on natural science. At the beginnings of this modern development the thought of Georg Friedrich Wilhelm Hegel had fully integrated sacred and profane history in an idealist program of philosophy that rationally traced the unfolding of the divine Idea in the historical forward march of human consciousness. Hegel identified this Idea with the Logos of the Anselmian-Neoplatonic interpretation of the Christian doctrine of the Trinity.[9] This impressive edifice of progressive thought, particu-

4. LW 73:509–15.
5. BoC 382.
6. BoC 381.
7. BoC 382.
8. Hinlicky, "Exorcism."
9. Hinlicky, "Hegel."

larly in the US,[10] self-consciously claiming a Christian, even "orthodox" way forward in modernity, however, began to break down into its heterogenous components after Hegel's death.

The entire effort to credential Christian theology as a scientific discipline worthy of a place in the modern university, as Johannes Zachhuber has shown,[11] repeatedly broke down into its component parts, either profane historiography or profane philosophy of religion, neither of which would as science continue to countenance (Protestant) Christianity as the "consummate religion" in the way that Hegel and his Berlin rival, Friedrich Schleiermacher, had done. The trajectory of the "historical theologians" that runs, then, from the Berliners through Ferdinand Christian Baur and David Friedrich Strauss on up to Albrecht Ritschl and Adolph Harnack culminated in the devastating deconstruction conducted by Ernst Troeltsch. He called out the bad faith of surreptitiously privileging Protestant Christian theology's supersessionist and self-aggrandizing history of salvation over and above the sober history of religions while at the same time wishing still to be credentialed as a "scientific" enterprise rather than ecclesiastical propaganda. History of salvation enjoyed a reprieve in Karl Barth whose theological ambition formally resembles the initiating project of Hegel, preceded by Ritschl's attempt to redeem a historically grounded theology by return to Kant (although it is revelation in Barth that makes history, not history that is revelation as in Hegel). Perhaps the great systematic theology of Wolfhart Pannenberg represents the final attempt to make "systematic" theology succeed as a university-recognized science.

As "parochial," if not Christianly hegemonic, doctrinal theology is being pushed out of the academy in favor of "cosmopolitan" religious studies, it looks anew for hospitable habitat in the existing, fragmented, more or less demoralized churches. But these are blown to and fro by every new wind of propaganda, having long since lost interest in "scientific" theology other than in the pseudo-scientific apologetics favored in fundamentalism, while on the other side of polarization theology gilds an alternative propaganda in a search for fresh symbols and new similes by hitching its wagon to contemporary movements claiming the cutting edge of social progress. How did this dire strait of double loss in audience and theme[12] come about? Can doctrinal theology find orientation

10. Gura, *American Transcendentalism.*

11. Zachhuber, *Theology As Science.*

12. On the double loss of audience and theme, see Stout, *Flight from Authority.*

and nerve to assert anew the confession of faith? Yes, but only at the risk of something truly scandalous.

As this book has been reiterating the "apocalyptic" framing of doctrinal theology from the originating event, in this chapter we come head-on to meet the conversation-stopping objection, particularly as the one term of the confession, Jesus, refers to him whose proclamation of the reign of God initiated a particular combat. Historically speaking, the New Testament sources and Martin Luther after them[13] can hardly speak about "God" without also speaking of God's foe, nor of God's salvation without speaking of the devil's defeat. Why was this moral dualism of God and devil, to speak minimally, necessary theologically? How does retrieving the apocalyptic frame unveil the church's need for robust doctrinal theology as the subversive work of the sanctifying Spirit in undermining the devil's kingdom of mendacity with its murderous pomp and circumstance? As second-order theology in this book explores the terms by which third-order theology could vigorously debate the reality of the devil, it does not actually do that work but only invites it by preparing for it. The question of this chapter is not whether the devil exists but what the devil and its legions mean in narrative antithesis to the sanctifying Spirit by which Jesus silences and expels them. Thus, that meaning can be reasoned from its antipode, Messiah Jesus in the power of the Spirit breaking into the house of the strong man to bind him and redeem his stolen goods by a generous act of self-giving love.

Fundamentally, this second-order preparation entails a profound break with the linear and tacitly teleological conception of human time informing modern theologies of progress as well as postmodern theologies of despairing disillusionment, now bereft of hope seeing time as only endless, pointless sequence going nowhere but perpetuating the vicious cycle of contests for power. Apocalyptic theology is not to be taken literally according to this notion as a linear timetable marking progress to the last day, in either premillennial pessimism or post-millennial optimism. Rather it summons alert watching (Mark 13:37), attentive to the breaking in of the time of the end, the *kairos* of God's purpose colliding with demonic titanism, as that in-breaking attends the proclamation of the resurrection of the crucified Jesus, where and when it pleases the sanctifying Spirit to grant this preaching the force of truth defeating lies. Apocalyptic theology is about the time of the end, the Creator's end, i.e., *purpose* for

13. Aulen, *Christus Victor*.

the creation transpiring on the earth as it is willed and fulfilled in heaven; it is *not* about the end of linear time. It does not map chronologically. Nor is it the history of what had actually happened according to the secularist analogies informing modern historiography. It is the event of the reign of God advancing against the *regnum diaboli* on the earth by the gospel in the mission to the nations, creating the ecclesia from it as harbinger on this earth of the beloved community of God and enlisting the ecclesia in mission to it. Several recent authors help us in this preparation.

Philip Ziegler's *Militant Grace*[14] is a seminal work providing a brisk immersion in what he calls the "originating idiom" of the Christian faith and with that a perfectly bracing exercise therefrom in swimming against the stream of "modern" theologies. The thesis is that God is known in his powerful, gracious and yet militant initiative. We have to re-think theology, then, from the ground up, i.e., out of its scientistic pretensions and academic captivity in modernity, a real neo-scholasticism. Apocalyptic framing entails the "loss of a world" to generate a new theological subject on this very earth on which stood the cross of Jesus. Here the sanctifying Spirit by means of the gospel word concerning Jesus plays the indispensable role of author of the theological subject's confession, "Jesus is Lord." The apocalyptic nuance in meaning is that "revelation" is primarily to put something into force and only thusly to unveil a particular divine purpose and design for creation's redemption, the "economy" of God (Rom 16:25–27). The gospel's Easter inauguration of the saving lordship of Jesus consequently *also* registers epistemically. It is not "revelation" as a mere disclosure of a timeless truth somehow obscured to finite minds, but "adventitious, agonistic, and disjunctive," the assault of militant grace which contests reality as it presently pretends to fixity, setting aside old antinomies but creating a new one (Gal 3:26–28!). Divine apocalypse is deed: "the saving apocalypse of God in Christ unhinges the existing order of creation, an order that itself had already previously been unhinged by the Adamic incursion of sin."[15] Consequently, we quite properly despair of the presumption that a permanent and perspicacious moral order of creation lies before us. Rather, ours is a world marked by what Martyn calls "'startling and uncompromising discontinuity' between creation and '*this* world' and, all the more, between 'this world' and the new creation that is the ripening fruit of the cross."[16]

14. Ziegler, *Militant Grace*.
15. Ziegler, *Militant Grace*, 130.
16. Ziegler, *Militant Grace*, 135.

Of course, then, "the catastrophic invasion of God's saving love from the future must register epistemically . . . [But] Christ [is] the advent of divine and saving truth, and only just so [also] revelation."[17] Pauline promeity does not

> proffer an abstract concept of divine benevolence but rather [means] to fix one's eyes on the saving act centered in the death of Jesus wherein God concretely exegetes his own identity and purpose. And in this marriage of power and agape, power is properly ordered to love: God's saving acts in Jesus Christ disclose that divine power is the power of gracious, divine self-giving. Here revelation is clearly less a matter of drawing back the curtain to afford a glimpse of the otherwise obscure identity and purposes of God than it is to acknowledge, as J. Louis Martyn has put it, that the "One who has been on the other side rips the curtain open, steps through to our side, altering irrevocably our time and space."[18]

"Revelation is 'no mere disclosure of previously hidden secrets, nor is it simply information about future events.' But revelation is an event that initiates, even as it discloses, a new state of affairs."[19] Ziegler's "militant grace" thus parallels Aulen's *Christus Victor* model of the atonement, though Ziegler smartly acknowledges how in Aulen's mature dogmatics he integrates reconciliation of the sinner to the holy God with Christ's victory over the anti-divine powers of sin and death.

For our purposes of reconstruction in doctrinal theology stemming from the tradition of Luther, we highlight Ziegler's claim "that the focus, form, and substance of Christian theology itself are all at issue in the effort to appropriate the fundamental impulses of Pauline apocalyptic into the heart of our practice of theology." Acknowledging that apocalyptic is a "distinctive and difficult idiom," he argues that it is "uniquely adequate both to announce the full scope, depth, and radicality of the gospel of God, and to bespeak the actual and manifest contradictions of that gospel by the actuality of the times in which we live."[20] Christian theology reconfigured this way will not shy from the "unexpected, new, and disjunctive character of the divine work of salvation that comes on

17. Ziegler, *Militant Grace*, 14.

18. Ziegler, *Militant Grace*, 49. On "ripping the curtain open," cf. Mark 1:10 and 15:38.

19. Ziegler, *Militant Grace*, 172.

20. Ziegler, *Militant Grace*, 26.

the world of sin in and through Christ."[21] This boldness is mandatory because New Testament apocalyptic provides "an account of salvation as a 'three-agent drama,'" of the redemption of human beings "from captivity to the anti-God powers of sin, death, and the devil" as a "realistic gesture of notable explanatory power."[22] An ecclesiology of discipleship[23] is created by the powerful apocalypse of God in Christ Jesus: "a provisional and pilgrim community gathered, upheld, and sent to testify in word and deed to the gospel for the sake of the world."[24] This ecclesia is a community of hope in "an imminent future in which God will act decisively and publicly to vindicate the victory of Life and Love over Sin and Death." In sum, "hearing the apocalyptic gospel drives us to receive the theological vocation as a call to serve the mission and service of the pilgrim church in the time that remains."[25]

To be sure, we might press Ziegler for greater precision on how it is that apocalyptic revelation is an event. As the book argues for a true interpretation and appropriation of the apostolic theology of Paul, one fails to see engagement with a statement like 1 Thess 1:9–10 regarding Jesus's saving lordship *as rescuing us from the approaching wrath of God.* Acknowledging the problems besetting satisfaction theories of the atonement, one must still account for Paul's affirmation of Christ's unique substitution, as Simon Gathercole has smartly argued.[26] Moreover, the sinner is not only a hapless prisoner crushed to moral helplessness under the dominion of sin, but willingly complicit in its own subjugation, as Ziegler also acutely describes (Gal 4:9!). Consequently, the burden of guilt exposed under God's scrutiny, as we heard Howard Thurman exposit, cannot justly be whisked away with a divine fiat of "unconditional love," really, some wave of a magic wand, no matter how powerful, a merely omnipotent but morally arbitrary act of indulgent sentiment. So, some account is needed of how Christ's victory in the weakness of the cross is *not* an unintelligible assertion of victory in manifest defeat (a problem besetting J. Louis Martyn's account[27]) but *mediates* the victory of

21. Ziegler, *Militant Grace*, 27.

22. Ziegler, *Militant Grace*, 28.

23. See the forthcoming volume of this series (2026), Jensen, *Call to Discipleship.*

24. Ziegler, *Militant Grace*, 29.

25. Ziegler, *Militant Grace*, 30.

26. Gathercole, *Defending Substitution.*

27. Eastman, "The progression of the argument is quite clear; what is not clear is exactly *how* and *why* Christ's death on the 'law-cursed cross' means God's victory over

militant love mercifully undertaking the guilty burden of sinful failures who may wish to rectify themselves, but cannot in power do so, such that forgiveness and acceptation is lavished upon them *justly*. For Paul, in any case, God is the avenger, and leaving retribution to God's judgment is one of the good reasons why believers can leave self-vindication aside, instead to overcome evil by returning good. It is important, then, to spell out not only the powerful but still *embattled* royal work of Christ the King,[28] as Ziegler does, but also the priestly office in which he offered not a scapegoat but himself in the place of the guilty *justly* to win, not simply to overpower by force, but by incarnate obedience to gain the sinner's justification. The heavenly intercession of the ascended Christ is not least of the messianic tasks undertaken during this fraught interim.

There are resources to do this in a way that avoids the pitfalls of Anselm's theory in Luther's joyful exchange, and the interpretation of the Trinity as beloved community, themes which Ziegler mentions in passing in connection with Jüngel.

> The final judgment is judgment *unto eternal life* because it means final deliverance from that annihilating power of death, which is "God's enemy and mine." And we should recognize that it is it is exactly the apocalyptic form of the saving work of cross and resurrection and its close identification with the final judgment that makes it possible and then necessary to link the philanthropy of saving divine justice with the vision of God's ultimate triumph over death's inimical misanthropy.[29]

All of these concerns are congenial, because Ziegler pointedly remarks that "unconditional grace" is "too abstract" in that what Paul the apostle is really talking about is the transformative encounter with Jesus Christ in the event of his becoming present as saving Lord. In other

---

the enslaving powers," in "Apocalypse and Incarnation," 172; Hinlicky, *Luther and the Beloved Community*, 242–53.

28. In the emphasis on the *embattled* Lordship of Christ, Ziegler subtly differentiates his position from that of Barth who seems closer to the already prevailing cosmic Lordship portrayed in the letter to the Colossians. Arguably, the stance Reinhold Niebuhr took at the end of *The Nature and Destiny of Man* with its sober Christian political realism provides a better resource for the apocalyptic turn in theology. Niebuhr there actually engaged the Second Temple apocalyptic literature to critique modern theologies of progress "which regard history itself as the God of redemption." He portrayed an intensifying opposition from the forces of darkness in tandem with the ascended Lord's expanding reign, anything but a Hegelian "end of history." Niebuhr, *Nature and Destiny of Man*, 2:313–21.

29. Ziegler, *Militant Grace*, 109.

words, the dogmatic issue may be posed whether the advent of grace in the gospel of Christ amounts to a flat and undialectical assertion that Jesus is God, credentialing the authority of his supposed kindness. Isn't Paul's proclamation of the "Christ crucified" the intentional offense of the catachrestic paradox that this man hanging on a cross, i.e., *as innocently yet willingly bearing the shame and sin of our world*—that precisely *he* is the Son of the heavenly Father? Isn't that Mark's apocalypse? Paul's too if we recall 2 Cor 5:21!

There is also a concern with ecclesiology. It is certainly Pauline to say that the world, not the church, is the intended object of salvation, that the scope of redemption is universal. But one worries that this affirmation too easily elides the defiant refusal of grace by the world God so loved. We could call this the Johannine problem, "that they preferred darkness" (John 3:19). Thus, discernment is required if one is not enthusiastically to endorse secularist movements and their propaganda as some "new thing" in history that God is doing (instead of boring old church led by boring old pastoral ministry). Ziegler's own interpretation of the royal office is carefully qualified in that he stresses that Christ's is an *embattled* reign, and so a matter for the discernment of spirits (Mark 3:20–35). A thicker account is needed, then, of the Pauline ecclesia as the beachhead of the apocalyptic invasion (so Martyn) and accordingly a Bonhoeffer-like reading (as Michael Dejonge is showing us;[30] see further below) of the two kingdoms differentiation as an *event* ever generated by the Spirit's novelty in calling and gathering the ecclesia subversively from within the realm of contending political sovereignties, thereby reordering wayward authorities to the Creator's institution. Finally, the apocalyptic turn in theology needs to advance to the Johannine literature as the final canonical development of Paul's christologically qualified apocalyptic in its journey through the Synoptic Gospels, beginning with Mark. John executes the deliteralization of apocalyptic as a timetable to the last day and yet affirms it as a properly metaphorical knowledge of God's disrupting *kairos*.[31] The Johannine *krisis* is precipitated by the coming in principle and power of God's end on and for this earth in the person of Jesus Christ presented in gospel proclamation.

Another recent author who helps with reframing apocalyptic as a properly metaphorical knowledge of God is Simeon Zahl. But the story

30. DeJonge, *Bonhoeffer's Reception of Luther*.

31. Bultmann, *Faith and Understanding*, 165–83.

here begins with Karl Barth's discussion in CD IV/3.1, "Jesus is victor," based upon John 16:33, "I have overcome the world." This statement, "Jesus is victor," comes from the witness of Johan Christian Blumhardt who himself took it, Barth comments, from a very "curious source." It was voiced "in Mőttlingen on December 28, 1843 at the climax of the two-year story of the suffering, now about to become a story of healing, of someone called Gottliebin Dittus who was entrusted to [Blumhardt's] pastoral care." The words were spoken in a shriek, "a cry of despair . . . which the demonic power uttered through her lips at the very moment when a superior opponent forced it to yield its control over Gottliebin."[32] Barth allows three possible explanations: 1) in the sense of ancient and modern mythology; 2) in terms of modern psychopathology; 3) spiritually on the assumption that the former two explanations are both possible and each even justifiable in its own way.

Yet the true fruit borne by the story lies

> in a new and unhesitating action in the light of the superior life of the risen Jesus Christ; and a new power and joy in the proclamation of the remission of sins that has taken place and is found in him; in a new and self-evident apprehension of the reality of the kingdom of God as it has been set up in him; and a new intercession with the unquenchable expectation and indestructible hope that there will be fresh declarations of this lordship and a fresh outpouring of the Holy Ghost on all flesh . . . [33]

This elder Blumhardt proclaimed "the new outpouring of the Holy Spirit which was to precede the true and new beginning and the return of the mighty works and miracles which, in apostolic times, had proclaimed the imminent kingdom of God in time."[34] Taking note of Blumhardt's apocalyptic hope echoing within circles of late pietism, Barth formulates the Blumhardts' (i.e., father Johan with son Christoph who followed him in his ministry) trenchant critique of contemporaneous church life from within these circles:

> a complete and utter lack of the characteristic hope which is so distinctive in the message of the New Testament and New Testament faith, of diluting to a purely individual hope for the future life of the soul the confidence and unsettled expectation of the

32. CD IV/3:169.
33. CD IV/3:170.
34. CD II/1:633.

> kingdom of God which will rectify the whole world and all life even to its deepest recesses . . . [all this] in conflict with the most earnest representatives of the anthropocentric Christianity of the post-reformation period.[35]

Barth is prompted by this discussion of the elder Blumhardt to critique his own youthful endorsement of the religious socialism of the younger Blumhardt for its anthropocentric "identification" of the "Christian expectation of the kingdom of God and the socialist expectation of the future." Barth's famous statement from his commentary on Romans was intended as a protest against such naïve identification: "Hope that is visible is not hope. Direct communication from God is not communication from God. A Christianity that is not wholly and utterly and irreducibly eschatology has absolutely nothing to do with Christ."[36] But regarding his then Platonizing affirmation of eternity in the supratemporal eschatology in his Romans commentary, Barth now sees this as also one-sided. He references the biblical scholars' rediscovery of apocalyptic, Overbeck, Weiss and Schweitzer: "the whole of primitive Christianity was chiefly concerned with the end of all things,"[37] i.e., God's end goal for the creation which occurs on the earth as it prevails in heaven where and when the will of God is done. Because the literal return of Christ did not happen, however, these scholars concluded that "all its other statements are radically affected and that all that remains is the mysticism of reverence for life and nothing more."[38] For Barth, consequently, one-sided reductions of God's eternity to *any* particular modality of time is exactly the problem: the one true God is at once pre-temporal, supra-temporal and post-temporal, i.e., God's eternity wholly envelopes created time as the end intended from the beginning. Consequently, with deliteralized apocalyptic one rather says that God's eternal being is in becoming,[39] such that God comes from God as God into the time of creatures, the reign of God in the event approaching like an army of liberation on the march.

Simeon Zahl picks up the story of the nineteenth-century exorcism in his fascinating study of the younger Blumhardt, *Pneumatology and*

35. CD II/1:633.
36. CD II/1:634.
37. CD II/1:636.
38. CD II/1:637.
39. Jüngel, *Doctrine of the Trinity.*

Theology of the Cross.[40] Zahl correlates the elder Blumhardt's "Jesus is the victor" ministry at Bad Boll with the irruption of the worldwide Pentecostal movement at the Azusa Street Revival—not a causal connection but parallel emergent phenomena. The younger Blumhardt, Christoph, grew up into the ministry of his father and shared his critique of academic theology during the heyday of neo-Protestant liberalism on behalf of pietism's tradition of the theology of the heart. Jesus must not merely be thought; Jesus must be experienced. The affect-transforming experience of Jesus is worked by the Holy Spirit who blows where he will, even apart from the institutional ministry of the church. Jesus can be experienced even without knowing that it is Jesus!

In the period between 1888 and 1896 however, the younger Blumhardt became disillusioned with the same "old Adam" egoism manifesting itself in the excesses of his own revivalist circle which Lutheran theology had traditionally disdained as "enthusiasm." He sarcastically tagged the otherworldly religious egoism which he witnessed as a decadent pietism's "sacrament of death"—an enormous reduction from the New Testament hope of the visible reign of God on the earth to the pious soul going to heaven on separation from its mortal coil. Blumhardt thus came to a turning point in 1888 in which the older motto "Jesus is the victor" is now reframed in a new motto according to the theology of the cross: "Die, so that Jesus may live." Zahl associates this demand to surrender life to Jesus the Lord with a marked anthropological pessimism, another connection between these nominally Lutheran ministers in nineteenth-century modernity with the tradition of theology stemming from Luther: only the crucified and risen Jesus is the truly human being, the Spirit-endowed new Adam, and for him to be victorious in anyone the old egoist needs to die so that he may live in us and through us. Zahl connects this summons with what he calls an under-realized eschatology: the cosmic transformation associated with the final victory of Jesus Christ is *not yet*. Salvation is the coming to this earth on which the cross of Jesus stood of the reign of God in visible fullness, nothing less: "Thy kingdom come! Amen, come Lord Jesus!"

Most scholarship has been preoccupied with Christoph's—at the time bold and shocking—decision to join the Social Democrats, reputedly an "atheist" party; defrocked, it cost him his status as an ordained minister. In fact, not only did Christoph join but he was elected to the

40. Zahl, *Pneumatology and Theology of the Cross.*

regional parliament and was active there for six years and thus became a pioneer of what was called at the time "religious socialism." Yet Christoph was soon disillusioned in a secular way that parallels his earlier religious disillusionment with revivalism. Here also an overly enthusiastic identification of the approach of the kingdom of God with socialism fell to pieces and in the final stage of his life he entered a "quietistic period." Yet disillusioned quietism is not the whole story of his final years. Almost singularly during World War I Christoph preached and published stinging critiques of German war enthusiasm and uncritical nationalism. It was not that he had abandoned the prophetic spirit but that he had seen that partisan secular triumphalism is no more a remedy of the endemic human predicament than is religious triumphalism for the sin-sick world's endemic egoism with its contending propagandas manifest in the demonic fury of five insane years of trench warfare.

What does Zahl make of this? He wants to put contemporary Pentecostal theology and that of Martin Luther into dialogue with his story of Christoph Blumhardt. He makes a stunning correlation here with John 16:8–10 to cast the sanctifying Spirit as also a *prosecuting attorney*. When the Paraclete comes, "he will prove the world wrong about sin and righteousness and judgment: about sin, because they do not believe in me; about righteousness, because I am going to the Father, and you will see me no longer; about judgment because the ruler of this world has been condemned." But it had been the testimony of Old Testament Scripture, particularly the book of Job, that it is the Satan who is the accuser. What differentiation is required here? The devil exploits the sinfulness of sinners to imprison them under his cruel regime, but this leverage of death-dealing accusation has now been condemned on account of the unjust overreach by which the devil condemned righteous Jesus for his solidarity of love with these guilt-bound sinners. Now the true and salutary prosecution of the sanctifying Spirit takes the devil's place with the admonition of severe mercy, "Die, that Jesus may live." Regulated now by the theology of the cross, Christoph's revision of his father's motto, "Jesus is the victor," exposits the experience of the sanctifying Spirit as in the first place the negating experience of *holy* judgment which exposes egoism and delivers it to its own just desserts, *spiritual* death. Exorcism, then, comes about by baptismal death into the death of Christ (just as the premodern rites indicated). This is true, not phony delivery of the self from the desperate pretensions by which it is ensnared in the strong man's house.

Zahl writes in conclusion about a

> charismatic theology of the cross: this theology is charismatic because it expects, and indeed has little hope apart from, God's acting in the world and in human lives in an "experiential" way, not just rationally, but effectively in bodiliness . . . [It] is a theology of the cross because, as a result of low anthropology, it expects God to act primarily in the form of "negative" experience. And it does not replace triumphalist "certainty of" with cognitive or "word-event" certainty, both of which tend to be abstracted from effective "experience." In their place, this theology's trust is in the certainty that suffering and the frustration of human self-determination are reliable features of Christian existence.[41]

This latter character of human experience of the prosecuting of the sanctifying Spirit might be called "patiency" as an antonym of "agency" in theological anthropology, and in Christian particularity, "the Gethsemane of the soul." It is at Gethsemane that the devil is defeated by surrender to the will of God. Zahl's accent on the sanctifying Spirit's prosecution in actual human experience, at least when it is taught and identified as such, satisfies in part the objection to Lindbeck's "cultural linguistic" model for over reliance upon ritual working *ex opere operato*. It indicates that liturgical preachers of the gospel must teach in their preaching to excavate intelligently and persuasively the frustrated human experience of their listeners and thereby to attune them to this prevenient but "severe" grace of the Spirit in the form of the experienced negation of sinful incurvation. But, with Luther, we must always sharply distinguish the Holy Spirit from the unholy one by adding the purpose clause: God does an alien work *in order to* do his proper work; God kills *in order to* make alive. In the maw of critique, otherwise, true God becomes indistinguishable from false god who accuses solely to destroy. But distinguished by the Spirit's introduction to the accused of the friend of sinners, the joyful presence of Christ exchanging righteousness for sin will be experienced for the transformation of human affect.

Faith is not faith in faith but it is existentially warranted in personal experience, specifically as the affective experience of the proclamation-portrayal of the crucified Jesus by the apostles of his resurrection (Gal 3:1). The healing-forgiving presence of the thusly identified risen Jesus with the gift and gifts of the Spirit are experienced only at the foot of his

41. Zahl, *Pneumatology*, 194.

cross in his act of subsuming the believer's cross. Faith comes into experience as this strange bundle of gift: new life precipitated by spiritual death. Moreover, faith's experience is often lonely, only one of ten lepers healed returned to give thanks. Those gifted and burdened with faith believe vicariously on behalf of a thankless and unbelieving world, that merrily and in healthy self-esteem "prefers darkness." Believers believe, however, without resentment at their election to faith, both a privilege and the sad cross of experiencing unrequited love. John 16:7–10 about the promised Paraclete must be balanced by 1 John 4:1–4, the requirement to test the spirits. It is misleading in these matters to speak of mediated as opposed to unmediated experience of the Spirit; the critique of enthusiasm stemming from Luther assumes that there will be spirits speaking, whether mediately or immediately. The point is to test all by the word of God concerning the coming of Christ in the flesh. When the word of God concerns the crucifixion of the incarnate Son and his Easter vindication, it is deeply congruent with the identification of the experience of the sanctifying Spirit as the divine work of negation playing holy prelude to the free justification of a real, not fictitious sinner by the grace of the present Christ.

Great issues for the future of Christian doctrinal theology in post-Christendom are raised here: how do we deliteralize the apocalyptic hope of cosmic redemption without losing God's end for the creation? How do we confess, "Jesus is Lord!" in a world that refuses grace because its deeds are evil? How do we confess jubilantly, "Jesus is victor!", without a devil to be vanquished? These are ever urgent questions of third-order theology. Our purpose here remains the clarification of the terms in which such issues may be debated. To affirm the victorious Lordship of Jesus as the Christ, the Son of God one must clarify the antithesis under which creation groans which is the regime of the devil.

Diabology: Spiritual Forces of Wickedness

Traditionally, Christian dogmatics interpreted the devil as the fallen angel of light, Lucifer, who in a rage of envy rebelled against God's plan to make lowly earthlings covenant partner. And so, this liar and murderer from the beginning became hell-bent on subverting humanity, despoiling creation and frustrating its divine destiny of redemption and fulfillment. This theologoumenon of the fall of Lucifer has the merit of seeing the root of all evil in the *malice of envy*. Kant, by contrast, explicitly excludes malice as humanity's propensity to "radical evil." He instead defines radical evil as the subordination of the good will to obey the moral law of the rational self, inalienably stamped upon human nature, to the lesser motives of mere animal inclination and egoistic desire.[42] This idealism, a reprise of Platonic ethics, is not nearly "radical" enough. Returning to the dogmatic tradition, then, the devil as fallen *angel* remains the good creation of God in spite of its wicked envy, only gone astray. For this reason, Origen could hope even for the devil's final reconciliation. The alternative was either to project its eternal damnation as in the Book of Revelation (Rev 20:7–10) or, as in modern theologies, to see the devil's fate in annihilation, returning to the nothingness from which it was first created. The scriptural sources for this aitiology, however, are sparse to nonexistent. Given the privative theory of evil as the absence of the good, one indeed *has* to wonder with Origen whether the good creature of God, even in the devil, must also be redeemed, if God's creative purpose is to prevail and not finally be frustrated. Or, one might question the privative theory of evil if it allows for the redemption of the devil, contrary to Rev 20.

Leaving these ontological questions about the origin and fate of the devil to the deliberations of third-order theology, we may here observe for the doctrinal purposes of second-order theology that the material account of the devil in the theological tradition was largely reached by inferential reasoning to conceive the "anti-Christ" antithesis to "the generosity of the Lord Jesus who was rich but for our sakes became poor" (2 Cor 8:9), paradigmatically in docetic denial that the divine Son of God visited humanity in the poverty of human flesh. Thusly constituted in his incarnate person, Christ Jesus in his life-deed performed the new-creativity of unmerited agape love, making worthy the unworthy. Despite this material reliance on the Second Article of the Creed to conceive the evil one by antithesis as the actual malice to damn and destroy the unworthy as it is met and overthrown in Christ, the traditional account of the "fall" of the devil located it in the First Article of the Creed; as Ziegler pointed out, its seeming purpose there was to protect the Creator from the accusation of being the author of evil. But the devil was *ex hypothesi* created the angel Lucifer whose author is God! This move only deferred the fault for sin and evil up a step in ontological ranking. What explains this incoherence? The "fall" of the devil represented the epitome of the

42. Kant, *Religion and Rational Theology*, 82–83.

so-called "free will defense" of the goodness of the Creator, necessitated in the patristic era by the ongoing threat of gnostic denigration of this world. Here too help from Platonism was gladly received. The moral fault for creation's woe belongs to the free-willing sin of creatures, not the creator who gave them a choice. The doctrine of the devil was thusly hijacked for the apologetic purpose of a seemingly rational but question-begging theodicy. For if the devil is a good creature of God in spite of its moral wickedness, then God is no less the devil's author and so responsible ultimately for his creature's evil will.

If that sketch sums up the traditional doctrine of the devil, the modern argument against superstition in this connection seems theologically shallow, even if medically and scientifically necessary. "The idea that demons are a personal representation of evil expresses the conviction that evil is a cosmic force that rules over humanity and nature and is not a constituent part of them."[43] Apart from this realistic representation of ruling cosmic forces, it has historically proven impossible to prevent the lethal decline in secularized modern culture into propaganda demonizing human opponents. The naturalistic alternative to discover the root of human wickedness in genes or social systems only licenses biological or political engineering as witnessed in the evolving biopolitical authoritarianisms that would force malleable humanity into behavioral norms. It is in any case hard to reject the devil as a superstition and not, by the same token, also to reject the similar-in-kind narrative figures of the saving Lord Jesus, his heavenly Father and their sanctifying Spirit as also fantastical figures of the imagination. But in New Testament apocalyptic narrative, all these extraordinary figures appear together as a package deal. The heart of superstition in any case is magical thinking, i.e., of an occult causality that can be deployed by those in the know to manipulate the causal nexus of physical reality.[44] The critical thinking of doctrinal theology has nothing whatsoever to do with such magical thinking insofar as the causal nexus is itself good creature of God. But then, what about the devil?

43. Rőhl, "Demons."

44. How the saving wonders of God neither bypass nor manipulate the physical nexus of causality is a topic for third-order theology, but the lines of a solution may be indicated in Chapter 6's consideration of the person of the man Jesus Christ as the saving wonder of God.

In the Warfield lectures delivered at Princeton Theological Seminary in 2024,[45] Philip Ziegler traced the steady eclipse of the doctrine of the devil in Reformed dogmatics to its virtual disappearance on the contemporary scene. In the story he tells, the devil succumbs to the Enlightenment critique of magical thinking. Yet Ziegler argues that this adversary of Christ necessarily figures in the gospel narration as the old evil foe over whom Jesus is the victor. This observation should locate the doctrine of the devil in the Second Article of the Creed (e.g., as Luther catechetically exposited the saving lordship of Christ to mean "that he has redeemed and released me from sin, from the devil, from death, from all misfortune. Before this I had no lord but was captive under the power of the devil"[46]). In accord with this relocating of the doctrine from the traditional First Article to focus on the devil as the adversary of Christ, Ziegler seeks a responsible discourse about the devil in theology which 1) avoids a pitfall of the antecedent theological tradition as if the fall of the devil provided a theodicy needful or persuasive; and, 2) strictly correlates it with a christological soteriology informed by Pauline apocalyptic, i.e., the Second and Third Articles. He erects the skeleton of such a new "diabology" by working out the antitheses to Christ as the way, the truth and the life. We are to know the devil strictly by its opposition to the saving lordship of Christ. If the victory of Christ over the devil can be thought out in terms of truth defeating the lie by the physical act of confession under trial, critical, not magical thinking will carry the day in doctrinal theology on this difficult topic.

This is a strikingly original project both in its diagnosis of the dead-end to which the traditional doctrine has come, and, in its thought-provoking counterproposal of the agency, identity, and nature of the devil as nihilistic, anarchic, and adventitious, respectively. The devil's agency is parasitic vampirism, its identity defies categorization as boundlessly multiform to appear even as an "angel of light," its nature self-concealing, episodic and unanticipated. The argument for the adventitious nature of the devil seems to have some kind of relationship to Karl Barth's doctrine of *das Nichtige* as the nothing which God does not will which nevertheless

45. Superseded now by the revised and expanded Ziegler, *God's Adversary and Ours*, which has come to my attention too late for consideration in this book. Hence any reservations expressed here about the Warfield manuscript should be taken *cum grano salis.*

46. BoC 434.

asserts itself destructively to undo what God creates.[47] This relation to Barth, however, was not articulated in the lectures which developed instead the triad of predications, nihilistic, anarchic and adventitious as mentioned, by antithetical inference from Christ as the life, the truth and the way. That omission is perhaps deliberate. Barth's doctrine implies an ontological placement of *das Nichtige* within the divine mind as those possibilities from the infinity of possibilities rejected in the decision to actualize this particular world to be redeemed and fulfilled in Christ by the Spirit. Envious for existence, these rejected possibilities breakout chaotically wreaking havoc upon the creation.

This very problem of the doctrine of the devil figuring evil, of course, also perplexed German idealism with its theological notion of God as the omnicausal Absolute, perfect and supreme in being, especially Schelling who influenced Tillich in the latter's notions of "the demonic" as the "abysmal" aspect of the divine. Idealism inherited certain readings of Luther's distinction between the hidden and the revealed God to speak of the divine "abyss." Is the devil the dark side of God? Strict monotheism seems to force this reflection, especially if, per Ziegler's case, the devil is *not* a fallen angel/creature, the reality of which can be explained in terms of the First Article. But, the accuser, the Satan within the heavenly court seeking permission to attack righteous Job, is an aspect of the divine (council). In recent time in this connection, one could also consider Walter Brueggemann's varying accounts of YHWH's self-regard exploding in destructive wrath against an unfaithful Israel.[48] Is the devil but a figure of *that*? Is the satanic accuser the harbinger of the wrath of God unchecked by the countervailing mercy of Christ? Is God apart from Christ the devil? The notion is not utterly repugnant. It could be argued that in mythological form it represents the divine drama within the life of the God of love enacted in the cross and resurrection of Christ by which "Satan" was cast out of heaven when the wrath of God's love was overcome by the mercy of it. Yet debating such things is a matter for third-order theology.

Given the argument that the doctrinal location of the devil in the article on creation in the patristic tradition was motivated by concerns of theodicy to spare the creator from the accusation of being the author of evil, and yet, at the same time, the dependence of Ziegler's argument on

47. CD III/289–368; Krōtke, *Sin and Nothingness in the Theology of Karl Barth.*

48. Brueggemann, *Theology of the Old Testament.*

the priority (over forensic justification) of the *redemption* of the beleaguered but *good* creation of God, treatment of the patristic problematic and sources in his lectures was cursory. What is the relationship of the patristic battle against gnostic dualism and christological docetism, as we have unfolded in this book, to a proper account of the devil, granting its Second Article location in the doctrinal affirmation of the true humanity of Jesus Christ as savior? 1 John, after all, identifies the docetic heresy as *antichrist* when it pertinently demands testing the spirits. Why does antichrist appear here lying about the coming of Christ *in the flesh*? The reliance of the fathers on angelology to articulate the fall of the devil in *envy* at the appointment of humanity as God's covenant partner, moreover, provides a penetrating analysis of the nature of Irenaeus's diabolic "apostasy" (which Ziegler references later in connection with Charles Hodges) which cannot be reduced to the truism that Augustine blamed pride for the fall in *City of God* XI.9. Rather contempt for the flesh and the saving incarnation in turn led Irenaeus to conceive of antichrist as etherealizing Christ, turning salvation from redemption of the creation to escape from matter and embodiment.

So far as Ziegler is correct that the doctrinal aitiology of the devil as the fallen angel Lucifer was meant to serve as First Article protection from the accusation that the creator is the author of evil, together with his insight that the devil is forced into the open by the coming of Christ to be exposed, named, and expelled, we can nevertheless, albeit with appropriate reticence, personify the malice of envy in this figure of the ancient foe and exposit its role and reality as it is exposed by the apocalypse of crucified Jesus as Christ the Son of God. *In faith, theological subjects struggle against that which only truly becomes known in the confrontation with Jesus Christ, and in the power of his sanctifying Spirit, they likewise struggle* for *the beloved community of the Father.*[49] The devil is theologically identified in the event by its enmity to this divine purpose of creation's redemption by the justification of the ungodly and the sanctification of the earthly body. A proper doctrine of the devil prepares for *this eventuality but only discovers its reality in the tumult elicited by the proclamation and enactment of Jesus Christ.* Prejudicial typecasting of perceived earthly opponents as demonic, by contrast, is itself demonic deception making theology into ideology, i.e., propaganda.

49. The following part of this section supersedes Hinlicky, "'Powers and Principalities.'"

The biblical "seat of doctrine" for reconstruction of the doctrine of the devil reads: "Our struggle is not against flesh and blood, but against the principalities, against the powers, against the world rulers of this present darkness, against the spiritual hosts of wickedness in the heavenly places" (Eph 6:12). This statement comes in the context of the early catholic development of Paul's evangelical theological legacy in the treatise we call Ephesians. These words come *after* the historical apostle's imminent expectation of the literal end of time had faded from view, that is to say, *with* the emergence of the church in mission to the nations and, as such, the Spirit's good in its own right here and now, prefiguring, as the ecclesia does, the victorious coming at the last of the beloved community of God upon the peoples of the earth.

What doctrinal theology is *for* under the sanctifying Spirit's struggle *against* the usurped powers and principalities, i.e., the structural elements of human society on the earth, is to build up engaged and caring communities of Christ's people as *knowing* alternatives to the wicked lust for domination springing from the malice of envy; these usurped authorities manifest as, and in the light of Jesus Christ we are to know and to name them, structures perverted by malice working injustice. As instrument of God's eschatological purpose and the Spirit's here and now good in its own right (Eph 1:3–23), the renewing, realigning and reuniting post-Christendom ecclesia emerging today in the spiritual ruins of the West is to be built up as a structure of love working justice. In this renewed existence, the ecclesia will also serve as the stick which the sanctifying Spirit pokes into the spokes of the wheel (Bonhoeffer) of the unsustainable juggernaut on which Euro-America is being driven to catastrophe, be it ecological or economic, if not already moral. Such ministry requires a kind of prophetic criticism of culture, far more insightful and penetrating than the borrowed bromides and bombast from partisan politics as usual that characterize political parties organized equally by envy into unsustainable greed. Scholarly pastors and pastoral theologians in the Euro-American context are to understand that in the making and sustaining of holy community in Christ, locally and universally, they ipso facto protest the false choices demanded by today's partisanships, rivalries in envy.

The struggle for clarity about the entailment of a demonic adversary in predicating Lordship to the crucified and risen Jesus just described takes place in the so-called First World context of Euro-American post-Christendom, which reflects different cultural challenges than those confronting many of the younger churches, where presumably the powers and principalities show another face (2 Cor 11:14). Yet it is, per hypothesis, a common struggle against the same spiritual forces of wickedness in high places that is occurring here as there. The point is merely that the present case acknowledge the particularities of our historical and cultural location in critically self-aware dogmatics. We in Euro-America live in the unprecedented situation of post-Christendom, a territory renamed by secularism as "the West," over against the Orient, the Far East and the Global South. This very re-naming has not a little to do with the global juggernaut that afflicts the two/thirds world. But we must—urgently, also for the sake of afflicted sisters and brothers in the postcolonial world—attend to our own struggle.

In what follows, the welter of issues that arise in our context to the proposal of apocalyptic diabology for clarifying the term *Kyrios* confessed of crucified but vindicated Jesus must first be assessed and the significant objection to the thesis that is voiced both from within and from outside the churches must be met. In defense of the modern status quo ante, the objection to the diabology of our Ephesians text is that it is a mystification, propagandistically, a superstition that obscures hard-nosed analysis of the root causes of human oppression which an enlightenment humanity is good enough, wise enough and powerful enough to remedy. The objection maintains that the enlightened world with the contemporary West at the helm, with its science and technology and virtual monopoly on both capital and the means of coercion, can and should set the agenda for the church as its compliant chaplaincy. The result is that this "secular" age—the very one which *prima facie* apocalyptic theology regards as passé (1 Cor 7:31)—claims unqualified sovereignty, tolerating religion within the limits of its rationality. The Western secular is the Tribunal of Reason incarnate, calculating the greatest possible good available here and now for the greatest number (thus eliding the necessary sacrifice of the lesser number to the putative greater good).

The thesis from Ephesians, however, does not simplistically contradict secularism or merely invert its values, but on behalf of holy secularity wants to expose the co-optation of powers and principalities by the spiritual forces of wickedness in high places. Stated as a rule, diabology requires us to speak of "the devil" as the adversary which emerges from hiding whenever the controversial Christ "in the flesh" is proclaimed in the power of the Spirit for us, *pars pro toto*, for the salvation of humanity. The devil hides in the powers and principalities which it presents as idols, fascinating and alluring: e.g., the nation-state, great power imperialism, the global intifada, family values, capitalism, socialism, fascism, technology, Christendom, the Islamic Umma and many other and lesser permutations.

Two Kingdoms: Demystifying the Powers That Be (Or Would Be)

From the Hebrew Bible/Old Testament Christian theology inherited its view of the divine counsel in which the holy One, Elohim, presided over the divine court populated with lesser divinities assigned to rule especially over the various peoples on behalf of the holy One. With the modification of this henotheism by apocalyptic dualism, the lesser divinities were converted into angelic powers with some of them in full rebellion. Pre-Socratic Greek philosophical theology, however, had tried to demythologize such gods as primitive representations of the forces and structures of nature, the *stoicheia tou kosmou,* the elemental substances undergirding cosmic reality (fire, air, earth and water). These might also be referenced by the terms "authorities," "principalities" and "powers" as they became, congruent with the mythological background, objects of religious veneration, such as Paul discovered among his Galatian converts: "Then, when you did not know God, you served beings not gods by nature. But now having come to know God, or rather having become known by God, how can you be turning again to the weak and impotent *stoicheia* which you are wanting to serve once more? Why, you are observing days and months and seasons and years!" (Gal 4:8–10).[50] The final reference to the ritual calendar connects these supposed "gods" with the ritual veneration of the powers on display in natural cycles. But crucially, Paul represents these *stoicheia* as *idols, not demons*, i.e., as creatures usurped by spiritual forces of wickedness to enslave human beings with seductive lies. Elsewhere, Paul writes that the demons are at work *by means of* the idols (1 Cor 10:20–21). Idols allure, demons enslave.

> Among the soteriological idioms of the New Testament, perhaps the most radical is that of Pauline apocalyptic, for it conceives of human beings as captive to anti-God powers that have "rendered humanity incapable of repenting, seeing God's good gifts, and resolving in the future to do what is right" [Gaventa]. Chief among our slave masters of "this present age" are sin,

50. de Boer, *Paul,* 99.

> death, and the devil, rogue cosmic agents inimical to God and God's purposes and to humanity who has been, as Paul says, "handed over" . . . The situation is one of fundamental captivity and within that captivity also a baleful complicity as humans have become the "settled inhabitants" of the world of sin, "actively habituated" . . . to its ways as subjects devoted to the service of its false gods.[51]

The question of sinful complicity is articulated in Gal 4:9: why do you desire your own subjugation? The human sinfulness of complicity in one's own captivation may not be overlooked in what follows.

At least some of the powers can be re-ordered to serve the purposes of righteousness, peace, and life of the impending divine sovereignty inaugurated and made known in Jesus Christ. Indeed, the deutero-Pauline treatise we know as the letter to the Colossians goes over board with this hope, insisting that

> all things in heaven and on earth were created, things visible and invisible, whether thrones or dominions or rulers or powers—all things have been created through [Christ the image of God] and for him. (1 Col. 1:16; cf. 1 Cor 8:6)." They belong to Christ from creation's origin to its consummation. "He is the Lord of the powers and principalities (cf. 2:10, 15; Eph. 1:21; 1 Peter 3:22) . . . In this way not only statements about the origin of creation are summarized, but also the goal of creation is indicated: creation find finds its goal in no one save Christ alone.[52]

The coordination of origin to the eschaton by the mediation of the eternal Christ here is important; whatever powers and authorities exist are created for the reign of Christ. But proclaiming already now the complete dominion of the exalted Christ, the realized eschatology of the Letter to the Colossians both sanctioned and motivated a doctrine of the two kingdoms as the fixed order of creation, obscuring the embattled character of the reign of the ascended Christ "until all enemies are subdued under his feet." Yet some of the usurped powers have become so totally depraved that remediation has become impossible and creation's preservation depends upon their defanging, even final destruction. A viable doctrine of the two kingdoms must penitently acknowledge this in sober Christian realism.

51. de Boer, *Paul*, 107.

52. Lohse, *Colossians and Philemon*, 51–52.

Thus, situating political sovereignty within the doctrine of the powers and principalities articulates its divine mandate (Rom 13:1–7) as an "emergency order" (and so also the conscientious political vocation of the baptized within it) over against the invasive powers of Sin and Death to serve as a check against the ever imminent devolution into suicidal violence, the creation disintegrating into chaos. As the highly contested Lutheran theology of the "two kingdoms" descends from the magisterial Reformation, this political vocation of Christian political responsibility[53] will differ[54] from the great contributions that Stanley Hauerwas[55] and his student, Daniel Bell, have made to our renewal of apocalyptic ecclesiology in postmodernity. It is the proclaimed gospel in the sanctifying Spirit's mission to the nations that sets the theological agenda in making the making and keeping of the ecclesia as holy community to be the *sine qua non* in anticipating the final victory of God for captivated humanity. The Colossians text designates "the church as the place where in the present Christ exercises his rule over the cosmos. Christ is Lord over the universe (cf. 2:10, 19), his body, however, is the church. For this reason the worldwide rule of the Kyrios is proclaimed everywhere in the preaching of Christ among the nations (1:27) . . . " The Colossians Christ hymn goes on to declare that "the fullness of deity was pleased to dwell in Christ making peace through the blood of his cross," that is, by reordering the rebellious or wayward powers and principalities to the creator's purposes.[56] In other words, the reordering of the principalities and powers occurs concretely and historically by the intervention of the Spirit in gathering and forming the church into their midst, robbing them of pretensions to ultimacy and saving power and just so reordering them to a fraught temporal service. But this dynamism can be stifled by a realized eschatology that obscures the ambiguity of the institution of political sovereignty as a reactionary power poised against chaotic violence.

This accent on the ecclesia as the apocalyptic novelty in the world generating the distinction between the two regimes of God corrects the static tendency of a fixed "two kingdoms" doctrine which de facto concedes an idolatrous "paternal" authority to the political regimes of this world in violation of the gospel's gain of disruptive allegiance to the one Lord Jesus Christ, as the Barmen Declaration expressed in its first thesis.

53. Lazareth, *Christians in Society.*

54. Lösel, "*Kirchenkampf* of the Countercultural Colony."

55. Hauerwas and Willimon, *Resident Aliens.*

56. Lohse, *Colossians and Philemon*, 59.

The wounded and bleeding fragments of the Christian ecclesia in the ruins of Christendom in this light contradict the intended purpose of the gospel's God. The fragmented churches are themselves usurped, no longer the sanctifying Spirit's instrument to put into effect the salutary differentiation by which the community of Jesus's disciples is harbinger of God's new humanity within the coerced and conflicted political sovereignties under which humanity otherwise exists. The political urgency of an ecumenical realignment for a confessing church is a direct and pointedly political implication of the Lordship of Jesus Christ in this current "ecumenical winter," retreating into denominational ideologies competing with one another by way of religious propaganda over ever shrinking pieces of Christendom turf while leaving the world to the devil.

In Lutheran principle and in fact, the very distinction between the right and left hands of God in the rough governance of a creation gone astray is generated ever anew by the apocalyptic incursion of the gospel, generating the new community of faith, hope, and love in the midst of this world and therewith differentiating it in kind from the political sovereignties of an evil and corrupt generation whose root mechanism is and must be coercion. Coercion is reactive; the "power of the sword" cannot analogize the redemptive reign of God whose power is the persuasion of the word of God by the Spirit. The apocalyptically generated distinction between the impending reign of God and the corrupting regime of the devil generates a fraught and tentative hope for reordering political authority for greater justice and peace. Greater justice and peace are possible, but are not scripted into the very nature of things, least of all into the institution of political sovereignty wherein the temptation to tyranny and propaganda is endemic, indeed overwhelming, absent Christ's inbreaking and binding, the proclamation of which is the chief responsibility of the stewards of the gospel. Thus, to expose political idolatry, exorcize demons and reorder political sovereignty to divine purpose, it is the actual event of generating the two kingdoms differentiation which is ever necessary, not least of all because the gospel's very intention to be culturally indigenized (as in Colossians) brings with it an ever-present danger of being accommodated, indeed captivated by the kingdoms of this world.

Apocalyptic proclamation of the ecclesia as creature of the gospel is the concrete form of the scandal of the particularity in the "now time" between the resurrection of Christ and his parousia. The two kingdoms distinction of sixteenth-century Lutheranism (Augsburg Confession

XXVIII) is not just there in the air for one and all to see (usually thought on the basis of the anthropological dualism of soul and body as in John Locke's authorship of political liberalism[57]). Indeed, in the world enthralled by the liar and murderer from the beginning, there is visible only one kingdom of coercive power with its politics of the contest for such power. When the gospel comes on the scene it disrupts this mentality and practice by the establishment in its midst of another kingdom of the sanctifying Spirit whose Lord is, so far as the world can see, the crucified, dead and buried Jesus, i.e., whose power is powerlessness. But in this new perspective of the ecclesia, the demonization of social institutions is exposed in turn and the summons of responsibility to the Creator for the care of the creation is freshly issued, even as Christians in political vocations undertake conscientious participation in the temporal kingdom in the theological knowledge that the principalities and powers are to be reordered accordingly.[58]

For the present thesis from Eph 1:20–22 regarding the church as the place of formation for the ministry of the people of God in the world, the two kingdoms differentiation entails, albeit "for the time that remains," being subject under some *political sovereignty* albeit *conscientiously* (Rom 13:5), i.e., according to its divine institution and emergency purpose (Rom 13:4) despite all the anomalies and paradoxes that this interim existence entails.[59] In extremity, conscientious obedience to the divine institution entails conscientious disobedience when a regime manifestly and with public intention violates its divine purpose. Just so, all the more is the need to attend to the ever-urgent mandate "to test the spirits to see whether they are from God" (1 John 4:1). The task of discernment is the deliberative work of third-order theology in concrete reference to the reality of this present world. With respect to diabology and the threat of a demonized political sovereignty, the argument now proceeds to making the difficult notion of the contra-divine powers intelligible in our context, meeting the aforementioned objection which accuses it of mystification in place of scientific knowledge of root causes.

57. Locke, *Letter Concerning Toleration*. But see Waldron, *God, Locke, and Equality*.

58. Larson, *Ubi Deus Dixit Where God Has Spoken*.

59. Niebuhr, *Moral Man and Immoral Society*; Niebuhr, *Irony of American History*.

Sociology: Powers, Authorities, and Principalities

In this apocalyptic context of struggle, it becomes abundantly clear that Christian beliefs are articulated in doctrine for life, not doctrine for doctrine, i.e., for theoretical speculation that seeks to transcend the apocalyptic battle in which we are placed by the coming of the Spirit through the gospel. In his influential and well-intended books of the past generation, *Naming the Powers* and *Engaging the Powers*,[60] Walter Wink argued that Pauline powers and principalities ambiguously denote *both* "human/institutional" *and* "spiritual" powers,[61] and thus are to be taken together as simultaneous aspects of "one concretion of power." But this latter may be a non sequitur. It does not follow that if two things appear confusedly or ambiguously as one thing that this appearance is one thing. It does not follow that if the state, for example, appears as Stalin's gulag that the state is gulag, as anarchists might suggest, obliterating the relative but humanly significant difference, say, between contemporary North Korea and the United States. The basic contention of Wink is that Pauline language about "spiritual forces" has wide scope so that under it one may critically consider and theologically evaluate all claims for an authoritative principle of origin and/or for lordship with power liberating and vengeful; this claim has withstood scholarly scrutiny and is here appropriated.[62] But the other proposal of Wink, that institution and demonic spiritual power form one concretion of power, has been subjected to withering exegetical and hermeneutical criticism on the basis of Rom 13, as just discussed.[63] That the state may be demonized is one thing, Wink's "concretion of power." That the state is demonic is quite another thing. Paul quite concretely and explicitly declares that it is divinely instituted for our good in the fraught world he had described in Rom 1–3. Powers and authorities are aspects of the divinely intended good of creation, social structures in which creaturely life is generated and preserved, even if subject to demonic usurpation.

60. Wink, *Naming the Powers*; Wink, *Engaging the Powers*.

61. Forbes, "Paul's Principalities and Powers"

62. Forbes, "Pauline Demonology and/or Cosmology?"

63. Lynch, "How Convincing Is Walter Wink's Interpretation of Paul's Language of the Powers?" Fellow evangelical theologian, Gerald McDermott, has argued from a different angle for the non-reducible reality of the principalities and powers as "other real supernatural powers besides God" in his *God's Rivals*, 67–83.

A lot of contemporary theological thinking based on responsible biblical scholarship,[64] but insufficiently hermeneutical and systematic in method, seeks a different kind of intelligibility for the "one concretion of power," along the lines of the soft, but finally incoherent demythologizing proposed by Wink. This work suggests that under the "code language" of the principalities and powers we are talking about *empire*, about imperialism. The most sophisticated contemporary advocate of this view is the otherwise excellent N. T. Wright.[65] One can hardly fault a contemporary Englishman for heartfelt repudiation of imperialism but Wright's version of Wink's "one concretion of power" as empire has been decisively qualified, both methodologically and substantively, by John M. G. Barclay.[66] The continuity of Christian theology with its "mother," anti-imperial Jewish apocalyptic, is qualified by the *unexpected* cross of the Messiah, as the deed by which the wickedly usurped powers and principalities underwriting imperial oppression are exposed and defeated. This *skandalon* brings about a division of the division, retooling apocalyptic and its categories as well.

In his *Auseinandersetzung* with Wright, Barclay articulates the perceptive thesis that "Paul's gospel is subversive of Roman imperial claims precisely by not opposing them within their own terms" since "even turning Roman values on their head entails a kind of confinement within the ideological system in which those values are defined."[67] "Opposing them within their own terms" is precisely what happens when we demythologize rather than deliteralize the powers and principalities by reducing this reference to the *mystery* of evil usurping the good creation to the merely mundane *fact* of empire, as if, short of the eschaton, there could be *any* political sovereignty that was not in *some* way animated by the *libido dominandi.* The sinful desire to dominate animates not only the powers-that-be but also the powers-that-would-be in the carousel of contending forces pretending to make progress, as Barclay grasps when he rejects opposing Roman values within their own terms. While discriminate and as such highly fallible political judgments and commitments are required of Christians in their vocations as citizens amid such contests for power, it is academic child's play not to reckon with how

64. E.g., Portier-Young, *Apocalypse Against Empire.*

65. Wright, "Paul and Caesar," 173–93.

66. Barclay, *Pauline Churches and Diaspora Jews* criticizes Wright's "reading between the lines" to discover a "hidden transcript," 379.

67. Barclay, *Pauline Churches and Diaspora Jews*, 386.

endemically "the Gentiles lord it over one another," as known by reason from historical experience[68] if not by faith from revelation.

By the same token, Paul's God institutes and thus employs also empire (alongside other political regimes) as a structure for rough justice and tolerable peace that militates against the kind of nationalistic zealotries that tormented Palestine in the first century and, likewise, the Europe of the twentieth century in the guises of Italian fascism and German Nazism and Soviet communism, and, painful truth be told, some forms of Israeli Zionism today, not only Hamas, Islamic Jihad, or Hezbollah. Empire, by contrast with nationalism, can in principle represent a multicultural cosmopolitanism that forces diverse peoples to live together in tolerable peace and rough justice. That empire *forces* people to do so as a monopoly on the means of coercion is, to be sure, its fatal flaw as only another form of political sovereignty in which some sinners govern other sinners. That is why, theologically, the state is but a temporary order, mutable in form, and one that is eminently reformable as ever in need of reform to conform to God's institution. Whatever its historical failures, however, empire's best aspiration for cosmopolitan tolerance is not simplistically to be demonized, especially when the political alternative, as we in the West have seen in the twentieth century, is the bottomless pit of ethnic-group self-determination over against other ethnicities in a desperately violent struggle for *Lebensraum*.[69]

Thus the Paul who also authored Rom 13, according to Barclay, "reads political history according to a different script" such that "his stance towards the Roman Empire is neither simple opposition or obedience: it is a field of human reality crisscrossed and contested (like all others) by the opposing forces of flesh and spirit, and is subject to powers far greater than itself in the battle created by the gospel."[70] In this way, Paul "more radically reframes reality"; he demythologizes political sovereignties and reduces them to a "bit-players in a drama scripted by the cross and resurrection of Jesus." This does not mean, according to Barclay, that Paul's gospel is "apolitical, only that the political is for him enmeshed in an all-encompassing power-struggle which covers every domain of life"

68. Burleigh, *Earthly Powers*.

69. See Leithart, *Defending Constantine*. Lewis, *God's Crucible*. Greater awareness of Western political theology in this connection should provoke Western theology to a thorough-going reconsideration of the filioque controversy; see Haugh, *Photius and the Carolingians*.

70. Barclay, *Pauline Churches and Diaspora Jews*, 386.

i.e., neither separating the personal from the public nor reducing politics to the contest for the reins of power. Accordingly, "his theology concerns *the subversive and redemptive power of divine grace in Christ, which creates and empowers new communities of social (and therefore broadly political) significance*."[71] This claim supports the previous section's case for a dynamic version of the doctrine in which the distinction between the two kingdoms is ever generated and sustained by the gospel's authorization of Paul's new society of broadly political significance. What scholarly pastors and pastoral theologians are to do today, precisely as cutting edge political praxis, is to create and sustain engaged and caring communities of Christ's people as the knowing and articulate alternative to politics as usual, based on the customary secularist separation of the private and the public.[72] Just this frees up a place in the world for the formation within the nations of new vocations, including the political vocation, of the baptized, working to reorder the powers to the purposes of God.

Still the question cannot go begging: if the powers and principalities are not reducible to concretions of demonic power qua secular institutions, even when they deviate from God's institution and purpose, what *in the world* aside from mind numbing resignation to mystery are we talking about when we reference "spiritual forces of wickedness in high places"? Reference to fallen angels or, more abstractly, elements of creation claiming the power and principle of origin but gone astray by asserting autonomy over against their creator, do not much illuminate the question; they merely state it in mythological form. Just so, however, they do make one important point: we are talking about something high yet "in the world," i.e., creature, not creator. What concerns us, then, is the mystery of genuine evil within the good creation of God, that is, of knowing, willful, hence "personal" *rebellion* against the Lord and giver of life. That conundrum remains unabated in the biblical depictions. Käsemann's comment on Rom 8:31–39 illuminates the force of this conundrum: "only the apocalyptic worldview can *describe* reality thus, just as this outlook alone can catch in it the cry of an enslaved creation and

71. Barclay, *Pauline Churches and Diaspora Jews*, 383, emphasis added.

72. The dualism of public and private that arises with Cartesian-Kantian subjectivity and its political theology articulation in Locke is what most contemporary theologians think of under the term, "the doctrine of the Two Kingdoms," as if this supposedly represented Luther's political theology. I disentangle this confusion in *Luther and the Beloved Community*, 301–57 and *Before Auschwitz*, 183–87.

see the messianic woes taking place therein. In Paul apocalyptic does not lead to enthusiasm but to a somber experience of the world."[73]

More broadly, as we have argued, the idea that the devil can be named and engaged concretely as some concrete social formation—say, as capitalism or as communism, as patriarchy or as the dehumanizing anarchy of the sexual revolution—contravenes the intention of the Ephesians text. The text rather wants to *distance* the spiritual powers of wickedness in high places from such human-all-too-human demonizing of flesh-and-blood opponents populating the mundane social institutions in which they are found; it wants to provide an insight into a true conflict over our heads and behind the scenes, as is the wont of the apocalyptic genre; it does so, however, in order to specify precisely what is new and redemptive about the action of God in Christ by the Spirit, namely, the holy struggle for sanctification of the usurped earth, to make and keep the new polity in the world that is the ecclesia by which other claims for allegiance are relativized and humanized. Here the spiritual power of God's righteousness on the earth is to be sought and found in the grace that gives what is not deserved, not, then, in politics as usual (Mark 10:35–45) as contention over merit for the keys to coercive power. But by the sanctifying Spirit's powerful institution of the body of Christ on the earth protruding into politics as usual, powers and principalities may well be decoupled from subservience to spiritual forces of wickedness and reordered as instruments preparing the earth for the reign of God, as happens whenever through them God's will is done on earth as it is in heaven—as in Luther's expositions of the petitions for daily bread and mutual forgiveness. We should follow these intentions of the text, at least if we wish to be justified in deploying its revelation of the earthly struggle for holiness against demonic forces as a warrant in theology today.

Moreover, we recall here from the earlier discussion that any theologian today who thinks in the tradition of Luther must surely and with unreserved self-critical force repudiate the great man's descent into the sin of demonizing flesh and blood opponents.[74] Disastrously, Luther came to see one demonic "concretion of power" in the institution of the papacy, and, in the same vein, in the flesh and blood fellows who were peasants justly angry at their feudal overlords and the (to Luther) exotic rabbinic scholars questioning his messianic exegesis. Indulging himself

73. Käsemann, *Commentary on Romans*, 251.

74. Hinlicky, *Luther and the Beloved Community*, 379–85.

with verbal violence in manifest violation of his own reformatory principle that the true people of God are they who bring to bear the judgment of the cross upon themselves,[75] Luther did not follow the intention of the Ephesians text patiently to bear with evident opponents, as per Daniel Bell's wonderfully apt turn of phrase, in the "refusal to cease suffering."[76] Such patience even with malicious others, including apparent enemies, is the difficult and demanding cost of affirming that our true struggle is *not* with flesh and blood—even in a justified war to thwart the incorrigible violence of a totally depraved regime.

Having said that, Wink is right that naming and engaging the powers in holy struggle is an inalienable aspect of the ministry of the gospel that we discard at our peril. We are not done with the demonized powers by discarding them as illusory remnants from the pre-scientific past; rather we become their "enlightened," but just so doubly deceived pawns, all the more blinded because of the light of modernity we now have. In any event, the theology of the powers and principalities is, if it is anything, instruction for spiritual *battle* which is prosecuted by naming the powers when usurped by spiritual forces of wickedness in high places to reclaim them under the institutional mandates of the good creation and so to reorder them to the Lordship of Christ, as Bonhoeffer argued.[77] Wink has rightly seen this and made the theological problem of Christian diabology acute again so far as the New Testament is read and heard as scripture.

Indeed, as every preacher who strives to be faithful to New Testament texts quickly discovers that, whatever the ontology, she cannot retell the gospel narrative apart from that uncanny figure of malice and deception, the devil. That this rhetorical necessity creates profound problems of intelligibility is, of course, true; indeed, it accounts for the tendency in Wink's work softly to demythologize, so to say, the spiritual forces of wickedness into the human institutions they captivate to form the "one concretion of power" of which he speaks. We will conclude this chapter addressing that acute problem of intelligibility. For the moment, the point is that this book's thesis is indebted to Wink, who has rightly lifted up the holy struggle against the spiritual forces of wickedness in high places, for providing the *raison d'être* of doctrinal theology in that it designates one pole of the reality test incumbent upon meaningful

75. Obermann, *Roots of Anti-Semitism.*

76. Bell, *Liberation Theology After the End of History.*

77. Bonhoeffer, *Ethics.*

theology.[78] It is the task of third-order theology to argue these concrete correlations. For the present purpose in second-order theology of clarifying the terms by which these arguments can be Christianly meaningful, it suffices to indicate that in today's world where progress in science and technology has not ended institutional violence but all the more powerfully equipped it, indeed *entrenched* it through the now total system of technologically enabled propaganda, what is urgent and perilous is and remains the overarching Cartesian narrative of spirit versus nature rather than the apocalyptic battle of spirit versus spirit.

That is to say that the human predicament has been understood in modernity as its conflict with indifferent nature so that human victory comes with the technological conquest of it, beginning with our own embodiment. To this predominant modern propaganda, as Ellul detected, the apocalyptic gospel speaks a sharp No! What is needed is reconciliation with nature not its unqualified exploitation via human domination. What is needed is gracious acceptance of human finitude not infantile fantasies of immortality.[79] What is needed is to be at home on the earth, not an alien spark of light trapped in thick darkness. Deliverance from last enemy, the apocalyptic power of Death, is not deliverance *from* creaturely finitude but the deliverance *of* it. The conflict driving human history is not human spirit against indifferent nature but between sanctifying spirit and unholy spirit. Apocalyptic instructs that the actual conflict supervening the human predicament is between spirits unholy and holy—a battle of the Word, a battle between the sanctifying Spirit and the father of lies and murderer from the beginning (John 8:44).

To be sure, the perception of physical nature's indifference to human concerns raises acutely the problem of the doctrine of creation in apocalyptic framework, namely, the reality of the invasion of the powers of Sin, Death and Devil actively opposing the Creator's goodwill on the field of the creation. Oswald Bayer has smartly addressed this problem in his probe of Luther's catechetical theology.[80] What is striking is the modern emergence of the concept of nature as an autonomous and self-regulating system as opposed to the doctrine of creation telling of the creator's initiation and perseverance in the divine project for righteousness, life and peace on the earth. The ensuing modern protest is highly ironic in that

78. Helmer, *Theology and the End of Doctrine.*

79. CD III, 625–33.

80. Bayer, "I Believe that God Has Created Me with All that Exists."

the indifference of the machine of "nature" to human concerns justifies deep questioning of the goodness of God the Creator when the terms of the creator's care have been switched out, namely, reconceived now as first cause or demiurge of a mechanical system indifferently, necessarily and arbitrarily crushing innocent human aspirations.

A striking attempt to tackle this modernized problematic (i.e., on these terms of the concept of creation replaced by the concept of nature) was Marilyn McCord Adams, who argued for a christologically low but metaphysically high doctrine of the Incarnation assuring divine and healing contact with the traumatized.[81] But that is problematic for all the reasons previously discussed in privileging incarnation over resurrection in christological construction. Bayer's proposal points in a better direction. Creation is to be conceived eschatologically neither as a fixed platform on which the human drama then plays out, nor as a dynamic cosmic evolution which, Shiva-like, gives and takes away human life and aspiration. Creation is rather the divine project from the beginning for the righteousness, life, and peace of creatures dwelling at last in the eternal life of the triune God.[82] Creation is teleologically ordered to its redemption and fulfillment, as Luther says in the Large Catechism.[83] The apparent indifference of its relatively autonomous order to human concerns reflects the Creator's abiding mandate for the human vocation (Gen 1:26–28), and indeed the creator's presence in the mask of nature exerting pressure for humans to cooperate to cultivate the earth as a garden that may be bequeathed to every new generation. It is also a challenge gracefully to accept finitude, to be human and at home in the humus on the earth, as Gustav Wingren argued at the initiation of the new Scandinavian creation theology.[84] All this follows because it is first of all a challenge to see the divine Son of God in "the man, the man, nothing but

81. Adams, *Christ and Horrors*.

82. Greene, *Imagining Theology*.

83. BoC 439.

84. Uggla Bengt, *Becoming Human Again*. If the incarnation includes nature as well as history, as Niels Henrik Gregersen proposes in his notion of "deep incarnation," we have a radical overthrow of the Cartesian paradigm which launched modern thought and determined modern theology. The implications of Gregersen's proposal should be worked out in third-order theology. It is worth mentioning here that the near contemporary Lutheran theologian who took radical aim at Cartesianism in theology was Helmut Thielecke.

the man"[85] who, in the grip of the sanctifying Spirit, battles the devil to free its prisoners and cleanse the earth.

Throughout this chapter we have spoken of creation without giving an apocalyptic account of it, particularly the Pauline correlation of divine creation with the resurrection of the dead in Rom 4, which is the source of the doctrine of creation out of nothing. As Ian McFarland has quite acutely argued, we misunderstand the doctrine of creation *ex nihilo* as a somewhat bizarre premodern attempt at physical science (in that, as the ancients knew, "nothing comes from nothing"). Rather, the creation account in Genesis is Bonhoeffer's hope projected backwards,[86] the origin imagined in Israel through the prism of the exodus. Creation from nothing is not physics but discourse about God as the creator of everything that is not God. When this title for the divine is christologically "framed," as in the prologue to the Gospel of John, Colossians, or Hebrews:

> it points to the fact that divine self-sufficiency takes the form of love that is realized in the mutual communion of the Father with the Son in the power of the Spirit. *Nothing apart from* God proposes a vision of divine omnicausality as the extension outside of God of the sharing of being that constitutes God's own triune life. *Nothing limits God* means that divine sovereignty is perfected in God's making the life of a creature to be God's own, as a means of ensuring creation's flourishing . . . God's total and unrestricted dedication to [creatures].[87]

Predominantly, however, the received theological tradition is marked by a theological propensity other than "creation's flourishing" and the Ephesians text's summons that we, here on the earth, struggle in the Spirit against mysterious spiritual forces of wickedness. It has articulated angelology as a more or less disciplined speculation about the cosmic harmonies hidden beyond the veil of earthly conflict and confusion. In curiosity about our text's intimation that phenomenal appearances of merely human, purely social struggle do not tell the whole story, the tradition was thus tempted to overlook the crucial assumption the Ephesians

85. Hinlicky, "Luther and the 'Repair of Chalcedon.'"

86. DBW 3:22. "[T]hat the universe was created in both matter and form out of nothing [was] absolutely basic to belief in the one and only God . . . The real starting point for the doctrine of creation . . . was the mighty act of God in raising Jesus Christ from the dead, for it was there that the absolute power of God over life and death, over all being and nonbeing, was uniquely exhibited." Torrance, *Trinitarian Faith*, 97.

87. McFarland, *From Nothing*, 106.

text makes, namely, that the Christian life is a *social* one ("*our* struggle") against forces of *malice*. In an antecedent iteration of the Platonic diagnosis of conflict between soaring human spirit chained to the physical body of this material world, it misconstrued the sense of the Ephesians struggle as the individual ascetic's ascent from the earthly realm to a heavenly one, cognitively, then, beyond the "deformed imagery used by scripture in regard to the angels"[88] to the ideal forms which they are. Imagining a celestial world of pure harmony of ideal forms behind the earthly veil of evident conflict in the Neo-Platonic speculations of his *celestial hierarchy*, Pseudo-Dionysius thus overlooked the urgent, on-the-ground *militancy* of the Spirit who makes holy war against "the flesh," as the usual Pauline idiom has it (in distinction from the Johannine usage). As a consequence, Pseudo-Dionysius construes the Pauline conflict between spirit and flesh as one of overcoming earth-bound sensuality and passions to attain the passionlessness of angelic existence, i.e., purely intellectual existence, as he imagines it.[89] This is simply *not* the struggle of the ecclesia on the earth for an embodied righteousness, as our Ephesians text projects.[90]

Deplatonizing Pauline interpretation in favor of apocalyptic as the "mother of Christian theology" (Käsemann), we should register in this light that the Pauline conflict between the Spirit *of God* and "the flesh" is the conflict in the field of human consciousness between reliance on the God who has come for us in Jesus Christ by the Spirit's preaching of the gospel and creaturely reliance on its own brain-power or muscle-power to do what this God alone can do and does for creatures, namely to give life to the dead and call into being worlds that do not yet exist. It is thus a struggle of faith, over what is first and above all to be trusted, believed, obeyed, hoped and loved with ultimate concern. Precisely when we recall and hold fast to that usual Pauline way of speaking, the Ephesians text makes the crucial clarification that this holy militancy is a struggle

88. Luibheid, *Pseudo-Dionysius*, 153. We owe to Platonism both the great mandate to think critically by distinguishing appearance and reality and the sub-Christian tendency to locate the source of human sin in individuation and embodiment. By this we divinize mind and demonize body. Platonism must be far more critically received than in Pseudo-Dionysius.

89. This judgment does not express in the first place a Lutheran judgment on Eastern Orthodoxy, but an Orthodox self-critique. See Meyendorff, *Christ in Eastern Christian Thought*, 47–68, 91–111 respectively. It does, however, correspond to Luther's considered opinion.

90. For an alternative analysis of Dionysian cosmology and Lutheran theology, see Mattox, "Cosmology."

within the church itself to believe the God of the gospel rather than alluring idols and seductive demons, indeed, positively to identify *in order to disbelieve* idols by exposing the demons animating them.[91] It is the gospel that demythologizes the powers and principalities in robbing them of soteriological pretenses and putting them back to work for the creator's purposes of righteousness and life.

Christians do not struggle with swords of steel on behalf of God or, more subtly, with the verbal violence of political propaganda against fellow human beings similarly armed in the usual contests of the *libido dominandi* of this present age. But by the word of God and in the mode of critical thinking that tests the spirits, Christians struggle against an elusive, supra-individual, trans-human force of incorrigible *wickedness*. To know *this* enemy is not a matter of ordinary observation or curious speculation; it is matter of learning the One who is God truly by the coming into the world of the beloved Son in the power of the Spirit, sent to break into the strong man's house to bind him and plunder his goods (Mark 3:27). It is revealed knowledge ever in this event and sustained as such, not least, because that strong man *fights back*, exposing itself. "What have you to do with us, Jesus of Nazareth? Have you come to destroy us? I know who you are, the Holy One of God!" (Mark 1:24).

Is taking gospel narrative seriously this way, though not literally, as knowledge of God, a relapse into fundamentalism? Mark Lilla's issued an important brief against the recurring outbreaks of christologically *unmodified* apocalyptic theology, as in fundamentalism, crusades, inquisitions and wars of religion, where demonizing opponents exacerbates secular political conflict into unmanageable fanaticism sustained by incorrigible dogmatism. In the process, however, he acutely diagnosed the sickly state of civil religion in secular, "democratic" regimes, the accommodated public theology of modernity.

> Liberal theology began in rational hope, not fevered dreams. Its moderate wish was that the moral truths of biblical faith be intellectually reconciled with, and not just accommodated to, the realities of modern political life [separating church and state institutionally]. Yet the liberal deity turned out to be a stillborn god, unable to inspire genuine conviction among those seeking ultimate truth. For what did the new Protestantism offer to the soul of one seeking union with his creator? It prescribed a catechism of moral commonplaces and historical

91. Morse, *Not Every Spirit*.

> optimism about bourgeois life, spiced with deep pessimism about the possibility of altering that life.[92]

Lilla thus wistfully describes exactly where most of us tired Euro-American Christians are at today, especially in the old Protestant denominations. There is no change we believe in. We are the end of history. And thusly thinking so well of ourselves, we acquiesce to renditions and detentions without due process, waterboarding, government spying on citizens and outsourcing of censorship, not to mention predator drone strikes to preserve our way of life. Failing that, we for are for peace at any price. But Lilla ignores the rise of "political religions" in the cultural space vacated by the stillborn God of liberal Protestantism. We hear today new gospels telling us what must be done to save the situation: technological imperatives; market imperatives; imperatives to maximize personal freedom or social equality; imperatives for revolutionary praxis, law and order, or sectarian separation from a corrupt and dying world. This list of urgent calls to saving action in our naked public square could be multiplied, each registering intensity in direct proportion to the impending sense of crisis, yet in sorry truth each expressing only some immanent aspect of the common human predicament rather than going to the root, as each one falsely claims to do. Reconciliation to the God who comes to reclaim his creation by the missions of his Son and Spirit for the purposes of righteousness and life is the saving resolution of the endemic human crisis under spiritual forces of wickedness in high places because it lays axe to the root.

Consequently, penetrating prophetic criticism of ideology/propaganda was summoned in 1964 by Harvard professor Amos Wilder, who invoked the recovery of the biblical kerygma in its eschatological dimension—here previously termed "christologically modified apocalyptic" (Mark 14:33–39)—that proclaims, in J. Louis Martyn's words, the cross of the messiah as "the best of news in a still unredeemed world."[93] Wilder called this recovery an "exhilarating" rediscovery of "the deepest levels of Christian understanding . . . with momentous insights and affirmations" for articulating a timely Christian social ethic.[94] In the aftermath of Hitler, Hiroshima, and Stalin, Wilder wrote of an

92. Lilla, *Stillborn God*, 301.

93. Martyn, "Epistemology at the Turn of the Ages."

94. Wilder, "Kerygma, Eschatology and Social Ethics," 509.

> almost unparalleled demand upon the church for ethical guidance. Those same totalitarian pressures which have forced Christians to clarify their faith and its biblical ground, have similarly compelled them to search the scriptures for light on fundamental decisions as to the nature and limit of the state, the political witness of the believer and ultimate questions as to the relations of the church and world.[95]

In want of such guidance, however:

> [m]any modern men with important responsibilities in society have despaired of finding clear light for conduct and policy in the Bible, whether as regards law, politics, business, labour, marriage or property, [i.e the basic social institutions ordering human life on the earth, the "principalities and powers"]. In absence of such light, they turn to secular moral philosophy or the great rival views of man which today oppose themselves to the gospel, or, in private dilemmas, to secular psychiatry or some esoteric cult.[96]

But "if we put at the centre of our Christian message the theme that God has visited and redeemed his people, that in the cross God dethroned the powers that which hold men in bondage, that in the redeemed community there is neither Jew nor Greek, slave nor free, male nor female, black nor white, but all are one in Jesus Christ . . . ," a genuine and timely engagement with the powers becomes possible today. Drawing on Barth, Bonhoeffer and Bultmann (though critical of Bultmann's existential reduction to the individual's decision of faith in that, prioritized, it eclipses the social dimension of corporate faith), Wilder especially lifted up the church's biblical-prophetic calling as "watchman" over the city and the nations, asking how "aggressive" this guardianship is to be.[97]

That is perhaps a misleading formulation of the truth mentioned above that the very presence of the Christian community in society *as the zone of freed thinking* in the vigorous deliberations of third-order theology to make reality correlations, on the model of early Christianity,[98] patiently pressuring the usurped powers, exposing their co-optation by spiritual forces of wickedness, and thinking out their reordering under the Lordship of Christ. But the Lordship of Christ is actual in the world

95. Wilder, "Kerygma, Eschatology and Social Ethics," 515.

96. Wilder, "Kerygma, Eschatology and Social Ethics," 515.

97. Wilder, "Kerygma, Eschatology and Social Ethics," 515.

98. Kreider, *Patient Ferment of the Early Church.*

in the concrete form of the community called out by the gospel; its very existence is the divine novelty and harbinger of human salvation. The saving Lordship of Christ in the body of the ecclesia is the term by which such debates can be Christianly meaningful. The question is not about degrees of "aggressiveness," then, but whether theologically informed criticism of culture which *is* the new community of Jesus and his disciples executes the sanctifying Spirit's mission "to prove the world wrong about sin and righteousness and judgment" (John 16:8). This is a "spiritual" battle, a battle *of the spirits*, addressing *conscience*.[99] Christologically modified apocalyptic does not think, as does modern secularism in its capitalist, socialist, or least of all fascist, modes of a battle of human spirit against indifferent nature, and thus against rival iterations of the same modern attack on nature. "Flesh" for Paul designates humanity, not in its base animal emotions or motives but in its highest, "spiritual" powers, brain-power no less than muscle-power. Flesh is the *spirit* of self-reliance in the absence of Creator God over against reliance on the presence of the sanctifying Spirit of Jesus and his Father. The biblical battle is a battle of spirit against spirit. Thus, prophetic critique in the Spirit is not to be gauged by its level of "aggression," but by its capacity to lighten our darkness with a critique of human culture that necessitates the crucified Messiah as activating God's saving purpose of beloved community (Gal 2:21) already now concretely manifested in the ecclesia, harbinger of human salvation.

Wilder does better in answering his own question. He notes that "[n]o political authority in the ancient world was devoid of religious and metaphysical connotations," so that "the hostile rulers and angelic powers in question include transparently what we would speak of in non-mythological terms as structural element of unregenerate society, the false authorities of culture." While this formulation is still too vague and we have to question whether our modern sociological way of thinking is as demystified and non-mythological at it claims, Wilder derived from this basic insight the important mandate for theology: "the dethroning of such authorities and the weakening of such power-principles constitute the central task of Christian social action."[100] That is to say: the central social-ethical task is *public preaching* of the gospel announcing the inaugurated Lordship of the crucified Jesus and accompanying

99. Hinlicky, "Spirit of Christ amid the Spirits of the Post-Modern World."

100. Wilder, "Kerygma, Eschatology and Social Ethics," 528.

theological reflection that makes such proclamation precise, pertinent and powerful in destabilizing the metaphysical, or more precisely, the *soteriological* pretensions of sovereignty.[101] Genuinely Christian social action, then, is anything but mute activity as if it were self-interpreting; it is public and articulate kerygma and liturgy and works of mercy (cf. 2 Cor 10:4) enacting the Lordship of Jesus that as such and only as such contests the thralldom and wins over hearts and minds to the beloved community in anticipation of the reign of God.[102] Unlike "political Barthianism"[103] (though he does not name it), yet following Paul, Wilder realizes that the reconciliation of the world to God in Christ is incomplete, that battle still rages, that the coming Christ in glory still has work to do presently in subduing the powers, negating the negations, that last of which is Death—not creaturely finitude, but a hostile power demanding payment on the debts of human sinfulness, let it be emphasized, to be *destroyed* (the Greek verb is *katargeo*) like sin—*not* reconciled or re-ordered (1 Cor 15:26)—in the eschaton of judgment, executing the "death of death and hell's destruction." The anti-divine spiritual forces of wickedness are thusly forced back upon themselves as a house divided in final furious self-annihilation.

In this light, today's contextual theologies are not wrong, as we see in Wink, to demand that we name and engage the powers here on earth in the apocalyptic situation of dire need. But the question is who names who and how we so identified are to engage in a struggle that is *holy*, not more of the same old cycles of envy and revenge; this is for Paul, and should be for us, a matter of knowing Jesus Christ by the sovereign work of the Spirit who sanctifies theological subjects by conforming them to his way of love *for enemies*. The sovereignty of the Spirit of Jesus and his Father entails, accordingly, this firm specification of the politics of gospel: the gospel forms holy communities of Christ the crucified but vindicated Lord to whom at last every knee will bow when death is forever swallowed up in divine life, provided only that in the interim this new existence of the ecclesia in the world is not mute but itself proclaimed and understood as the divine beachhead making an alternative to the politics and propaganda of the *libido dominandi*.

101. Bertram, *Time for Confessing*.

102. Boulton, *God Against Religion*.

103. Hinlicky, *Beloved Community*, 712, 802, 840.

The Problem of Intelligibility

If the foregoing discussion succeeds in its modest purpose of fleshing out what is at issue in the thesis that humanizing the powers comes about by the formation of the church in the Spirit's gospel mission to the nations, we are confronted with an immediate and formidable objection. This is not an objection to the mixed record of Christianity in its 2000 years of history, as for contemporary example, Ephraim Radner has so acutely analyzed.[104] Nothing human, including the church, has other than a mixed historical record; as Augustine knew, precisely as a catholic Christian: in this life our righteousness consists for the most part in the forgiveness of sins. Thus, the true problem in this regard is triumphalist resistance to acknowledging penitently the sinfulness of the holy church, indeed, penitence *as* the holiness of the church. Rather, the salient objection in connection with our proposed diabology stands behind Bultmann's existential reduction of the mythology of the powers and principalities to the individual's decision of faith, taken as existentialist freedom in the act of defying fate. Yet it stands as well behind the softer demythologizing in Wink to human political and institutional powers that are to be identified as demonic in his "one concretion of power." But this objection at its root stems from a Feuerbach or a Durkheim who would expose the theological thesis about spiritual forces of wickedness in heavenly places usurping social forms as a mystification.

And indeed, it is the case that we are now confronted with an acute problem of intelligibility to which this chapter at the outset alluded but set aside until now, namely, that according to our Ephesians text, social appearances, to which we have natural access, do not tell the whole story, or penetrate to the true roots of apparent conflicts, and accordingly settle for a salvation less than the Pauline eschatological defeat of the elusive, trans-individual, supra-human powers of Sin and Death, personified in the figure of the devil, as spiritual forces of wickedness in high places. In a sense, the critics are right that there is no solution to the problem of evil in Christian theology other than the solution which is the victory of God for us and over it, as Luther claimed for the eschaton of judgment at the resurrection of the dead.[105] Why else would Jesus have announced and enacted the impending reign of God dispersing the legion forces of evil?

104. Radner, *Brutal Unity.* See the author's response to Radner, in Hinlicky, "On the 'Sacrifice of Conscience,'" 11–17.

105. Luther, *Bondage of the Will*, 316.

Thus, to insist that there is a problem of evil—of powerful malice afflicting the good creation of God—such that it resists not only theological but any human cognitive mastery itself constitutes a powerful recognition and needed defensive maneuver in the apocalyptic battle of the ages. Intelligibly to describe this mystery of evil in theological dimension as the surd of actual defiance of the creator's sovereignty aimed at destruction of the creator's work is the task now before us.

A distinction between appearance and reality is, of course, at the basis of critical thinking. Theology too is a form of critical thinking. It differs from philosophy in holding that epistemic access to the root conflict afflicting human experience is not available to what Paul calls "the natural man" (1 Cor 2:14), but rather it must be apocalypsed, revealed. This is an axiomatic distinction and the reason why doctrinal theology is not self-consciously freethinking, but conscientiously freed thinking: it knows the devil in that it has been freed from its grip by the Lord Jesus. If for a Feuerbach or a Durkheim, the very notion of God, let alone the self-giving, and so, self-revealing God of the gospel, is already an ideological mystification produced by purely human-social aspiration in combat with other social forces, how much more so, then, must the notion of the contra-divine adversary be an all the more anesthetizing mystification of purely human conflict! Marx put it famously in speaking of religion as the opium of the people: this diabolical world a hopeless veil of tears, heaven true home. As Nietzsche said about the forgiveness of sins—an imaginary solution to an imaginary problem—so we might also say about sin, death, and devil as apocalyptic powers: an imaginary problem evoking an imaginary solution.

Reconstruction of Lutheran doctrinal theology will have at least a little sympathy with such critics in this regard.[106] Much "God-talk" is idolatrous. Apocalyptic literalism has given critics a rich fat target. Here are indeed "devil made me do it" mystifications that evade ethical responsibility, that maintain order at the expense of love, law at the expense of wisdom, and invocations of mystery to conceal muddles in thinking about the obligations of conscientious discipleship. Such mythological literalism surrenders agency and makes victimhood a badge of personal identity with a get out of jail free card: "I was only following orders." "I had no choice." Christian theology of the powers and principalities today cannot go forward without wholehearted acceptance of the Enlightenment's

106. Hinlicky, "Luther's Atheism," 53–60.

critique of such superstitious but self-serving mystification. But the Christian point of endorsing such critique is not so much to demythologize as to render all flesh accountable to God our creator and redeemer for that to which hearts falsely cling in every time of trouble.

Having acknowledged that, we also acknowledge after the secular century of Hitler, Hiroshima, and Stalin that the tradition of the European Enlightenment indulges its own superstitions: an imperious faith in Reason anointing itself the Tribunal ruling discourses in or out of bounds. To be sure, Marx, Nietzsche, and Freud, the masters of suspicion, all children of the Enlightenment, in a fashion reminiscent of Luther's exposé, unveiled Reason subservient to unconscious powers, willing and able to rationalize anything according to unacknowledged self-interest or mimetic desire. Historian Robert Ericksen described this as the "double crisis of modernity," the Enlightenment's discrediting of the antecedent ideology of Christendom, and the subsequent discrediting of the Enlightenment's credulous faith in Reason, as Ericksen sought to explain the spiritual vacuum in which the most educated nation in Europe could fall for Hitlerism.[107] This double crisis of modernity anticipates contemporary postmodernism which to a degree has leveled the playing field by discrediting foundationalist epistemologies which have ruled out of rational bounds theological discourse responding to the putative word of God in contest against spiritual forces of wickedness in high places. Of course, it has also ruled in bounds not only lots of foolishness, but the propaganda free-for-all in which today we live and move and have our being.

To go forward in renewed confidence with the intention of the Ephesians text for today is, as mentioned, to deliteralize the apocalyptic metaphors of military struggle by removing them from the human plane of politics as usual, where, as history shows, Christians too have readily been misled by literalism into the bloody fanaticism of crusades, witch-hunts, persecutions and inquisitions, self-deceived about their own lust for domination that always animates the struggle for power in politics as usual, no matter the religious dress. Again, as mentioned, the intention of the Ephesians text is to refer instead and so direct us to the ecclesia as the Spirit's new community in the world where politics are not to be as usual, but to provide the alternative to structures of malice working injustice by erecting and sustaining a structure of love working justice.

107. Ericksen, *Theologians Under Hitler.*

Needless to say, this implication mandates a thorough-going ecumenical realignment in the existing denominations along the apocalyptic battle line in order to gather the holy remnant of a confessing church from Euro-America's ruins of Christendom (which will also fulfill in principle the promise of twentieth-century ecumenism for the visible unity of the churches publicly confessing the Lord Jesus Christ the Son of God). Its confessing theology should trump the Enlightenment's abiding charge that devil talk amounts to a mystification of what is really going on by displaying a critical power of prophetic insight in third-order theological operations that out-enlightens the enlighteners (as Oswald Bayer suggested in his interesting study of Hamann[108]).

But to meet the objection substantively, we have to ask: what *in the world* are we actually talking about when, in the light of Jesus Christ, we expose what we name and engage here on the earth as manifestations of spiritual forces of wickedness usurping powers and principalities that in any case structure human social life on the earth? That is the *crux intellectus*. It confronts every preacher every time she is required to make intelligible to her audience the kinds of biblical texts we have considered in this chapter. We cannot give a glib answer to this question, for we have learned that the spiritual forces of wickedness are a revealed mystery: ever elusive, disguising themselves as angels of light, masters of deceit at work with super-human cunning and murderous malice. What is revealed is this *mystery* of evil, precisely as appearing in the good creation of God in defiance of the Creator's goodwill (2 Thess 2:7), thereby precluding the very possibility of uncovering its secret reality so as to root it out once and for all. Metaphysics of the devil cannot succeed and if it is thought to succeed, it is the devil who has just so deceived. Engaging this *mystery* for theological understanding phenomenologically by descriptive ontology which discloses *being there* rather than metaphysics which would penetrate behind *being there* to its timeless spaceless ground is thus a matter *only* of equipping on-going discernment. Biblical texts that figure Satan in various guises grant epistemic access for informed consideration of this *mystery*, and just this consideration makes the notion of *usurped* powers and principalities intelligible, so far as the *mystery of evil* can be made intelligible at all. It is best in theology to openly confess bafflement at actual evil in the figure of the devil as the surd of evil will in the good creation of the good God, if only to be able to reject dehumanizing

108. Bayer, *Contemporary in Dissent.*

reductions of the mystery of evil to some supposedly knowable and humanly manageable "root cause."

By way of conclusion the following descriptions of the *event* of the devil drawn from the foregoing may help in third-order theological deliberation and discernment.

Commenting on Wis 2:24, "through the Devil's envy, death entered the world," Augustine picked up an early Christian tradition about the angel of light, Lucifer, who, enraged upon learning that the lowly earthlings were elected as God's covenant partner, resolved to destroy the creation and the covenant. Just so he seduced humanity with the false promise, *sicut deus eritis*, that tickled their pride.[109] Augustine predominantly discusses the mystery of evil under the concept of *superbia*, pride, thinking that inordinate self-confidence is presupposed in envy. But notice that the false promise, "you shall be as God . . . ," is not premised on a false estimate of human power which is actually felt to be lacking in comparison to the creator God. It is precisely because they *lack* ultimate power, and, however vaguely, know that they lack it, that they are willingly seduced and eat the forbidden fruit that falsely promises to bestow the missing clout. So, the devil figured as a serpent (as the sanctifying Spirit is figured as a dove) tempts them with its own sin, envy; it captures their desire for power by enticing envy, insinuating that the Creator jealously forbids eating the fruit in order to keep them in a subordinate place as powerless inferiors. The sin of envy succumbing to vain pride violates the First Table of the Decalogue, thus forming a circle with the prohibition of envy on the plain off human relations at the conclusion of the Second Table. Augustine understood this circle as well. Disordered love, *concupiscentia*, dominates the sinner who in irrational pride, as the latter-day Augustinian Martin Luther put it, "wants to be God and does not want God to be God."[110] Envy is ontologically prior to greed and the secret motive of prideful overreach; greed is but the envy of the rich. In all permutations, envy *of God* is the malice on which the fallen world now turns—but especially when this theological interpretation of the mystery of evil is lost from consciousness, no longer available to discern and to keep evil in check.

Human bondage to the tyrannical powers at work in human concretions of power whereby the good of social institutions is usurped for

109. Case, "Devil's Envy," 474–95.

110. LW 31:10. Cf. Luther on envy, LW 49:337.

purposes of domination is not innocent victimhood; the bondage is *sinful* in the non-moralistic sense of apocalyptic theology's interpretation of the universal scope of the sin of origin in Adam (Rom 5). This easily misunderstood claim is meant in the precise sense of the *ordo caritatis*, where sinfulness refers to the person's relation to God (*coram Deo*), not, then, to its relation to other creatures in political life (*coram hominibus, coram mundo*) where reference is to visible acts of trespass or crime, personal and social injustices. There are here indeed significant degrees of guilt or criminality and equally significant differences between victims and perpetrators. But envy is the sin that seduces one and all to sell themselves, body and soul, to idolatrous "powers and principalities" themselves usurped by spiritual forces of wickedness. (Think, illustratively, of the Bernie Madoff Ponzi scheme: while he sinfully abused his victims they just as sinfully, though not criminally, became his victims in their own greed for a disproportionate financial bonanza.) Envy is sinful in the way that yielding to a seduction captivates the restless heart that rests truly only in the God of love; and this sinfulness becomes second nature in fallen humanity, in turn requiring patient pastoral therapy in the ecclesia by ministries of exorcism, inducing willing repentance, forgiveness, cleansing, healing and re-ordering of the treasurings of the human heart in those who are now slowly learning to have in them the same mind that was in Christ Jesus (Phil 2:5–6), who did not envy divine status but rather gave himself for lesser and morally unworthy beings in a generous act of creative love.

As Hans Conzelmann pointed out in his commentary on 1 Cor 15, it is the contra-divine powers of Sin and Death which from a high place wickedly oppose the divine purposes of righteousness and life that are represented in the "mythological," i.e., narrative figure of the devil. As sin opened the door to the dominion of death and death is named as the "last enemy," so the figure of the devil

> becomes a means of representation. It can express the facts (a) that death is primarily God's adversary before being man's enemy . . . ; (b) that it has to do with the whole existence of man . . . ; (C) that it is a *historical* power; (d) that the victory over death does not consist in man's escaping death and its (abiding) power, but in death itself being overcome.[111]

111. Conzelmann, *1 Corinthians*, 273–74.

The lying devil, murderer of humanity, is overcome by the vindicated righteousness of truth-telling Jesus in whose death and resurrection faith now participates.

Second, then, against the tendency in Wink and Wright (let alone lesser imitators) to underplay the reconciliation of the holy God with the sinful creature in the thrall of envy enticing pride in favor of the liberation of the innocent from oppression, we might better hold tightly together these New Testament atonement motifs, along with the call to cross-bearing discipleship in imitation of the Lord who thus shows us his way in self-giving creative love for enemies. As it is stated in the Apocalypse:

> Now have come the salvation and the power and the kingdom of our God and the authority of his Messiah, for the accuser of our comrades has been thrown down, who accuses them night and day before our God. But they have conquered him by the blood of the Lamb and by the word of their testimony, for they did not cling to life even in the face of death. (Rev 12:1–11)

Here we see an indication of the unity of all three atonement motifs found in the New Testament: liberation from the tyrannical powers, atonement at the cross, and Spirit-given freedom to follow Jesus through the cross to the crown.

Commentator Joe Mangina insightfully remarks: "The devil is the original bearer of false witness. His lies are legion, like his multiple personalities. At the social level, they include all the stratagems of deception and doublespeak by which corporations, governments, and the vast enterprises of technocracy seek to keep people from a knowledge of the truth."[112] In today's total system of propaganda one and all are seduced by multiform lies, so that our own moral fault must be *apocalypsed*, shattering the convenient propagandistic self-deception that we are not sinners but innocent victims of someone else's sin. That we are sinners *coram Deo* is the truth even when we had been sinned against *coram mundo*. The final lie, however, is that we have not been victoriously befriended. Luther helps here:

> There was no counsel, no help, no comfort for us until this only and eternal Son of God, in his unfathomable goodness, had mercy on us because of our misery and distress and came from heaven to help us. Those tyrants and jailers have now

112. Mangina, *Revelation*, 154.

> been routed, and their place has been taken by Jesus Christ, the Lord of life, righteousness, and every good and blessing. He has snatched us poor lost creatures from the jaws of hell, won us, made us free, and restored us to the Father's favor and grace. As his own possession he has taken us under his protection and shelter, in order that he may rule us by his righteousness, wisdom, power, life and blessedness.[113]

Note again how all three atonement motifs combine here. By winning our forgiveness before God at the cross, Christ dethrones the evil powers whose only real power is the half-truth they possess in accusing sinners with threat of death. Made unworthy of God and fearful of death, sinners are made submissive to demonic tyranny, even to desire it. But making us worthy of God by his own action of generosity, Christ gives his own Spirit to free believers from the threats of death temporal and eternal and for the newness of life in hope and love. The ultimate sanction of the tyrannical powers, the powerful threat of death plausible enough on account of inchoate awareness of sinfulness and its due, is now contested in the holy battle of public witnesses, the martyrs fortified by the sanctifying Spirit.

Third, if political sovereignty is not as such the enemy of God, but is, as Paul affirms in Rom 13, instituted to be God's temporary servant for our good in a post-paradisical world in which evil-doing persistently happens, and as such, is a place of conscientious obedience to God (Rom 13:5), by the same token, the state is all the same, as the same text indicates (Rom 13:4), an ambiguous, postlapsarian monopoly on the means of violence (1 Sam 8:4–22) by which at best some sinners deter fellow sinners from spiraling one and all downward into anarchic violence. If that is right, Agamben is right, contra Hobbes and Carl Schmitt,[114] to describe political sovereignty, not as the social contract on which civilization is built but as an unstable emergency order that lawlessly enforces law by appeal to a perpetual state of emergency in the time between humanity's fall and its redemption. Likewise, then, Marx was not wrong to imagine that in the coming of the beloved community, the state, like the temple, will wither away. The state and organized religion are postlapsarian emergency orders which functionally interact but have different mandates in the common task of preserving humanity from self-destruction, lost as humanity is in sinful blindness to its own sinful envy provoking prideful overreach in the downward spiral of contests

113. BoC 434.

114. Schmitt, *Political Theology*.

for power. In this interim, however, the nations to which the gospel is addressed in the Spirit's mission find themselves under political sovereignty of many kinds that may, or may not, serve according to God's institution to enforce rough justice and tolerable peace. If the ministry of pastors and theologians is *to* the word and sacraments that they be faithfully and aptly spoken, making in the world a zone of freedom for such discernment in the holy communion of Christ's people, the ministry of all the baptized is *from* the word and sacraments to the suffering world in need and under thralldom. Often, these ministries are frustrated by the institutional organization of religion and the state respectively. These powers and principalities, then, become scenes of spiritual battle.

Bonhoeffer's ruminations are helpful here. He identified "mandates of creation" from Gen 1:26–28 that continued to be in force as structures of life, even as, in humanity's post-paradisical exile, they take on the institutional forms of organized religion, the family and economy, and the state. These institutions have become, as it were, "second nature" but are open as such to the coming of Christ. Yet these social formations can all and each be demonized which means that they become closed to the "coming of Christ." Bonhoeffer writes:

> The concept of the natural must, therefore, be recovered on the basis of the gospel. We speak of the natural, as distinct from the creaturely, in order to take account of the fact of the Fall; and we speak of the natural rather than of the sinful so that we may include in it the creaturely. The natural is that which, after the Fall, is directed toward the coming of Christ. The unnatural is that which, after the Fall, closes its doors against the coming of Christ.[115]

According to this interpretation, institutions which exploit rather than steward the aspects of creation under their care have become unnatural; by contrast, stewards work naturally in expectation of accountability at the master's return. When the unnatural becomes utterly destructive of creation as ordered to divine judgment, redemption and fulfillment in Christ, institutions become demonized as powers and principalities usurped by spiritual forces of wickedness. In this exploration, composed during the death rattle of Christendom in his Nazi prison cell, Bonhoeffer put his finger on the problem of the doctrine of creation, it's preservation under providential care, Christian vocation and social

115. Bonhoeffer, *Ethics*, 144.

responsibility when the apocalyptic conflict between the reign of the ascended Lord and the dethroned but all the more raging *regnum diaboli* becomes newly perceptible on the earth.

What matters for doctrinal theology is not a theoretically satisfying definition of the figure from the gospel narrative, but the identification of the devil's manifest agency as the spiritual force of wickedness coming from a high place within the creation. How can one capture the "nature" of the surd of malice contradicting the goodwill of the creator for righteousness and life, whose *modus operandi* is deception, including ever fresh self-disguise? One can only stand watch and be on the alert against a lion prowling about seeking to devour. Even to insist that it is, for classical example, an angel at the head of a cosmic fall, entails the creator's responsibility for evil, whether by permission or out of gross incompetence. The free-will defense of God to absolve him from responsibility for evil in creation fails; in the case of the devil as fallen angel it only moves the fall into sin up a step on the ontological ladder. The supposed fall of Lucifer not only fails to justify God but epitomizes the moralistic understanding of sin as a free choice rather than the subjugation precipitated by an irrational seduction to complicity in the tempter's envy of God according to a false conception of God as jealous for power rather than the overflowing and creative power willing, able and wise to give life, peace, and righteousness. The Lucifer theodicy perpetuates the propagandistic veil of free will, that is, "consumer choice," concealing the envy which ensnared the primal couple and motivated the fratricidal murder in the first generation and the tower-building of their descendants. Ziegler is right to call the "nature" of the devil *adventitious*, an incomprehensible mystery *erupting unexpectedly*, mad to destroy whatever it cannot possess. The devil is what it does and that description of a recurring happening suffices for doctrinal theology to identify its agency as murderous usurper and father of lies. That fury to destroy what cannot be had for one's own is what in the world we are talking about when we identify the foe flushed out of hiding by the coming of Christ, who gives what is his own.

This argument locates the ecclesia in what is sometimes misleadingly called the "pre-political" realm of culture. The church's modern defection from this station and catechetical vocation therein is at the root of destructive culture wars which trade in propaganda.[116] Engaging the powers and principalities (which are good creatures of God) usurped by

116. Hunter, *Before the Shooting Begins;* see further the noble, literally quixotic effort of Helmer and Carr, *Ordinary Faith in Polarized Times.*

the devil does not happen by preachers abusing the pulpit to indulge in the partisan bromides and bombast of propagandistic politics as usual, but in the very serious business of edifying the laity in Christ and thereby empowering the laity for political vocations of responsibility to God for the creation under one's care.[117] Amos Wilder, for pertinent precedence, lifted up in 1964 the great work of the post-war Evangelical Academies in Germany bringing together "jurists, philosophers and sociologists as well as theologians" in *die Zone der Freiheit*, that is, as ecclesia, to brainstorm the problems of public life in the task of post-war reconstruction.[118] That kind of engagement of the "whole church," as Wilder put it, will be the catechetical method that empowers Christians to see and to say what in the world they are talking about when they take up, not only Paul's words, but his program of holy struggle "against the principalities, against the powers, against the world rulers of this present darkness, against the spiritual hosts of wickedness in the heavenly places."

117. Benne, *Paradoxical Vision.*

118. Wilder, "Kerygma, Eschatology and Social Ethics," 510.

V

Critical Dogmatics out of the Tradition of Luther

Tying together several of the interlocking arguments made in the preceding, this chapter focuses on the need for critical dogmatics going forward from the theological tradition stemming from Luther. It begins by tracing the deliteralization of apocalyptic metaphor accomplished by the Gospel of John to refer to the God who comes in judgment for the purpose of mercy. This important hermeneutical work of deliteralization becomes apparent when John is read as a midrashic commentary on the Synoptic tradition which in turn allows the Gospel to function as the Spirit's bridge from the earliest traditions about Jesus to the developed dogmas of the Trinity, hence Trinitarian Christology and pneumatology. By and large these dogmas of the patristic era are, as putative knowledge of God, the subject matter of the discipline of dogmatics along with the anti-gnostic/docetic canon of Scripture and the doctrine of salvation by grace articulated against Pelagianism, the cause especially taken up and renewed by Luther. Prefaced by a retrospect on early Christian baptism, the chapter shows how in his catechisms and in his treatise against Erasmus, Luther is the great but critical renewer of patristic dogmatics who breathed new life into the old language by way of apocalyptic reframing of the creedal formulas as rules for identifying Christ. Thus creeds are gifts of the Spirit fending off fatal deviations from the truth of the gospel, beginning with the antichrist's propagation of docetism (1 John 4:2–3). But reclaiming such a legacy from Luther requires an account of the failure of the subsequent

Lutheran tradition to sustain doctrinal theology along these lines. This failure is traced to an eclipse of the knowledge of the sanctifying Spirit who is humanly, indeed bodily experienced in affect-transformative ways in the preaching of God's word as righteous demand that mortifies and gracious promise that vivifies those thusly mortified in conformation to the crucified and risen Christ. So, there is no event of the word of God without the reality of the God who comes to humans from God with the reality of human beings transformed by that coming. In this double correlation, critical dogmatics attends to reality.

What Has John Done?

A COLLEGE PROFESSOR TEACHING New Testament from a "history of religions" perspective once remarked with a smirk in this author's presence, "There is nothing historical whatsoever in the Gospel of John." This unnuanced *obiter dicta* by a quester after a credible Jesus of history, intended as an expert verdict of "guilty" upon the Gospel as Christian propaganda, will be familiar to many readers of this book. The verdict is a much attenuated descendent of the proper kind of interest in the faith of the man Jesus we observed in considering Howard Thurman's *Jesus and the Disinherited*. The professor's judgment is unnuanced, however, because the very existence of the book is witness to something importantly historical in early Christianity; the judgment of value from the contemporary perspective of scientific historiography, concealed under the assertion, is that verifiable evidence about Jesus of Nazareth in analogy to contemporary human self-consciousness is what is of value for knowledge of this person, rendering the incipient Christology of early Christianity nothing but a distorting bias rigorously to be set aside by scientific scholarship. If, however, Christology in an inchoate sense began with the Jesus of history (Mark 1:1!), as is more than plausible in the context of Second Temple Jewish apocalyptic, one is arguing in a circle with this supposed scientifically-objective methodology.

Second-order theology describes the terms in which debates about historicity are meaningful. In this perspective there is indeed a "future for the historical Jesus"[1] in "third-order" theology in which it is meaningful

1. Keck, *Future for the Historical Jesus*. The incisive critique of Jonathan Rowlands in *Metaphysics of Historical Jesus Research* has come to my attention too late for detailed

to argue for a correlation between the faith of Jesus and those poor in power in this world (1 Cor 1:26–29), as we have seen. But such inquiry is *theology* working out its term, "Jesus," not "history of religions" dissolving him into a type. Broadly speaking, the difference is this: an historical Jesus reconstructed apart from his intense relationship to the God of Israel as known from the Scriptures is above all an ahistorical abstraction, little more than a polemical trope, indeed a blank page upon which questers construct a Jesus in their preferred image, as the gnostic docetists pioneered and as Albert Schweitzer pointed out more than a century ago looking back upon his century.[2] For present purposes, as doctrinal theology proceeds from the primary normed norm of canonical Scripture, John's *literary* distance from the Synoptic Gospels, to put the matter precisely and *historically*, is a long-standing and widespread truism, *not only* in modern biblical scholarship. *This* problem of the Gospel of John is a real one for doctrinal theology today in that, as biblical scholar James Dunn once remarked,[3] John is the historical bridge between the earliest traditions about Jesus and the developed doctrine of the Trinity and consequently Trinitarian Christology.

Indeed, the college professor was correct to insinuate that if traffic on this bridge cannot credibly be restored, the very project of Christian doctrinal theology, not least in the tradition of Luther in which the Gospel of John figures prominently, is cut off at the source. The problem of this chapter in our effort to provide a fresh theology of theology in the tradition of Luther for post-Christendom was signaled earlier on when it was argued that the apocalyptic turn in theology today needs to

---

discussion in this book. Suffice it to say, however, that his critique, which envisions coexistence between historical criticism and theological exegesis in that Christian Scripture is *both* a human artifact *and* canonical testimony to the word of God corresponds to my use of Scripture as *norma normata prima* in this book. Cf. DBW 3:22.

2. Schweitzer, *Quest of the Historical Jesus*. Marcus Borg in his exchange with N. T. Wright openly acknowledges this tendency to inventiveness: "I have trouble imagining that Jesus saw his own death as salvific. Tom and I differ substantially on this topic." Further: "Honesty compels candor: I find this not only a strange notion, but an unattractive notion to attribute to Jesus. I don't want Jesus to have seen his own death as having the significance Tom gives to it. As a Christian, I want Jesus to be an attractive figure. Obviously, wanting Jesus to be attractive cannot be a criterion for making historical judgments, and I must factor this desire into my historical judgment not only about this matter, but about every other historical decision I make about Jesus." Borg and Wright, *Meaning of Jesus*, 81–82. Nothing has been gained when critique of supposedly "post-Easter creations" have simply been replaced by the contemporary scholar's "pre-Easter creations."

3. Dunn, "Let John Be John."

advance to the Johannine literature as the final canonical development of Paul's christologically qualified apocalyptic in its journey through the Synoptic Gospels.[4] It is, as mentioned in the previous chapter, John who executes the deliteralization of apocalyptic as a timetable to the last day and yet affirms it as a properly metaphorical knowledge of God's disrupting *kairos*, the time of God's end for his creation, the Johannine *krisis* precipitated by coming in the flesh of God's purpose on and for this earth on which the cross of Jesus stood.

It is, as indicated above, widely and rightly acknowledged that the Gospel of John belongs to the later stages of New Testament literature, even if upon analysis one detects traces of earlier editions, perhaps as far back as the "community of the beloved disciple" (whose testimony is cited only in connection with the Passion), as Raymond Brown argued.[5] Be that as it may, John 20:31 seems certainly to have concluded a penultimate version of the gospel very close to what presently appears in the canonical New Testament: "These things have been written in order that you believe that Jesus is the Christ, the Son of God, and believing have life in his name." No hidden agenda here! What is unmistakably and emphatically articulated, moreover, is not simply vague trust in a heavenly parent but articulate belief focused upon the object of trust, answering the questions about who Jesus is and why trust in him bestows eternal life. The articulation of this belief is implicit and preliminary in Matthew, Mark and Luke but John makes it explicit and accordingly directs the line of doctrinal development in early Christianity, leading to the formulations of ecumenically binding dogma in the trinitarian doctrine of God and accordingly of the persons of Christ and the Spirit.

Johannine beliefs developed towards the trinitarian statement of the ecumenical councils of Nicaea 325 and Constantinople in 381, namely, that the Son of God, while identical with his God and Father in being the one creator of all that is not God, yet as person/hypostasis differs personally as that of son from father and economically as mediator from source in the acts of creation and its redemption. Likewise in 381 came the clarification that the sanctifying Spirit is no vague and impersonal energy but person/hypostasis in the same sense as the Father and the Son; as such the Spirit proceeded from the Father to dwell upon the Son and so bound them together in mutual indwelling, a circulation of love. Following from

4. Following Joel Marcus that the Marcan gospel is informed by Pauline theology. See also in this connection Hultgren, *Rise of Normative Christianity*.

5. Brown, *Community of the Beloved Disciple*.

this articulate Trinitarianism, clarified by the novel, subtle but acute distinction between abstract being (*ousia* or *physis*) and concrete way of being (*hypostasis*), the christological doctrine of the council of Chalcedon in 451 followed. It was there affirmed that uniquely and inseparably the one person/hypostasis of the eternal Son incarnate in Jesus Christ bears two natures, his own divine and newly his own human, creator and creature whose respective properties are in communion and deployed as befits the need of the messianic mission. It is not the nature that bears or "supposits" the person like a cloak that may be put on and off, but the hypostasis that owns its natures, human and divine, as one and the same "Christ Jesus." The legitimacy of this doctrinal development and its continuing significance for reconstruction of doctrinal theology in the tradition of Luther is what is at stake in our understanding of the Gospel of John. The historical role of John as the bridge between the Synoptic tradition and the dogmatic development of early catholic Christianity is indisputable. But why should this be a problem?

Because intellectually honest observation of the profound literary differences between John and the Synoptic Gospels seemingly forces a choice: *Either* John is a marginal tradition representing a sect outside the mainstream of early Christian development only later and artificially conjoined to the Synoptics in the canonical New Testament with the profoundly distorting effect of turning Jesus into a god striding on the earth; *or* John is quite deliberately published as a narrative-theological interpretation of the Synoptic account, the sense of which can be well argued and its legitimacy understood. The first choice would undermine the doctrinal development to Nicene Trinitarianism and indeed regard it as a distortion of what should have developed from the Synoptic deposit of faith: i.e., an Antiochian Spirit-Christology of divine indwelling of a man, radiant in his personality, as for modern example in Schleiermacher's *Life of Jesus*, which we will engage in chapter 6.[6] The narrative-theological interpretation of the Synoptic account is surely the right one historically, even though John's bold rewriting of the Synoptic plot caused its canonicity to be challenged as also its misunderstood engagement against gnostic/docetic forms of early Christianity caused doubts about its orthodoxy as measured against the unflinching treatment of the mortal humanity of Jesus in the Synoptic

6. This contemporary either/or excludes Schleiermacher's treatment of John as eyewitness testimony to the self-consciousness of Jesus—the source of the continuing modern misunderstanding of the meaning of docetism in Christology. This will be argued in detail in chapter 6.

Gospels. In all directions, the problem boils down to the sense of docetism as a christological deviation, whether it indicates lack of psychological plausibility in our portrait of Jesus by the historical principle of analogy or repudiates a full and true divine embodiment in mortal Jesus. The latter is the anti-docetic concern of the Gospel of John.

The Gospel of John, however, has had to deal anew with an accusation of its docetism since the rise of historical critical interpretation of the New Testament; it has seemed that the doctrinal development turned a marginal Jew[7] of the first-century Palestine into a deity "striding upon the earth," as Ernst Käsemann once put[8] it with typical polemical flourish, laying charge at the foot of the Gospel of John for obliteration of the humanity by presenting a "divine man," a superhuman in mortal guise, sovereignly above torture and gruesome death by crucifixion. So Käsemann, following Bultmann, and like Raymond Brown, a half-generation later, opted for a sectarian interpretation of John on the border between primitive Christianity and Mandean Gnosticism. Notice, however, that this way of framing the question about a "God striding on the earth" obscures a crucial nuance of early Christian doctrine, namely, that the identity of divine nature in the Father and the Son is not the only thing at stake but rather and indeed crucially the distinction in person between them.

The crucial advancement beyond such attempts to identify a sectarian Johannine community on the borders of emerging Gnosticism, a position that can claim the authority of Bultmann's influential commentary on John, relocated the Johannine community historically in a Judaism in turmoil. This advancement uncovered the Gospel's situation in life in the first-century fallout from the destruction of the temple in Jerusalem after the first Jewish revolt. The seminal study of J. Louis Martyn[9] read the Gospel, accordingly, as a story on two levels: ostensibly the story of Jesus's conflict with the temple authorities leading to his martyrdom, but also a subterranean story of a Jewish Christian community's expulsion from the synagogue for the blasphemy of acknowledging the crucified Jesus as the Son of God whose risen body has become the site of a new and spiritual temple, no longer localized in destroyed Jerusalem.

7. Meier, *Marginal Jew.*

8. Käsemann, *Testament of Jesus.*

9. Martyn, *History and Theology in the Fourth Gospel*; Ashton, *Understanding the Fourth Gospel.*

Martyn's historical critical advancement helps to make sense of the most important theological feature of the Gospel of John: its deliteralization of apocalyptic (by means of the rearrangement of the Synoptic plot) to focus on the coming of Christ in the flesh as the event dividing the eons, the *krisis* of God. The freedom with which the evangelist rearranges the storyline and reimagines the Synoptic story is also explicable from the situation in life of Second Temple Judaism, as it exemplifies rabbinic practices of midrash to make ethical and theological points by narrative means, rather than through conceptual argument. Likewise, as current scholarship locates the origin of early Gnosticism in Jewish circles disillusioned of apocalyptic literalism by the crushing of the revolt and the destruction of the Jerusalem temple, the points of contact between the Gospel of John and the docetic interpretation of Christ is also accounted for historically (even as careful exegesis demonstrates the Gospel's anti-docetism).[10]

While John seems to know the plot line of the Synoptic tradition and in places follows it in detail, for example, in the feeding in the wilderness in John 6, he also quite willfully, as it seems, alters it. For instance, the cleansing of the temple is placed at the very beginning of Jesus's ministry rather than at its end; and accordingly, the event which precipitates the conspiracy to kill Jesus is not the cleansing of the temple but the raising of Lazarus, a story with no parallels in the Synoptics. Rather than an extended Galilean ministry, the narrative course of Jesus's ministry is organized around three trips to Jerusalem on the occasion of Jewish festivals. Notable key episodes in the Synoptic plot are absent in John, specifically the ones that apocalyptically identify Jesus as the Son of God: there is no narrative of Jesus's baptism by John with the voice from heaven identifying him as the beloved Son nor of the Transfiguration likewise identifying Jesus. If we regard Jesus's agony in the garden as the final scene in this Synoptic triptych of revelatory events showing the relationship of the Father and the Son, it too is absent in the Gospel of John.

Yet it is not as if John is ignorant of these episodes. Instead, he has John the Baptist proclaim Jesus as the Lamb of God to indicate what divine Sonship consists in. The discourse of Jesus after he is informed that the gentiles are seeking him in John 12:27–30 seems to retool both the Synoptic Gethsemane and Transfiguration episodes. Likewise, absent are exorcisms, so characteristic of Jesus's Galilean ministry in the

10. Schnelle, *Antidocetic Christology in the Gospel of John.*

Synoptics, reduced to Jesus's statement in John 12:31, "Now is the judgment of this world, now shall the ruler of this world be cast out." Also absent in John is the Synoptic articulation of salvation as the approaching reign of God; the parables of the kingdom are replaced by the figures of speech in which Jesus predicates to himself various scriptural images of salvation by the sovereign enunciation of the divine "I am." Several miracles unknown to the Synoptic tradition are told but they are quite deliberately named "signs" in distinction from the Synoptic Jesus who refuses to give "signs." Jesus's teaching in the Gospel of John finds nothing like Matthew's Sermon on the Mount or Luke's Sermon on the Plain but only the new commandment that the disciples love one another as Jesus has loved them. When we gather up these literary observations, we understand the problem. What has John done?

As mentioned, there have been chiefly two ways to resolve these difficulties in modern scholarship. The first has been to locate the Gospel of John as a development peripheral to the mainstream of Jesus tradition, i.e., the Synoptic Gospels. Rudolf Bultmann argued that at the base of the Gospel of John lies a gnostic-Mandean source organized around seven miraculous signs authenticating Jesus as the revealer of God.[11] The source was taken over and retooled by a redactor who took advantage of the gnostic tendency to demythologize the apocalyptic ideas of a literal future resurrection and in its place to assert the bald, tautological paradox that what Jesus reveals already now is that he is the revealer—that's it, no props historical or mythological provided for the sheer assertion of revelation in Jesus summoning to the risky decision of faith, taken as resolute existential abandonment of all worldly securities to own one's being towards death. A conservative version of this way of resolving the historical difficulty of John's difference from the Synoptics was made by Raymond Brown, as previously mentioned, who likewise located John on the periphery of the mainstream early Christian development as the community of the Beloved Disciple, whose special testimony and authority appears in John's passion and resurrection narrative. This conservative version of John's marginality both saved an element of historicity for the Gospel and allowed for a catholic view of the development of doctrine from a deposit of faith.

The second resolution of the difficulties initiated by Martyn consists of a twofold move. First, recognition of the thoroughly Judaic

11. Bultmann, *Gospel of John*, 6–9.

character of the Gospel enables us to see how the evangelist deliberately makes conflict with the Jerusalem temple establishment the starting point of the entire narrative aimed at proclamation of Jesus as the tabernacling of God with humanity, more precisely with all those who will worship the Father in spirit and truth. Recognition of the Jewishness of the Gospel of John also makes visible a second insight, namely that the discourses about the identity of Jesus have their origin in the christological conflicts that finally led to the expulsion of Jewish Christians from the synagogue (John 7:13; 9:22; 12:42; 16:2) in the time following the destruction of the Jerusalem temple in A.D.70 when the normative Judaism of the early rabbis was consolidating in the need to find a new basis for Jewish unity after the catastrophe.

What are we to make theologically of these literary observations and their several historical resolutions?

First, the Jesus who speaks throughout the Gospel of John is the risen, indeed ascended Christ in his unveiled identity as the divine Son of God. To be certain, his glorious identity to bestow the grace upon grace which he speaks is only perceptible to faith in the risen one *as the same person who was crucified;* as such, he predicates of himself the saving attributes of life, spirit, shepherd, resurrection, and the like. What is otherwise visible (also for faith!) is "the man, the man, nothing but the man" (Luther), hence the controversy/*krisis* which must attend his coming. Indeed, the conspiracy to eliminate Jesus for the threat he represents to the temple by conspiring a judicial murder is predicated upon his visibly mortal humanity belying his divine self-predications. The Gospel insists upon this apparent paradox. Bultmann following Luther, was not wrong to insist upon a christological paradox in this sense but it was reductionist abstraction by far to say that what Jesus reveals is that he is the revealer. The revealer reveals that he is the *saving* Lord by self-predicating scriptural images of healing, wholeness, and abundance of life in knowing antithesis to the father of lies and murderer from the beginning.

Second, what John has thus done is to re-narrate the Synoptic story of the man Jesus to articulate for faith this unveiled identity of Jesus as Son of God and Savior. For example, in the Synoptic story of Jesus's agony in the garden of Gethsemane he prays to be delivered from the cup of the divine wrath that he must drink. But in the Gospel of John, we hear Jesus instead stating to his disciples, "Now my soul is troubled. And what should I say—'Father, save me from this hour'? No, it is for this reason that I have come to this hour" (12:27). Here John's Jesus does not deny his troubled soul as in the Synoptic depiction but resolutely overrides his own human and natural aversion with the determination to accomplish the Father's severe, strange but saving will, just as the Synoptic episode also eventuates.

Third, in rewriting the Synoptic story to articulate this unveiled identity of Jesus, John also interprets all the miracles of the Synoptic tradition as signs of the saving will of God, not as proofs of Jesus's divine identity (12:37) but as his enactment of divine purpose. Johannine signs are disclosures or revelations of the disambiguated will of God that creatures have life and have it abundantly. In other words, signs in John have a dogmatic rather than apologetic purpose. This is especially evident in the famous story of doubting Thomas. Thomas does not doubt that the disciples have seen something wondrous but rather doubts that the apparition that they have seen is the very Jesus who was crucified. It is upon recognizing that it is Jesus who was crucified that now stands before him that Thomas falls down to worship his Lord and God—the very picture of anti-docetic Christology according to John.

Fourth, John has entirely refocused the conflict between the reign of God and the kingdom of the devil according to apocalyptic mythology, taken literally. Gone are the exorcism stories and in their place comes the one decisive act of casting Satan from heaven so that on the earth truth-telling Jesus may overcome the murderous father of lies. Jesus wins this victory over the purveyors of propaganda in his confession before Pontius Pilate: he is the original and paradigmatic *martyr* who witnesses to the truth in defiance of the death threats of the liar. In the same way disciples of Jesus will witness and confess in combat with the *regnum diaboli*, cast from heaven but now raging upon the earth.

Finally, John simplifies the ethical teachings of Jesus to the enactment of his love for the disciples which entails their love for one another; he makes this new community of mutual love on the earth the cutting edge of the divine advance into the world of darkness separating, in Augustinian parlance, the city of God from the earthly city. The self-giving mutual love of the community of disciples is the sanctifying Spirit's holy work on the earth contesting in deed the unholy politics of the earthly city.

What are we to make of the obvious development we see when we grasp that the Gospel of John is a theological midrash, an exercise in narrative theology that intentionally retells the Synoptic story for manifestly doctrinal purposes, presupposing an audience that will be attuned to the transformations? Provided we acknowledge this movement with intellectual honesty, we can see in it precisely the Paraclete's promised ministry to lead disciples to all truth by recalling the word of Jesus. In other words, the deposit of faith is given and exists from the beginning as the external word of the Easter kerygma concerning the divine vindication of the Crucified, eliciting in turn the primal confession of the Lordship of Jesus motivating stories about the ministry of Jesus which provoked his crucifixion and their collection. The Synoptic Gospels are written as this confession of faith in a perspective "from below," i.e., accentuating the imperceptiveness of the pre-Easter disciples who are incapable of grasping the humanity of Jesus as the locus of divine apocalypse until the executioner's confession. John is written as the same confession of faith in a perspective "from above," i.e., retelling the story of the humanity of Jesus as the locus of divine apocalypse in the post-Easter perspective, unveiling the divine and saving "I am" who is the true, supervening subject of the human being's actions and passions. Doctrinally the Synoptic narrative initiates the rejection of docetism while the Johannine incorporates the anti-docetism in anticipating the rejection of Arian subordinationism. Admittedly, if one reads John as a literal representation of how it actually happened rather than as a Spirit-inspired theological interpretation of the Synoptic tradition, it produces what Hegel called a "monstrosity": the picture of a human being inhabited and instrumentalized by an otherworldly spirit. But we need not do so. Indeed, Schleiermacher, who above all contended for psychological plausibility, regarded the Gospel of John to be the most historically authentic! He was wrong on both counts, as we shall see in the next chapter. But at least in reading John he did not see a human puppet inhabited by a divine spook.

So, the Synoptics clarify one term of the confession, Jesus of Nazareth, while John clarifies the other term, Lord. Seeing these two witnesses *together* we are given the canonical one Lord Jesus Christ, the Son of God. Of course, seeing together means that we cannot see John as a replacement of the Synoptics, but rather as their doctrinal interpretation making explicit the saving action of God who so loved the world in giving the beloved Son as this particular human being attested in the Synoptics. In the felicitous exposition of John Meyendorff regarding the outcome of this trajectory in doctrinal theology centuries later:

> In Chalcedonian Christology the unique hypostasis or person of Christ is that of the Logos. Obviously, then, the notion of hypostasis cannot be identified with either the divine or the

> human characteristics [i.e., "natures"]; neither can it be identical with the idea of human consciousness. The hypostasis is the ultimate source of individual, personal existence, which, in Christ, is both divine and human.[12]

The concrete way of being God as the Son who became incarnate is the source-subject of the particular existence of the human being Jesus of Nazareth from birth through death and resurrection and beyond. This is precisely not an Apollinarian Christology of a soulless body, i.e., lacking human consciousness or mind, a mannequin orchestrated by implantation of a divine ghost in a physical machine. It is confession of faith and doxological wonder before the person, visible in his humanity, believed as the divine Word made flesh. What is equally significant about this Johannine christological synthesis, then, is that it dispenses with apocalyptic literalism without abandoning apocalyptic metaphor as the theological matrix of knowledge of God. "No one has ever seen God, but the only Son who is in the bosom of the Father, has made him known" (John 1:18). By the aid of the promised Paraclete, the evangelist recalls the word of Jesus from the Synoptic tradition to bring forth all its truth, way and life.

The Canonical Synthesis and *Sola Scriptura*

Acute practitioners of history of religions research openly and in principle disregard canonical boundaries, in that the very selection and assignment of authority as rule of faith to various documents of early Christianity is in this perspective the essence of a retrospective and exclusionary dogmatization of literature for purposes alien to writings in their historical particularity. As an historical artifact, a text is to be known precisely without the artificial harmonizing imposed by canonicity. Certainly, however, this intentional disregard for the survival and preservation of texts as canonical is a boundary-busting maneuver subverting early catholic construction of orthodoxy and heresy. The doctrinal function of the baptismal *regula fidei* as summation of the gospel knowledge of God by which literary candidates were tested for admission to the New Testament canon is thereby exorcised methodologically, even though historically as we saw earlier precisely this proto-creedal crystallization of the gospel functioned as *norma normans*. Scholarly projects as

12. Meyendorff, *Byzantine Theology*, 48.

widely ranging as from the reconstruction of an historical Q document[13] to alleging traces of historical authenticity in the second-century Gospel of Thomas[14] to titillating exposé of self-serving ecclesiastical power grabs at the heart of defining orthodoxy against heresy[15] followed upon this apparently methodological but in fact theologically substantive repudiation of scriptural canonicity, not as a formal list of included literature, but as in Irenaeus, the baptismal rule of faith fleshed out by ruling in literature that linked essentially creation and redemption by depicting realistically the incarnation and the crucifixion of creation's redeemer. Nothing makes clearer than this the alternative between theological exegesis of canonical Scripture and the history of religions methodology. Moreover, as we shall see, theological exegesis is not the mere conservativism of dogmatism; it shows its critical power in disrupting theological tradition for premature closures which quench the Spirit, whose project of doctrine true to the gospel remains unfinished business.

Yet from the origin, doctrinal theology as knowledge of God proceeded onward by means of the Johannine bridge. Effectively, though not yet officially, doctrinal theology now assumes the canonical synthesis of the New Testament literature judged apostolic by the baptismal "rule of faith" together with the Scriptures of Israel as the authoritative human testimony to the word of God. In a situation of being "threatened by a seemingly uncontrolled plethora of theological and exegetical speculation which sapped the strength of the Church in its resistance against the wiles of the 'evil one,'" William R. Farmer explains why the Gospel of John was ruled in.

> The New Testament canon is a martyr's canon which can be traced through Origen, Hippolytus, and Irenaeus to a particular traditional idealization of Christian martyrdom exemplified by Polycarp and Ignatius and reflecting the martyrdoms of Peter and Paul in Rome. In this tradition the letters of Paul have always been united with books which witness to and emphasize the reality of the death as well as the resurrection of Jesus Christ.[16]

13. Oakman, *Political Aims of Jesus.*

14. "As a wisdom teacher, [Jesus] is more like Lao Tzu or the Buddha than he is like a teacher of conventional wisdom." Borg and Wright, *Meaning of Jesus,* 68. Borg's claim is based on the authenticity of traditions in the Gospel of Thomas.

15. Bauer, *Orthodoxy and Heresy in Early Christianity.*

16. Farmer, *Formation of the New Testament Canon*, 42.

Indeed, given John's dramatic portrait of the confrontation between agnostic Pilate and truth-telling Jesus, one might well consider John's gospel as bearing the exemplary theology of the martyr, holding tightly together doctrine and ethos. No one performs the confession of faith in Jesus Christ the Son of God consequently, apart from the vulnerable posture of a witness to a subversive new *persona* breaking into the strong man's house.

As mentioned, the baptismal confession of faith developed into the rule of faith which, expanding into a tacit summary of the emerging canonical story from Genesis to Revelation unified by redemption in Christ, tested literature for inclusion into the Scriptures of the church. It played this role not only because baptism into the death and resurrection of Christ turned for its saving significance on "the reality of the death as well as the resurrection of Jesus Christ," but also because it unified creation and redemption against gnostic dualism by attesting the true humanity of Jesus by his bodily birth from a human mother of the chosen people of God and his cruel death by crucifixion at the hands of Israel's oppressors. Effectively this way of norming the literature of the emerging New Testament canon made the Easter kerygma of the resurrection-vindication of the crucified Jesus the *norma normans* and canonical Scripture as the primal, i.e., prophetic and apostolic confession of faith, *norma normata.* Recognition of the norming function of the baptismal creed as summary of the apocalyptic gospel to perform human renunciation of the kingdom of the devil thus entails recognition that canonical Scripture is authoritative as the primally elaborated confession of faith: *prima Scriptura* (in the Latin nominative), not the misunderstood *sola Scriptura* (a Latin ablative).[17]

This historical-theology reconstruction of the organic emergence of doctrinal theology in primitive Christianity thusly issues in a subtle but important refinement of the (second generation) Reformation's doctrine of *sola scriptura*. It is first of all to be noted and well registered that the Latin expression is in the ablative case, *by* scripture alone, just like the parallels *by* faith alone, *by* grace alone. Only the "Christ alone" is in the nominative case. The sense of this grammar is that Christ is the subject-object of justifying faith who is accessed through Scripture by way of the sanctifying Spirit's mediation of the grace of faith. The interminable morass of conflicting Protestant readings of Scripture, as if

17. Hinlicky, "Prima Scriptura."

apart from knowledge of the gospel key it is self-interpreting, produces unending schism, factions each with their own propaganda, official and de facto. This "paper papalism" comes from treating canonical Scripture as if, like the holy Qu'ran of Islam, it was dictated by direct divine inspiration with a clear and unquestionable sense for all honest readers, with everything equally weighted as equally words of God. This magical view of inspiration is precluded by the present reconstruction. The sanctifying Spirit's inspiration of Scripture is rather to be seen in the prophetic and apostolic testimony to the coming of Christ in the flesh; the Spirit subsequently *selects* (which is what *sanctification* is) this testimony for preservation as witness to the originative event of the gospel word of God. But also precluded by this refinement is the mirror image of this magical morass in the historical reductionism of contemporary biblical studies, ignorant or disdaining of the Easter kerygma confessed in the baptismal *credo* which in historical fact pulled the literature together into the canon of faith and so preserved it historically. Consequently, there is little choice in the history of religions methodology but to reduce the canonical literature into piles of archaeological rubble, each piece with its fragmented meaning unrelated to the next with the result that the authority of canonical Scripture as early Christianity understood it and intended it is effectively blocked. Theological exegesis can and must do otherwise and in good, hermeneutical conscience.

Apocalyptic Baptism in Cyril of Jerusalem's Doctrinal Instruction

To illustrate how early Christianity in fact understood Scripture in its practice of doctrinal theology as normed by the baptismal gospel of incorporation into the death and resurrection of Christ, we revisit the catechetical lectures of the bishop of Jerusalem, Cyril, from the fourth century, expositing the rite of baptism to the candidates.[18] Cyril's account is typical[19] of the developed rite of baptism in early Christianity.

18. Cyril of Jerusalem, "Catechetical Lectures, Lectures 19–21." I have taken the liberty of modernizing the Victorian English of this translation. For a modern English translation see Cyril of Jerusalem, *Works of St. Cyril of Jerusalem*, 2:153–80. What appears in the NPNF as Catechetical Lectures 19–21 are now typically regarded as a separate set of lectures commonly referred to as lectures 1–3 (of five) of "The Mystagogical Lectures." Thanks to Dave Delaney for this update.

19. Whitaker, *Documents of the Baptismal Liturgy*.

Cyril explicated the significance of the ritual of water immersion into the name, i.e., ownership of the Triune God "in order," as he states, "that the baptized may know the effect wrought upon [them] on that evening of [their] baptism . . . know the symbolical meaning of the things which are there performed." The sign is not empty but efficacious; understanding the meaning of the rite is an aspect of its efficaciousness. Catechetical teaching is thus an act of apocalyptic warfare.

The candidates assemble and, facing the West where the sun disappears in darkness, they renounce Satan. This is a declaration of personal independence, as it were, a claim of liberation: "I fear your might no longer; for Christ has overthrown it, having partaken with me of flesh and blood, that through these He might by death destroy death, that I might not be subject to bondage forever. I renounce you . . . I renounce you." Here the doctrine of salvation in Christ typical of patristic Christianity is owned by the candidate in a personal confession of the faith that is believed. Confession of faith delivers the baptized from the tyrannizing work of the devil by the acknowledgment of the work of the triune God, liberating, first of all, from sin, but then also from the devil's "pomp," i.e., the culture and ceremony of the surrounding world: "the madness of theatres and horse-races," the meat-markets associated with idol worship, the incantations and pharmacology of occult healing arts, sorcery and divination. Now turning to the East, the place where the sun rises signifying paradise, the candidates confess the Father, the Son, and the Holy Spirit as the one who is God truly coming now to liberate and reclaim his creation in these very persons about to be baptized. In this act a *public transfer of allegiance* is both signified and put into effect: In the "holy washing of regeneration . . . ," as Cyril tells the baptized, "you have put off the old man and clothed yourself in the garment of salvation, even Jesus Christ."[20] Baptism is Christification.

As the candidates entered the church they removed their tunics, "an image of putting off the old man with his deeds." Naked, "imitating Christ who was stripped naked on the Cross," then, like the dead anointed with oils, the baptized are "led to the holy pool of divine baptism, as Christ was carried from the cross to the sepulcher." Immersed three times as Christ lay in the grave for three days, "at the self-same moment you were both dying and being born; and that water of salvation was at once your grave and your mother." In this full, watery immersion, Cyril sees the sanctifying

20. Cyril of Jerusalem, "Catechetical Lectures, Lectures 19–21."

Spirit's extension of the death of Christ for the baptized into and upon them personally. Here the salvation Christ won for humanity is concretely and individually communicated by the Spirit. Cyril exclaims: "Christ was actually crucified, and actually buried, and truly rose again; and all these things He has freely bestowed upon us, that we, sharing His sufferings by [ritual] imitation, might gain salvation in reality. O surpassing loving-kindness! Christ received nails . . . while on me without pain or toil by the fellowship of His suffering He freely bestows salvation."[21]

The agency of Christ in the baptism is complemented by the agency of the Spirit. More transpires in this than deliverance from eternal death. "Let no one suppose that Baptism is merely the grace of remission of sins, or further, that of adoption." Baptism also means putting on Christ, thus, being endowed with Christ's own Spirit. Baptism thus "ministers to us the gift of the Holy Spirit," just as Christ himself was anointed with the Spirit at his baptism in the River Jordan. This is symbolized by the anointing in oil, the chrism or unction, which follows emergence from the pool of water, "the antitype of that with which Christ was anointed, and this is the Holy Spirit." Now those newly baptized into Christ are equipped for battle. Like "Christ after His Baptism, and the visitation of the Holy Spirit, went forth and vanquished the adversary, so likewise you, after Holy Baptism and the Mystical Chrism, having put on the whole armor of the Holy Spirit, are to stand against the power of the adversary and vanquish it . . . " as ready martyrs boldly to testify before the adversary's persecutors. The self-giving of Christ even to death on a cross brings an end to the expiatory sacrifice of self or others in ritual violence. Symbolically imitated and appropriated in baptism, this mimesis reorders desire from the demonic will to destroy what cannot be possessed to the divine will to redeem what has been lost for righteousness, life and peace.[22] Such formation of the new and theological subject is the indispensable prerequisite to authorship in Christian doctrinal theology.[23]

Here are a number of significant themes, therefore, for our theology of theology: the apocalyptic framing of baptism, baptism as incorporation into Christ crucified and risen, the catechetical nature of doctrinal theology as doctrine for life in the fraught interim between the resurrection of Christ and the believer's resurrection, and the ecclesial location

21. Cyril of Jerusalem, "Catechetical Lectures, Lectures 19–21."

22. Girard, *Violence and the Sacred.*

23. Cyril of Jerusalem, "Catechetical Lectures, Lectures 19–21."

of doctrinal theology. We also note again the right understanding of the docetist error: affirming of the deity in the person of the Son "having partaken with me of flesh and blood, that through these He might by death destroy death, that I might not be subject to bondage forever." Docetism is not about a psychologically implausible Jesus but about the divine *power* of compassion *to be weak and humble in solidarity* with captivated humanity, not of course to remain so, but to gain hold thereby of the strong man's prisoners to deliver them. We shall find these themes retrieved and renewed not only in Luther's catechisms but particularly in his great doctrinal treatise on the captivity of human choice and liberation by the Spirit to which we turn next in this chapter.

Luther's attempt to break out of the anthropological optimism of late medieval nominalism was no small undertaking. The *facere quod in se* semi-Pelagianism of "God helps those who help themselves" was reinforced by a hermeneutic which treated authoritative texts of the past as if making straightforward but seemingly contradictory propositions and so in need of logical reconciliation. If such is the academic method of theology, the actual sense of Scripture on matters of sin and grace cannot but be obscured by the ready citation of authoritative propositions to the contrary. Just this procedure stands behind the skepticism of Erasmus concerning the apparent contradiction between free will and predestination: he could cite scriptural texts apparently on both sides of this issue, allowing him to throw up his hands in professed agnosticism. The breakout from skeptical paralysis came from Luther's rediscovery and retrieval of apocalyptic theology by means of the literary tools of Renaissance humanism. But complications arose from the need to make his fresh formulation of theological anthropology intelligible in the familiar concepts and terminology of his day, e.g., Luther's notorious utilization of the metaphysical sounding "necessity of immutability" to conceive divine fidelity to the promise of the redemption and fulfillment of the beleaguered creation. Moreover, as mentioned previously, the modern reception history of Luther's most significant doctrinal treatise has been biased by the towering figure of the European Enlightenment, Immanuel Kant, who retrieved both Erasmian doctrinal agnosticism and positively commended a practical theology of moral merit.

A summation thus far in this chapter and reminder: it is the Gospel of John which sends us now to Luther's controversial brief for confident doctrinal assertion in timely confession of the originative gospel of the resurrection of the crucified Jesus revealing him the incarnate Son of

God. "Very truly I tell you, everyone who commits sin is a slave to sin. The slave does not have a permanent place in the household; the Son has a place there forever. So, if the Son makes you free, you will be free indeed" (John 8:34–36). In short, "the bondage of the will" is about the apocalypse of the glorious liberty of the children of God.

New Readings of Luther's *De Servo Arbitrio*

We began in this book by citing Luther's claim against the skepticism of Erasmus about "making assertions." The citation came from the writing of Luther that he regarded, alongside of his catechisms, as his best contribution to theology and of abiding value. One could randomly open to almost any page and do a comparison of references to "the Holy Spirit" and to "the bondage of the will." In such a poll, the Holy Spirit will easily win; given this predominance, the treatise might better have been titled, *de Spiritu sancti*. At the same time, the treatise is among the most problematic in Luther's literary legacy for the difficulty in understanding his meaning. This is a root difficulty of a "theology of theology," such as in the present endeavor, in that statements about the epistemic nature and purpose of doctrinal theology are not justified universally upon a neutral foundation but inevitably presuppose material doctrinal commitments. So, it can seem that such work argues in an epistemological circle, presupposing exactly what must be demonstrated. How can Luther make assertions when the validity of assertion, especially in matters divine, is itself what is at issue?

Epistemological circles can be vicious when the purpose is to found a knowledge regime, but they can also be virtuous when the purpose is to specify *epistemic access* to a particular domain. It depends upon purpose. If for example a court theologian would say to a medieval Jew hauled before the Inquisition, "Can you not see the clear testimonies to Jesus Christ and his cross in the Old Testament?" The circle would be vicious because for the Jew the Hebrew Bible, the Tanakh, is not the canonical Christian "Old Testament." The Christian reading of the Hebrew Bible is question-begging for a Jew in that the construction "Old Testament" sets the terms for a meaningful yay or nay to the asserted testimonies to the Messiahship of Jesus. But the defenseless Jew does not share this construction (if any did, they would be Christians). It is the inquisitors here who are arguing in a circle. (The medieval Luther, to be sure, commits exactly the same hermeneutical blunder in demanding the civil authorities punish recalcitrant Jews.) On the other hand, if a theologian argues with another Christian theologian that she is neglecting the testimony of the Old Testament regarding expiation in her case for an Abelardian-exemplarist Christology, the circle is virtuous because her standing as a Christian theologian entails heeding the witness of the Old Testament as Christian canon for providing the very terms in which a case for or against expiation might be judged. Christian theology always begins within such a virtuous circle *in media res*. Bearing this in mind, we now investigate Luther's treatise in order to further orientation on the plane of anthropology in the reconstruction of doctrinal theology.

The most comprehensive historical account of Luther's text available in English is by Robert Kolb.[24] Kolb avoids translating into English the title *de servo arbitrio* as "bondage of the will," as has been customary, and instead translates "bound choice." This is decisive because for Luther the will to sin is not forced or under duress, but one sins happily in innocent self-assurance, *willingly* and in that sense freely. The point in Luther's reading of biblical narrative is rather that after the exile from Paradise, all the subsequent choices of Adam's posterity are bound to sinfulness, having lost in perpetuity the paradisical possibility of free and willing obedience to the good command of God for life, not death. In this original loss of true choice, Kolb agrees with Robert Jenson[25] that when Luther is talking about human will as *voluntas*, willingness, he means the natural freedom to desire the good and to decline what is repugnant relative to the goods and evils that humans encounter in the world. Therefore, Luther can argue that true human freedom of *voluntas* is the freedom of beloved children of God willingly to do the will of their Father in heaven. The notion of freedom of desire here operative goes back to Augustine, who contrasted such free, for relationally *filial* willingness with *servile* will, grudgingly doing another's will for something undesirable under duress of coercion. In the treatise Luther also considers freedom of choice and freedom of action, although he confuses himself and readers by interchanging these discrete senses of the equivocal notion of freedom of the will. Luther treats both freedom of action and freedom of choice apocalyptically as captive in the kingdom of the devil. Notably, in all three of these distinct senses of the will and

24. Kolb, *Bound Choice, Election, and Wittenberg Theological Method.*

25. Jenson, "Ontology of Freedom in the *De Servo Arbitrio* of Luther."

its freedom (or bondage), the question is about the relation to God, or rather the Creator's relation to the will of the human creature.

The heart of the book is Kolb's interpretation of "the necessity of immutability," Luther's claim that "all things happen by necessity." This formulation was the source of much controversy during Luther's lifetime and on through the Formula of Concord. Kolb points to a passage in Luther's Genesis commentary more than ten years later in which Luther seems to express regret for his use of the philosophical terminology of "necessity" as too harsh for his intended meaning. In the same passage Luther clarifies that what he wants to affirm is that God is immutably faithful to his promises. This constitutes an important differentiation. God's will is free, not bound by any necessity of "nature," but itself sovereign and, at the same time and as such, it is freely *decided* to create, redeem and fulfill the creation by the missions of the Son and Spirit. This eternal counsel of the triune God initiates, sustains and brings the creation to its consummation in the resurrection of the dead and the life everlasting. By "necessity of immutability," Luther is not talking about the iron cage of the causal nexus but the supervening end of God to redeem and fulfill the creature. Illusions of free will are the anthropological pivot, however, upon which propaganda turns, the flattery which seduces consumers into manipulated choices for controlled behaviors. Conversely, the more one knows how manipulated human beings are by forces beyond them, the freer they become until they are freed indeed. Those seized by the sanctifying Spirit to become "slaves" of Christ the liberating Lord have in him a *freed* will to love as they have been loved as newborn children of God.

The strength of the book is Kolb's devotion to the *Wirkungsgeschichte* (history of reception) of Luther's doctrine in subsequent generations which illuminates much of the confusion over Luther's volcanic theology, compounded by his penchant for rhetorical overkill and resort to the inherited metaphysical terminology such as "the necessity of immutability" to express his meaning. Kolb notes Luther's affirmation that "God is not responsible for evil," even if this affirmation seems to be betrayed by Luther's "necessity of immutability," taken metaphysically. There can be no question, however, that at the conclusion of the book Luther takes up the question of theodicy which haunts the entire debate with Erasmus.[26] Thomas Reinhuber, in an excellent exposition of Luther's appropriation of the doctrine of the three lights of nature, grace, and glory at the end

26. Reinhuber, *Kämpfender Glaube*.

of the treatise, demonstrates how Luther indeed engages the question of theodicy in order to defer answer to God's own act in the eschaton, visible in the light of glory. Faith in the interim believes that God is righteous even *sub contrario*, i.e., when God appears to be evil, notably at Golgotha. As we shall see, Ruokanen sees that the chief motivation of Erasmus was to relieve God of responsibility for sin by giving creatures enough free will to take the blame. It is certainly true that Luther excoriates this kind of philosophical theodicy, the so-called "free will defense" of God's goodness in creation ruined only by the culpable sin of creatures of "free will." But it is not true that Luther evades the force of the question about the righteousness of God and indeed concludes the treatise with an eschatological affirmation about it.

Extending Kolb's analysis, Andrea Vestrucci[27] has recently published an exceedingly rich, albeit in places equally demanding, treatment of Luther's text in the light of contemporary philosophical logic to contest a problematic history of interpretation which has read Luther's theology, against his intention, as philosophy. Hence, he registers significant differentiations from modern subjectivism, transcendentalism, ontology and dialectics. That is the sense of the title, *Theology as Freedom*, inasmuch as theology's utterly unphilosophical dependence on divine apocalypse is also in this world a daring declaration of intellectual independence, a stance of defiant freedom vis-à-vis all would-be epistemological tribunals with their propagandistic aspiration to totality. The difficulty, however, is that this freedom of theology must account for itself in the extant vocabulary of philosophy in order to make itself clear to those outside the theological circle, not to mention to others within the theological circle!

Vestrucci recognizes that the concept of the hidden God in Luther's text has been a stumbling block in its reception especially in the twentieth century, beginning with Karl Barth and continuing in Robert Jenson. These theologians feared that the distinction undermined the certainty of faith in the *Deus revelatus pro nobis* if at any moment the God hidden in absolute arbitrary freedom (*Deus exlex*) could emerge to rescind the revealed God and thus breach fidelity to its promises. Luther, historically, could not have thought this, however, since his entire argument against the skeptical Erasmus was on behalf of the "immutable" certainty of faith in the revealed God. Either then, Luther contradicts himself by misunderstanding the import of his teaching of a hidden

27. Vestrucci, *Theology as Freedom*.

God or, worst of all, we have an unbaptized remnant of nominalism's absolute and arbitrary deity encroaching here.

For present purposes, the most important chapter in Vestrucci's book is the one on Luther and Kant which includes a subsection titled, "Kant is not a theologian" followed by one titled, "Theology and philosophy conceive the *Sollen* differently." For Luther, "ought" does *not* imply "can" as is the case in the latter-day Erasmus, Immanuel Kant. Rather, the divine "ought" in the mouth of the sanctifying Spirit demanding the lost paradisical choice for wholehearted love of God above all and all creatures in and under God reveals instead human impotence and bondage to inordinate self-love as sinfulness. The final part of Vestrucci's book is a reflection on theological subjectivity as freedom, "life as a celebration of divine grace," which includes the most sophisticated dissection of the twentieth-century existentialist misunderstanding and misappropriation of Luther yet to appear: "The concept of existential choice makes no sense theologically, because this concept presupposes that existence is its own 'revelation.'"[28] "In sum, theologically, existence has sense as what is no longer meaningful in itself, given that any self-formulation of meaning is already overcome by divine revelation. Theological reflection upon existence coincides with the reflection upon this overcoming."[29] This overcoming declares and puts into effect the divine claim in election to faith: it is not *who* you are, but *whose* you are that matters. Decision theology about the self-determination of carnal identity is undone by the "immutable" decision of the Father to redeem and fulfill the creature by the missions of the Son and the Spirit. The gospel proclaiming this divine decision by the resurrection of the crucified Jesus is not a solution to the existentialist experience of meaninglessness and heroic resolve creatively to carry-on nevertheless[30]—the gospel provides and communicates the divine end of the creation and in so doing divides the city of God from the earthly city, thusly making history on the earth.

As noted, the fallacy of equivocation haunts understanding of "*the bondage of the will*" as Luther's Latin has been mistranslated into English. To review and reiterate: several distinct usages may be found in Luther's text and should be held in mind to avoid confusion: freedom of desire (*voluntas*) according to which one does willingly whatever one does; freedom of choice (*arbitrium*) between varying paths to the same

28. Vestrucci, *Theology as Freedom*, 247.

29. Vestrucci, *Theology as Freedom*, 248.

30. Helmer, *How Luther Became the Reformer*.

satisfaction of desire; and freedom of action (*vis*) according to which one has the power to enact a choice freely willed. All three senses of "will" are present in Luther's text, but Luther's central contention in these usages is for a genuinely theological anthropology, i.e., *of creature in relation to creator*. In Miikka Ruokanen's words:

> According to Luther, humans never had the capacity of absolutely free choice: in the state of integrity, the human being's *arbitrium* was a "servant" of God, but after the fall it became the "slave" of sin. For Luther, then, in relation to "things above oneself" the true freedom of humanity equals humble and obedient servanthood under the creator by loving the creator above everything else, whereas after the fall, seduced by Satan by his lie of absolute freedom as independence from the creator, humanity fell under the imprisonment of sin and evil.[31]

For Luther, it is an analytical truth: one wills willingly what one desires. In this sense free will is not at whim free to desire just anything but is rather bound to what one in fact willingly desires as such objects of desire or aversion are presented as possibilities actually beckoning from beyond the finite and embodied self. This sense of *voluntas* is crucial for Luther's theological anthropology for which the *fides ex corde* which justifies *must* be freely and joyfully willed, never coerced, upon hearing of God's gracious election in Christ. In this sense, Luther agrees with his patristic mentor Augustine: "God who created us without our will does not will to redeem us apart from our willing." However, after the exile from paradise the original human choice to freely will the will of God and do so in filial fear, love and trust has been lost; all choices are henceforth bound to the diminished alternatives attending the state of exile, also the highest religious and moral choices therein. Finally, even if hypothetically one could willingly will the will of God, the power to do so is lacking because that power is none less and none other than the departed Spirit of God. Conversely, ecstatic love for God, in which the creature's rectification ultimately consists, is not within its own power. Rather, God must make himself lovable to the alienated creature, *incurvatus in se*, by the rectifying event of divine self-giving in Christ, hence revealing "the Father's heart." Justifying faith *ex corde* is thus a sovereign

31. Ruokanen, *Trinitarian Grace in Martin Luther's* The Bondage of the Will, 35, cf. 89. See Paul R. Hinlicky, Review of Miika Ruokanen, *Trinitarian Grace in Martin Luther's The Bondage of the Will* (Oxford: Oxford University Press, 2021) in *Modern Theology* 38/1 (January 2023) from which the following is adapted.

work and gift of the Spirit who sheds this love of God abroad in human hearts even as by the Spirit's enabling the heart beholds and desires the Lamb of God who takes away the sin of the world.

Ruokanen's study is long overdue. It should serve to reorient radically the reception of Luther's most "apocalyptic" and at the same time most "systematic" theological work. It is long overdue because the framework of thought inherited from the High Enlightenment philosophy of Kant has biased conceptualization of the Luther text in favor of Erasmus's case for human freedom of choice and a corresponding calculus of moral merit in relation to the divine. Within this Kantian framework, Luther's indisputably Augustinian doctrines of the captivation of desire by contradivine powers fatally compromising postlapsarian human choice have become all but invisible to modern scholarly interpretation. And with this invisibility Luther's vigorous contention for the person and work of the Holy Spirit as the powerful saving *persona* of God given to will the will of God and do it has also disappeared—*not* excepting in twentieth-century kerygmatic theologies, as Ruokanen pointedly argues. The Holy Spirit is not a pious gloss on performative utterance.

Luther's robust account of the Holy Spirit in this text becomes intelligible, however, in the alternative framework of a Trinitarian theology according to which the Word alone is never alone but always accompanied by the sanctifying Spirit and vice versa. The incisive critique of modern German Luther scholarship which Ruokanen executes along these lines, however, is accompanied by an equally probing revision of the Finnish Luther scholarship (in which school he stands) for the misleading deployment of metaphysical concepts like "ontic-real" to articulate the saving presence and efficacy of the Spirit-anointed Incarnate Word. "Luther's *The Bondage of the Will* has very often been treated as a book concerned mainly with the classical problems of the freedom of the will and the question of divine predestination."[32] Indeed, this was already how in the immediate aftermath Ulrich Zwingli's treatise on divine providence[33] cast the matter and in the process repudiated Luther's critical distinction—so Ruokanen—in the argument against Erasmus between the "things above us" and the "things below us." For Luther the human powers at issue refer strictly to the human relationship to its Creator where the "necessity of immutability," i.e., God's unchanging fidelity to

32. Ruokanen, *Trinitarian Grace in Martin Luther's* The Bondage of the Will, 12.

33. Jackson, *Latin Works of Huldreich Zwingli.*

his creative and redemptive purpose prevails. In turn, Luther affirms human powers in relation to creation where mutability, i.e., contingency is admitted. Zwingli, whose treatise originated in sermons delivered to Philip of Hesse following the Luther-Erasmus exchange, found Luther's distinction metaphysically untenable since the entire nexus of secondary causes necessarily enacts the immutable will of the sole omnipotent causality, the First Cause, sovereign almighty deity.[34] Unlike Luther, Zwingli drew positively and affirmatively the dire doctrine of double predestination from such metaphysical *Alleinwirkamseit Gottes*, the *sole* causality which the deity *is*.

In distinction, Luther affirmed the *Alleswirkamseit Gottes*, a causality which permits no creature to stand idle, the *universal* creativity of God moving in all that is not God. Yet Luther's concern in the treatise is not philosophical metaphysics but apocalyptic theology. "The transcendence of human existence, a person's relation to God's Spirit or to the opposing spiritual power—understood in terms of realistic biblical language—has a decisive role."[35] What hermeneutical difference does this claim make? "Here the German existentialist interpretations of Luther echo the rationalism of Erasmus . . . . Not recognizing the compelling captivity of the human *arbitrium* by a superhuman power drops the question of conversion and of the reception of grace onto the level of theological anthropology. This is what happened to Erasmus, and this is what happens in the modern liberal interpretation of Luther. For Erasmus, the drama of sin and salvation takes place in the sphere of human life, in anthropological reality, whereas for Luther, this is a drama of the transcendental powers which are beyond human comprehension and intervention"[36]—precisely as in apocalyptic theology's warfare of the embattled Lord Jesus against "the spiritual powers of wickedness in high places."

Ruokanen rightly sees with Robert Kolb that the dilemma of "God's responsibility for evil" is the root problem in the debate between Erasmus and Luther. "Following the commonplace teachings of the *via moderna*," Erasmus defended a "minimal freedom of the human decision in matters of salvation with the intention of establishing an image of a 'just God.'"[37] Luther's hyperbolic counter-attack on the moralistic and rationalistic theodicy of the so-called free will defense of God's permission of evil

34. Hinlicky, *Luther and the Beloved Community*, 159–69.

35. Ruokanen, *Trinitarian Grace in Martin Luther's* The Bondage of the Will, 12.

36. Ruokanen, *Trinitarian Grace in Martin Luther's* The Bondage of the Will, 59.

37. Ruokanen, *Trinitarian Grace in Martin Luther's* The Bondage of the Will, 190.

readily gives rise to the impression that he teaches in counterpoint a *Deus exlex*. Drawing that conclusion (which would put Luther into the *Alleinwirkamseit Gottes* camp of his opponent Zwingli), however, misses the point to which Luther is arguing. That point is what I have (elsewhere in a critical discussion of Leibniz) called the "theodicy of faith"[38] in sharp distinction from any self-bootstrapping philosophical theodicy constructing a deity who plays fair by human rules. "According to Luther, the human beings must be content with the fact that the final solution to the problem of God's justice is an eschatological one"[39] The only solution to the problem of evil, materially as well as intellectually, is God's victory for us over it, as we concluded in the previous chapter. By contrast with the free will defense of God's permission of evil, "Luther follows Augustine who openly admits that there is no solution to the very origin of evil will,"[40] although there is indeed an illuminating account of the serpent's murderous lie inciting envy in the seductive *sicut Deus eritis*. Understood along the lines of Erasmus, then, indeed "the *classical* problem of theodicy finds no solution in Luther's *The Bondage of the Will*."[41]

But what Luther does affirm in the dramatic conclusion of his treatise is that to believe God when he appears to be unrighteous is the essence of faith—as Jesus believed at Gethsemane. With the prophet Habakkuk, as taken up by the apostle Paul, this is Luther's theodicy *of faith* which justifies God in his judgment by trusting in his righteousness presently concealed under the opposite, yet fully to be revealed. This is not blind faith, a leap in the dark. The revelation of God's righteousness in the light of glory can be trusted on account of the astonishing revelation of the righteousness of God in the light of Easter morning's disruptive grace, giving to the dying and sinful not their due but precisely what is not deserved and—astonishingly!—thanks to the human Jesus who believed against appearances in consenting to drink the cup once and for all of us.

So understood, Luther's eschatological theodicy sheds light on the apparently dualistic teaching of the *Deus absconditus* in Luther's treatise which greatly troubled Karl Barth and his American disciple Robert Jenson. Rhetorically, the most extreme statement in Luther's text "sets against each other *Deus revelatus*, Jesus lamenting over the hardness of his

38. Hinlicky, *Paths Not Taken*.

39. Ruokanen, *Trinitarian Grace in Martin Luther's* The Bondage of the Will, 79.

40. Ruokanen, *Trinitarian Grace in Martin Luther's* The Bondage of the Will, 79.

41. Ruokanen, *Trinitarian Grace in Martin Luther's* The Bondage of the Will, 79, emphasis added.

people, and *Deus absconditus*, his Father not granting them conversion by the power of the Spirit."[42] But Luther's doctrine is not, as they feared, the affirmation of a whimsical and unprincipled deity, whose might makes right, hovering in the background and always threatening to override the compassion of the revealed God electing the rejected to salvation. Allowing for rhetorical excesses, recognition of the hidden God in fact expresses the proper fear of the revealed God, balancing the filial love and trust elicited by the light of grace with sober awareness that the light of glory has not yet dawned. The apocalyptic battle between God and Satan over captive humanity still rages, a battle in which the believer is not immunized by a magically causal grace so irresistible that it would effectively force faith upon the unwilling. But rather, ever aided by the sanctifying Spirit's free favor, faith is renewed through each believer's lived tribulation in the Gethsemane of the soul, conforming the self to Christ. *Anfechtung*, the necessarily accompanying perception of God still hidden in the fog and friction of apocalyptic war inaugurated by his gracious self-revelation in the Christ event rightly evokes the fear of God as a needed check against human-all-too-human cheapening of grace into a human religious trophy already securing heaven on earth in possessing the mere idea of a loving God, as the supreme religion, to boot, of the Christians. So, Dietrich Bonhoeffer complained. Grace without repentance in the proper fear of God is grace cheapened beyond recognition. Rather, it is as Bultman rightly stressed always "the grace of the judge."

The concept of the hidden God articulates theologically this requirement "only to fear and adore" God.[43] Corresponding to this fear of God is the salutary despair of self in the lifelong repentance of the Spirit-led life, lest the Spirit's assurance of saving faith becomes new grounds for religious boasting. This fear of God strikes home by "facing even the horrible possibility that he/she is left outside God's saving grace and shall face eternal separation from God's goodness . . . " Yet, so Ruokanen argues, none but the one grasped by the sanctifying Spirit worries about the holy danger of exclusion! In other words, "the life that thinks about damnation is *already* the object of salvation."[44]Any person who has thus become totally "desperate about him/herself" is, paradoxically, "already

42. Ruokanen, *Trinitarian Grace in Martin Luther's* The Bondage of the Will, 123.

43. Ruokanen, *Trinitarian Grace in Martin Luther's* The Bondage of the Will, 120–21.

44. Ruokanen, *Trinitarian Grace in Martin Luther's* The Bondage of the Will, 129.

in the state of grace."[45] Of course, this Romans 7 counsel must be pastorally communicated to those in the grip of *Anfechtung* feeling forsaken by God. Here the hidden God "is a way of speaking about the sovereign divine mercy and about the human being's assurance of salvation *which is not within his/her own control.* Paradoxically, both of the concepts of God, the revealed and the hidden God, serve the same end of the assurance of salvation"[46] i.e., as salvation which is *ours ever as gift to be trusted but never as a merited possession* under our command and control.

What, then, is the genuine alternative to the fear and adoration of the hidden God arising *with* trust in and love for the revealed God? For Luther it would be blasphemy or atheism. That would represent falling back into an apprehension of God solely in the light of (fallen) nature as alienated from its divine purpose as creation. That the revealed God retains this aura of mysterious hiddenness beyond human fathoming blocks excessive theological conceptualization; with Andrea Vestrucci, Ruokanen maintains that there remains "a gap between divine revelation and inferred concepts." There is accordingly no rule for God's predestination enacted in history because there is no formal distinction between election and rejection which are simply our subjective takes on the revelatory reality of God's love for enemies as pure immutable grace.[47] Thus, God's hidden will "cannot be scrutinized, it can only be respected and worshiped in humility."[48] Optimistic attempts to close the gap between God hidden and revealed inevitably crash against the hard rock of eschatological transcendence which Luther's distinction protects.

> Erasmus requires transparent and fair rules in God's dealing with humanity; Luther denies all that. Here human logic does not avail and there is no eternal law above God's will ruling his decisions. This is exactly what makes him God and not just a projection of the human imagination.[49]

What remains is Spirit-given trust in God's revealed will in Christ to redeem and fulfill the creation.

45. Ruokanen, *Trinitarian Grace in Martin Luther's* The Bondage of the Will, 128.

46. Ruokanen, *Trinitarian Grace in Martin Luther's* The Bondage of the Will, 130, emphasis added.

47. Ruokanen, *Trinitarian Grace in Martin Luther's* The Bondage of the Will, 119.

48. Ruokanen, *Trinitarian Grace in Martin Luther's* The Bondage of the Will, 120.

49. Ruokanen, *Trinitarian Grace in Martin Luther's* The Bondage of the Will, 123.

The *locus classicus* in Scripture debated between Luther and Erasmus is the motif of the hardening of the heart of the wicked slave master, the Pharaoh of Egypt. "In those to whom God grants his Spirit a conversion takes place; those who lack the Spirit become irritated and angry at God . . . permitting his ungodly corrupt nature under the rule of Satan to catch fire, flare up, rage, and run riot with a kind of contemptuous self-confidence."[50] Scripture gives no explanation of this withholding of the Spirit but Luther acknowledges that "in his foreknowledge and omnipotence, God may use the immutable bad will for his good purposes. This kind of instrumental use of evil is part of God's providential care of his creation."[51] Human sympathy for the hapless slave master driven to self-destruction should not, for Luther, deflect attention from the Lord who in fidelity to his own sovereign, creative, and redemptive purpose take sides with Pharaoh's victims and acts in history to bring about the end of his slaveholding by driving his evil to the extremity of self-destruction.

> Luther's concept of the necessity of immutability does not include a doctrine of predestination of individuals, not to speak of a concept of double predestination. He avoids using the term . . . . Luther connects the idea predestination . . . with his defense of the sovereignty of God's grace in his eternal plan of salvation . . . [52]

The "immutable" fidelity of the God of love to his own purpose for his creation entails the bad fact that his love must be and effectively manifest against what is against love.

Today as we navigate the postmodern breakdown of the certitudes of the European Enlightenment which cast into outer darkness Luther's assertion of the captivity of human choice to the malice of envy, propagandized in the lie of the devil that we can be like God (as we crookedly imagine God to be), it is striking to observe how in his wartime radio broadcasts to the resistance within Nazi Germany, Paul Tillich employed exactly Luther's biblical argument, namely, that the Lord of the Exodus was now driving the Nazi regime to catastrophic self-destruction from which ruins alone could a new birth of freedom come about.[53] Just as striking was Martin Luther King Jr.'s question whether the rich young

50. Ruokanen, *Trinitarian Grace in Martin Luther's* The Bondage of the Will, 77.

51. Ruokanen, *Trinitarian Grace in Martin Luther's* The Bondage of the Will, 77.

52. Ruokanen, *Trinitarian Grace in Martin Luther's* The Bondage of the Will, 82.

53. Tillich, *Against the Third Reich.*

ruler who went away sad from his encounter with Jesus stands for the contemporary West now in trial and under testing.[54] In an epoch in which theological sentimentalism prevails, wanting only an emotionally sympathetic *idea* of deity on which to model human behavior, but in the process unwittingly accommodating *real* structures of malice and injustice, Ruokanen's pathbreaking exposition of a classic text of doctrinal theology merits wide reading and discussion.

But under two conditions! First, methodologically, clarity, clarity, clarity! Fuzzy language, equivocation, the fallacy of treating innovative metaphor delivering reference to something in the world instead as ethereal, merely evocative similitude, contempt for logic and systemic coherence—all this demand for rigor for the sake of meaningful communication of the gospel of the controversial Jesus, requires the intellectual virtues at work in the scholarly hermeneutics of doctrinal theology. Second, substantively, as much as Luther's "assertion" concerns the captivity of human choice, just as much and more so does it concern the liberating gift and human experience of the sanctifying Spirit. And this doctrinal need to articulate the person and work of the Spirit may be developed to meet Simeon Zahl's critique of the cultural linguistic model for inordinate, subtly rationalistic reliance on the Christian language game not merely to inform but to capture human desire. Indeed, Zahl himself has begun this critique by arguing for a "low anthropology" of natural limits (i.e., the captivated human will just described from Luther) over against social construction (supposing an infinitely malleable human nature easily remade by ideas embraced with willpower) in his *The Holy Spirit and Christian Experience*.[55] In other words, neither performative language nor social construction substitute for knowledge and proclamation of the sanctifying Spirit in understanding, indeed, in authoring Christian experience.

The *Experience* of the Sanctifying Spirit

"It is a core assumption of this book," Zahl writes, "that for human beings there is no such thing as experience of fear or joy or delight apart from the physical body and brain, embedded in the material world"[56]

54. Motivation Ark, "One of the Greatest Speeches Ever."

55. Zahl, *Holy Spirit and Christian Experience*. See Hinlicky, "The Experience of Incongruous Grace," Review Essay on Simeon Zahl, The Holy Spirit and Christian Experience, *Anglican Theological Review* (2022) 1-13, from which the following is adapted.

56. Zahl, *Holy Spirit and Christian Experience*, 77.

and accordingly that there is no experience of God apart from such physical events. This anthropological affirmation of corporeal materiality is actually far more than an "assumption," as Zahl assembles compelling arguments drawn from contemporary psychological science in support of a unitary theological anthropology harkening back to Augustine's doctrine of desire as the motive force and unitive form of human behavior. But long-standing habituation in anthropological mind-body dualism divides desire into two; continued in modern Idealism and on to its contemporary permutation in social constructivism, this wholly immanent antagonism between lower animal desire and higher intellectual desire dies hard. Zahl deploys Manuel Vasquez's notion of "somatophobia" against the prevalence of social constructivism in contemporary theology and religious studies:

> We cannot reduce to human texts the materiality of our bodies in the world in which and through which we live . . . Nature . . . is not opposed to culture . . . as a mere passive or empty surface upon which we inscribe our meanings. Nor is nature a mere artifice of reiterated, reified discourses. These attitudes betray a Cartesian dualism and the underlying anxiety to establish human exceptionalism . . . [57]

But with Bonhoeffer, we have affirmed "the natural" as that which in the fallen creation remains open to the Lordship of Christ, awaiting conformation in the redemption of our bodies. The redemption of our bodies is indeed microcosm of the macrocosmic apocalyptic hope of cosmic redemption.

The salience of this material dogmatic concern for Zahl is that it questions the "social and linguistic constructivism undergirding the cultural-linguistic model of religion that we see theorized in Lindbeck"; his model has rightly been "heavily criticized in recent years" for underestimating the power of non-discursive factors in shaping experience, thus placing a weight on language and discursive practices that they cannot bear. Constructivism is significantly limited in its "ability to make sense of what human beings actually feel and do—to explain what 'makes bodies move.'"[58] Emergent Affect Theory consequently "targets post-enlightenment convictions of the autonomy of the atomized rational subject,

57. Zahl, *Holy Spirit and Christian Experience*, 147. From the Roman Catholic perspective building upon John Paul II's theology of the body, see O. Carter Snead, *What It Means to Be Human: The Case for the Body in Public Bioethics* (Cambridge MA & London: Harvard University Press, 2020).

58. Zahl, *Christian Experience*, 149.

pointing to the phenomenology of emotion to expose the 'myth of our own sovereignty over our emotions'" as emotions register, often subconsciously, the body's physical response to environmental stimuli. Reminiscent here is the way in which the Masters of Suspicion undermined the Tribunal of Reason by unveiling the unconscious forces moving human minds through unacknowledged emotions, Affect Theory pulls "humans out of the domain of the angelic—which means out of the domain of self-determination through sovereign reason—and into the bodily, the material and the animal."[59] It is re-naturalizing.[60]

Human beings, of course, are the animals which have language by means of which they reason and communicate; any unitive theological anthropology must accordingly account for this universal web of language. Reminiscent of Hamann's critique of Kant, Zahl is professedly not rejecting rational discourse nor the primal power of language to name (or misname) but rather relativizing it: "language and reason are just two dimensions in the play of many powerful forces, and they acquire power primarily in so far as they become attached to affects." The salience of these observations for reconstruction in theology is that they retrieve the Reformation suspicion that abstract reason pretending sovereignty can be in the thrall of powers of which it is unconscious, or worse, it can half-consciously betray itself to the highest bidder; moreover, that language can be weaponized by cunning rationality to bear false witness in propaganda manipulatively to capture desire. Zahl cites Alastair McFadyen to this effect: "The traditional doctrine of Original Sin appears to run counter to the most fundamental affirmations of the modern turn to the subject: that the individual is autonomous, and that autonomy is the sole basis for establishing responsibility and guilt."[61] Such modern anthropological assumptions are

> baffled by pathological situations that cannot be reduced to the deliberate willing of free moral agents: economic, social and institutional forces that apply massive pressure on individual willing; biological predispositions and physiological habituations; the shaping effects of the cultures and environments in which we are raised as children; and so on.[62]

59. Zahl, *Christian Experience,* citing Donovan O. Schafer, 150.
60. Sharpe, *Spinoza and the Politics of Renaturalization.*
61. Zahl, *Christian Experience*, 158.
62. Zahl, *Christian Experience*, 160.

But equally, the turn to the subject as would-be "captain of its own ship, master of its own destiny" has reduced the Christian doctrine of human sinfulness to the moralistic assessment of visible, calculable and culpable transgression, predicated upon the inflated view of the moral responsibility of an autonomous agent. Inevitably this focuses sin solely upon manifest transgressions by competent agents for the purpose of establishing legal culpability *coram hominibus* in contrast to the Reformers following Pauline apocalyptic for whom sin is an uncanny *power* both experienced and known, *sensus peccati*[63] when brought before scrutiny of the God of the prophets who knows and judges the heart to expose the complicity of consent to prevailing evils. As mentioned at the conclusion of the previous chapter, such critical observations of modernity direct theological attention to the domain of culture which is the social place and vocational task in every generation of preparing the next for adult responsibility—or not.

Under the regime of the modern self of sovereign agency the discursive labeling of the experience of bondage to polluting forces is different than the New Testament representations of demonic possession, of course, but the *sensus* is the same: "we still encounter the world as a place full of large-scale injustice and structural evil, and we still long for healing and repair on societal as well as individual levels. And we still experience 'death anxiety,' when we have not distracted ourselves too much to think about it."[64] The alternative to ethical idealism in theology is not, of course, a plunge into its binary opposite in classical Epicureanism but, as mentioned, a third way: the common body of humanity on the earth is neither essentially plastic nor is it wholly static but manifests a "basic affective continuity in the experiences of bodies across contexts and eras, including between the New Testament and the present." Thus, the Christian doctrine of sin "can help us to recognize, understand, interpret, reconfigure, and make use of affects that bodies are already experiencing, rather than to try to generate a feeling of plight from scratch where it does not already exist . . . ,"[65] as happened in modern revivalism's fire and brimstone preaching. As previously mentioned, the *spiritual* use of the law, i.e., the law *of God* in the hands of the sanctifying *Spirit* at work for *divine* purposes (John 16:8)—precisely *not* the law in the hands of sinners for purposes of self-justification and scapegoating—works knowledge of

63. Zahl, *Christian Experience*, 160.

64. Zahl, *Christian Experience*, 162.

65. Zahl, *Christian Experience*, 163.

a *common* bondage to sinfulness in order to break down the walls of the strong man's house for his prisoners' reconciliation and liberation. Zahl thusly aims with this theological anthropology

> to retain the advantages of traditional Protestant disjunctive theologies of grace, which emphasize the work of the Spirit over and against the resistance of the sinful human agent and which seek to engage honestly and compassionately with the problem of moral non-transformation in Christians, while maintaining a robust connection between the saving work of the Spirit and embodied experience, thus avoiding the problems sometimes associated with "extrinsicist" models of grace.[66]

A better understanding of "disjuntive" participation "is that the work of the Spirit takes place in and through bodies embedded in the world"[67] the effects of which should be in principle discernible, i.e., amenable to practical recognizability, in transformed human affect, however inchoate. Zahl's brief is for old-fashioned pastoral care of souls; it is, moreover, resolutely Trinitarian, as we shall see, and thus anti-docetic. Consequently, there are divine-human relationships or putative participations which are *contested* and such holy *militancy* is an aspect of Christian *salvation* as the time-and-space *sanctification* of mundane creatures in the *thrall of sinful idolatries*. Note well, however: the need and desire for bodily experience of the Spirit is not for some kind of epistemic evidence of uncertain divine reality, but rather the assurance of reality that the grace proclaimed *pro me* has in fact changed the "me."

Root Failures in Lutheran Doctrinal Theology

Zahl's story of the eclipse of bodily experience of the Spirit in Protestant theology begins with Luther, but it is worth careful observation and consideration that Zahl's Luther is an *Augustinian*,[68] for whom participation in the action of God in creation is Trinitarianly specific: it is the union of Spirit-given faith with Christ the Son, concretely into the historical particularity of his death and resurrection by way of the joyful exchange of his life for our death and righteousness for our sinfulness. This specific union of *Christification* (Cooper) consists in a *filial*, not servile,

66. Zahl, *Christian Experience*, 81.

67. Zahl, *Christian Experience*, 239.

68. Zahl, *Christian Experience*, 195–97.

relationship of trusting goodwill in the new-found heavenly Father, in which "the good must be done out of love and delight rather than fear."[69]

> Luther's early soteriology was profoundly focused on affect and desire as core dimensions of human experience that are of particular significance in life before God. In this, Luther's soteriology functions quite differently than critics of classical justification models have tended to assume."[70]

Affective justification by way of *fides ex corde* is not generic theosis but becoming in Christ a little Christ to the neighbor in need, as Luther characteristically put it.

Robustly affirming Luther's Augustianism in anthropology today is not trivial. It rubs against the grain of much nineteenth- and twentieth-century Luther scholarship under the influence of Kantian ethical idealism with its repudiation of Augustine's alleged eudaimonism (Nygren), theologically, of Pietism's *Heilsegoismus* (Ritschl). For Kant, the radical evil of humanity is *not* the malice of envy over against the Creator but the carnal inclination to subordinate (or even merely to coordinate) rational duty to lesser motives or incentives. Such for Kant is the "radical" corruption of the rational self in surrendering to the animal loves of the body.[71] What is at stake in this differentiation?

> That Luther, in particular, subscribes to a broadly Augustinian ontology of creation is evident in his development of the distinction between the "use" and the "substance" of a thing, in which "use" is theologically prioritized over "substance" without denying the importance as well of the inherent goodness of "substance." This distinction depends upon "an Augustinian account of creation and its ordering to God.[72]

It is Augustine's ontology of creation according to the hierarchy attested in Jesus's double love commandment, the *ordo caritatis*[73] and the attendant *uti/frui* instruction to enjoy the gifts of creation by proper usage under the Creator, never in place of the Creator. This Augustinian doctrine materially undergirds Luther's important discussions of the First Commandment, the prohibition of idolatry, and justifying faith in turn as

69. Zahl, *Christian Experience*, 193.
70. Zahl, *Christian Experience*, 118.
71. Kant, *Religion and Rational Theology*, 82–83.
72. Zahl, *Christian Experience*, 19n52.
73. Zahl, *Christian Experience*, 191,196, 222.

the fulfillment of the First Commandment, the inchoate justice of giving God the glory that is God's due as the God of surpassing grace. Augustine's most favored Bible verse, Rom 5:5, about the love of God poured into human hearts by the Spirit meant also for Luther the infusion of delight in God echoing back in praise of God's unmerited favor. Indeed, this doxlogical human experience of delight *is* the immediate presence of the uncreated sanctifying Spirit in person, not merely of created graces. So, Luther expressly teaches as late as the Genesis commentary, where he describes the loss of the Spirit in Adam's sin, not merely loss of the theological virtues, as lethal loss of the likeness that constituted humanity as theological subject. The departure of the Spirit issues in the fatal corruption of human nature itself, its loss of original righteousness.[74]

In the Osiander controversy of the 1530s, the circle around Luther was confronted with a difficult ambiguity of language in its own ranks. Osiander picked up the image of the *infusion* of divine righteousness into the soul as the ground of the sinner's justification. This picture clearly did not accord with the Spirit-mediated trust in the personal self-giving of the present Christ in his own righteousness achieved once for all by his obedience to death on the cross, offered now in exchange for the penitent's burdens of sin and death, "the joyful exchange." Osiander, however, understood the Spirit's infusion of essential divine righteousness to be the new birth, regeneration. In fact, he used the very formulations of Luther and Melanchthon, including their regular description of the Spirit's gift of justifying faith as the new birth, regeneration. But, as Zahl sees, Melanchthon interprets regeneration primarily in experiential rather than ontological terms. Indeed, the very accusation Melanchthon makes against his [papist] opponents is that they turn the gift of the Holy Spirit working faith trusting in the righteousness of Christ *pro me* into a metaphysical reality that works mechanically—*just like* pouring water into a vessel. Understood experientially as repentance and faith, "regeneration, for Melanchthon, is therefore inextricable from justification."[75] So both sides spoke of regeneration but meant different things.

To the Wittenberg reformers in the 1530s, infusion sounded much too ontological-mechanical and they came to prefer the Pauline language of reckoning, i.e., imputation, as referencing an historical event of communication through word and sacrament. Given their existential

74. LW 1:65–68.

75. Zahl, *Christian Experience*, 128.

focus on changed affect effected in Spirit-wrought repentance and faith, they further worried that Osiander's teaching of infused righteousness would lead believers into the uncertainty of introspection whether they had been truly born again, thus turning attention away from the ecstasy of Spirit-bestowed faith in the Christ who had loved them and so come to deliver them. Such anxious introspection would be a kind of anxious inquiry that would put believers once again back under the law's demand to be born again rather than deliver them as newborns into the freedom of Christ-for-them.[76]

So, a wall had to be erected against these dangers represented by Osiander[77] and this eventually happened in 1577 when the Lutheran Formulators were bold to scold the Luther and Melanchthon of the 1520s for the loose talk equating justifying faith with regeneration which Osiander had exploited. The Formula consequently made justification by Spirit-given faith incoherent and opened the door to accrediting at least a tiny act of Spiritless human will power in triggering divine acceptance. The purely forensic model of imputed alien righteousness and the rigid sequence—justification first, only then sanctification—resulted. In removing the electing Spirit from enabling human willingness in the new birth to justifying faith by presenting the righteous Christ in his act of self-giving, Lutheranism was henceforth fated to the Orthodox-Pietist cleavage where justification came about *either* "by grace" in a transcendental act of the heavenly court room above *or* by the "down in my heart" experience of the new birth as affective transformation of desire. Zahl indeed sees this.[78] He wants to retrieve and rehabilitate the original correlation of the new birth with justifying faith as the Spirit's work in justification here and now on the plane of immanence and so palpable and identifiable in human experience. Consequently, Zahl argues, we may now "take the many dimensions of human subjectivity seriously without having to turn them

76. Zahl rejects a "prescriptive" approach to regeneration which turns the experience of disjunctive grace into a kind of law, a regulative order of salvation: "in so far as the experience of grace becomes an experiential standard that one "must" meet it is no longer authentically grace." Psychological variability "is simply to be expected of the work of the Spirit. Biblically speaking, a fundamental feature of the Spirit's work from the perspective of human encounter is its freedom, which is often experienced as dynamism, resistance to comprehensive description, and resistance to instrumentalization" (*Christian Experience*, 201–2).

77. Zahl, *Christian Experience*, 130.

78. Zahl, *Christian Experience*, 131.

into theology's "starting point" or apologetic basis."[79] Progress depends on taking experience seriously without making it into the "ground and foundation of dogmatics."[80] The solution lies in defining "experience" by the particularly Christian way[81] of testing the spirits.

Identifying the Sanctifying Spirit

"Experience of God is to be understood and described first and foremost as experience of God the Holy Spirit."[82] Yet God is unseen. "What does it mean to speak of a person's perception of the presence of God if that presence is invisible, cannot finally be tested, measured, or proven, and tends to elude attempts to pin it down or generate experience of it on command?"[83] One thing this incisive question broadly implies is that the anxious attempt to justify theology as a scientific discipline since the Enlightenment is simply doomed to failure, inevitably in view of divine *Unverfügbarkeit*. More specifically, the usual attempts to assign to the Spirit the role of mediation or bridge building to assert the presence of the otherwise invisible and intangible God in human experience are "still rather vague." "Present" in what way, we might ask, "and to whom, and for what purposes and with what effects?"[84] How does Christian theology identify the sanctifying Spirit?

The Holy Spirit, it is often said, is the personal "agency that mediates the presence of God to human beings by establishing the connection between the risen Jesus and the faith and experience of Christians."[85] Yet even this ontologically correct Trinitarian answer is "curiously abstract." "Presence" seems to be used simply as

> a solution to a logical or conceptual problem: that of the metaphysical gap between God and humanity and a related chronological-historical gap between the Jesus of history and the faith of contemporary persons. . . . The Spirit's role in such accounts seems to be simply to fill up space perceived to be otherwise empty rather than to display a distinctive identity and this lack

79. Zahl, *Christian Experience*, 35.
80. Zahl, *Christian Experience*, 48.
81. Zahl, *Christian Experience*, 47.
82. Zahl, *Christian Experience*, 52.
83. Zahl, *Christian Experience*, 53.
84. Zahl, *Christian Experience*, 56.
85. Zahl, *Christian Experience*, 57.

> of specificity creates a danger that such pneumatologies will either collapse back into Christology or else revert to . . . generic ideas about "religious experience . . . "[86]

The classical doctrine of the Holy Spirit as person along the same lines as the Father and the Son are person, distinct agents essentially related to each other as the agents of the singular deity, has been reduced to a cipher for a generic notion of divine presence substituting for Jesus whose body has been removed, either metaphysically or historically, from the human scene.

So, there are problems of vagueness and abstraction that fail to satisfy the eminently practical need to test the spirits (1 John 4:1–3), reflecting a deeper failure "to demarcate adequately the Trinitarian distinctiveness of the Spirit . . . " due to "an insufficiently Trinitarian concept of the divine unity."[87] Zahl lifts up Ralph Del Colle's penetrating question: "Is the distinction between *Christus praesens* and *Spiritus praesens* anything beyond a nominal predication on the part of the theologian? If not, can we seriously hold to the hypostatic differentiation?"[88] Indeed, the perennial doctrinal question about the Holy Spirit arising from Scripture and persisting in the doctrinal tradition is *whether* to conceive it *vaguely* and *impersonally* as an energy mediating between divine and human natures *or personally* as that One of the gospel Three who eternally mediates the relationship of the Father and the Son in the freedom of love and so also in time mediates the relationship of creatures to the Creator by uniting them with the Son of the Father.

Unverfügbarkeit! "God is invisible"—but in what sense? A fundamental decision in theology is whether to take divine invisibility as the metaphysical background of the cosmos or as the absence yet of the promised future of the creation. In the New Testament, Zahl notes, salvation is future, an

> eschatological reality rather than something that has already taken place or is currently taking place in our present experience. In so far as we understand soteriology to be about the overcoming of physical death and the final and complete transformation of sinful human beings into creatures capable

86. Zahl, *Christian Experience*, 57.
87. Zahl, *Christian Experience*, 57–58.
88. Zahl, *Christian Experience*, 65.

> of eternal communion with the holy God, then in this life Christians clearly are not there yet.[89]

For the reign of God, albeit inaugurated and so announced in the resurrection vindication of the crucified Jesus for the judgment and justification of the ungodly, has not yet come upon the earth in fullness of power and glory for the redemption of the body. Such invisibility of a promised future specifies present experience of the Spirit as "a proleptic participation in a future eschatological reality." Particularly important here are the notions of hope and faith as language "that speaks about Christians engaging in a present-tense participation in Christ's death and resurrection in some sense." So, "what precisely is the sequence of events by which believers come to have faith" that conforms them to Christ's death and resurrection? How does a person's Pentecost come about?

It is important to stress here that the experience of the Spirit of God under discussion is not an apologetic matter of authenticating the reality of the invisible object of faith in face of skepticism but a dogmatic matter of identifying that faith which is the work of the Spirit of Jesus Christ. In other words, faith is faith in Jesus Christ whose saving work has begun but not yet finished. The theological concern for identifying the experience of the Spirit who works faith very much reflects a pressing concern for perseverance in a fraught and contested world. Between the ascension and the parousia there are many Pied Pipers singing siren songs to hawk alternative messages of liberation, justice and peace, as Luther saw in Karlstadt and Müntzer and Bonhoeffer and Sasse saw in the German Christian adulation of Hitler. In the same vein, Zahl sees that what is needed theologically is a practically recognizable sequence of the Spirit at sanctifying work moving human affects from one state to another—a plot, a pattern, a model, a grammar, or a symbol system, as he variously describes, an *ordo salutis*. As Luther was wont to put it, God does an *opus alienum, ut faciat opus proprium*. Essential here is the Latin particle, *ut*, which expresses purpose: "God kills *in order to* make alive" which formulation captures John Barclay's uncanny "incongruity" of grace[90] as corresponding to Zahl's "disjunctive grace" and to Ziegler's "militant grace." Just so, we identify the experience of the sanctifying Spirit as transformative love, as Luther would put it, value bestowing creative love upon "real not fictitious sinners."

89. Zahl, *Christian Experience*, 84.

90. Zahl, *Christian Experience*, 144.

At the heart of his book, Zahl executes a retrieval of the law-gospel sequence in the enunciation of the word of God as identifying the experience on the earth of the Holy Spirit, ever (Luther: daily) giving new birth to repentance and faith by conformation to the death and resurrection of Christ. Both Luther and Melanchthon understand experiential encounter with the law in terms of the *alien*, i.e., prosecuting agency of the Spirit on the way to the gospel of unmerited grace, the sanctifying Spirit's *proper* agency of vivification, assurance and edification. When the law is "used" to reveal sin and effect mortification, "the 'user' is God the Spirit";[91] when the Spirit uses the law to prosecute the controversy of the Lord with his people in the manner of the prophets of Israel, we have "the beginning of man's justification and of his true baptism" preparing the way for the faith-generating experience of divine grace[92] where "grace" is not another theological abstraction but delivering and so revealing the self-donating Son personally present to say as in nuptials, "I am yours and you are mine."

> The Spirit's communication of the gospel is never less than a Christological event as well. To believe the promise of the gospel in and through the Spirit is at the same time to receive the gift of Christ. . . . The message of divine grace is thus not a generic word of forgiveness but a specific, Christologically ordered gospel . . . [93]

The gospel as experienced is thus "more than just an explanatory label." Christian theology introduces "a new possibility within the closed system of self-inflicted suffering: the possibility of hope for deliverance that originates outside the system"[94]—grace *in person* breaking into the strong man's house to bind him and plunder his goods. Grace is rendered "emotionally as well as conceptually compelling through a particular kind of account of the atonement"[95]—Luther's "joyful exchange," the work of the *risen* Christ, as previously alluded.

The pastoral implications are profound. The discursive labeling provided by the sanctifying Spirit's law-gospel "symbol system" of mortification and vivification can

91. Zahl, *Christian Experience*, 168–69.

92. Zahl, *Christian Experience*, 169.

93. Zahl, *Christian Experience*, 170.

94. Zahl, *Christian Experience*, 175.

95. Zahl, *Christian Experience*, 175.

> interpret affective experiences without having to make overly strong claims about the power of discourse either to generate affects from scratch or to overcome affective intransigence in a straightforward manner . . . This is a kind of process of excavation to forces and feelings that are present in the body but which have been shrouded, misinterpreted, or numbed.[96]

A proper "self-love" is thusly grounded in God's redeeming love for his own creature as it is in its earthy realities of sinning and being sinned against,[97] a love which simultaneously locates the human self in bodily solidarity with all creatures of the one creator.

To be sure, the Holy Spirit acting in the divine offices of prosecutor and judge often renders problematic affects more acute at the beginning of the exorcism:

> to recognize that our efforts to justify ourselves to the world, our attempts to hide our flaws or to blame external circumstances or other people for them, our labors to manipulate relations with others to guarantee love, our unwillingness to resist oppressive and destructive structures of power out of fear of losing perceived benefits to ourselves, and so on, are not morally neutral.[98]

In revealing the state of sinful complicity under the *regnum diaboli*, the creator God kills in order to make alive. Overly optimistic views about Christian ethical transformation do not grasp the requisite "rhetoric of passivity" entailed in the very notion of the person of the Spirit at sanctifying work in human life. "Much of the force of the Christian message is precisely its efficacious protest, in and through the work of Christ, against the natural human tendency to freight our day-to-day actions and feelings with soteriological or crypto-soteriological significance."[99] The *saving* work of the Spirit is *disillusionment* of such self-deception. In any case, it is "biological matter through which affects circulate in between bodies," Zahl concludes, so that

> in so far as we are failing to look for the Spirit's' work of conviction in the realm of bodily experience we have blinded ourselves to a major site of Pneumatological activity. It is no wonder that the Spirit might thus appear to be absent from the world. . . . Cut

96. Zahl, *Christian Experience*, 172.
97. Carr, *Facing Divine Affliction*.
98. Zahl, *Christian Experience*, 173.
99. Zahl, *Christian Experience*, 116.

> off from the Spirit by being cut off from bodies, it is no wonder that the idea of sin can be viewed as hollow and moralizing, and can get co-opted for use in human power games . . . [100]

Divine law as the Spirit's prosecuting hermeneutic of human experience is, to be sure, subject to important qualifications if it is not to be misunderstood as the sanctification of demonic hegemonies. "There really are quite significant theological differences between the judgment of God and the judgment of our boss, our spouse, or our parents, and these in turn will have effects on how we 'experience our experience.'"[101] That is why the purpose clause, "God makes us sinners *in order to* make us righteous," is absolutely crucial to the proper deployment of the law-gospel hermeneutic of Christian experience. "It is only in the Spirit that the *revelatio peccati* is put in its proper context of divine love, as an instrument of compassionate diagnosis that is always ordered to an infinite grace."[102] Conviction here is a matter of conscience before the scrutiny of the Father in heaven, not feelings of guilt before the tyrannies of public opinion in propaganda, peer group or even of frowning intimates.

We have come with Zahl's help, then, to an amendment to the cultural linguistic model specifying that its culture refers concretely, and more than symbolically, to the living body of Christ, the body once crucified for us but vindicated and exalted to become the body of each and every physical body joined by the Spirit to it as members of Christ the head; assembled and united by eating and drinking from the one loaf and the one cup, in this physical act fearfully proclaiming the Lord's death until he comes again. Consequently, the interpretation of the human experience of new life in Christ becomes the burden of liturgical preaching which surely aims at the on-going transformation of human affect by the prosecution of sin and the consolation of grace. "We believe in the Holy Spirit, the Lord and giver of life." Taking this doctrine as a rule stipulates the saving purpose of proclamation and liturgical leadership: to give grace to the disgraced, love to the unloved, God to the ungodly, in all promising life to the dead, in this way answering the why question that gives the good reason for the severe mercy of the sanctifying Spirit: God kills in order to make alive.

100. Zahl, *Christian Experience,* 181. Cf. McGilchrist, *Master and His Emissar;* Crawford, *World Beyond Your Head.*

101. Zahl, *Christian Experience,* 179.

102. Zahl, *Christian Experience,* 181.

VI

What in the World Does the Word *God* Mean?

The word "God" is an empty title. It gains meaning only when claimed, as a claimant to the title refers to something in the world. This reference in turn specifies the content of the empty title, indicating what kind of God God is. The Exodus/Easter reference of the scriptural witness clarifies the title to belong to the One who is creator and so also redeemer of all that is not God. Doctrinal theology, accordingly, learns what the word God means from the divine self-presentation in the gospel narrative of the man Jesus and likewise learns what the human creature means in terms of Jesus's relationship to this self-giving God.

This final chapter returns to the second term of the primitive christological confession, Jesus is Lord, by asking what on earth the word God is supposed to mean if indeed the man Jesus is Lord. Confused use of the title, "God," i.e., the numerical One that is creator of all, as a personal name reflects at the profoundest level of linguistic usage the deleterious influence of the unbaptized God; this usage subverts the vital confessing of the One who is God truly as namely the Father who eternally generates the beloved Son on whom he breathes his Spirit and so enacts truthfully in turn the gift of eternal life for creatures, lost and disgraced, by the incarnation of his Son and the sanctification of the Spirit. By this voluntary act of generosity, this One who was rich for our sakes became poor that by his poverty we might become rich (2 Cor 8:8). The anti-foundationalist argument here works by the virtuous, not vicious circle of John 1:18: "No one has ever seen God, but the only Son who is close to the Father's heart has made him known." The named God tells us what in the world Christians are talking about even as the claimed title appropriately defers final validation to the God so named. In the interim the antifoundationalist claim is validated ethically in the lived discipleship of the Crucified on the earth.

In this light, the doctrine of the Incarnation can be redeemed from besetting vagaries as the fitting expression of eternal divine Sonship in and as the human consent of the man Jesus on his path to Golgotha for us and for all. The important critique of the unbaptized God is thus sustained without collapsing into the idealist philosophy of history of right-wing Hegelianism. And if such Trinitarian interpretation of the "hypostatic union" prevails to disambiguate and repair the Chalcedonian formula, then the Nicene doctrine of the eternal and immanent Trinity can be justified as a sound induction, turning on the truthfulness of the generous God, from the gospel narrative of Jesus, the God of Israel who is his Abba-Father, and the sanctifying Spirit who binds them together. This doxological confession anticipates the fulfillment of creation, singing glory to the Father and to the Son and to the Holy Spirit, the eternal and coequal Trinity, world without end—the final reality.

Critical Dogmatics

In the previous chapter we have met one significant objection to the cultural linguistic model of doctrine by the amendment that specifies the doctrine of the person and work of the sanctifying Spirit defeating unclean spirits to heal human affect such that the human experience of conformation to the crucified and risen Christ can be recognized and pastorally attended "in the mutual conversation and consolation" of the community. We have yet fully to meet the objection, however, that the model, relocated in New Testament apocalyptic, amounts to a ghettoized fideism, a self-referential, in-house language game alongside many other such sectarian jargons in the conflicted world, thus declining a claim to truth and falling into self-serving ecclesiastical propaganda. The objection rings out, what *in the world* are you talking about (other than yourselves)? What public claim to truth are you making that can be engaged appropriately so that it may meaningfully be denied or affirmed in a fashion appropriate to its claim? What in the world does the word *God* mean? The term must be clarified if bearing a claim to truth.

Theology is language about reality,[1] as Christine Helmer has argued in *Theology and the End of Doctrine.* As language about reality, theology arises from the reality of the *Christus praesens.*[2] And because of the living experience of the *Christus praesens* in the transformed subjectivity of faith, theology is about the living God encountered in the reality of lived history.[3] The living God is the One who ever surprises us there when we have locked God up in a closed and self-referential circle of merely inherited certitudes.[4] Theology, to be sure, produces knowledge; it identifies God by articulating doctrinal formulations for discernment in a conflicted and contested human world in which what counts as "reality" as opposed to "appearance" is not least of all at stake. In this connection as a form of critical thinking, theology scrupulously employs a scholarly method as a check against deception and self-deception. It inherits a tradition of precedents in this regard. Historically contingent (though not fortuitous), locally and temporally apt (but also humanly inept and so reformable) formulations of doctrinal knowledge of God are received as timely, perhaps historic as Spirit-guided confessions, but not timeless captures of the living God. It is the *reference* of theology's metaphorical language about God, not adequate representation taken literally, that counts in the reality correlation with the believer's concrete experience. This latter correlation with experience forged by the prevenient grace of the Holy Spirit, according to the argument of the previous chapter, is the open matter of third-order theology's discernment and deliberation. The problem of reference to the reality of God, however, is the matter of second-order doctrinal theology to which this final chapter attends.

Titles and Names

For it seems that the word, God, is polymorphous, lending particular utility to its deployment in propaganda from multiple angles. Polytheism seems to be the cultural default, monotheism sheer abstraction from polyglot

1. Helmer, *Theology and the End of Doctrine*, 134, 144.

2. Helmer, *Theology and the End of Doctrine*, 43, 57, 113, 124.

3. Helmer, *Theology and the End of Doctrine*, 61, 65, 69, 77, 87, 106, 144, 151–52, 160.

4. Helmer, *Theology and the End of Doctrine*, 105.

human religiosity, or in secular idiom, "spirituality." As Christian theology looks for renewed orientation in the ruins of Christendom, return to the originative event informs us that this cultural situation is the human default and that abstract monotheism, backed by political force whether in Christian nationalism, Islamic fundamentalism or any of the host of aspiring totalitarianisms of contemporary secularist "political religions"[5] is the social world into which the gospel enters. "Hence, as to the eating of food offered to idols, we know that "no idol in the world really exists," and that "there is no God but one." Indeed, even though there may be so-called gods in heaven or on earth—as in fact there are many gods and many lords—yet for us there is one God, the Father, from whom are all things and for whom we exist, and one Lord, Jesus Christ, through whom are all things and through whom we exist" (1 Cor 8:4–6).

Paul answered the question of what Christians mean when they enunciate the word, God, in a peculiar way. He acknowledges that the world is full of loose God talk which upon critical examination has an air of unreality, even though this multi-form God talk has great purchase on human beings. He prima facie locates his Christian speech about God amid this bewildering maelstrom of spiritual propaganda, which requires him to make its meaning clear and its purchase on reality precise. "Yes," he writes back to the "spiritually strong" faction in Corinth who feel secured by an abstract knowledge of monotheism, "there is in reality only one God." Paul characterizes this "oneness" *numerically*: there is one Creator from whom and through whom all things are. This one Creator, however, manifests as a linked pair: the Father, designated the source of all things, and the Lord Jesus, designated mediator of the creation of all that is not God. These two, in this early "binitarian" formulation, are the numerical "one" who is "God" truly "for us." This peculiar characterization of the singular deity entailing universal scope to the exclusion of parochial "idols" at the same time differentiates agencies within the one God and specifies its actual purchase on the earth "for us" in Paul's little communities, audaciously referred to—so the letter continues—as Spirit-wrought harbingers of a new humanity in the midst of one old and dying.

One may know, as the spiritually strong Corinthians knew from the Scriptures of Israel, the title *Elohim* to enumerate the one and only that is over all and so over against the many idols. They might also know that the divine name, the Tetragrammaton, YHWH, of this one and only Elohim

5. Burleigh, *Third Reich;* Burleigh, *Earthly Powers.*

is not to be voiced lest in violation of the commandment the name be taken in vain; that it is rather paraphrased as *Adonai* = *Kyrios*, the Lord. But titles like Elohim and Adonai and Kyrios and *ho theos* ("the Deity") are not names which pick out in the world the someone bearing the title. They are titles designating sovereignty making any such naming a political assertion in a broad sense. The apocalyptic term, kingdom of God, is a tautology clarifying this scriptural sense of the title. So, the apostle fills in the blank, naming "God" as simultaneously "the Father" and "the Lord Jesus Christ." This naming holds, he writes, "for us," who have been called out by the Spirit's proclamation of the gospel as the redeemed of an inbreaking new creation, the reign of God which Jesus proclaimed and enacted against the *regnum diaboli* as finally vindicated by his Father in the power of their Spirit by his resurrection from the dead.

This Pauline analysis yields a double implication for this chapter's task of clarifying the reality reference of the God of the gospel. The phenomenal figures appear on the plane of immanence in the gospel narrative, namely, the so-called economic Trinity of Jesus, the God of Israel whom he addressed as Abba-Father and from whom he heard himself addressed as beloved Son, in the unity of their sanctifying Spirit. These are named in the gospel as the one who is God truly. This "economic" Trinity is what we are talking about here and now in the world when we say "God." But the title, God, on the other hand refers to the One who proves to be creator of all that is not God. Since public demonstration of that reality is and remains outstanding, any claim to the naming and hence knowledge of God is made only in self-entrusting faith to a named candidate for the title, God, a risky venture of obedient faith with a rigorous martyr ethic for life on the earth amid conflicted humanity.

By this naming Christians today, who live today in a Corinthian-like cultural situation in post-modern Euro-America, tell what in the world they are talking about. Their faith is informed. They know and mean "one God, the Father" through the mediation of the "one Lord Jesus Christ." Explaining this predication by way of this mediation is an illustrative exercise in critical dogmatics in that the theological exegesis exercised in this book, culminating in this chapter, shows its critical power in disrupting and reforming the dogmatic tradition in the Spirit's unfinished work of ecumenical orthodoxy on the precedent of Luther's Reformation theology.

The gospel's claim to truth regarding the reality of God is formulated by the primitive christological confession, Jesus is Lord, made by faith in the Easter word—putatively—of God the Father—a virtuous circle provided that it is embraced with intellectual honesty and corresponding moral risk. Along the way we have developed some specifications of both terms of this confession of faith. The first term of this confession refers to something in common human history and is thus epistemically accessible, so far as the sources allow, to any competent inquirer. In brief, the man Jesus proclaimed and enacted the impending reign of the God of Israel[6] which ministry implicated him as a blasphemer and condemned him to death by crucifixion as an insurrectionist. That, together with his human faith in his God and Father, is the reference in this world named by "Jesus." The second term, Lord, denotes a common human experience of *political theology*,[7] whether of a tyrant or of a liberator, an oppressor or a savior, signaling fear of wrath or hope of deliverance. The conjoining of the two terms by the copula is the acknowledgment by faith of the event of the Easter vindication of the crucified Jesus.

In the tradition of doctrinal theology stemming from Luther, christological doctrine attuned to the gospel assertion and Christian confession[8] predicating Jesus as Lord for us and our salvation has been a centrally important concern as it is the deep truth of the doctrine of justification by faith alone in Christ alone in the power of the Spirit alone. The assertion of the gospel points to Jesus, born from Mary of Israel and crucified under Pontius Pilate, and to his resurrection-vindication-exaltation by his God and Father to inaugurate his saving Lordship, as confessed ecumenically in the ecclesia. Accordingly, it tells of the reality of God who gives life to the dead and calls into being worlds that do not yet exist, creator of all that is not God. Incarnation of the creator God in the person of the Son, then, underwrites the *reality* of the eternal life freely given by right and in power by the Lord Jesus Christ, *Dominus Mortis*.[9]

In chapter 3, however, we attended to the significant hermeneutical difficulty that arises in treating the notion of incarnation as settled and henceforth axiomatic. Such a dogmatism can overshadow the originative event of the resurrection-vindication-exaltation of the Crucified Jesus from which it actually arises and which determines its sense. Incarnation dogmatism can shade from clear view the controversial life Jesus lived for us, as Howard Thurman complained, in the process depriving

6. This specification is not trivial. Heschel, *Aryan Jesus*.

7. Hobbes, *Leviathan*; Elshtain, *Sovereignty*.

8. Hinlicky, "Confession."

9. Luy, *Dominus Mortis*.

us of the concrete and particular human reality in need of vindication to gain the justification of the ungodly. In this chapter, the task is to redeem the doctrine of the incarnation by the critique that abstract incarnation Christology presupposing abstract monotheism is de facto *docetist*. What incarnation *could* mean, however, if strictly predicated of the man born of Mary and crucified under Pontius Pilate for understanding the *reality* of God is that the God of the gospel is antecedently the fullness of a social life of love so that out of no need but from gratuitous freedom to love, this One who is God truly initiates, redeems, and fulfills a world of creatures other than God by sharing a place in God's own eternal life in the promise of the resurrection. Such a clarification resolves the problem of reality reference in the claim of the Nicene Creed by the differentiated equation: the economic Trinity expresses fittingly and so adequately the eternal Trinity in our human time and space for its purpose of salvation of the sinful and the perishing. The eternal Trinity in turn provides the good reason for the economy of God who freely loved the dark Egypt of this world at the cost of the cross of the incarnate Son. The meaningful question of belief is clarified by the doxological confession of the eternal Trinity as declaring for faith humanity's ultimate destiny. Clarified, one can entrust oneself in life and death to this promise of the glory of God in redeemed humanity—or not.

And such clarification is needed. The regulatory approach to doctrine pioneered by Lindbeck, and continued thus far with significant amendments in this book, was complicated by Jenson's discovery of the basic flaw in ecumenical theology and his own unsuccessful attempt to remedy it. Broadly speaking, the argument has been *with* Jenson to dePlatonize the doctrinal tradition but to do so *beyond* Jenson by reframing the issues, not with futurology but with the christologically modified apocalyptic that stamps the New Testament writing; this accords with a more careful appropriation of Luther's christological legacy (siding with Chemnitz and Gerhard against Brenz[10]). In other words, granting that we have in the foregoing chapters made sense of the originative doctrinal predication, Jesus is Lord, by clarifying the references of the several terms, and the Easter sense of their identification, what must that clarification mean for the most basic term in theology, God? And how in turn does that Trinitarian meaning clarify the sense of "incarnation" by moving away from a naked and presumptuous assertion of contact with immortal but unknown deity

10. BoC 544–65.

towards the costly and creative love which does not seek the good but confers good on the lowly and unworthy?

The burning issue here in modern theology has been whether we can have an incarnation without succumbing to docetism. If the Word became flesh and dwelt among us does the flesh named Jesus remain truly human? What difference does it make in answering this question about docetism if the meaning of the word "God" includes within divine life a becoming-other yet without self-cancellation? How does such a *natural* divine becoming-other (as in the Father eternally generating the Son and breathing the Spirit) clarify not only a specific and fitting sense of incarnation as a *hypostatic* becoming-other but answer the underlying question of what *truly* is human and humanizing, hence what would count by contrast as only *apparently* human and thus truly dehumanizing?

A Singular Claim to Truth

What in the world does the word *God* mean? It may be, as mentioned, among the most promiscuous terms in the entire human dictionary. The operating hypothesis, evident in our procedure hitherto, is that humans may have a vague *sensus divinitatis*, but they do not *know* what the word means until "the only Son, who is in the bosom of the Father, has made him known." Lacking such knowledge, there is no such thing as natural *theology*, only groping in the dark (even in the form of sophisticated speculation). Theology, however, is knowledge of God or it is nothing at all; it is the knowledge of faith, to be sure, which must be validated in its claim to truth about God by the God so named, as befits language about the ultimate *reality*. As we have seen in chapter 3, Christology, provided that it is constructed from the originating event of the resurrection of the Crucified, in fact culminates in the incarnation confession of doubting Thomas, "my Lord and my God!" This confession fills out the Christian naming of the word "God" to form the hermeneutical circle of Christian theology which, upon understanding, anyone doing due diligence can affirm or deny meaningfully and in terms of which all other theological questions of the third order may be intelligently deliberated and debated. As we shall see, however, this advance comes with a codicil against in-house theological speculation in that the consequent doctrine of the eternal Trinity establishes a boundary beyond which *both* speculation may not trespass *and* by which dogmatism is precluded. This apophatic boundary means that only the God who proves to be God truly validates human knowledge of God; consequently, Christian knowledge of God remains the risky knowledge of faith as informed by the Christ event, never in place of the Christ event—the subtle but noxious error of self-satisfied orthodoxy in its theological dogmatism.

Because ongoing retrieval and reformulation of gospel tradition in doctrinal theology is always a critical process in the light of the originating and authorizing gospel event, not to mention its function of testing the proclamation and behavior of the contemporary church, the need today in the tradition of Luther in Euro-American post-Christendom is for *critical dogmatics*. The reticence of Lindbeck to venture truth claims with ontological force, while exhibiting appropriate humility in doctrinal theology as just mentioned, in fact can also stymy the regulative function of doctrine for which he contended. Forfeiture of the claim to truth, Luther's "assertions," begs pressing questions why anyone should be convinced of the rules about Christian speech and behavior or want to be convinced or remain convinced in adhering to the confessing community of Christian faith. For centrally this involves, as Zahl noted in the previous chapter, confessing a divine *being there* which "is invisible, cannot finally be tested, measured, or proven, and tends to elude attempts to pin it down or generate experience of it on command." In what way can the gospel claim to divine presence be true? That is the question about reality reference in language concerning God here and now. In any case, the force of doctrinal regulation depends on doctrinal beliefs about the truth being spoken or obeyed and hence the need to speak clearly and correctly and to behave accordingly. Speech and behavior thus are dependent on the articulation of a singular cognitive claim to truth regarding of the *being there* of God—to be sure, in view of Greene's *Unverfügbarkeit* an intrinsically risky claim in that ultimately it can only be validated definitively by the God in question. That is as it should be. Doctrinal theology cannot transcend the posture of faith and the epistemically vulnerable status of witness. But we have argued that the theological circle here is virtuous—and thusly *critical*.

How so? Over against the propositionalist past which dogmatized all sorts of things found in Scripture and tradition but today suffers disillusionment at the progressive unraveling of falsely dogmatized beliefs,[11] when rather reform by reformulation is that ongoing task of

11. Hart, *Tradition and Apocalypse*.

critical dogmatics, this singular cognitive claim represents a clarifying *simplification*: theology is *about God* and if it is not knowledge of God, "theology" is *nothing* but the idle chatter contemptuously but justly rejected by the critical thinking of our age. An arbitrary laundry list of beliefs, say, Jonah and his whale, or young Earth creationism, or the rapture and the millennium, the immaculate conception of Mary as backed by papal infallibility, or grace so cheap it cannot be given away, even "justice" and "liberation" are not theology as knowledge of God but only random religious propositions opportunistically and propagandistically deployed which collapse of their own weightlessness under critical questioning about *being there* as reality of God-talk. The singular claim to truth in the second-order theology of critical dogmatics, confessing knowledge of God by contrast, emerges from reflection on and clarification of the primary theology attesting the word of God in the Easter event, elevated to explicit status as the critical principle of doctrinal theology going forward in the ruins of Christendom: "*God*," *taken as a title for the creator of all that is not God, is identified truly as the being there of the Almighty Father who is freely determined to redeem and fulfill his creation by the missions of his Son and his Spirit.*

Fully clarified in this light, Christology is *Trinitarian* Christology and likewise patrology and pneumatology. In this light and faith, the *Christus praesens* is known on the earth as *bodily* present in the new mode of his glorified humanity, sent by the Father to be made available "for us" by the sanctifying Spirit. The "being there" of God is this *event* of the mission of the embodied Son by the sanctifying Spirit in our world even as the *Christus praesens* points forward to the eschaton when the God and Father reigns "as all things to all," the ultimate being there. Again, the reminder: doctrinal theology does not presume to prove the Christian claim to truth but only provide the terms in which its assertion is meaningful. As such, however, it opens up wide and often urgent theological discussion but does not and cannot settle such third-order questions; it only referees debate as abiding within the virtuous circle of genuinely theological deliberation intending ecumenical orthodoxy. It defines the boundaries of Christian theological discussion in humble awareness of the scandal of this hermeneutical circle of particularity in the world. But an ecclesial habitat of such genuine theological debate is precisely what the moribund churches in post-Christendom need to regain health, orientation and renewed purpose. It is the free-for-all replacing such doctrinal theology with moralistic one-upmanship in a desperate bid for cultural relevance that polarizes and demoralizes contemporary church life.

Trinitarian Christology

"Why is Christ necessary?" Melanchthon repeatedly posed this question to papist opponents in the Apology of the Augsburg Confession IV. This was the form that the why-question took in early Lutheran theology. Melanchthon was redeploying the Pauline thought in Galatians that if justification were by works, then Christ died to no purpose. But Christ's death was purposive, *divinely* purposive, and the critical thinking of theology must pose the question until it uncovers the good reason in the life of God for the cross of the incarnate Son. So far so good, and through the centuries much of the tradition of theology stemming from Luther has held, whether tacitly or explicitly, to christological doctrine as providing this backbone of the doctrine of justification by faith. Faith alone is not faith in faith but faith in Christ; justification is not on account of faith, but on account of Christ. In a candid statement in the Smalcald Articles, Luther equates if not subsumes the doctrine of justification by faith to a robust statement of the christological doctrine accentuating its salvific promeity.

> Here is the first and chief article: that Jesus Christ, our God and Lord, "was handed over to death for our trespasses and raised for our justification" (Rom. 4 [: 25]); and he alone is "the Lamb of God who takes away the sin of the world" (John 1 [: 29]); and "the Lord has laid on him the iniquity of us all" (Isaiah 53 [: 6]); furthermore, "all have sinned," and "they are now justified without merit by his grace, through the redemption that is in Christ Jesus . . . by his blood" (Rom. 3 [: 23–25]). Now because this must be believed and may not be obtained or grasped otherwise with any work, law, or merit, it is clear and certain that this faith alone justifies us . . . [12]

And yet through the course of Lutheran theological tradition, the doctrine of Christ has been far from stable. De facto assimilation to the predominant Western Chalcedonian interpretation of Christology early on led to the Brenzian controversies in early Orthodoxy[13] continuing on

12. BoC 301.

13. Baur, *Luther und seine klassischen Erben.*

into the nineteenth-century clashes over kenoticism as well as between right- and left-wing Hegelianism on to the present kaleidoscope of opinion still agitated by the question of the Jesus of history which influentially entered into dogmatics with Schleiermacher.

This tortured history of Christology in Lutheranism is indicative of a deep problem in the Western interpretation of Chalcedonian Christology; it is the source of a broad confusion but particularly vexing for Luther's intended correlation of the Christ *pro me* and justifying faith, of a "Cyrillian Christ for Pelagian humanity."[14] The Chalcedonian formula, acknowledging two "natures" in Christ "without confusion, without change, without division, without separation . . . combining in one Person and *hypostasis*—not divided or separated into two Persons, but one and the same Son and only-begotten God . . . ,"[15] is neither *prima facie* lucid nor as a result stable as a doctrine.[16] The Western interpretation of Chalcedon is represented by the Tome of Leo, the contemporaneous Pope who intervened at Chalcedon to mitigate the condemnation of Nestorianism and validate the Antiochian Christology by underscoring the two "natures" distinction as absolute and inviolable, i.e., the Platonic doctrine of *forms* as hermeneutically axiomatic. Fatefully, he treated the "natures" as if they were real agents rather than mental classifications of commonalities. Eclipsed in the event was the leading affirmation in the Chalcedonian formula concerning the *unity of person* (*hypostasis*) as agent. With this eclipse, the fecund distinction between person (*hypostasis*) and nature (*ousia, physis, substantia*) worked out in the Trinitarian doctrine preceding Chalcedon was likewise overshadowed. Christology ceased to be strictly Trinitarian Christology;[17] consequently, the hypostatic union was increasingly rendered mere lip service[18] until it became unintelligible, thought to be a mere redundancy as we saw in Jenson's revisionism, and its vital insight into the *personal,*

14. For the fulsome argument, see Hinlicky, *Beloved Community*, 393–611. In the argument there on behalf of a "Cyrillian Christ for Augustinian humanity," I take pains to resituate the Antiochene Theodore of Mopsuestia's biblical case for the Spirit-inspired, grace-elicited obedience of Jesus within the soteriological interpretation of Christ's person by the Alexandrian Cyril.

15. Hardy, *Christology of the Later Fathers*, 373.

16. David J. Luy, drawing upon the analyses of Eberhard Jüngel and Werner Elert, helpfully describes the conundrums attending reception of Chalcedon in modern Lutheran theology in his *Dominus Mortis*, 197–209.

17. Schleiermacher, *Christian Faith*, 2:400; #97.2.

18. Jenson, *Unbaptized God*, 124.

i.e., *voluntary* communication of properties was consigned to the dustbin of history by Schleiermacher.[19]

Modern Christology consequently transmuted into symbolization of the general problem of the relation of generic divinity and generic humanity which could be thought apart from Christ and only then somehow applied to, or rather, imposed upon the figure of Jesus Christ, as Bonhoeffer acutely diagnosed.[20] For human salvation, to be sure, there had to be in Christ some special connection between the life-giving creator and perishing creature effectively to communicate the gift of eternal life, as also Schleiermacher held regarding the "constant potency of [Christ's] God- consciousness, which was a veritable existence of God in him."[21] But that generic approach quickly presents unsolvable problems. The de facto deifying of the human nature of Christ, especially the human mind (*nous*) which as ruler was thought to mediate deification to the body, soft peddled the narrative insignia of finitude for the understanding of Jesus Christ to the extent that the exhibition of psychological features of finitude throughout the gospel narrative were said to be playacting[22]—or, in Schleiermacher's case, mistaken memories or inventions of the early church community. But is a deified, as opposed to a sanctified humanity truly descriptive of the human Jesus of the gospel narrative, even John's? In the other direction, the communication of human anguish and pain to the divine nature had to be strictly excluded as ontological nonsense lest the natural immortality of the divine desired for salvation be compromised. A divine nature that can suffer and die simply ceases to be divine according to the Platonic axiom of divine apathy and has no value for salvation understood as generic deification.

The Western expedient on the horns of this dilemma was to argue that divine nature assumes a human nature (as if "donning a coat"—Luther) whereby the marks of mortality are superficially endured but do not penetrate to the underlying substance. But this proved to be an equally difficult solution. What can it mean for the perfect divine

19. Schleiermacher, *Christian Faith* 2:411, #97.5

20. DBW 12:333.

21. Schleiermacher, *Christian Faith*, 1:385; #94.1

22. "He had no need of these and similar things either as God *or as a human being*. He was only making a show of behaving in a human way, in accordance with what was demanded by necessity or profit, such as when he prayed in order to show that he was not a rival God but to honor the Father as his cause. He asked not because he was ignorant but in order to show that he was truly a human being as well as God." St. John of Damascus, *On the Orthodox Faith*, 270–71, emphasis added.

nature to *add* to itself in a *real* relation something ontologically *alien* and yet so intimately as Luther's notion of incarnation requires? Must this not in the process betray unrealized possibilities in the divine being, and, to boot, novel becoming in time, compromising its purely actual perfection? Reservations about this implication pushed the thought of incarnation back to the eternal idea of God: if there is in fact a creation and if in it there occurs an incarnation of God, then creation and incarnation are eternal necessities entailed by the very divine and fully actual perfection of being; consequently, in the temporal unfolding of creation and incarnation nothing new occurs for God at all. The necessitarianism is evident, robbing the deity of freedom in creation and redemption as also robbing the human creation of the dignity of free consent to divine purpose, willingness, *voluntas*. Incarnation in time and space as Jesus Christ accordingly becomes nothing but the exemplification of an antecedent ontology, supposedly superior in clarity, but not different in kind but only in intensity from other revelatory manifestations of eternal necessity, as in the saints. And if not willing to admit such evacuation of the contingent historicity of Jesus, and, as *the* incarnate Son of God, unwilling to acknowledge a corresponding historicity of God,[23] the metaphysical distance presupposed in the Western reception of Chalcedon abides: the metaphysical gap between the divine revealer and its finite human instrument perpetually subverts the christological teaching of the divine assumption of flesh, not to mention Chalcedon's forgotten "unity of person." Luther already wrestled with these problems of Chalcedonian Christology, particularly in the terms of late medieval Western scholasticism.[24] His struggle is pregnant with possibility for reconstruction in doctrinal theology and richly informative for answering the question of this chapter: what in the world are Christians talking about, if Jesus is Lord when they think, speak, and act on the word, God? But Schleiermacher took this question about the meaning of the word, God, for granted—as provided by philosophical ontotheology of perfect being (which may have been borrowed from Kant).[25]

23. McCormack, *Humility of the Eternal Son*.

24. Hinlicky, "Luther and the 'Repair of Chalcedon.'"

25. "Even if God were to make an immediate appearance, I would still need rational theology as a presupposition," Kant once argued. "For how am I to be certain that it is God himself who has appeared to me, or only another powerful being? Thus, I have need of a pure idea of the understanding, an idea of a most perfect being, if I am not to be blinded and led astray." Kant, *Lectures on Philosophical Theology*, 161.

Schleiermacher's *Life of Jesus* and Bonhoeffer's Christological Correction

What stands in the way of a contemporary Lutheran repair of the doctrines of God and Christ in the light of the theological exegesis[26] deployed in this book is the monumental modern influence of Friedrich Schleiermacher's *Life of Jesus*,[27] which theologically stands behind the past two centuries of the *dogmatic* quest for a useful Jesus in accord with present consciousness. What is influential about this late career attempt at a historical critical biography of Jesus is certainly not its solutions to the various difficulties of the ensuing quest for the *historical* Jesus. It suffices to say in this connection that Schleiermacher regarded the Gospel of John as a coherent account of Jesus by an intimate eyewitness in position to attest to the perfect human consciousness of God which governed Jesus in his life's way. Short years later, David Friedrich Strauss devastated Schleiermacher's reconstructed historical Jesus with the sharp indictment: "A sinless, archtypal Christ is not one whit less unthinkable than a supernaturally begotten Christ with a divine and human nature."[28] This indictment is sharp because the pivot on which Schleiermacher's reconstruction of the Jesus of history to replace the "supernaturally begotten Christ with a divine and human nature" turned on his demand for psychological plausibility on the analogy of contemporary consciousness. Attributing divine omniscience to the human mind of Jesus "destroys what is essential to human existence, and that is Docetism, and abolition of the true humanity of Christ."[29] The theological task, then, undertaken in *The Life of Jesus* is to understand Christ as the adequate basis of human salvation for all time by conceiving "*of his whole existence in the perfectly human way* . . . "[30] A natural explanation of Jesus comes about by a psychological analogy: "matters stand similarly with the Holy Spirit as the life principle of the Christian church as with the divinity of Christ."[31] The virtual being of God in Christ is to be understood as the truly human Christ's self-consciousness as beloved son of God which compelled the

26. Hinlicky, "How Theological Exegesis Disrupts Theological Tradition," 143–57.
27. Schleiermacher, *Life of Jesus*.
28. Strauss, *Christ of Faith and the Jesus of History*, 29.
29. Schleiermacher, *Life of Jesus*, 15. Cf. 31.
30. Schleiermacher, *Life of Jesus*, 33.
31. Schleiermacher, *Life of Jesus*, 33.

uniquely God-conscious Jesus to share his self-consciousness with others and so to spread the spiritual kingdom of God on earth.

What counts as illegitimate "docetism" is an implausibly divine consciousness animating the man, replacing a rational soul (as in the ancient Apollinarianism, see below) which Schleiermacher detects in naïve embellishments in the Gospels. But such a divine consciousness in Jesus was dogmatized, he charges, in the hypostatic union and artificially said to be concealed during the lifetime of Jesus, in the process unwittingly attributing an undignified deceptiveness to Jesus. Yet to stress Strauss's critical point, Schleiermacher's solution is no less docetic than the alleged problem. At the critical point, it requires him to protest as unhistorical the agony in Gethsemane and the cry of dereliction from the cross as incompatible with perfect human consciousness of God. Yet what has survived from Schleiermacher and had massive dogmatic influence is the underlying claim that an authentically human Jesus is a psychologically plausible one on the analogy of contemporary consciousness. The only difference is that subsequent questers do not so much look to found a consciousness of blessedness on the personality of the Redeemer but rather seek in Jesus an ethical exemplar who serves to deconstruct christological dogma. This quest, which *cannot* follow the gospel narrative of the Spirit-anointed man on his messianic mission "to serve and not to be served and give his life a ransom for many" (Mark 10:45), deflects attention from a needed dogmatic repair and reclamation operation on Chalcedonian Christology which both integrates it with Trinitarianism and in the process clarifies the fully Trinitarian doctrine of God to articulate the *being there* of the deity.

A major concern in patristic Christology was the challenge of docetism, the teaching that Christ only appeared to be human. In the second century (as in Ignatius of Antioch, Polycarp, Justin Martyr and Irenaeus), however, the issue was whether transcendent *deity could truly be a human being*, born of a woman, born under the law, crucified, dead and buried—and thence raised *bodily*. In other words, there was no controversy about the special, even unique "presence of the divine" in Christ, to use Schleiermacher's generic terminology, but whether the divine Christ is truly human. The Nicene Creed and its completion at Constantinople in 381, on the other hand, settled the Arian controversy by affirming the coequal deity of the *personal Son* of God who became incarnate in Christ by virtue of the distinction between person and nature. Consequently, one could say the Son of God was crucified *personally* in his human body and soul *without* saying that divine nature was crucified (which implied either modalism or a radical ontological kenosis, the death of God). The kenosis of the divine Son in the incarnation was not ontological diremption, but personal humility *coram Deo*, undertaken as human obedience. Nevertheless, the issue of docetism resurfaced in new ways.

A follower of *homoousios*-champion Athanasius, Apollinaris, taught that the divine Logos took the place of the rational human soul (the mind, *nous*) in the person of Christ. But on the soteriological principle that what is "not assumed is not healed," as articulated by the Cappadocian Gregory Nazianzus, it was affirmed against him that Christ had to have a human mind if our human minds are to be healed by him. But this affirmation of Christ's human mind still presented a difficulty in view of the human sinlessness affirmed of Christ's incarnate person. How could a finite soul subject to error avoid sin? How could a weak human will in fact will the will of God? What, more broadly, does it mean to be *truly* human? It could be thought that the human mind was deified by incarnation. It could also be thought that the human mind was sanctified by the messianic endowment of the Spirit so that it wills the will of God. These two thoughts are not the same. The first is generic, the second specifically Trinitarian.

The standard Chalcedonian attempt to solve this problem was to fortify the mind of Christ via deification, i.e., its union with the divine nature on the anthropological supposition that human reason was the quality most like the divine; consequently, the deified rational human soul was fit to mediate divinity to the flesh, subduing its passions.[32] This

32. E.g., "The Word of God, then, is united to flesh by means of mind, which mediates between the purity of God and the materiality of flesh. For the principal element governing both soul and flesh is mind, the purest part of the soul, but God is also the principal element governing mind . . . " John of Damascus, *On the Orthodox Faith,* 175. Yet elsewhere John writes, "It is impossible that uncreated and created nature [in Christ] should have a single nature, power, or activity. If we were to say that Christ's activity is simply one, we would be attributing to the divinity of the Word the passions of the intelligent soul, by which I mean fear and sorrow and anguish." By the same token, the will of the divine Son would no longer be the same "activity as the Father nor would he be of the same essence" (201). That need to separate divinity from humanity in Christ explains John's repeated invocation of the Western *Tome of Leo* to insist upon the humanity of the one incarnate Son—*as a buffer* between the divine nature and the incarnate experience of shame, grief, pain and the terror of death. John quotes Leo in order to separate: "One shines with miracles, while the other has succumbed to outrages." This reliance upon Leo is what made John's summation of the Eastern Orthodox tradition amenable to Western appropriation, as it was translated into Latin early on and was influential especially on Thomas Aquinas.

appeared to preserve the separation of the two natures in the buffering provided by the deified rational soul. The Monophysites, committed to the unity of person, had argued that Christ was composed "out of" two natures, but finally it seems that deified human nature was, as it were, absorbed into the divine nature like a raindrop in the sea and ceased to be meaningfully human. The Nestorian party in opposition wanted to insist upon the biblical testimony to the abiding humanity of Christ to the extent that it virtually affirmed a double personality-and-agency in the son of Mary and the Son of God, functionally aligned in willing the will of God, a moral not hypostatic union. In this latter case the human soul of Christ was fortified by the Holy Spirit to constitute the new and true Adam. In truth, however, as Jenson saw, both parties were motivated by a Platonic commitment to protect the apathetic divine nature from ontologically damaging entanglement with human finitude, not to mention sin. Nestorians did this by dividing the person. But on the Monophysite side this required, as mentioned, the expedient of explaining Christ's ignorance, anxiety, even despair as playacting. And this problem of a playacting Christ persisted in Western Chalcedonian orthodoxy. It was a riddle how to acknowledge the suffering humanity of Christ without undermining his significance as divine Savior; metaphysical apathy overrode hypostatic sonship.

Compounding the difficulty, the medieval Western tradition fatefully rendered the Greek *hypostasis* by the Latin *suppositum*.[33] This is a literal translation based upon etymology. Etymologically both terms mean that which underlies as a foundation. Normally you don't see the foundation but the structure which rests upon it. So suppositum meant the foundation of the divine nature upholding the phenomenal appearance of the human nature, the man Christ. But the Trinitarian doctrine expressed in the Greek language had generated an innovative meaning, disregarding the etymology: *hypostasis* in distinction from generic nature, *ousia*, *physis*, *substantia*, represented a concrete way of being, *prosopon* or *persona*, a particular face or figure in the world, and as such perceptible unlike intellectually grasped essences, i.e., the noumenal *suppositum*, as the medieval Latin's thought, undergirding the phenomenal appearance. Specifically, the Son is God by nature but in the concrete way of being

33. According to Richard Cross, a theory of *suppositum*, foundationalism or undergirding, predominated in the Western medieval tradition in place of the received but opaque terminology of *hypostatic* union in the Nicene-Chalcedonian tradition. Cross, *Communicatio Idiomatum*, 26–27.

the Son (and likewise the Father and the Spirit) as these appear as figures on the plane of immanence of the gospel narrative. So, it was fitting that it was particularly the Son who became incarnate in obedience to his Father's redemptive purpose and in the power of the Spirit undertook the Messianic mission as the human son of Mary. It was fitting that the eternal Son was humble before his God and Father and thusly "emptied" of equal status in the incarnation, declining to manifest or exercise natural divine authority as incompatible with the weakness voluntarily but just so fittingly undertaken in the human flesh he has made his very own. Made truly human by the agency of the Spirit, the incarnate Son was endowed with the Spirit from conception through life and death and finally to resurrection and exaltation, all to fulfill the divine saving purpose in humanity as human, as *truly* human, as *Spirit-endowed* humanity. So, the incarnation was a fully Trinitarian operation. This is crucial for understanding Trinitarian Christology. The incarnation of the divine Son in the hypostatic union and this humanity's anointing by the Spirit are neither incompatible nor rival explanations of Schleiermacher's "presence of the divine" in Christ but its Trinitarian explication.

But all this was obscured in the Latin mind by rendering *hypostasis* as the divine *suppositing* of a human person (hypostasis!) so that the suppositum wore the humanity like a cloak that one could put on and off depending upon the temperature (i.e., environment, circumstances). This obscurity funds a Nestorian tendency since the distinct natures of the suppositum and its human cloak can only be accidentally united, being two integral hypostases. There is not in Christ's person a unique personal communion of the natures but only an intense association. Luther militated against this christological teaching; he wanted the far more intimate personal union of communion to the extent that the divine Son of God in his own flesh bore our sins and endured in his own human soul the curse upon them. So, Luther renovated the patristic *admirabile commercium*, the personal communication of properties in Christ in its soteriological intention ("God became human in order that humans might become divine"), meaning that it is the specific *person* of the divine Son who freely employs divine and human properties as befits his mission of redemption. In view of 2 Cor 5:21, Luther further Paulinized the patristic *admirabile commercium* in his rhetoric of the joyful exchange, mindful that its reality was gained at the cross and is there for us as *Christus praesens* only by virtue of resurrection-vindication-exaltation. In all this, moreover, it is to be registered emphatically that Luther issued an acute critique and sharp polemic against renewed docetism in the figure of Casper Schwenckfeld in his *Disputation on the Divinity and Humanity of Christ.*[34] Unlike Schleiermacher, however, the point of rejecting docetism was not that we relate psychologically to Christ's inner life but to affirm that the Trinitarian infinity of circulating, other-regarding love is truly capable of the finite, making the composite person of the incarnate Son in truth the wonder of a divine capacity of willing compassion and free favor for disgraced and perishing humanity.

Beginning with Zwingli, traditional Western theologians, whether Roman or Reformed, rejected Luther's christological doctrine of God whose glory it is to come down to the depths. To the Western mind, Luther's doctrine of Christ seemed absurd. It implied to them that in eating and drinking at the Lord's Supper, one cannibalized the body of Christ, even though Luther insisted on the catachrestic-metaphorical meaning of body, in that the natural body born of Mary and crucified under Pilate is now translated into an exalted mode of resurrected existence by virtue of which the personal promise to nurture believers in the Supper may be kept. By virtue of the *ubivolipraesens* ascribed to the humbled and incarnate, but now glorified hypostasis of the Son incarnate, moreover, Christ Jesus can be bodily wherever he promises to be. As in the Nestorian reaction of old, however, Luther's doctrine of Christ seemed to destroy the essential finitude of human body (which can only be in one place at a time) as well as entangle the deity in ontologically compromising human bodiliness, sin and spiritual suffering. By the time of the high Enlightenment, Kant's rational idea of God as the ontotheological perfect being *rules out a priori* any such entanglement with imperfection. All that is left beyond the ontotheological postulate of perfect being is the idea of a prototype of humanity in the symbolic Son of God who wills the will of God, that is, the duty to act in a universalizable way.[35] Emulating the prototype, the human being can trust that it merits the divine pleasure. So, we end up with a Nestorian Christ for a Pelagian humanity.[36]

34. Hinlicky, "Luther's Anti-Docetism," 139–85.

35. Kant, *Religion and Rational Theology*, 105.

36. "The Nestorian conception of Christ . . . qualifies Christ for being an example of what man can do, and into what wonderful union with God he can be assumed if he is holy enough; but Christ remains one man among man, shut in within the limits of a single human personality, and influencing man only from outside. He can be a Redeemer of man if man can be saved from outside by bright example, but not otherwise. The Nestorian Christ is logically associated with the Pelagian man . . . the Nestorian Christ is the fitting Saviour of the Pelagian man." Gore, "Our Lord's Human Example,"

Here Schleiermacher enters the scene and fundamentally alters theology for the next several hundred years, ironically, in the name of anti-docetism. In many ways his doctrine is the modern renewal of the Antiochian emphasis in Christology on preserving the true humanity of Christ, but with the twist that Schleiermacher, unlike the Antiochians, jettisons the Nicene doctrine of the hypostatic Son. (In his dogmatics, *The Christian Faith*, the doctrine of the Trinity is relegated to an appendix at the end of the book and subjected to an historical deconstruction accusing the hypostatic distinctions, as unified by the "monarchy" of the Father, of tacit "subordinationism."[37]) In the *Life of Jesus*, his fundamental methodological decision is consistently to oppose any "docetism" in the doctrine of Christ by seeking to understand his human mind *on the historical analogy of our experience of personhood*. Bear in mind here, however, that the historicist principle of analogy is itself historically conditioned, i.e., that after Kant, "personhood" emerges as the "self-consciousness" of living according to duty as that which distinguishes rational human beings from barnyard animals. Bear in mind as well, how differently this modern anxiety about human uniqueness forces interpretation of the docetism heresy away from its original articulation in the second century where the point was to affirm truly divine *being there* in the suffering but vindicated human body and soul of Jesus of Nazareth. With Schleiermacher the problem of docetism becomes the psychological plausibility of Jesus (along Kantian idealist lines) rather than the divine capacity of the eternal Son for the creature who is Spirit-anointed Jesus innocently bearing the sin of the world in his body on the tree. And this modernized notion of "docetism" is elevated to function as a criterion in assessment of what is and can be historical in the gospel narrative!

Now it is true and often pointed out that in distinction from Kant, Schleiermacher did not reduce Christ to a symbol of prototypical humanity pleasing to God. Quite the contrary, he intended and sought a truly human and historical Jesus and valued his reconstructed Jesus of human history as "Savior." But what he "found" was an historical Jesus who actualized Kant's prototypical humanity pleasing to God. For him, faith is generally a historically generated articulation of the feeling of absolute dependence, i.e., the vague awareness of divine causality universally and constantly impressing itself upon us. Specifically, faith in Jesus

---

298, cited in McGrath, *Christian Theology Reader*, 196. For Kant's "Nestorianism," see *Religion and Rational Theology*, 103–4.

37. Schleiermacher, *Christian Faith*, 2:738–51.

Christ as savior articulates the blessed assurance that this omnicausality is good and means us well. This can work because for Schleiermacher Jesus is the perfect human being in that he lives an entire life in perfect consciousness of the benevolent heavenly parent and thus delivers to his believers his own idea of God which they too can trust and obey.

In his *Life of Jesus* Schleiermacher had utterly dispensed with the Protestant Orthodox doctrine of verbal inspiration that had usually been theorized as divine dictation; he embraced the emerging historical criticism of the biblical writings, treating them like any other human literature. But, as mentioned, he makes highly implausible *historical* decisions here, regarding the Gospel of John as the work of an eyewitness with superior insight into Christ's human self-consciousness. With Strauss's radical critique of *both* Chalcedonian orthodoxy *and* Schleiermacher, more fuel was thrown on the fire of the anxious quest for the real historical Jesus that dominated the nineteenth century. But the devastating blow to Schleiermacher's precedent-setting quest in theology (but according to the argument of this book, the ground clearing away of Christian Platonism for reorientation in apocalyptic) came at the end of the century when Johannes Weiss fundamentally contradicted the notion of Kant and Schleiermacher that the building of the "kingdom of ends," i.e., "of God" on earth was the meaning of Jesus's proclamation and the continuing task of the regenerate. Weiss pointed out that the notion of the reign of God in Jesus's proclamation was "antithetical," i.e., fundamentally opposed to the kingdom of Satan. In place of Schleiermacher's perfect human being with his perfectly rational ethic of duty supposited by the divine presence in him, after Weiss a disturbing new picture of the controversial Jesus of history emerged, a picture to the Enlightenment mind bordering on madness.

It is important to observe here the methodological turn to historiography, i.e., to the critical writing of history by the criterion of the reconstruction of what had really happened according to the doctrine of analogy with the historian's contemporary experience in history. The important study of Johannes Zachhuber previously referenced demonstrated how this methodological turn had everything to do with the desire to establish theology as an academic science eligible for disciplinary recognition in the modern university. With Schleiermacher, theology has become historiography with a double focus: 1) on the historical sources in Bible and the doctrinal tradition and 2) the contemporary consciousness of the church. By contrast with his Berlin rival, Hegel, who opted for philosophy of religion as the academic platform to credential theology, Schleiermacher turned to historiography for this credentialing.

In his *Brief Outline on the Study of Theology*[38] Schleiermacher created and defined for the future the now entrenched *division of labor* in academic theology which in time had the debilitating consequence of separating biblical study as pure historiography from theology increasingly taken as free artistic construction of consciousness for the contemporary context in a people's church. He had an initial role for philosophical theology in regard to apologetics and polemics but from this meta-theological space he essentially affirmed the profane positivity of the Christian faith as a religion alongside others, thus requiring a historical method appropriate to the plane of immanence for its self-understanding. Although this division of labor has been modified down through the years, it is ironic that this basic scheme aimed at university recognition of theology as a scientific discipline has been imitated in church seminaries which might think better of such artificial divisions of labor, not to mention conceiving of theology as piggy-backing on the modern discipline of history-writing: its scientific ideal of presuppositionless inquiry cannot tolerate what in its eyes can only be a bias, imposed by canonicity, fronting for the would-be hegemony of Christian dogma.

Zachhuber concluded his study:

> In light of this, much seems to speak for a theology that consciously relinquishes the claim to a prior, external verification of its basic assumption; in other words, a *non-foundationalist* theology. Such a theology presupposes the existence of the Christian faith in its historical social form, the Church, as a fact to be interpreted. Its use of the concept of religion, as far as this is necessary, is hermeneutical, that is it aids the interpretive task and internal communication between members of the faith community.[39]

While Zachhuber's conclusion comports with this book's appropriation of an amended cultural-linguistic model of doctrine, the relocating of the model in the external word of a christologically modified apocalyptic is not as compatible, strictly speaking, with the tradition of historical theology flowing from Schleiermacher through Ritschl to Troeltsch in so far as that was historically undermined by Johannes Weiss's recovery

38. Schleiermacher, *Brief Outline on the Study of Theology*.

39. Zachhuber, *Theology as Science*, 291–92.

of the apocalyptic framing of the New Testament gospel which knows otherwise "the mind of Christ." We are thusly advocating theological exegesis in place of history of religions.

In this latter connection, mention must be made of the counter proposal of Hans Frei.[40] In studying the work of Karl Barth, Frei noticed how Barth developed his initial method of "pneumatic exegesis," i.e., to exposit the biblical text in view of its subject matter, which is putatively the God-given knowledge of God. Such theological exegesis of course has no reservations about appropriations of historical critical insights which can illuminate much about the circumstance of the given biblical text as the text is also, and essentially, a human artifact. Nor does pneumatic exegesis resort to the precritical doctrine of verbal inspiration to secure historical plausibility on the basis of miraculous inerrancy. Least of all, does it uncritically adopt the doctrine of analogy behind Schleiermacher's psychological criterion of authenticity. Rather it receives the testimony of the prophets and the apostles contingently recorded and handed on in and by the contingent emergence of the community of faith as the historical witness to the putatively God-given event of the knowledge of God. Scripture in *contingent* historical fact thus constitutes the theologian's *equally contingent* epistemic access to revelation. Acknowledging these contingencies, there is nothing foundationalist about such a foundation!

Barth not only embraces this lack of a philosophical foundation for theology to accentuate the vulnerability of the theologian *as corresponding to the reality* of the God who cannot be controlled, manipulated or predicted. But also revelation here is not the supernatural communication of information about all sorts of things but is strictly God's *self*-revelation. What all this amounts to, according to Frei, is that the narratives of Scripture cumulatively render a character, a persona, in the phenomenal world: The God of Israel, the God of the exodus and of the exile, with Jesus Christ the Son of this God and their sanctifying Spirit prosecuting sin in order to proclaim good news to those thusly convicted. Naming these figures, scriptural witness renders them identifiable by relative clauses, "who" did such and such, thus *being there in the narrative world* into which the auditor is drawn so that the auditor with its world is interpreted by the narrative rather than vice versa. Consequently, the knowledge of God provided in biblical narrative is for the cognitive purpose of identification, picking someone out of a crowd

40. Frei, *Eclipse of Biblical Narrative*. See Greene, *Imagining Theology*, chs. 4–5, on Frei.

by name, further specifying the name with relative clauses describing its characteristic work. Significantly for Frei, the truth of the Bible is its reference, yet *not* to critically reconstructed history, but rather to the God so rendered by the narratives of Scripture. Such pragmatic, not theoretical knowledge of God is the subject matter of theology which receives Scripture as its normed norm and matrix so that the self and ultimately its antecedent world is interpreted by this external word, as believers learn to speak its new language of the Spirit in the community of faith. The sanctifying Spirit captures human desire by binding it in Christ to the loving obedience of faith in his God and Father; and the Spirit accomplishes this for the discipleship of the mind which is theology. In the matrix of the Bible, the sanctifying Spirit captures the rational faculty of imagination, dreaming dreams and seeing visions.

Garrett Greene ably articulates the necessary dialectic involved in doctrinal knowledge of the gracious God who ever evades human instrumentalization. The rational faculty of imagination can run wild rather than serve to hypothesize better understanding of the realities of God and world, so whether in science or in theology, one "must wrestle with the question of how to govern use of imagination, how to employ it properly in the service of truth . . . to identify the normative use of imagination, some set of rules or guidelines to govern its use and to curb its excesses."[41] The Spirit disciples the imagination of the believer's mind by immersion in the matrix of Scripture. "The Bible embodies the concrete paradigm on which all genuine Christian theology is based, enabling the faithful to rightly imagine God."[42] This is possible because the same Spirit inspiring the prophets, scribes, sages, priests, and apostles, first selected and preserved their testimony in writings to transcend the occasion and continue *as written* to form the identity of the community of faith. This is not the literalism of a dictation theory, as Islam reads the Qu'ran, but historically contingent testimony to Jesus Christ as the incarnate Word of God, hence "not by putting words into the mouth of passive ancient authors but by capturing their imagination and enabling them to utter truthfully—using their own culturally specific and time-bound conceptuality—the mysteries of the one eternal God, Creator of the heavens and the earth."[43] As a consequence of this divinely intentional contingency, "no appeal to a 'literal' reading of the

41. Greene, *Imagining Theology*, 12.

42. Greene, *Imagining Theology*, 13.

43. Greene, *Imagining Theology*, 13.

Bible can bypass the need for right interpretation—that is, for a hermeneutic that enables us to find in Scripture the normative way to imagine God"[44]—namely, as the One who justifies the ungodly and gives life to the dead. Chiefly that consists in not reading the apocalyptic metaphors literally (which would make them nonsense, e.g., "God is a warrior") but discerning the reference made in the literally nonsensical representation, e.g., the God of love acts against what is against love.

We have here a virtuous circle of the new and spiritual subject knowing the new and spiritual object in the apocalyptic correlation of saving divine deed and human transformation. "Right imagination of God is a movement not only of the head—our mind or intellect—but also of the heart, our feelings and effective responses." Consequently, "the theological use of imagination must always remain open to the mystery of God, resisting every temptation to rationalize, demystify, or control the divine."[45] This imperative follows because the theologian's object of study "is the one holy God, who in his aseity is not at our disposal, who in his freedom remains ever mysterious who, as we might say simply *is* mystery." God is mystery, however, as the "infinitely *knowable* one,"[46] providing no excuse for agnosticism. Knowledge of God is always a gift and hence by its very nature necessitates humility on the part of the knower of the God who is always new without changing or losing his identity.[47] Paradigmatic imagination is ordinarily similitude, metaphorical "seeing-as," telling what something unfamiliar is like by the comparison with the familiar. But how is the theologian to find a likeness to the One utterly unique? The man Jesus Christ is given to the believer as the image of God: familiar to us as a human like ourselves but received in transformative faith as the paradoxical apocalypse of the heavenly Father's heart by his resurrection-vindication. For there is no paradigm of such a God "unless it be revealed by God himself. Thus, theologians have followed the Bible and emphasized the essential role played by the Holy Spirit, the one who inspires the imagination of the witnesses"[48] as also believing reception. "Because theological imagination is dependent

44. Greene, *Imagining Theology*, 14.

45. Greene, *Imagining Theology*, 15.

46. Greene, *Imagining Theology*, 16.

47. "In accordance with its biblical paradigm, theological imagination always remains open to novelty, eschewing every attempt at metanarrative or systematic closure." Greene, *Imagining Theology*, 16.

48. Greene, *Imagining Theology*, 18.

on the Holy Spirit, it is an enterprise of faith, appearing uncertain and circular from a worldly perspective, depending on the certainty of God's revelation for its claim to truth."[49] Hence, faith is not Platonic opinion but "the right way, the only way" to know the One who is God truly, thus not at our disposal. The certainty of such faith is always as recipient of a gift of divine grace forming a "virtuous circle."[50]

Greene's illuminating account of the dialectic of first- and second-order theology also tells how these enable the third-order theology of discernment and deliberation as the gospel encounters new challenges, new contexts and new difficulties.

> The sources of [theologians'] paradigms, the likenesses they discover in the scriptural witness, are open-ended like all paradigms, but never arbitrary. The temptation to indulge their own imaginations and fantasies always lies close at hand and can be restrained only by faithful adherence to the scriptural norm, which has been defined and disciplined by the long tradition of exegesis and articulated in doctrine, which codifies the "grammar" of Scripture. But just as the discipline of grammar does not prevent the poet or philosopher from employing the language in new and creative ways, so the church's doctrine does not confine the theologian to a boring traditionalism but rather provides guideposts and warning signs along the way to new insights into the meaning and application of the biblical witness to the real life of the world today.[51]

In this light, what we have seen in Schleiermacher is a modern incapacity in second-order theology to follow the gospel narratives, beginning with the Gospel of Mark (as we began this book in chapter 2). He regards the Synoptics as pearls (along with some clunkers) on a string. He frequently says he can make no sense of the story these stories tell, that only John has a coherent presentation. But notice how his reading of John is also narratively imperceptive. Why should John's Jesus cleanse the temple at the very beginning of the narrative? Or likewise tell the Samaritan woman of the new and spiritual worship, following upon the prologue's identification of Jesus as the event of the divine tabernacling? Why should Jesus travel to Jerusalem on the occasion of three significant Jewish festivals? Why should Jesus replace the Synoptic parables of the

49. Greene, *Imagining Theology*, 19.

50. Greene, *Imagining Theology*, 19–21.

51. Greene, *Imagining Theology*, 22.

kingdom with the I AM statements expositing his saving person and work? Why should it be the unparalleled story of the raising of Lazarus that precipitates the conspiracy to kill Jesus? Many more such questions could be put to Schleiermacher's *literary* reading of the Gospel of John, so narrowly focused on dogmatically excavating the presence of the divine in the historically available human consciousness of Jesus, that it misses utterly the climactic anti-docetic articulation of the gospel when Thomas, the apostle thought to represent docetism, exclaims before the Risen One's wounds, "my Lord and my God!" As Strauss rightly pointed out, Schleiermacher's perfectly human but wholly God-conscious Jesus is no less a product of mythological imagination than the more natural reading of John presenting the divine Logos/Son made flesh. Indeed, the latter provides the actual sense of early anti-docetism.

What we should note in all this methodologically is what Oswald Bayer has called the erasure of the christological communication of idioms in modern theology,[52] in other words, the rejection of the hypostatic union as the trinitarian exposition of the incarnation. What do we mean when we say with the Gospel of John that the divine Logos became flesh? We *don't* mean metaphysical transubstantiation such that divinity turned into flesh or flesh into divinity. *Nor* do we mean that a perfectly receptive human being, providentially provided, grew into a perfect consciousness of God as Schleiermacher portrays the salutary, prototypical Jesus-possibility for us. What we mean is that the eternal person of the Logos/Son gave himself fully to be the very human son of Mary who was crucified under Pilate so that it is true to say the Son of God suffered for us as his ownmost and only human body and soul, indeed, in his Spirit-anointed body and soul. But it is also true to say that this incarnate Son of God suffered in a truly *divine* way: in the *patience* of creative love even in the face of persistent incomprehension and hostility. The divine Son suffered spiritually cruel human rejection, false witness, betrayal with a kiss, abandonment by his own, denial by his chosen, the ignominy of the taunting crowd demanding a display of divine power to save himself—in all this, the righteous wrath of God poured out on the sinfulness that ruins the creation, the sinfulness that this divine Son bore, body and soul, out of willing solidarity of unfathomable love with failures and persecutors. He suffered divinely the true death of his very own sin-bearing humanity, its loss to the grave, its redemptive future evidently contradicted,

52. Bayer, "Das Wort ward Fleisch," 5–34.

canceled. The divine Son suffers spiritually in helplessness, having given up status and authority, divinely waiting in trust upon the vindication of his incarnate life, which vindication he may not give to himself (*nemo iudex in causa sui*),[53] but in divine patience waiting upon the restoration of his own humanity for the future intended by his God and Father of life, righteousness and peace.

Bonhoeffer's sharp and ironic judgment is that Schleiermacher and those following him are in truth the modern docetists.

> Why is this docetism? Because, once again, it is not the real human being, but rather an image of the human being obtained from a particular concept of history, which is then applied to Jesus. One starts with a particular religious idea that one already has and applies it to this historical Jesus. Thus, it is decisive that Jesus as a historical person is reduced to the embodiment of a religious idea. Here his becoming-human once again becomes the means to an end . . . From this point on, all liberal theology must be understood in the context of a docetic Christology. Liberal theology only wanted to see, in Jesus, the embodiment of a certain doctrine. Thus, the humanity of Jesus is basically not taken seriously, even though liberal theology has much to say about Jesus as a human being. The idea of Jesus as humanity bypasses here the reality of Jesus as a human being, confuses the ideal of his humanity with its reality, in short makes his humanity into a symbol.[54]

Bonhoeffer's positive point from this critique will be that the divine becoming as this particular human being is the enduring sense and purpose of the incarnation.

It is difficult simply to derive a reparative instruction from Bonhoeffer's early lectures on Christology which we have only from a reconstruction of student notes in which the young lecturer is trying out various ideas without tying things together neatly. It is certain, however, that he wants to make a Luther-like assertion of the "who" of Jesus Christ, bypassing the misleading "how" question. In other words, Bonhoeffer would confront us with the God-given and established reality of the unique God-Man as the person who works and whose works as saving can only be understood in the light of this asserted identity. The lectures accordingly deliver a nuanced critique of the christological tradition.

53. Malysz, "*Nemo iudex in causa sua*," 363–86.

54. DBW 12:336–37.

> The Chalcedonian formula is an answer to the "how" question, but it is an answer in which the "how" question has already been surmounted . . . We must carry on in this Chalcedonian sense. This can only happen when we have overcome our way of thinking about the divinity and humanity of Christ as objects that are before us, when our thinking does not begin with the two natures in isolation, but rather with the fact that Jesus Christ is God. The *is* may not be interpreted any further. It has been established by God and is therefore the premise of all our thinking and not subject to any further constructions.[55]

In terms of Chalcedon, then, the "unity of person" presides hermeneutically for it asserts definitively the priority of the who over the how. We might therefore see in Bonhoeffer a tentative exploration of the repair of Chalcedon in his reiterating the unity of God and man as the "who" of Christ apart from any explanation of its "how." If so, it may also be the precedent upon which Jenson's revisionism was based, i.e., taking the explicit and more radical step of jettisoning the hypostatic person as an illicit theory explaining the how of the incarnation by providing an agent of this union. As such, the mythological hypostasis is no more than a redundant fifth wheel which obscures the divinely established, direct identification of Jesus as the God-man, for Jenson the "second identity" of God.

Similarly, Bonhoeffer expresses skepticism that the Chalcedonian unity *of person* is in fact an answer to the who question and is rather an attempt to answer the how question. Over against soft criticism of Reformed Christology (as if Luther's tradition did not say the same!), which supposedly does not unite two natures in any other way "than indirectly through the person [so that] what can be said about one of the two natures can be said of the person,"[56] Bonhoeffer wants to affirm the deeper insight of *Luther's* own Christology that "God is no longer other than the one who has become human. God is bound up in the human being . . . The concrete existence of one nature is expressed by the concrete existence of the other nature." Yet in keeping with Luther, Bonhoeffer nonetheless rightly qualifies that "you may say that God is the human being, but not that divinity is humanity. The two natures remain separate." Bonhoeffer thus hovers indecisively here over alternative possible reforms of Chalcedon.

55. DBW 12:350.

56. DBW 12:346.

For the Alexandrian precedence accorded to the unity of person, the union of ontologically distinct natures is precisely the work of the divine hypostasis of the Son who communicates its divine properties as appropriate to its humanity for the messianic work. This personal mediation is indispensable if indeed "the concrete existence of God and that of the human being must be expressed by each other."[57] Bonhoeffer along the same lines, however, criticized the patristic doctrine of the *enhypostasis*, meaning that Jesus had no human hypostasis of his own, but that his human nature was *uniquely* formed in the divine hypostasis.[58] He questions whether *enhypostasis* is "an ultimately concealed form of docetism" in denying that Jesus has a hypostasis of his own, even though he knows well that Jesus can be *followed* in the power of the Spirit (as he showed in his later commentary on the Sermon on the Mount), but *not emulated* as the unique God-man who alone saves. Likewise, Bonhoeffer criticized the Chemnitz-Gerhard doctrine of *ubivolipraesens* (even though it originates in Luther's account of the freedom of the glorified Christ to be bodily present as he promises over against the Zwinglian Christology confining Jesus locally to heaven) for reinforcing the supposedly Reformed insistence upon a mediating divine person between the human nature and the divine nature. Like to others in modern Lutheran Christology, the notion of the divine hypostasis or person as agent of the union seemed little other than a buffer to keep divine nature from fatal compromise by a real union with the mortality and shame of the human Jesus. Yet his concession to Luther's affirmation of hypostasis for the good reason of rejecting an ontological kenosis of the divine nature dissolving into the human causes him to swing back and forth without resolution in the lectures. But alleged buffering is not the motive nor necessity of the doctrine of the hypostatic union. It is not the problem of the Chalcedonian formula in need of repair but rather the solution, when and if hypostasis is rightly taken in its Trinitarian sense.[59]

57. DBW 12:344.

58. DBW 12:335.

59. As the later Barth wrote, we have "to affirm and understand as essential to the being of God the offensive fact that there is in God himself an above and below, a *prius* and a *posterius*, a superiority and a subordination . . . it belongs to the inner life of God that there should take place within it obedience . . . His divine unity consists in the fact that in himself he is both one who was obeyed and another who obeys. Not in unequal but equal, not in divided but in the one deity, God is both one and also another, his own counterpart, coexistent with himself." McCormack, *Humility of the Divine Son* is a sustained development of these thoughts from CD IV/1:200–201. What follows is adapted from Hinlicky, "Luther and the 'Repair of Chalcedon.'"

Indeed, just as Bonhoeffer fair-mindedly acknowledges, the personal union means precisely that the Chalcedonian union is *not* a fusion of natures but a personally willed communication of divine properties to the humanity, based neither upon a metamorphosis nor a hybridization but on a divine and personal appropriation of humanity, constituting a genuine and unique *novum* in the life of God to redeem guilty and perishing humanity. What we can take away from Bonhoeffer's critique of liberal Christology and his attempt to retrieve the gravamen of the Lutheran christological tradition is that the gospel narrative indeed asserts that "the concrete existence of God and that of the human being are expressed by each other." By this he should have understood that the concrete way of being God *as the Son* and the concrete way of being human as *Jesus born of Mary and crucified under Pilate* are expressed by each other. By "concrete existence," however, Bonhoeffer, like Jenson and Brenz overlooked the personal characteristic of the eternal Son as one concrete way of being God-in-relation to others; thus, he does not think being God in the concrete way of being Son as immediately and directly related to the ways of being God as the Father and as the Spirit. He seems to want with Brenz a union of natures direct and unmediated. Yet the attempt to repair Chalcedon by eliminating the divine hypostasis of the eternal Son by interpreting it as a gratuitous buffering device rather than an intra-divine relation fails. In reality, the person of the eternal Son provides the unity of the incarnate person precisely as simultaneously it constitutes its constitutive relational unity with the Father and the Spirit. Absent the free and willing personal obedience and humility of the eternal Son in becoming human, so that being God concretely as the Son is expressed as the concrete humanity of Jesus freely consenting to the will of his Father, the gospel assertion that the Son of God *is* the son of Mary collapses into a dumbfounding *obiter dicta*: Jesus is God, take it or leave it. Least of all does such nonsensical predication posing as christological paradox illuminate the wonder of Jesus's Spirit-enabled *human* consent at Gethsemane—the true test of anti-docetism in Christology!

The persistent problem of thinking two "substances" in one Christ resurfaced following Chalcedon in controversies about the two wills, human and divine, in the one person. Eventually the right kind of distinction was suggested and, in the process, the genuine necessity of the humanity of Jesus, body *and soul*, for human salvation was identified. The promising synthesis in this connection is that of Maximus the Confessor and it commends itself to reconstruction in Lutheran Christology.[60] Here the human will of the *anhypostatic* human nature is embedded by the Spirit (*enhypostized*) from conception in the divine hypostasis of the Son of God, as indeed Jesus then appears in the gospel's narrative world as growing in grace into the Spirit's man on a mission, endowed with the Spirit to do the Father's will in sending/giving his Son. Jesus lives his life for us into this messianic vocation. Recalling that enhypostasis is meant as a conceptual description of the foregoing narrative rendering of the persona, not a theory of the "how" of incarnation, enhypostasis tells that the human mind of the man Jesus is without an autonomous "personality" (to use the misleading anachronism after which questers chase), formed as are the rest of us by the overwhelming experience of an alienated creation. Indeed, the gospel narrative shows no interest whatsoever in the psychology of Jesus on the analogy of modern self-consciousness. Rather, the human mind of Jesus from the outset is portrayed as utterly filial, hinting its formation in the One who expressed equality with God in the concrete and divinely powerful way of self-donating, humble and obedient Sonship. The narrative thus tells of a mysterious "who" requiring doctrinal description for its faithful retelling; such description of a way of being in the world is not an explanation of "how" but a safeguard and provocation to wonder. Paul describes in doxological language the unique person, the "Christ Jesus" of Phil 2:5, sent, going, and returned, describing a mystery and a wonder, inviting worship but resisting comprehension. In just this way, the entire mission turns dramatically upon the human consent of Jesus in the obedience of faith which could have been refused, if the testing was real as also the humanity, not playacting. The humiliation of the divine Son of God incarnate is not least such intimate *dependence* on the final willing consent of its own humanity to drink the dreadful cup. To focus on that is the point of christological doctrine with respect to the issue of docetism.

Closer to home, reconstruction in Lutheran Christology might consider, as previously discussed, the key theme of *faith* in any theological account of the integrity of human nature assumed and preserved and glorified in the incarnation. The human faith of Jesus, as articulated in the Lord's Prayer[61] and performed in the garden of Gethsemane, could fruitfully combine with the recent rediscovery of the Pauline *pistis*

60. Louth, *Maximus the Confessor*, 186–87.

61. Hinlicky, "Retrieving Luther on Prayer."

Christou,[62] as previously discussed in chapter 3. According to Luther's *fides Christi*,[63] Jesus Christ is not only the object of the believer's faith but the very subject in the believer's faith (cf. Gal 2:20). When believers believe, it is Jesus Christ by the Holy Spirit who believes in them. Thus, their faith is first of all the faith of Jesus, a vicarious faith on behalf of the unbelieving world, then, beginning with their own conflicted selves wherein Christian life is constantly renewed by the sanctifying Spirit in the experience of the Gethsemane of the soul. Following the Phil 2 plotline in any event reflects the gospel narrative in attesting public purity of purpose in fidelity to his messianic vocation under the profound trial of an "obedience to death, even death on a cross." Apart from voluntary human consent, however, it would not be filial obedience to his God and Father but a forced death march. His public obedience of faith in and to his calling is to live humanly as the Son of God just as the divine Son lives divinely as this son of Mary: the one and same person.

The narrative character sketch centering on the *human* obedience of faith cannot be understood as puppetry orchestrated by a divine spook (let alone baiting the devil to pounce). The true and profound humility of the divine Son in the incarnation is his divine dependence on his own true Spirit-anointed humanity for the accomplishment of the mission. When glory is sung to Jesus in Lenten hymns, the reference is to the agonizing human surrender in Gethsemane to his Abba Father's uncanny will that he, the beloved Son, drink the bitter cup. In Robert Bridges translation of Johan Heermann's *Herzliebster Jesu* the human and divine characteristics are entirely integrated in the one divine person living to the end the saving human solidarity with the guilty and the perishing.

> Ah, holy Jesus, how hast thou offended that man to judge thee
> hath in hate pretended? By foes derided, by thine own rejected,
> O almost afflicted.

62. Hinlicky, "Faith."

63. Lotz, *Luther and Ritschl*. Lotz acutely distinguishes the liberal Protestant interpretation of Luther in Albrecht Ritschl from Luther himself in a way that anticipates accents of the Finnish school of Luther interpretation. "In the matter of justification, one must supposedly opt for either imputed righteousness or infused righteousness; either God's forensic sentence outside of us (*extra nos*) or his sanative of process within us (*in nobis*); either "for Christ sake" or "in view of the new obedience." Luther himself would not have recognized these options as mutually exclusive. His theology of the real presence of Christ, affected in the believer by the Spirit through faith in the living Word, held together what his interpreters have not infrequently put asunder" (136).

> Who was the guilty? Who brought this upon thee? Alas, my treason, Jesus, hath undone thee. 'Twas I, Lord Jesus, I it was denied thee; I crucified thee.
>
> Lo, the Good Shepherd for the sheep is offered; the slave had sinned, and the Son hath suffered; for man's atonement, while he nothing heedeth, God interceedeth.
>
> For me, kind Jesus, was thine incarnation, thy mortal sorrow, and thy life's oblation; thy death of anguish and thy bitter passion, for my salvation.
>
> Therefore, kind Jesus, since I cannot pay thee, I do adore thee, and will ever pray thee; think on thy pity and thy love unswerving, not my deserving.[64]

The Reality of God Is the Eternal Trinity

What must it mean for the *being there* of God if Jesus is Lord? The legitimate concern of Antiochene Christology had been to preserve this human dimension of the incarnate life of the humble Son of God who so exercised *divine* Sonship as *human* obedience to death, even death on a cross. As we have seen, the wrong way to conceptualize this is to think of two sons, the son of Mary and the Son of God as if sign to thing signified. The right way is to think of the union in Christ is of the sign *as* the thing signified: son of Mary from the beginning uniquely formed by the Spirit as the self-donating Son of God's own. But *how* may we conceptualize this genuine union in the one person of Christ Jesus? With the provision that it is and remains to all eternity an ineffable wonder invoking the confession of praise, this much may be said by way of clarification.

Inasmuch as human nature *qua creature* is malleable ("clay in the potter's hands"), its "gnomic" will, as Maximus termed the equivalent of the Latin *voluntas* (willingness), is a *disposition*, not so much a "free will" as, so to speak, a "free won't," i.e., in withholding consent. As the natural freedom of *consent*, it does not initiate spontaneously as if a creator but only responds willingly as patient of the Creator's will (which it can also—notoriously but freely—refuse). By contrast, *the sole creator* is *freely* formative in relation to creatures. It alone spontaneously initiates in free self-determination *ad extra* which is at the same time a sovereign expression of pure benevolence towards all that is not God. Even so clarified, however, to conceptualize the asymmetrical beings of the Lord who forms and of the servant who is formed under the common concept of

64. "Ah, holy Jesus, how hast Thou offended" by Johann Heerman, translated by Robert Bridges.

"nature/substance" cannot but be misleading. This equivalence or rather equivocation by an abstract common concept Schleiermacher rightly rejected.[65] Caution is needed here. In his humanity Jesus knew and lived into his calling as the beloved Son because in his divinity the same eternal Son freely chose to become dependent upon this, his own humanity, by way of the sanctifying Spirit contesting the *regnum diaboli*. In the gospel of Luke, the evangelist tells that the tempter departed Jesus in the wilderness for a more "opportune time." In his account of the passion, the evangelist makes the point that the adversary has now returned again to challenge: "If you are the Son of God, do this to save yourself!" which is three times repeated by taunting onlookers to shame the dying Jesus. In surrendering his life's breath to his Father, the dying man Jesus shows his full and true divinity *as the Son* of that Father. The theological response to this human consent of the One who thereby overcame the satanic temptation that he demonstrate divine Sonship by *sinful* self-justification is *the* confession of praise, "Ah! *Holy* Jesus!"—*or* offense.

The pragmatic point of doctrine for life concerning this saving person is to *identify*, not to theorize. We must bear in mind here the clarification that this baptized terminology of "natures" is descriptive *ontology*, *no longer* metaphysics; it locates, describes and classifies realities for purposes of *orientation*, it does not pretend to explain them ultimately. Describing the person of Jesus Christ as the one in the world who deploys from two otherwise separate baskets of "species-typical" potentialities serves strictly *to point* to the gospel narrative of the incarnate Son of his Abba Father, the God of Israel, on a mission to save precisely as the new Adam on whom the Spirit rests, utilizing freely the attributes of both "natures" *personally* as befits the needs of the mission. This clarified *reference (*biblically, *witness!)* is the sole *meaning* of christological doctrine. To try to get behind this and uncover the mystery, whether historically or metaphysically, is to take offense at the gospel which for good reason tells who but not how. If we knew the "how" of the Creator's way, we would be the creator. For our own true good as earthlings on rare and precious planet Earth, Creator God in his self-giving revelation bars this path in hiddenness.

Hence our true good is to be at home on the earth with a new "taste for the finite."[66] That too belongs to the saving reconciliation in Christ, just as the humanity of the Lord made known at Gethsemane singles out the Savior as human among humans, our brother and friend. To be

65. Schleiermacher, *Christian Faith*, 2:392.

66. Bayer, "I Believe That God Has Created Me with All That Exists."

certain, one can take offense at this and insist upon the how question; Christian theology can respect that objection, provided that it is done with intellectual honesty. But it is no less intellectually honest for the Christian theologian in virtue of this barrier to acknowledge true doctrine within the limits of the theological circle of faith alone by the Spirit's grace alone in Christ alone. Just so, we come to know what in the world we are talking about as Christians when we employ the word, God: a fiery furnace—aflame with love for us, *severe* love, *holy* love for us all as we really are and not as we fancy ourselves to be. At home on the earth in new lives of righteousness, life, and peace we await in the patient obedience of faith the consummation which comes upon the earth from above.

> A doctrine of the Trinity which takes seriously the mutuality of loving communion opened up for humanity in Christ by the Spirit suggests the ultimate identification of the source of being in the communion of the Trinity. The communion of God is in no sense to be conceived as a qualification of a more foundational category of "Being" or "Substance." The triune communion characterizes Reality (Being) at the most fundamental level—it is that in which we live and move and have our being. The communion of the Trinity as such constitutes the *arche* and the *telos* of all that is. It provides the hermeneutical criterion of all that has existence (good as well as evil) and compels us to conceive and reinterpret being in terms of divine personhood and the ultimacy of the intra-divine personal communion. That the critical controls on the understanding of this would have to remain radically theological (and therefore *a posteriori*) and not anthropological is expressed in Barth's emphatic reminder, "this is the unique divine trinity in the unique divine unity."[67]

So, knowing this, the objection to Lindbeck's model of doctrine that it declines to make ontological claims is met and the feared collapse into inbred and self-referential propaganda prevented on account of making no claim to truth that can in the appropriate way be verified. The pragmatic verification of the ontological claim that the God of the gospel is the One who is God truly consists entirely in the consent of human beings, beginning with Jesus the author and pioneer of our faith, to entrust themselves to this promise of eternal personal-social communion. That trust is ventured on the eschatological vindication of

67. Torrance, *Persons in Communion*, 258–59.

the promise of eternal life on the precedent of the Easter vindication of the faith of Jesus for us.

Lindbeck had expressed reserve about the doctrine of the eternal Trinity with its incarnation denoting the human visitation of the eternal Son as speculative transgression of the Trinitarian pattern of gospel language, accompanied to boot with a dogmatic demand for belief in the speculation. But the doctrinal status of the immanent and eternal Trinity need not be taken as metaphysical speculation; indeed, its doctrinal function as confession of praise is corrupted by metaphysical speculation. Its status is rather to be seen, as in Paul's use of the Philippians 2 Christ hymn,[68] as a doxology anticipating the promised future of the redeemed creation and from this forward perspective looking back upon its origin in the eternal life of God as the condition of its historical possibility. The doctrine of the immanent Trinity is an *induction* from the narrative Trinity of the gospel whom we meet in our human history; it is an induction on the grounds that the God of the gospel must be conceived to be truthful in his self-giving self-revelation and is powerful, wise and good to deliver the promise of fallen creation's emancipation, the final apocalypse of the glorious liberty of the children of God by the redemption of their bodies. These affirmations must be fleshed out in a robust account of the doctrine of the resurrection as the apocalyptic defeat of that last enemy. But that is a task for another day. As holding this belief entails the conviction that nothing in all creation can separate us from the love of God in Christ Jesus our Lord, the doctrine of the immanent Trinity indeed makes a claim to truth and as such is doctrine for life, grounding the confidence to live in the hope of the redemption of our bodies even as we regard what we do in our bodies here and now on the earth as having eternal significance. Our labor in the Lord is not in vain—here is a meaningful claim to truth that can be either be affirmed in faith or denied in unbelief.

68. Wesley Hill's instructive treatment of Philippians 2 concludes: "In terms of his identification with the *Kyrios* of the LXX, Jesus is not differentiated from God (with whom he shares the same form and to whom he is 'equal'). In terms of his relation to the *person or agent Theos pater*, Jesus is differentiated from God and ordered in such a way that he could be labeled 'subordinate.' Both of these affirmations are required by the theological grammar of Phil. 2:6-11 . . . " Hill, *Paul and the Trinity*, 110.

Conclusion

Siloed inside the total system of propaganda, a meeting of minds in common deliberation to live into a future together can never occur. But just this breakthrough, predicated upon a break-in, has been proposed in the preceding pages. This book has re-situated the cultural-linguistic model of doctrine proposed a generation ago by George Lindbeck into the christologically modified apocalyptic of primitive Christianity in order to ground the model in the external word of God which comes to the self from outside of itself to transform the self. This Word announces the originative event of the resurrection of the crucified Jesus; it is the gospel concerning the Son. Insofar as Lindbeck defined a religious community as determined by an "external word," which evoked a normative language in confessing what had been heard, the need for doctrinal thought arose as for a learned grammar to articulate intelligibly the originative event with its enduring force. In the case of Christianity, Lindbeck spoke of the "story" of God putatively given by God in the originative event. Despite the fact that Lindbeck borrowed from modern philosophy and sociology to justify his model before a broad audience so that it might be ecumenically received and used to facilitate ecumenical convergence and interreligious communication, the traces of his own Lutheranism were everywhere evident, particularly in the signature proposal that the meaning of doctrine is its use to regulate thinking, speech and behavior such that the community perseveres in its identity and mission through the changes and chances of time. Adapting Lindbeck's model for the reconstruction of doctrinal theology in the tradition of Luther, therefore, has not been intrinsically difficult, provided the reconstruction bears in mind, as stated in the Preface to the Augsburg Confession, the ecumenical intention of the Lutheran Reformation in its doctrinal theology. But in the process of adapting the model, it was found necessary to face certain significant objections to the model and to meet them with clarifying amendments. This influential revisioning of the model proved possible because re-grounding it in the apocalyptic theology of the New Testament correlated with the rediscovery and reiteration of apocalyptic in early Lutheranism, particularly documented in Luther's own impressive forays into doctrinal theology in his catechisms and the treatise against Erasmus.

It was hermeneutically important here to interpret apocalyptic as a genre of metaphorical narrative referring to deity. Deliteralization of metaphor to yield its knowledge of God is a hermeneutical operation in second-order theology which does not discard the apocalyptic narrative of the conflict of the ages as does the program of demythologization but interprets it theologically to refer to the coming of the creator God to reclaim his usurped creation from dark forces; this hermeneutical operation produces a reference to the *being there* of the heavenly Father who sends his Son in the power of his Spirit into the depths of human captivity to reconcile and liberate. It thus produces a meaningful statement in the confession, Jesus is Lord, which can be affirmed in faith or denied in unbelief, a meaningfulness that in turn required ongoing doctrinal clarification expressed in what Luther described as formulas of speech given by the Holy Spirit, promised to lead to all truth by recalling the word of Jesus.

It was important in the process of this apocalyptic rehoming of the cultural-linguistic model of doctrine to discriminate at least three orders of theological discourse entailed by greater precision in the doctrine of the Word inherited from Reformation times. The necessity was to disambiguate "the Word," which could mean Scripture, the divine Logos, the Logos incarnate, the eternal Son of God, the Son incarnate, the law, the gospel, or the law and the gospel in sequence or dialectical simultaneity, preaching (kerygma), the present Christ or the historical Jesus, the visible sacraments, even religious experience. Equivocation always produces confusion, particularly pernicious when what is at stake is the source and warrant of proposed regulation in theological doctrine. Clarity was attempted early on in this book by ranking a first-order description of the *norma normans* of *the* word of God in relation to a second-order *norma normata* articulating timely reception and confession with the force of formulations regulating proper thinking, speaking and enacting of that first-order word of God. Hence, by virtue of re-situating the model in New Testament apocalyptic, the external word of God was described as the gospel of the resurrection-vindication of the Crucified Jesus and put into relation with its primitive confession, Jesus is Lord, as the embryonic statement of Christian doctrine.

This resituating and differentiation corrected a fateful imprecision in the broadly Protestant doctrine of inspired Scripture as *norma normans* with the historical discovery that canonicity was determined by the baptismal rule of faith as a summary statement of the apocalyptic gospel, confessed in opposition to and renunciation of the *regnum diaboli.* This differentiation, far from demoting Scripture in doctrinal theology, however, instead elevates it anew as the primary matrix for the construction of ecumenically intended doctrine, as has been practiced illustratively throughout this book. It likewise allows a critical and appreciative appropriation of subsequent creed and confession which commends repair of, and amendment to, the doctrinal tradition rather than the mindless jettisoning or reckless revisionism current today, not to mention rote, merely habitual, hence spiritually vacuous repetition in lazy dogmatism.

Orthodoxy is the intention to think, speak and behave in accord with the gospel of God and as such it is the Spirit's work in progress. No claim to have achieved orthodoxy this side of the eschaton is credible, but neither is any theology that does not intend orthodoxy. This means that the normed norms of Scripture, creed, and confession in descending order of authority are open to the questioning of *Sachkritik* for their own adequacy to the originative event as conveyed in the gospel of God. Indeed, theology in the tradition stemming from Luther today may be all too eager to engage in wild questioning in the place of the intellectually demanding and spiritually patient, life-long work of listening to what these witnesses have to say in their own voices (as Hegel instructed us at the outset of this book against treating the word of God as a blank check to be cashed out with one's own opinionating). Much superficial revisionism in theology eschews the hard work of scholarly hermeneutics. In any case, reparative work may well be in order as we have seen with respect to the Chalcedonian christological formula. But just like the Chalcedonian formula, any constructive repair work must be intended ecumenically and submitted to the wider deliberation and judgment of all who intend orthodoxy, not just the in-crowd of one's own denominational or AAR grouping of the like-minded.

Much of this book has probed two chief objections to Lindbeck's model and provided amendments to it to meet these objections. One objection is to its pneumatological deficit in seemingly expecting the ritual performance of the external word to transform human affect in conformity with the story of Israel and Jesus without explicit naming, proclaiming and pastoral ministering of the correlative event of the love of God poured into human hearts by the sanctifying Spirit who has been given to us, bearing witness to our spirits that we are indeed the children of God. The economic Trinitarianism that Lindbeck more or less silently presupposed had to be explicated both in terms of Zahl's "low anthropology" and the sanctifying Spirit's personhood as Lord and giver of life in sovereignly electing to faith in the palpable human experience of Pauline conversion, explicated as Augustine's "severe mercy": God's word proclaimed as law that righteously demands for the sake of promise that mercifully gives what is demanded. The Word alone is never alone but truly the word of God when the word of God is deployed by the sanctifying Spirit—hence, *spiritually*—as event that kills in order to make alive.

The other important objection to Lindbeck's model was its apparent fideism in the sense that it turned the attention of the community of faith inward in concern about its own integrity as a survival strategy in a post-Christendom world rather than to its missiological mandate to connect living faith in the present Christ with real-world experience. Although Lindbeck gestured towards the biblical narrative as "world absorbing," mentioning the theological precedents of Augustine's *City of God* interpreting the fall of Rome and Reinhold Niebuhr's *Nature and Destiny of Man* in the face of ascendant Nazism, there was not great clarity in his proposal about this kind of theological work in relation to his regulative interpretation of doctrine.

This missiological deficit at least formally lent an air of unreality to his proposal for those urgently and rightly concerned with the gospel promises of Rom 8 for conversion of hearts and minds to long for the revelation of the glorious liberty of the children of God and so to work on earth now for greater justice and a better freedom in this frustrated and groaning creation in anticipation of its promised liberation. These have cried out in exasperation, "What in the world are you talking about?" And in fact, this objection indicates an urgently needed amendment to the model, namely, overcoming its reticence to make present and contextually apt claims to truth both concerning the reality of God and concerning the realities of the human world. We have argued that doctrinal assertion of second-order theology serves a unitive purpose in stewarding the gospel integrity of the ecclesia in common confession. In the process, it provides the terms by which lively debate in third-order theology can meaningfully adjudicate proposals for evangelization and greater justice as the community of faith engages the much-conflicted world. This is as it should be. The numerous social, economic, political, and cultural judgments that must be made in third-order theology, however, are by nature tentative and subject to correction on account of the sin and limited vision still attending theological subjects; just this necessitates an inclusive and deliberative procedure in third-order theology, as Wilder recommended in chapter 4. Here too the scholarly virtues of intellectual humility and open-mindedness defend against the danger of propagandization. But above all third-order theology is theology insofar as the certainty of faith, concrete in the confessing unity of the ecclesia, relativizes secular certitudes in the age of total propaganda.

In any case, we have answered the question put to second-order theology about what *in the world* are we talking about in the confession, Jesus is Lord. We are talking about this conflicted world which is at once the good creation of God yet fallen under alien powers by way of sinful human complicity; this earth, on which the cross of Jesus stood, the cross ever signifying its imperiled and contested *being there*. Invoking the christologically modified apocalyptic of the New Testament literature for formulating the originative confession of faith in Jesus as saving Lord, we have *not* meant a literalism denoting a revealed timetable for the end of time but rather the in-breaking of the time of the end, i.e., the metaphorical knowledge of God who comes from God to the purpose of reconciling sinners to the Holy One of Israel and redeeming creation from the tyranny of principalities and powers usurped by spiritual forces of wickedness. We are talking about the Jew Jesus of Nazareth who proclaimed and enacted the impending reign of the God of Israel, his Abba Father, in the sanctifying power of their Spirit, dispelling the legion forces of a mysterious malice personified in the figure of the devil, a confrontation which brought Jesus to the cross. We have predicated Lordship to this very Jesus, risen and vindicated, meaning saving authority and redemptive divine power to rescue and to redeem until all enemies of God are subdued under his feet, the last of which is Death, the brutal whip deployed in the devil's terrorism. In predicating Lordship to Jesus in our world, we have meant a truly integrated divine and human Sonship of humility and obedience actualized in the consent of the man Jesus to the Father's will that out of their common love he make the plight of captivated sinners his very own, himself bearing the sin he had forgiven in his Father's name in the act of taking responsibility for them before God. By the divine Sonship of the man Jesus Christ, we have further meant that he is this Son in intrinsic and inseparable relations of holy love to his Abba Father and the sanctifying Spirit. In naming these three figures of the gospel narrative we have identified the One who promises to be God truly by the redemption and fulfillment of this world as his creation. Asserting this claim to truth we have simultaneously acknowledged its provisional validity, subject to the final and definitive confirmation of the God so identified, yet prevailing here and now in the gathering on the earth of the new humanity, the Israel of God, the ecclesia as creature of the gospel and therewith, but only therewith, also mediator of the gospel in the world.

This conclusion leaves much hanging in the air because, as mentioned, it does not settle third-order theological questions, which are the debates and deliberations of competent theological interlocutors, internally about the adequacy and validity of the terms as formulated by the first two orders of theology, and externally about how these terms relate to challenging contemporary situations. The first two orders of theological discourse, in other words, merely establish the provisional epistemic platform on which context can be debated and the terms by which theological proposals for the church's mission and behavior there can be meaningfully affirmed or denied, or reformed.

Therefore, in conclusion it should be acknowledged that one can, of course, simply refuse, for good reasons or bad, the Easter proclamation and/or its christological confession generating the Trinitarian doctrine of God by which it is clarified and sustained communally in doxological anticipation of the victory of God for us and for all. But in that case, to use Paul Tillich's metaphor, one has departed from the theological circle, which in this book has been exposited as the virtuous circle of the knowledge of God in faith under the stipulation that true God is never at our disposal. Intellectual honesty in that case to depart would better serve the church and the world as well, if one indeed finds oneself outside this big but definite circle established by the word of God and its confession. As formulated in doctrinal theology, the church's speech and practice is thusly tested by the rule of gospel faith (Gal 6:15–16).

But this boundedness to the liberating Lord for freed thinking by no means suggests that the dogmatic tradition is a monolithic block to be accepted uncritically by surrender of conscience and intellect to any authority less than Christ Jesus the Lord. Such dogmatism betrays the very task of critical dogmatics. As this book has illustrated, orthodoxy is the Spirit's work in progress. In theologians it is an intention to think, speak and act true to the gospel of God by giving a reasoned account of the gospel. Such theology experiments as well as it tests. It is ecumenically intended, not a parochial denominational ideology justifying possession of a fragment of ecclesial turf on the rotting corpse of divided Christendom rather than attesting in penitent pain, and seeking healing of, the fractured body of Christ in which one and all are sinfully complicit. Above all, it interrogates the dogmatic tradition not only to retrieve what is good but also to overcome what has gone wrong. Inevitably, then, its articulation of doctrinal theology in any age is also a rigorous attempt to reform the tradition in which one stands, as also has been attempted in this book.

Our age is much and rightly concerned with theological context, meaning the specific social location with its concerns and problems in which the gospel is understood and appropriated for the help it promises, often with the challenge of finding fresh language and new conceptuality to articulate the Christian message fittingly.[69] We saw this concern lifted up in the work of Howard Thurman in which it is arguably the case that text is *not* swallowed up by context but rather like a two-edged sword effectively slices through it to dignify the poor in power with its sharp challenge of spiritual surgery on the heart to repair the soul for new agency in following Jesus. In any case, contextual theology is best understood as an exercise in third-order missiological discourse debating among competent interlocutors how second-order ecumenical doctrine as understood in the theological tradition stemming from Luther meets challenges of particular new contexts.

Here the perennial danger is the propagandistic over-generalization which misrepresents as it also misleads. For example, we witness today the ubiquity of philosopher Michel Foucault's influential reduction of human relations to power differentials so that a sweeping oppressor-oppressed binary emerges as procrustean bed devouring anomalous evidence, thus propagandistically evading difficulties. The reason for this caution against the endemic overgeneralizations of identity politics in third-order theology, then, is that any systematic apologetics built upon generalizations

69. See forthcoming in this series from Cascade in 2027, Apel, *Lutheran Missiology*.

about context may not only create dangerous blind spots by ignoring difficult particularities unique to concrete contexts but also that it may surrender the power to frame the questions posed to the context by the confessional assertions of doctrinal theology. The power to frame the question slips away from the stewards of gospel integrity into the hands self-appointed advocates claiming to speak for all in a particular classification as "voice for the voiceless"—becoming in sad fact, voice *in place of* the voiceless (as in Lenin's "democratic centralism"). The power of framing the question to which theology answers, however, derives from the apocalypse, i.e., *Jesus's* probing query to us, "Who do you say that I am?" But systematic apologetics bestows that power instead on its construction of the cultural context, transforming Jesus's probing question to us into our "constructive" answer, i.e., "who *we* say Jesus is."

As in his indictment of cheap grace, here too Bonhoeffer has been badly misunderstood and consequently misappropriated. The cultural context in any event is always contested within, as it is a confused exponent of human fallenness as well as created goodness; it is a dangerous conceit, therefore, to think one theologizes in context as a representative of all thusly identified by the theologian's gross act of classification apart from the incision of the word of God which make sides rather than take sides.

> Politics, in the normal course of things in the yet-unredeemed world, seems to involve something like an all-too-human struggle to cast out demons by the power of other demons, the effort to check the exercise of power by the deployment of other countervailing powers. . . . Jesus resists assimilation of his Lordship to the patterns of this age . . . Accordingly, the Christian's political service to Christ's reign can and must be politics by other means, the politics of the third Pneumatological article of the church's ancient creeds, we might say . . . a form of exorcism.[70]

Third-order contextual theology is an essential reflection in missiology, provided that we understand how naming Jesus as Lord will always be, this side of the eschaton, *controversial*, a stick in the spokes of the wheel of any mobilization of gentile politics whether imperialist or insurrectionist, conserving or innovating.

Lindbeck thought that the "depth of the present crisis" becomes evident in the observation that "even those who doctrinally agree that

70. Ziegler, *God's Adversary and Ours*, 66.

the story of Jesus is the key to the understanding of reality are often in fundamental theological disagreement over what the story is really about, over its normative or literal sense." He pointed to the diversity of distinct interpretive frameworks, "historical, phenomenological, existential, ethical, metaphysical, doctrinal" that "specify the questions asked of the text and shape the pictures of Jesus that emerge" yielding "implications for religious practice and understanding [that] are radically divergent." He regarded these "divergences" in method and outcome "theological issues" as opposed to "doctrinal ones," and thought them to be "more interesting,"[71] He thusly gestured toward what this book has identified as the open deliberation of third-order theology. But this concluding gesture left the crisis to its own devices and, in the retrospect of forty some years, the crisis has only deepened by the ever encompassing grip of the total system of propaganda. The apocalyptic theology of theology presented in this book, predicating theology on an incision from outside this totality, is a counter-manifesto of freedom, as Andrea Vestrucci has argued. "Theology as freedom" is the ecumenical gift and task of the tradition stemming from Luther.

In the event that this argument for theological theology has succeeded, let such deliberation of freed thinkers begin afresh!

71. Lindbeck, *Nature of Doctrine*, 119.

Bibliography

Adams, Marilyn McCord. *Christ and Horrors: The Coherence of Christology*. Cambridge: Cambridge University Press, 2008.

Apel, Dean. *Lutheran Missiology*. Eugene, OR: Cascade, forthcoming.

Asad, Talal. *Formations of the Secular: Christianity, Islam, Modernity*. Stanford, CA: Stanford University Press, 2003.

Ashton, John. *Understanding the Fourth Gospel*. Oxford: Clarendon, 1993.

Aulen, Gustav. *Christus Victor*. New York: Macmillan, 1931.

Barclay, John M. G. *Pauline Churches and Diaspora Jews*. Tübingen: Mohr Siebeck, 2011.

Bartsch, Hans Werner, ed. *Kerygma and Myth: Rudolf Bultmann and Five Critics*. New York: Harper & Row, 1961.

Bauer, Walter. *Orthodoxy and Heresy in Early Christianity*. Edited by R. Kraft and G. Krodel. Repr. Mifflintown, PA: Sigler, 1996.

Baur, Jörg. *Luther und seine klassischen Erben: Theologische Aufsätze und Forschungen*. Tübingen:Mohr Siebeck, 1993.

Bayer, Oswald. *A Contemporary in Dissent: Johann Georg Hamann as Radical Enlightener*. Translated by Roy A. Harrisville and Mark C. Mattes. Grand Rapids: Eerdmans, 2012.

———. "I Believe That God Has Created Me with All That Exists: An Example of Catechetical-Systematics." Translated by Christine Helmer. *Lutheran Quarterly* 8 (1994) 129–61.

———. "Das Wort ward Fleisch." In *Creator est creatura*, edited by Oswald Bayer and Benjamin Gleede, 5–34. Berlin: Walter de Gruyter, 2007.

Bell, Daniel M., Jr. *Liberation Theology After the End of History: The Refusal to Cease Suffering*. London: Routledge, 2001.

Benne, Robert. *The Paradoxical Vision: A Public Theology for the Twenty-First Century*. Minneapolis: Fortress, 1995.

Bergen, Doris L. *Twisted Cross: The German Christian Movement in the Third Reich*. Chapel Hill, NC: University of North Carolina Press, 1996.

Berlinski, David. *The Devil's Delusion: Atheism and Its Scientific Pretensions* New York: Basic, 2009.

Bertram, Robert W. *A Time for Confessing*. Edited by Michael Hoy. Grand Rapids: Eerdmans, 2008.

Bird, Michael F., and Preston M. Sprinkle, eds. *The Faith of Jesus Christ: Exegetical, Biblical and Theological Studies*. Peabody, MA: Hendrickson, 2009.

Bonhoeffer, Dietrich. *The Cost of Discipleship*. Translated by R. H. Fuller. New York: Simon and Schuster, 1995.

———. *Ethics*. Translated by N. H. Smith. New York: MacMillan, 1978.

———. *Sanctorum Communio*. Minneapolis: Fortress, 1998.

Borg, Marcus J., and N. T. Wright. *The Meaning of Jesus: Two Visions*. San Francisco: HarperCollins, 1998.

Bornkamm, Günther. "Das Wort Jesu vom Bekennen." *Pastoraltheologie* 34 (1938) 108–18.

Boulton, Matthew Myer. *God Against Religion: Rethinking Christian Theology through Worship*. Grand Rapids: Eerdmans, 2008.

Boyarin, Daniel. *Dying for God: Martyrdom and the Making of Christianity and Judaism*. Stanford, CA: Stanford University Press, 1999.

Brown, Raymond E. *The Community of the Beloved Disciple: The Life, Loves and Hates of an Individual Church in New Testament Times*. Mahwah, NJ: Paulist Press: 1978.

Brueggemann, Walter. *Theology of the Old Testament: Testimony, Dispute, Advocacy*. Minneapolis: Fortress, 1997.

Bultmann, Rudolf. *Faith and Understanding*. Edited by Robert W. Funk and translated by Louise Pettibone Smith. Philadelphia: Augsburg Fortress, 1987.

———. *The Gospel of John: A Commentary*. Translated by G. R. Beasley-Murray. Philadelphia: Westminster, 1976.

Burleigh, Michael. *Earthly Powers: The Clash of Religion and Politics in Europe, from the French Revolution to the Great War*. New York: HarperCollins, 2005.

———. *The Third Reich: A New History*. New York: Hill and Wang, 2000.

Carr, Amy. *Facing Divine Affliction: A Lutheran Theodicy for the Sinned Against* Eugene, OR: Cascade, forthcoming.

Case, Brendan. "The Devil's Envy: On Christ as Angelic Justifier and Demonic Stumbling." *The International Journal of Systematic Theology* 25 (2023) 474–95.

Chilton, Bruce, ed. *The Kingdom of God*. Philadelphia: Augsburg Fortress, 1984.

Coakley, Sarah. "What Does Chalcedon Solve and What Does It Not? Some Reflections on the Status and Meaning of the Chalcedonian 'Definition.'" In *The Incarnation: An Interdisciplinary Symposium on the Incarnation of the Son of God*, edited by Stephen T. Davis. Oxford: Oxford University Press, 2002.

Conzelmann, Hans. *1 Corinthians: A Commentary* trans. James W. Leitch. Philadelphia: Augsburg Fortress, 1975.

Crawford, Matthew B. *The World Beyond Your Head: On Becoming an Individual in an Age of Distraction*. New York: Ferrar, Straus and Giroux, 2015.

Cross, Richard. *Communicatio Idiomatum: Reformation Christological Debates*. Oxford: Oxford University Press, 2019.

Cyril of Jerusalem. "Catechetical Lectures, Lectures 19–21." Christian Classics Ethereal Library. https://ccel.org/ccel/schaff/npnf207/npnf207.ii.iv.html.

———. *The Works of St. Cyril of Jerusalem*. Translated by Leo P. McCauley S. J. and Anthony A. Stephenson. Fathers of the Church 65. Washington, DC: Catholic University of America Press, 1970.

Dalferth, Ingolf U. *Crucified and Resurrected: Restructuring the Grammar of Christology*. Translated by Jo Bennett. Grand Rapids: Baker Academic, 2015.

Davis, Joshua B., and Douglas Harink, eds. *Apocalyptic and the Future of Theology: With and Beyond J. Louis Martyn*. Eugene, OR: Cascade, 2012.

de Boer, Martinus C. *Paul: Theologian of God's Apocalypse*. Eugene, OR: Cascade 2020.

DeJonge, Michael P. *Bonhoeffer's Reception of Luther*. Oxford: Oxford University Press, 2017.

Dingel, Irene. *Die Bekenntnisschriften der evangelisch-lutherischen Kirche*. Gőttingen: Vanderhooeck & Ruprecht, 1967.

Dunn, James D. G. "Let John Be John: A Gospel for Its Time." In *The Gospel and the Gospels*, edited by Peter Stuhlmacher, 293–321. Grand Rapids: Eerdmans, 1991.

Eastman, Susan Grove. "Apocalypse and Incarnation: The Participatory Logic of Paul's Gospel." In *Apocalyptic and the Future of Theology*, edited by J. Davis and D. Harink, 165–82. Eugene, OR: Wipf & Stock, 2012.

Edwards, Mark U., Jr. *Luther's Last Battles: Politics and Polemics 1531–46*. Ithaca, NY: Cornell University Press, 1983.

———. Luther's Polemical Controversies." In *The Cambridge Companion to Martin Luther*, edited by D. K. McKim, 194–95. Cambridge: Cambridge University Press, 2003.

———. "Supermus: Luther's Own Fanatics." In *Seven-Headed Luther: Essays in Commemoration of a Quincentenary 1483–1983*, edited by P. N. Brooks, 123–46. Oxford: Clarendon, 1983.

Ellul, Jacques. *Propaganda: The Formation of Men's Attitude*. Translated by Conrad Kellen and Jean Lerner. New York: Vintage, 1965.

Elshtain, Jean Bethke. *Sovereignty: God, State, and Self, The Gifford Lectures*. New York: Basic, 2008.

Ericksen, Robert B. *Theologians Under Hitler: Gerhard Kittel, Paul Althuas and Emanuel Hirsch*. New Haven, CT: Yale University Press, 1985.

Farmer, William R. *The Formation of the New Testament Canon: An Ecumenical Approach*. Mahwah, NJ: Paulist, 1983.

Forbes, Chris. "Pauline Demonology and/or Cosmology? Principalities, Powers and the Elements of the World in their Hellenistic Context." *JSNT* 85 (2002) 51–73.

———. "Paul's Principalities and Powers: Demythologizing Apocalyptic?" *Journal for the Study of the New Testament* 82 (2001) 61–88.

Forstman, Jack. *Christian Faith in Dark Times: Theological Conflicts in the Shadow of Hitler*. Louisville, KY: Westminster John Knox, 1992.

Frei, Hans W. *The Eclipse of Biblical Narrative: A Study in Eighteenth and Nineteenth Century Hermeneutics*. New Haven, CT: Yale University Press, 1974.

Gadamer, Hans-Georg. *Truth and Method*. New York: Seabury, 1975.

Gathercole, Simon. *Defending Substitution: An Essay on Atonement in Paul*. Grand Rapids: Baker Academic, 2015.

Girard, René. *Violence and the Sacred*. Translated by Patrick Gregory. Baltimore: John Hopkins University Press, 1979.

Gore, Charles. "Our Lord's Human Example." *Church Quarterly Review* 16 (1883) 298.

Greene, Garrett. *Imagining Theology: Encounters with God in Scripture, Interpretation, and Aesthetics*. Grand Rapids: Baker Academic, 2020.

Greggs, Tom. *Theology Against Religion: Constructive Dialogues with Bonhoeffer and Barth*. London: T. & T. Clark, 2011.

Gura, Philip F. *American Transcendentalism: A History*. New York: Hill and Wang, 2007.

Hardy, Edward R., ed. *Christology of the Later Fathers*. Philadelphia: Westminster, 1954.

Hart, David Bentley. *Tradition and Apocalypse: An Essay on the Future of Christian Belief.* Grand Rapids: Baker Academic, 2022.

Harvey, Lincoln. *Jesus and the Trinity: A Beginner's Guide to the Theology of Robert Jenson*. London: SCM, 2020.

Hauerwas, Stanley, and William H. Willimon. *Resident Aliens: Life in the Christian Colony*, Expanded 25th Anniversary Edition. Nashville: Abingdon, 2014.

Haugh, Richard S. *Photius and the Carolingians: The Trinitarian Controversy*. Belmont, MA: Nordland, 1975.

Hays, Richard B. *The Faith of Jesus Christ: The Narrative Substructure of Gal. 3:1—4:11*. Eerdmans: Grand Rapids, 2002.

Hegel, G. F. *Lectures on the History of Philosophy*. 3 vols. Translated by E. S. Haldane with an Introduction by Frederick C. Beiser. Lincoln, NE: University of Nebraska Press, 1995.

———. *Lectures on the Philosophy of Religion: One Volume Edition*. Edited by P. C. Hodgson. Berkeley: University of California Press, 1988.

Helmer, Christine. *How Luther Became the Reformer*. Louisville, KY: Westminster John Knox, 2019.

———. *Theology and the End of Doctrine*. Louisville, KY: Westminster John Knox, 2014.

Helmer, Christine, and Amy Carr. *Ordinary Faith in Polarized Times: Justification and the Pursuit of Justice*. Waco, TX: Baylor University Press, 2023.

Hendrix, Scott H. *Luther and the Papacy: Stages in a Reformation Conflict* Philadelphia: Augsburg Fortress, 1981.

Heschel, Susannah. *The Aryan Jesus: Christian Theologians and the Bible in Nazi Germany*. Princeton, NJ: Princeton University Press, 2008.

Hill, Wesley. *Paul and the Trinity: Persons, Relations, and the Pauline Letters*. Grand Rapids: Eerdmans 2015.

Hinlicky, Paul R. *Before Auschwitz: What Christian Theology Must Learn from the Rise of Nazism*. Eugene, OR: Cascade, 2013.

———. *Beloved Community: Critical Dogmatics after Christendom*. Grand Rapids: Eerdmans, 2015.

———. "Complicity and the Truth of the Christological Path of Ecclesial Resistance: Summons to a New Catechesis for a Time of Despair." In *Truth-Telling and Other Ecclesial Practices of Resistance*, edited by Christine Helmer, 47–62. Minneapolis: Fortress, 2021.

———. "Confession: A New Look at Some Old Theology." *Academy: Lutherans in Profession* 39 (1983) 57–80.

———. *Divine Complexity: The Rise of Creedal Christianity*. Minneapolis: Fortress, 2010.

———. "Exorcism." In *Dictionary of Luther and the Lutheran Traditions*, edited by Timothy J. Wengert, 243–44. Grand Rapids: Baker Academic 2017.

———. "The Experience of Incongruous Grace," Review Essay on Simeon Zahl, The Holy Spirit and Christian Experience, *Anglican Theological Review* (2022) 1-13.

———. "Faith." *St. Andrews Encyclopedia of Theology.* www.saet.ac.uk/Christianity/Faith.

———. "Hegel: Simplicity Comprehending Differentiation." In *Divine Simplicity: Five Views.* Downers Grove, IL: InterVarsity, forthcoming.

———. "How Theological Exegesis Disrupts Theological Tradition," review essay on Robert W. Jenson, *The Triune Story: Collected Essays on Scripture*. *Harvard Theological Review* 114 (2021) 143–57.

———. "The Incarnation of the Eternal Son: Fitting, not Necessary." *Pro Ecclesia* 31 (2022) 542–58.

———. "Ingolf U. Dalferth, Crucified and Resurrected: Restructuring the Grammar of Christology." *Modern Theology* 33 (2017) 678–80.

———. "Irony of an Epithet: The Reversal of Luther's Enthusiasm in the Enlightenment." In *A Man of the Church: Festschrift for Ralph Del Colle*, edited by Michel Barnes and Mickey L. Mattox, 302–15. Eugene, OR: Wipf & Stock, 2013.

———. *Joshua*. Brazos Theological Commentary on the Bible. Grand Rapids: Brazos, 2021.

———. *Luther and the Beloved Community: A Path for Christian Theology After Christendom*. Grand Rapids: Eerdmans, 2010.

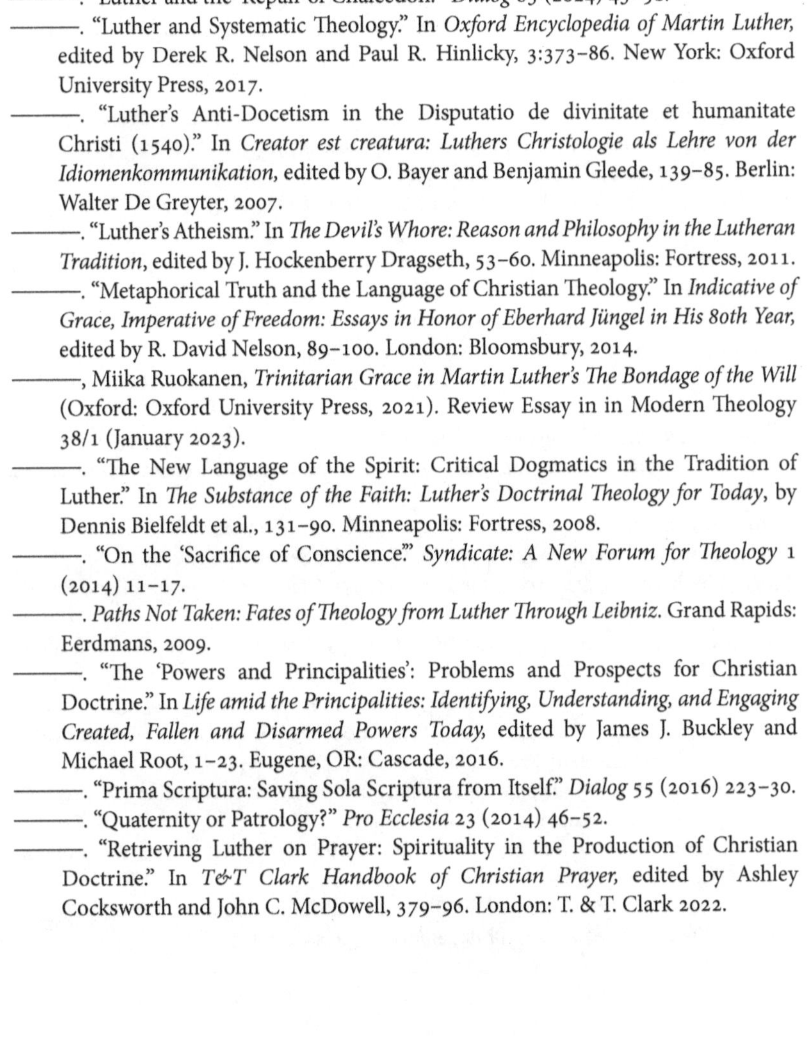

———. "Luther and the 'Repair of Chalcedon.'" *Dialog* 63 (2024) 43–51.

———. "Luther and Systematic Theology." In *Oxford Encyclopedia of Martin Luther*, edited by Derek R. Nelson and Paul R. Hinlicky, 3:373–86. New York: Oxford University Press, 2017.

———. "Luther's Anti-Docetism in the Disputatio de divinitate et humanitate Christi (1540)." In *Creator est creatura: Luthers Christologie als Lehre von der Idiomenkommunikation*, edited by O. Bayer and Benjamin Gleede, 139–85. Berlin: Walter De Greyter, 2007.

———. "Luther's Atheism." In *The Devil's Whore: Reason and Philosophy in the Lutheran Tradition*, edited by J. Hockenberry Dragseth, 53–60. Minneapolis: Fortress, 2011.

———. "Metaphorical Truth and the Language of Christian Theology." In *Indicative of Grace, Imperative of Freedom: Essays in Honor of Eberhard Jüngel in His 80th Year*, edited by R. David Nelson, 89–100. London: Bloomsbury, 2014.

———, Miika Ruokanen, *Trinitarian Grace in Martin Luther's The Bondage of the Will* (Oxford: Oxford University Press, 2021). Review Essay in in Modern Theology 38/1 (January 2023).

———. "The New Language of the Spirit: Critical Dogmatics in the Tradition of Luther." In *The Substance of the Faith: Luther's Doctrinal Theology for Today*, by Dennis Bielfeldt et al., 131–90. Minneapolis: Fortress, 2008.

———. "On the 'Sacrifice of Conscience.'" *Syndicate: A New Forum for Theology* 1 (2014) 11–17.

———. *Paths Not Taken: Fates of Theology from Luther Through Leibniz*. Grand Rapids: Eerdmans, 2009.

———. "The 'Powers and Principalities': Problems and Prospects for Christian Doctrine." In *Life amid the Principalities: Identifying, Understanding, and Engaging Created, Fallen and Disarmed Powers Today*, edited by James J. Buckley and Michael Root, 1–23. Eugene, OR: Cascade, 2016.

———. "Prima Scriptura: Saving Sola Scriptura from Itself." *Dialog* 55 (2016) 223–30.

———. "Quaternity or Patrology?" *Pro Ecclesia* 23 (2014) 46–52.

———. "Retrieving Luther on Prayer: Spirituality in the Production of Christian Doctrine." In *T&T Clark Handbook of Christian Prayer*, edited by Ashley Cocksworth and John C. McDowell, 379–96. London: T. & T. Clark 2022.

———. "Scripture as Matrix, Christ as Content: A response to Johannes Zachhuber and Anna Case-Winters." In *Refracted Luther: The Reformer's Ecumenical Legacy* edited Piotr J. Malysz and Derek R. Nelson, 299–317. Minneapolis: Fortress, 2016.

———. "The Spirit of Christ amid the Spirits of the Post-Modern World: The Crumley Lecture." *Lutheran Quarterly* 14 (2000) 433–58.

———."Tilted in the Direction of Scotus." *Pro Ecclesia* 19 (2018) 56–61.

———. "Verbum Externum: Dietrich Bonhoeffer's Bethel Confession." In *God Speaks to Us: Dietrich Bonhoeffer's Biblical Hermeneutics*, edited by Ralf Wüstenberg and Jens Zimmerman, 189–216. Berlin: Peter Lang, 2012.

Hinlicky, Paul R., and Brent Adkins. *Rethinking Philosophy and Theology with Deleuze: A New Cartography.* London and New York: Bloomsbury Academic, 2013.

Hobbes, Thomas. *Leviathan.* Edited by E. Curley. Indianapolis: Hackett, 1994.

Hockenberry, Jennifer. *Wisdom's Friendly Heart: Augustinian Hope for Skeptics and Conspiracy Theorists.* Eugene OR: Cascade, 2020.

Hollinger, David A. *After Cloven Tongues of Fire: Protestant Liberalism in Modern American His*tory. Princeton, NJ: Princeton University Press, 2013.

Hoskyns, Sir Edwin, and Francis Noel Davey. *The Riddle of the New Testament.* London: Faber & Faber, 1941.

Hultgren, Arland J. *The Rise of Normative Christianity.* Minneapolis: Fortress, 1994.

Hunter, James Davison. *Before the Shooting Begins: Searching for Democracy in America's Culture War* New York: MacMillan, 1994.

Jackson, S. M., ed. *The Latin Works of whom I Huldreich Zwingli.* 2 vols. Philadelphia: The Heidelberg, 1922.

Jensen, Gordon. *The Call to Discipleship: Baptism, Vocation, Discipleship and the Community.* Eugene, OR: Cascade, forthcoming.

Jenson, Robert W. *America's Theologian: A Recommendation of Jonathan Edwards.* New York and Oxford: Oxford University Press, 1988.

———. "An Ontology of Freedom in the *De Servo Arbitrio* of Luther." *Modern Theology* 10 (1994) 247–52.

———. *Systematic Theology.* 2 vols. Oxford: Oxford University Press, 1997.

———. *Unbaptized God: The Basic Flaw in Ecumenical Theology.* Minneapolis: Fortress, 1992.

John of Damascus, Saint. *On the Orthodox Faith.* Introduction, translation, and notes by Norman Russell. Yonkers, NY: St. Vladimir's Seminary Press, 2022.

Jüngel, Eberhard. *The Doctrine of the Trinity: God's Being is in Becoming.* Grand Rapids: Eerdmans, 1976.

Kant, Immanuel. *Lectures on Philosophical Theology.* Translated by A. W. Wood and G. M. Clark. Ithaca, NY: Cornell University Press, 1978

———. *Religion and Rational Theology: The Cambridge Edition of the Works of Immanuel Kant.* Translated by A. W. Wood and G. Di Giovanni. Cambridge: Cambridge University Press, 2001.

Käsemann, Ernst. *Commentary on Romans.* Translated and edited by G. Bromiley Grand Rapids: Eerdmans, 1980.

———. *Essays on New Testament Themes.* Translated by W. J. Montague. London: SCM, 1971.

———. *New Testament Questions for Today*. Philadelphia: Augsburg Fortress, 1979.

———. *The Testament of Jesus.* Philadelphia: Fortress, 1968.

Keating, James F., and Thomas Joseph White, OP, eds. *Divine Impassibility and the Mystery of Human Suffering*. Grand Rapids: Eerdmans, 2009.

Keck, Leander E. *A Future for the Historical Jesus: The Place of Jesus in Preaching and Theology*. Philadelphia: Augsburg Fortress, 1981.

Kingsbury, Jack Dean. *The Christology of Mark's Gospel*. Philadelphia: Augsburg Fortress, 1983.

Kolb, Robert. *Bound Choice, Election, and Wittenberg Theological Method: From Martin Luther to the Formula of Concord*. Grand Rapids: Eerdmans, 2005.

Kreider, Alan. *The Patient Ferment of the Early Church: The Improbable Rise of Christianity in the Roman Empire*. Grand Rapids: Baker Academic, 2016.

Kristensson, Uggla Bengt. *Becoming Human Again: The Theological Life of Gustaf Wingren*. Translated by Daniel M. Olson. Eugene, OR: Cascade, 2016.

Krötke, Wolf. *Sin and Nothingness in the Theology of Karl Barth*. Translated by P. G. Ziegler and C.-M. Bammel. Studies in Reformed Theology and History, New Series 10. Princeton, NJ: Princeton Theological Seminary, 2005.

Kunieriková, Michaela. *Acting for Others: Trinitarian Communion and Christological Agency*. Foreword by Paul R. Hinlicky. Minneapolis: Fortress, 2017.

Künneth, Walter. *The Theology of the Resurrection*. Translated by James W. Leitch. St. Louis: Concordia, 1965.

Lapide, Pinchas. *The Jewish Monotheism and Christian Trinitarian Doctrine: A Dialogue by Pinchas Lapide and Jürgen Moltmann*. Foreword by Jacob B. Agus and translated by Leonard Swidler. Eugene, OR: Wipf & Stock, 2002.

———. *The Resurrection of Jesus: A Jewish Perspective*. Translated by Wilhelm C. Linss. Eugene, OR: Wipf & Stock, 2002.

Larson, Duane. *Ubi Deus Dixit Where God Has Spoken: The Lutheran Doctrine of the Two Kingdoms*. Eugene, OR: Cascade, 2025.

Lazareth, William H. *Christians in Society: Luther, the Bible and Social Ethics*. Minneapolis: Fortress, 2001.

Leithart, Peter J. *Defending Constantine: The Twilight of an Empire and the Dawn of Christendom*. Downer's Grove, IL: IVP Academic, 2010.

Levinson, Jon D. *The Death and Resurrection of the Beloved Son: The Transformation of Child Sacrifice in Judaism and Christianity*. New Haven, CT: Yale University Press, 1993.

Lewis, David Levering. *God's Crucible: Islam and the Making of Europe, 570–1215*. New York & London: Norton, 2008.

Lilla, Mark. *The Stillborn God: Religion, Politics, and the Modern West*. New York: Vintage, 2007.

Lindbeck, George A. *The Nature of Doctrine: Religion and Theology in a Postliberal Age* Philadelphia: Westminster, 1984.

Locke, John. *A Letter Concerning Toleration*. Indianapolis: Hackett, 1983.

Lohse, Eduard. *Colossians and Philemon*. Translated by William R. Poehlmann and Robert J. Karris. Philadelphia: Fortress 1971.

Lösel, Steffen. "The *Kirchenkampf* of the Countercultural Colony: A Critical Response." *Theology Today* 67 (2010) 279–98.

Lotz, David. *Luther and Ritschl: A Fresh Perspective on Albrecht Ritschl's Theology in the Light of His Luther Study*. Nashville: Abingdon, 1974.

Louth, Andrew. *Maximus the Confessor*. London: Routledge, 1996.

Luibheid, Colm, trans. *Pseudo-Dionysius: The Complete Works*. Mahwah, NJ: Paulist, 1987.

Luther, Martin. *The Bondage of the Will*. Translated by J. I. Packer and O. R. Johnston. Ada, MI: Fleming H. Revel, 2000.

Luy, David. *Dominus Mortis: Martin Luther on the Incorruptibility of God in Christ*. Minneapolis: Fortress: 2014.

Lynch, Chloe. "How Convincing Is Walter Wink's Interpretation of Paul's Language of the Powers?" *Evangelical Quarterly* 83 (2011) 251–66.

Malcolm, Lois. "No Wisdom, No Trinity: Why (the Biblical Figure of) Wisdom Matters for Interpreting and Confessing the Trinity." *Word and World* 41 (2021) 221–30.

Malysz, Peter. "*Nemo iudex in causa sua* as the Basis of Law, Justice and Justification in Luther's Thought." *Harvard Theological Review* 100 (2007), 363–86.

Mangina, Joseph L. *Revelation*. Brazos Theological Commentary on the Bible. Grand Rapids: Brazos, 2010.

Marcus, Joel. *Mark 1–8, A New Translation with Introduction and Commentary*. The Anchor Bible 27A. New Haven, CT: Yale University Press, 2000.

———. *Mark 8–16, A New Translation with Introduction and Commentary*. The Anchor Bible 27B. New Haven, CT: Yale University Press, 2009.

Marshall, Bruce D. *Trinity and Truth*. Cambridge: Cambridge University Press, 2000.

Martyn, J. Louis. "Epistemology at the Turn of the Ages: 2 Corinthians 5:16." In *Christian History and Interpretation: Studies Presented to John Knox*, edited by W. R. Farmer et al. 269–87. Cambridge: Cambridge University Press, 1967.

———. *Galatians: A New Translation with Introduction and Commentary*. The Anchor Bible 33A. New York: Doubleday/Random House, 1997.

———. *History and Theology in the Fourth Gospel*. 3rd ed. Louisville, KY: Westminster John Knox 2003.

Mattes, Mark C. *Martin Luther's Theology of Beauty: A Reappraisal*. Grand Rapids: Baker Academic, 2017.

Mattox, Mickey M. "Cosmology." OREML 1:296–313.

McCormack, Bruce Lindley. *The Humility of the Eternal Son: Reformed Kenoticism and the Repair of Chalcedon*. Cambridge: Cambridge University Press, 2021.

McDermott, Gerald. *God's Rivals: Why Has God Allowed Different Religions? Insights from the Bible and the Early Church*. Downers Grove, IL: IVP Academic, 2007.

McFarland, Ian A. *From Nothing: A Theology of Creation*. Louisville, KY: Westminster John Knox, 2014.

McGilchrist, Iain. *The Master and His Emissary: The Divided Brain and the Making of the Western World*. Exp. ed. New Haven, CT: Yale University Press, 2019.

Meier, John P. *A Marginal Jew: Rethinking the Historical Jesus*. 2 vols. New York: Doubleday, 1994.

Meyendorff, John. *Byzantine Theology: Historical Trends and Doctrinal Themes* New York: Fordham University Press, 1979.

———. *Christ in Eastern Christian Thought*. Crestwood, NY: St. Vladimir's Seminary Press, 1975.

Miters, Benjamin. "From Faithfulness to Faith in the Theology of Karl Barth." In *The Faith of Jesus Christ: Exegetical, Biblical and Theological Studies*, edited by Michael F. Bird and Preston M. Sprinkle, 291–308. Peabody, MA: Hendrickson, 2009.

Moberly, R. W. L. *The God of the Old Testament: Encountering the Divine in Christian Scripture*. Grand Rapids: Baker Academic, 2020.

Morgan, Teresa. *Roman Faith and Christian Faith: Pistis and Fides in the Early Roman Empire and Early Churches*. Oxford: Oxford University Press, 2017.

Morse, Christopher. *Not Every Spirit: A Dogmatics of Christian Disbelief*. Harrisburg, PA: Trinity Press International, 1994.

Motivation Ark. "One of the Greatest Speeches Ever: Martin Luther King Jr." https://www.youtube.com/watch?v=Lsyi6lyAAhY.

Niebuhr, Reinhold. *The Irony of American History*. New York: Charles Scribner's Sons, 1952.

———. *Moral Man and Immoral Society: A Study in Ethics and Politics*. New York: Charles Scribner's Sons, 1960.

———. *The Nature and Destiny of Man: A Christian Interpretation*. New York: Charles Scribner's Sons, 1943.

Oakman, Douglas E. *The Political Aims of Jesus*. Minneapolis: Fortress, 2012.

Obermann, Heiko. *Luther: Man between God and the Devil*. Translated by E. Walliser-Schwarzbart. New Haven, CT: Yale University Press, 1989.

———. *The Roots of Anti-Semitism in the Age of Renaissance and Reformation*. Translated by J. I. Porter. Philadelphia: Augsburg Fortress, 1984.

Ochs, Peter. *Another Reformation: Postliberal Christianity and the Jews*. Grand Rapids: Baker Academic, 2011.

Pannenberg, Wolfhart. *Basic Questions in Theology*. 2 vols. Translated by G. H. Kehm Philadelphia: Augsburg Fortress, 1972.

———. *Systematic Theology*. 3 vols. Translated by G. W. Bromiley. Grand Rapids: Eerdmans, 1991.

Peterson, Cheryl M. *The Holy Spirit in the Christian Life: The Spirit's Work for, in, and Through Us*. Grand Rapids: Baker Academic, 2024.

Portier-Young, Anathea E. *Apocalypse Against Empire: Theologies of Resistance in Early Judaism*. Grand Rapids: Eerdmans, 2011.

Prenter, Regin. *Spiritus Creator*. Translated by John M. Jensen. Philadelphia: Muhlenberg, 1953.

Radner, Ephraim. *A Brutal Unity: The Spiritual Politics of the Christian Church*. Waco, TX: Baylor University Press, 2012.

Reinhuber, Thomas. *Kämpfender Glaube: Studien zu Luthers Bekenntnis am Ende von de servo arbitrio*. Berlin: Walter de Gruyter, 2000.

Riley, Gregory J. *Resurrection Reconsidered: Thomas and John in Controversy*. Minneapolis: Fortress, 1995.

Robinson, James M. "Introduction." In *The Nag Hammadi Library in English*, edited by James M. Robinson, 1–26. San Francisco: Harper and Row, 1988.

Rogers, Katherin A. *The Neoplatonic Metaphysics and Epistemology of Anselm of Canterbury*. Lewiston, NY: The Edwin Mellen, 1997.

Rőhl, Wolfgang G. "Demons." In *The Encyclopedia of Christianity*, translated and edited by Geoffrey W. Bromiley, 1:794. Grand Rapids: Eerdmans, 1999.

Rowlands, Jonathan. *The Metaphysics of Historical Jesus Research: A Prolegomena into a Future Quest for the Historical Jesus*. London: Routledge, 2023.

Ruether, Rosemary Radford. *Faith and Fratricide: The Theological Roots of Anti-Semitism*. New York: Seabury, 1979.

Ruokanen, Miikka. *Trinitarian Grace in Martin Luther's* The Bondage of the Will. Oxford: Oxford University Press, 2021.

Schleiermacher, Friedrich. *Brief Outline on the Study of Theology*. Translated by Terrence M. Tice. Atlanta: John Knox, 1977.

———. *The Christian Faith*. 2 vols. Edited by H. R. Macintosh and J. S. Steward. New York: Harper & Row, 1963.

———. *The Life of Jesus*. Edited by Jack C. Verheyden and translated by S. Maclean Gilmour. Philadelphia: Fortress, 1975.

Schmitt, Carl. *Political Theology: Four Chapters on the Concept of Sovereignty*. Translated by George Schwab. Chicago: University of Chicago Press, 2005.

Schnelle, Udo. *Antidocetic Christology in the Gospel of John: An Investigation of the Place of the Fourth Gospel in the Johannine School*. Translated by Linda M. Maloney. Minneapolis: Fortress, 1992.

Schweitzer, Albert. *The Quest of the Historical Jesus*. Introduction by James M. Robinson. New York: MacMillan, 1978.

Sharpe, Hasana. *Spinoza and the Politics of Renaturalization*. Chicago: University of Chicago Press, 2011.

Snead, O. Carter. *What It Means to Be Human: The Case for the Body in Public Bioethics*. Cambridge, MA: Harvard University Press, 2020.

Sonderegger, Katherine. *Systematic Theology, Volume 1, The Doctrine of God*. Minneapolis: Fortress, 2015.

Soskice, Janet. *Metaphor and Religious Language*. Oxford: Clarendon, 1987.

Stout, Jeffery. *The Flight from Authority: Religion, Morality and the Quest for Autonomy*. Notre Dame, IN: University of Notre Dame Press, 1981.

Strauss, David Friedrich. *The Christ of Faith and the Jesus of History: A Critique of Schleiermacher's* Life of Jesus. Translated by Leander E. Keck. Philadelphia: Fortress, 1977.

Thurman, Howard. *Jesus and The Disinherited*. Foreword by Vincent Harding. Boston: Beacon, 1996.

Tillich, Paul. *Against the Third Reich: Paul Tillich's Wartime Radio Broadcasts into Nazi Germany*. Edited by Ronald H. Stone and Matthew Lon Weaver. Louisville, KY: Westminster John Knox, 1998.

Torrance, Alan J. *Persons in Communion: Trinitarian Description and Human Participation*. Edinburgh: T. & T. Clark, 1996.

Torrance, T. F. *The Trinitarian Faith: The Evangelical Theology of the Ancient Catholic Church*. Edinburgh: T. & T. Clark, 1993.

University of Cambridge. "A Lutheran Timeline." https://exhibitions.lib.cam.ac.uk/reformation/artifacts/a-lutheran-timeline/.

Vainio, Olli-Pekka. *Justification and Participation in Christ: The Development of the Lutheran Doctrine of Justification from Luther to the Formula of Concord (1580)*. Leiden: Brill, 2008.

Vestrucci, Andrea. *Theology as Freedom: On Martin Luther's "De servo arbitrio."* Tübingen: Mohr Siebeck, 2018.

Vind, Anna. "Christus factus est peccatum metaphorice: Über die theologische Verwendung rhetorischer Figuren bei Luther unter Einbeziehung Quintilians." In *Creator est creatura*, edited by Oswald Bayer and Benjamin Gleede, 95–124. Berlin: Walter de Gruyter, 2007.

Waldron, Jeremy. *God, Locke, and Equality: Christian Foundations in Locke's Political Thought*. Cambridge: Cambridge University Press, 2002.

Whitaker, E. C., ed. *Documents of the Baptismal Liturgy*. 2nd ed. Naperville, IL: Alec R. Allenson, 1970.

Wilder, Amos N. "Kerygma, Eschatology and Social Ethics." In *The Background of the New Testament and Its Eschatology: In Honour of Charles Harold Dodd*, edited by W. D. Davies and D. Daube, 509–36. Cambridge: Cambridge University Press, 1964.

Wink, Walter. *Engaging the Powers: Discernment and Resistance in a World of Domination*. Minneapolis: Fortress, 1992.

———. *Naming the Powers: The Language of Power in the New Testament*. Philadelphia: Augsburg Fortress, 1984.

Wittgenstein, Ludwig. *Tractatus Logico-Philosophicus*. New York: Harcourt, 1922.

Wright, N. T. "Paul and Caesar: A New Reading of Romans." In *A Royal Priesthood: The Use of the Bible Ethically and Politically*, edited by C. Bartholemew, 173–93. Carlisle: Paternoster, 2002.

———. *Surprised by Hope: Rethinking Heaven, the Resurrection, and the Mission of the Church*. New York: HarperOne, 2018.

Wyschogrod, Michael. *The Body of Faith: God in the People Israel*. Lanham, MD: Rowman and Littlefield, 1996.

Zachhuber, Johannes. *Theology as Science in Nineteenth Century Germany: From F. C. Baur to Ernst Troeltsch*. Oxford: Oxford University Press, 2013.

Zahl, Simeon. *The Holy Spirit and Christian Experience* Oxford: Oxford University Press, 2020.

———. *Pneumatology and Theology of the Cross in the Preaching of Christoph Friedrich Blumhardt: The Holy Spirit between Wittenberg and Azusa Street*. London and New York: T. & T. Clark, 2010.

Ziegler, Philip G. *God's Adversary and Ours: A Brief Theology of the Devil*. Waco, TX: Baylor University Press, 2025.

———. *Militant Grace: The Apocalyptic Turn and the Future of Christian Theology*. Grand Rapids: Baker Academic 2018.

Zimmerman, Jens. *Recovering Theological Hermeneutics: An Incarnational-Trinitarian Theory of Interpretation*. Grand Rapids: Baker Academic, 2004.

Zuboff, Shoshana. *The Age of Surveillance Capitalism: The Fight for a Human Future at the New Frontier of Power*. New York: PublicAffairs, 2019.

Index of Names

Topical Index

I. Apocalyptic

II. God, Problems of the Doctrine of

III. Trinitarian knowledge of God

IV. Almighty Father, Problems of the Doctrine of

V. Almighty Father, the Doctrine of

VI. Christ Jesus (Philippians 2:5), Problems of the Doctrine of

VII. Christ Jesus, The Person of

VIII. Christ Jesus, the Work of

IX. Sanctifying Spirit, Problems of the Doctrine of

X. Sanctifying Spirit, Person of the

XI. Sanctifying Spirit, Works of the

XII. Method for Apocalyptic Theology:

XIII. The Word, Problem of the Doctrine of

XIV. The Word, Doctrine of

XV. Humanity, Problems of the Doctrine of

XVI. Humanity, Doctrine of

www.ingramcontent.com/pod-product-compliance
Lightning Source LLC
LaVergne TN
LVHW100516110826
845146LV00002B/659

* 9 7 9 8 3 8 5 2 2 2 8 6 5 *